# Indian Economic Growth in Historical Perspective

This book investigates the roots of rapid economic growth of India in recent decades, by exploring historical processes from the late colonial period.

Based upon decades-long archival and field research, this book deals with the period from the late nineteenth century to 2013 and offers an integral viewpoint of the economic history of India. While critiquing the conventional understanding that links recent economic growth only with the development of high-tech, export-oriented service sectors under the liberalised economy, the book suggests deeper and wider roots of development that had a cumulative effect in three stages. First, the agrarian development and rural socio-economic changes from the end of the nineteenth century. Second, the state-led import-substitution industrialisation since 1950 that established the industrial foundations for future economic growth. Third, the economic reforms since 1991 that helped technology-intensive industries find new markets with improved quality of production.

For the first time available in English, this book by the late Professor Haruka Yanagisawa, who was a leading figure in the South Asia studies collective in Japan, is an important contribution to the academic tradition of economic history of India It will be of interest to researchers in the field of social and economic history, sociology, anthropology and economies of South Asia.

The late **Haruka Yanagisawa**, who passed away in 2015, was a Professor Emeritus of the University of Tokyo, Japan. He was much loved and respected for his kindness and academic commitment. His publications include *A Century of Change: Caste and Irrigated Lands in Tamilnadu 1860s–1970s* (1996), *Towards a History of Consumption in South Asia* (co-editor, 2010), *Local Agrarian Societies in Colonial India: Japanese Perspectives* (co-editor, 1996, reprint: 2016), *Community, Commons and Natural Resource Management in Asia*, (editor, 2015). His articles have been published in *Indian Economic and Social History Review*, *Conservation and Society* and *Review of Agrarian Studies*. He has also published many books and articles in Japanese.

**Routledge New Horizons in South Asian Studies**
Series Editors: Crispin Bates, Edinburgh University; Akio Tanabe, Kyoto University; Minoru Mio, National Museum of Ethnology, Japan

**Modernity and Spirit Worship in India**
An Anthropology of the Umwelt
*Miho Ishii*

**Sustainable Development in India**
Groundwater Irrigation, Energy Use, and Food Production
*Edited by Koichi Fujita and Tsukasa Mizushima*

**The Dynamics of Conflict and Peace in Contemporary South Asia**
The State, Democracy and Social Movements
*Edited by and Minoru Mio, Kazuya Nakamizo and Tatsuro Fujikura*

**Caste and Equality in India**
A Historical Anthropology of Diverse Society and Vernacular Democracy
*Akio Tanabe*

**Language, Identity, and Power in Modern India**
Gujarat, c. 1850–1960
*Riho Isaka*

**Indian Economic Growth in Historical Perspective**
The Roots of Development
*Late Prof. Haruka Yanagisawa (ed. Tsukasa Mizushima)*

**The Rural-Urban Nexus in India's Economic Transformation**
*Tsukasa Mizushima*

**Inclusive Development in South Asia**
*Toshie Awaya and Kazuo Tomozawa*

For a full list of titles please see https://www.routledge.com/Routledge-New-Horizons-in-South-Asian-Studies/book-series/RNHSAS

# Indian Economic Growth in Historical Perspective

## The Roots of Development

**Haruka Yanagisawa**
**Edited by Tsukasa Mizushima**
**Translated by Gaynor Sekimori**

Routledge
Taylor & Francis Group
LONDON AND NEW YORK

First published 2023
by Routledge
4 Park Square, Milton Park, Abingdon, Oxon OX14 4RN

and by Routledge
605 Third Avenue, New York, NY 10158

*Routledge is an imprint of the Taylor & Francis Group, an informa business*



*British Library Cataloguing-in-Publication Data*
A catalogue record for this book is available from the British Library

*Library of Congress Cataloging-in-Publication Data*
Names: Yanagisawa, Haruka, 1944-2015, author. |
Mizushima, Tsukasa, 1952- editor.
Title: Indian economic growth in historical perspective : the roots of development / Haruka Yanagisawa ; edited by Tsukasa Mizushima.
Description: 1 Edition. | New York, NY : Routledge, 2022. |
Series: Routledge new horizons in South Asian studies | Includes bibliographical references and index.
Identifiers: LCCN 2022028924 (print) | LCCN 2022028925 (ebook) |
ISBN 9781032377216 (hardback) | ISBN 9781032377209 (paperback) |
ISBN 9781003341550 (ebook)
Subjects: LCSH: India--Economic conditions. | Economic development--India--History.
Classification: LCC HC435.4 .Y3613 2022 (print) | LCC HC435.4 (ebook) |
DDC 330.954--dc23/eng/20220811
LC record available at https://lccn.loc.gov/2022028924
LC ebook record available at https://lccn.loc.gov/2022028925

ISBN: 978-1-032-37721-6 (hbk)
ISBN: 978-1-032-37720-9 (pbk)
ISBN: 978-1-003-34155-0 (ebk)

DOI: 10.4324/9781003341550

Typeset in Times New Roman
by SPi Technologies India Pvt Ltd (Straive)

# Contents

# Figures

# Tables

# Preface

Dr Haruka Yanagisawa, Professor Emeritus, the University of Tokyo, passed away in April 2015 at the age of 70. Starting from earliest works on Indian cotton industry and moving towards agrarian relations in India, Yanagisawa continued to focus on the uplifting of the depressed classes placed at the bottom of the Indian society. Though originally an economist, Yanagisawa not only conducted archival research in London and in India but also did rural studies staying in a South Indian village near Lalgudi, Tiruchi, for months. One of his earlier works, titled *A Century of Change: Caste and Irrigated Land in Tamilnadu, 1860s–1970s*, was published in 1996 from Manohar, India, and has been highly reputed to become "a must book on Indian rural economy". A steady increase of landholding by the depressed classes was clearly verified by the work compiling dozens of village-level *Settlement Registers* (land registers recording the details of landholding of every land lot in the respective villages since the nineteenth century till today) and the analysis based upon them.

Yanagisawa further proceeded towards investigation on agrarian relations, including education, non-agricultural employment in and outside rural area, consumption, urban development and others, and deepened his understanding of the society.

In his late years Yanagisawa assembled his researches into a monograph in Japanese for the Japanese readers. The book was titled as *Modern Indian Economy: Roots of Development, Processes, and Prospects* (2014), which was awarded a prestigious "Award for International Development Study" (Okita Memorial Prize) in the same year. The present publication is newly rewritten by Mizushima and others for English readers after his demise.

What Yanagisawa argued in this book is the increasing consumption of rural classes in the recent decades, especially among the depressed classes. In contrast to the prevalent arguments that stress the consuming power of the emerging urban middle class, he stresses that the very root of economic development in present India lies not there but in rural areas. By presenting a term of "rural- and urban- informal economies" zone, Yanagisawa showed the critical importance of the synchronised increase of the lowly educated, lowly paid, irregularly employed migrant workers from rural area with the development of low-cost, low quality, "quasi-branded" industries.

Yanagisawa was, however, pessimistic about the future course of Indian economy. The nature of recent economic development poses constraints on further development because of the imperative and emerging competition with China in the same economic spheres. In addition, the continuing deep disparity between the manager and worker classes, the low incentive for low-skill workers to improve their skills in manufactures, and the short, irregular and unstable employment condition would, Yanagisawa argued, continue for some more decades to come.

Yanagisawa's demise was a great loss not only for the colleagues and friends in Japan but also for all those who know his extraordinary contribution to the understanding of Indian society. With this English publication, I do wish all the international readers can acknowledge his dedication to and love of India.

The translation work, a very laborious and time-consuming one, was funded partly by the Integrated Area Studies on South Asia (INDAS) under the National Institutes for the Humanities (NIHU) and partly by the Japan Society of Promotion of Science (JSPS), and was undertaken by Dr Sekimori Gaynor. Professors Akio Tanabe, Crispin Bates, Minoru Mio, Tom Tomlinson, Shigeru Akita and Aditya Mukherjee kindly assisted me for its publication. For all these supports, I am truly grateful.

**Tsukasa Mizushima**
(Professor Emeritus,
The University of Tokyo)
April 2022

# Introduction

## In Search of the Roots of Contemporary Economic Growth in India

For the last three decades, the Indian economy has flourished. From Independence until the end of the 1970s, its growth rate averaged around 3 percent. The 1980s saw this figure double and around 2003 it again accelerated. The period since the 1980s simultaneously witnessed a radical change in government economic policies, with the strategy towards state-led import-substitution industrialisation being officially abolished in the pro-market economic reform of 1991.

The widely accepted view is that this radical shift towards liberalisation and globalisation was the main trigger behind the escalation in economic growth. However, this outlook has been challenged by a series of studies, such as those by Rodrik and Subramanian (2004) and Kohli (2006). They criticise pro-market school approaches as being insufficient to explain certain aspects of Indian economic development in the 1980s and 1990s. First, the acceleration in the growth rate occurred around 1980, that is, about ten years before the 1991 pro-market reform marked a radical shift in economic policy. Furthermore, in spite of the epoch-making reforms, the growth spurt of the 1990s was marginal compared to the 1980s. Second, while the industrial sector, which the government regulations under the "Licence Raj" mainly targeted, should have been the sector most stimulated by the 1991 liberalisation reforms, the growth rate of this sector remained static or even slightly declined in the 1990s.[1] The third point pertains to the change in productivity. Contrary to the general expectation that the liberalisation would have resulted in a faster rate of productivity, some studies have pointed to a serious deterioration in the growth rate of total factor productivities within the industrial sector in the 1990s (McCartney 2009, 41–42).

Econometrical analysis has been used to challenge the argument that the shift to the pro-market policies was the major engine of economic growth. According to Balakishnan and Parameswaran (2007), there was only one break in GDP growth after 1950, in 1978–1979. Breaks in the growth of manufacturing however occurred three times. The first was in the middle of the 1960s, when its growth rate fell. The second break was seen in 1982–1983, when its growth rate rose, and the third in 1994–1995, when it lowered again. Balakrishnan and Parameswaran see the most important one of these as that of 1982–1983, which took place only after the 1978–1979 break in GDP

DOI: 10.4324/9781003341550-1

growth rate. They thus find evidence against the possibility that manufacturing led the acceleration of the growth rate. Wallack (2003), while admitting that the reforms in the 1980s were a stimulant, has found little evidence that they influenced the growth rate of important sectors like agriculture, manufacturing and services. These works therefore actively contradict the case for the pro-market reforms having contributed to economic growth by stimulating industrial investment.

The industrial sector, the core target of the policy reforms, experienced a sluggishness in the 1990s, but growth in the service sector sped up after 1991. It has been widely contended that the service sector's export expansion led its development and made it a catalyst for India's economic success, as exemplified by the IT software industry, which has seen a remarkable increase in its exports. Yet, recent work does not support this view. While acknowledging the rise in service sector exports, Verma (2012, 278–279) argues that they represent only a small part of the sector's GDP.[2] Moreover, as Chapter 8 will discuss in detail, statistical data presented by Bosworth et al. (2006/2007) seem to undermine the argument that the growth of such modern service sub-sectors as the IT and communication industries and financial services, which might have been encouraged by the economic reforms, led to Indian economic growth between 1980 and 2004. They have classified the service sections into two groups: The "modern" sub-sectors consisting of "communications, finance, business services, education, and medical care"; and "traditional" sub-sectors comprising "trade, transportation, public and personal services". Their data show that of the total output produced by the service sector, the modern sub-sectors accounted for as little as 40 percent even by 2004, and the percentage contribution to total services growth made by the modern sub-sectors was only 39 percent for 1993–1999 and 46 percent even for 1999–2004, indicating that the traditional sub-sectors were the main contributors to total services growth, even down to 2004. The recent work by Nayyar (2012, 213) also reveals that the sub-sector of services that accounted for the largest shares in total services employment, both in 1993–1994 and 2004–2005, are the ones characterised by low educational requirements and relatively low quality of employment. It is these generally "bad" employers that were responsible for the largest proportion of the increase in total services employment during that period. Therefore, it is problematic to say that, at least until the end of the last century, the modern services sub-sectors contributed most to Indian economic growth.

In connection with the debate over the role of the pro-market reforms and globalisation in the accelerated growth, a long-term estimate of GDP growth rate covering the whole twentieth century by Sivasubramonian (2000) has provided a new set of data. Nayyar (2006), viewing the twentieth century as a whole, posits that there were two turning points in economic growth: The first circa 1951 and the second circa 1980, with the first being more important than the second. As shown in Table 4.1 in Chapter 4 of this volume, in sharp contrast to the colonial period when the average growth rate was as low as 0.9 percent, the economic growth since the 1950s averaged 3–4 percent, which, though poorer than that experienced in East Asia, was higher than in African countries. The actual growth of output per worker in India was very close to the average across the world. The accumulative impact of economic policies or public actions over the preceding 30 years possibly played a significant part in the increase in the growth rate around 1980. Institutional capacities were created, and the capital goods sector was established. Entrepreneurial talents and managerial capabilities were fostered. A higher education system was developed. These advancements, Nayyar argues, probably provided the essential foundations for the second economic turning point. As we shall discuss later, in the first half of the twentieth century, while a protective tariff system was introduced in some industries, free trade remained the general principle of the regime. Therefore, in sharp contrast to the low growth rate averaging 0.9 percent under the free trade regime in the colonial period, the growth rate jumped to 3 to 4 percent after Independent India adopted general protective trade policies and started a state-led import-substitution industrialisation strategy. In addition, according to Sivasubramonian (2004, 230–321), the total factor productivity of the non-agricultural sectors grew at an annual rate of 1.21 percent between 1950–51 and 1964–65, indicating that the growth in the manufacturing sector after Independence was accompanied by a steady improvement in its productivity. Hence, as demonstrated by this Indian experience, an open economy regime does not necessarily led to economic growth.

It has also been revealed that some key industries – those that swiftly developed after the liberalisation reforms and successfully competed in the world market – had their origins in the pre-reform period under government protection, which had imposed severe restrictions on the activities of multinational enterprises. A typical case is the pharmaceutical industry. As we will see later in detail, in the 1970s the government started to control multinational companies in the pharmaceutical industry. Until then such industries had dominated the Indian market. The government revised the patents acts relating to the industry so that Indian companies could easily find entry into the production of pharmaceuticals (Chaudhuri 2004). Under this new protection policy, the industry witnessed a remarkable growth in Indian companies that developed as exporters to the world market in the 1990s. Government policies after Independence contributed to the growth in India of the IT sector, another successful exporting industry. Since the time of Jawaharlal Nehru, governments stressed the need to develop the sciences and a system of higher education, leading to the creation of a large number of scientists, engineers and other technical and scientific human resources. As in the pharmaceutical industry, tightened governmental control over multinational enterprises like IBM since the 1970s and other protective policies are reported to have helped the expansion of Indian companies in this field (Balakrishnan 2006). Hence the import-substitution strategy and other protective policies helped form the bases of some key industries that in the future, with the globalisation of the economy, became the foremost producers of Indian export products. Many auto-parts producers that later supported the development of an automobile industry in the 1990s had been established by the beginning of the 1980s under a government project to launch the Indian auto industry (see Chapter 4). Developments achieved in the pre-reform period therefore formed the basis upon which further developments in the post-reform period could be realised.

However, it is wrong to understand the Indian experience as suggesting that a closed system is always conducive to economic development. As previous studies have shown, there is no doubt that the Licence Raj and the lack of competition among companies under the import-substitution industrialisation regime helped form a "high-cost, low quality" Indian economy. As Chapter 10 will illustrate, the significant decline in the relative prices of consumer durables and communication charges would not have been realised without the pro-market reforms of the 1990s. Post-reform globalisation significantly contributed to an improvement in the quality of products in some formal sector industries. The acceleration in the growth rate around 2003 may have proved elusive without these changes. Thus the liberalisation and globalisation as witnessed in the 1990s seem to have been instrumental in upgrading the Indian economy towards a new stage of development. At the same time, this upgrading under the open economy system could not have been achieved but for various developments under the closed economy system before 1980.

Our brief examination of the Indian experience suggests that we have to go beyond a dichotomous framework of understanding economic growth, such as focusing on clarifying whether either an open or a closed system is conducive to development. The roles played by both systems have been historically mutually connected. It also indicates that it is not sufficient to interpret economic development only in connection with changes in government policy. In this connection, an observation made by Balakrishnan (2010, xxii) is illuminating. According to him, there was a tendency in India to be largely guided by the idea that growth is determined by the policy regime. "Naturally, it was to leave them ill-prepared to recognise a quickening of the economy while the policy regime remained unchanged. Not a dog had barked as the elephant deftly shifted gear to quicken her pace *circa* 1980". In this volume, I attempt to identify the roots of economic growth in various fields and aspects of the economy and society without confining our perspective only to changes in government policies.[3]

To present our conclusion in advance, I identify the following three developments as the most important factors behind contemporary economic growth: The long-term development of the agrarian economy and socio-economic changes in rural society; achievements in the import-substitution industrialisation; and the pro-market reforms, the liberalisation and globalisation of the economy. Growth since the 1980s has been particularly striking in the informal sector as well as in the technology-intensive industries. An analysis of the above three factors provides a key to understanding this characteristic of contemporary Indian economic growth.

Historical changes in various areas have led to the economic growth witnessed since the 1980s. The following sections will outline these.

## The Role Played by the Rural Economy: Rural Markets and New Entrepreneurs

A series of statistical studies suggests that the growth of the agrarian sector was the driving force leading to the acceleration in GDP growth rate. As early as 1992, Kumar (1992) pointed out that 1981/82 was the time when the real GDP experienced a break in its growth trend and that this fissure seems to have been prompted by the disruption of the primary sector's growth rate followed by the secondary and tertiary sectors.

Balakrishnan (2010, Chapter 3) further elaborates upon the role of the agrarian sector in growth acceleration. As indicated already, he argues, based on an analysis of GDP break years that suggests that the evidence for manufacturing having served as the engine of growth is weak, that a faster agricultural growth which had been maintained for at least three decades provided an expansion in demand that enabled improved growth in services, from which the growth impulse ran to industry. Thus he stresses the prominence of agriculture in the growth transition that took place in the late 1970s.

Using both an input-output (I-O) equation and a simultaneous equation framework, Sastry et al. (2003) examine the connections between growth in the agricultural, industrial and service sectors of the economy. They reveal that, despite a substantial increase in the share of the services sectors in GDP over the decades through to the early 2000s, the agricultural sector, due to its demand linkage with the other sectors, was still integral when it came to dictating the overall growth rate of the economy. The results based on I-O tables and econometric analysis indicate that a rise in agricultural output is bound to raise the demand for industrial goods, both for consumption and for investment. According to them, "demand originated from both agriculture and exports plays a major role in determining the overall growth in GDPR".

The consumption data corroborates the observations of Sastri et al., as will be seen in Chapter 6. Though slightly declining, the rural share in the total non-food expenditure remained around 60 percent during the 1980s and 1990s, proving the importance of rural demand as the major market for the industrial and service sectors.[4] Table 6.11 tells us that in terms of the total non-food expenditure, the bottom 90 percent group of the rural population accounted for 43–37 percent of the total, whereas similar figures for the top 20 percent group of the urban population ranged from 18 to 23 percent. Therefore, if we can view the latter group as representing the "urban middle classes", non-food expenditure by the "urban middle classes" is shown to have been as little as about half that of the non-elite rural population in the 1990s. This highlights the need to question the widely accepted view that regards the urban middle classes as the major consumer group leading economic growth since the 1980s.

In fact, the surveys undertaken by the National Council of Applied Economic Research (NCAER) in 1985 and 1989 (see Chapter 6) emphasised the importance of rural demand for consumer durables even in the 1980s, particularly drawing attention to the fact that non-rich groups in rural areas formed a core consumer group for such goods. In 1993/94 the rural markets bought up 60 percent of the consumer durables, and at the end of the 1990s, for the majority of the consumer-durable items, the share of the rural market exceeded 50 percent (see Chapter 6). In a survey of a Bihar village (Tsujita and Oda 2012, Appendix Table 2, p. 28), 63 percent of households were found to have owned a mobile phone in 2011. In terms of employment, the small scale and informal sectors in industry, services and construction have dominated since the 1980s. Chapters 7 and 8 will delve into how rural demand was the core market for these sectors and grew remarkably.

Rural involvement in Indian economic development has not been confined to the provision of receptive markets for goods and services. Socio-economic changes in village society have been accompanied by the emergence of new types of entrepreneurs with rural origins. Quite a few families with a farming background, enriched in the Green Revolution, started agro-based businesses before entering into newly thriving industries like pharmaceuticals from the 1990s (to be delineated in Chapter 10). The core business groups in the prominent apparel exporting centre of Tiruppur, for instance, had their origins in the surrounding rural areas. The agrarian sector and rural development have evidently sat at the heart of Indian economic expansion since circa 1980, and the first priority of this volume is to verify this hypothesis.

## Agrarian Development

Readers who correctly understand rural India to be characterised by poverty and inequality will perhaps not be comfortable with our argument that regards it as a dynamic source of development across the sectors. Admittedly, rural poverty and inequality still remain pressing issues, but I want to focus on remarkable achievements that have been made in two spheres since the early twentieth century: The expansion of agrarian production and transformations within the village social structure.

From the middle of the nineteenth century, Indian agriculture steadily raised its productivity and extended farming areas by reclaiming uncultivated "waste lands". Though by the end of the nineteenth century easily reclaimable waste areas had become scarce, forcing land expansion to come to a standstill, cultivators managed to maintain and often raise land productivity until around 1920. They did so by increasing the use of manures, including purchased fertilisers, and by digging more irrigation wells. However, Indian agricultural production suffered from the world agrarian depression starting in the 1920s and the Great Depression in the 1930s, which brought a radical drop in the prices of agrarian products in India, obliging farmers to curb their use of manure and stop building wells. This fall in agrarian prices was the leading cause of agrarian stagnation in the interwar period in India (see Chapter 1).

Affected by the world trading situation, agriculture became sluggish in the colonial period when a free trade regime dominated. In the 1950s, however, it resumed its vigour with a notable rise in land productivity. Agrarian prices had recovered from the slump, agrarian investments by the government began and farmers became more dynamic in their efforts to raise output. Against this backdrop, the spread of the Green Revolution from the middle of the 1960s led to a remarkable growth in agrarian production all over India, and a new set of technologies penetrated even among small farmers, resulting in an improved income in most segments of agrarian society. This was accompanied by a significant growth of non-farm activities in rural areas and nearby urban areas, which tightened rural labour markets and helped to gradually lift the real agricultural wage rate from the middle of the 1970s. Some enriched villagers began entering businesses in non-farm sectors.

This volume tries to locate the Green Revolution in the context of the long-term history of agrarian activity since the end of the nineteenth century. It also seeks to clarify the mechanism through which almost all classes, including agricultural labourers, succeeded in raising their incomes and, in this way, invigorated the rural markets for non-agricultural goods and services. Therefore, the second hypothesis that will be explored is that agrarian development from the end of the nineteenth century formed one of the historical roots of contemporary economic growth. It did so in the sense that it helped most classes of the rural population to increase their demand for consumer goods, engendered an expanded demand for agrarian inputs like manure and machines and, through both of these, fed the rural markets that have supported economic growth.

## Changes in the Village Social Structure: The Emancipation of the Lower Classes

It is not necessarily self-evident that improved agricultural production automatically increases income in all segments of the rural population, including among agricultural labourers and other lower-strata people. In rural society in the latter half of the nineteenth century and even in the first half of the twentieth century, a handful of dominant, elite villagers often owned more than half of the village lands, whereas the majority of the villagers scarcely owned any and worked on the land of others, either as agricultural labourers or as tenants. As indicated by the fact that many agricultural labourers were bonded workers unable to freely leave their masters or change jobs, the livelihoods of the lower classes of villager were under the economic and social control of usually upper-caste landowners. This system guaranteed that the elites would appropriate any benefits from increased agrarian production, and, therefore, without a radical weakening of that control, a substantial rise in real agricultural wage rates would have been unlikely.

The system, however, did begin to gradually weaken at the end of the nineteenth century in some regions in India. The proliferation of non-farm job opportunities – such as working on plantations overseas – encouraged a sense of independence among village agricultural labourers and other subaltern villagers, and upper-caste villagers started shifting to urban areas to get white-collar jobs and a higher education. Their control over the subaltern villagers in their native villages subsequently deteriorated. As seen in Chapter 6, in the latter half of the twentieth century, upper-caste elite landowners in many regions in India shifted to urban areas, reducing their ownership of village land and their hold over the labouring classes. On the other hand, previously landless or almost landless groups of villagers, like the OBC (Backward Castes), SCs and other lower castes, obtained small amounts of land through land reforms, waste-land distribution policies, or by purchase, and thereby moved towards socio-economic emancipation and an enhanced social status in village society. The waning power of local elites over subaltern villagers meant that they were unable to prevent wages rising in accordance with the tightening of the labour market. Thus, the structure of village landownership may remain basically unchanged with a handful of landowners still in possession of most village land, but agricultural labourers have successfully achieved a steady rise in their real wages. Hence my third hypothesis concerns the growth of emancipation movements since the beginning of the twentieth century and their fundamental role in crafting the foundation upon which agrarian growth rests.

## Consuming "Quasi-Branded Goods"

In connection with this third hypothesis, the fact that groups of subaltern villagers have had a keen interest in raising their status in hierarchical village society seems to have given a unique orientation to their consumption behaviour. In nineteenth-century south India, consumption patterns differed between the upper and lower strata, based on economic inequality and social hierarchy, and such differences were often based on social norms and rules. From the beginning of the twentieth century, those subaltern villagers who had started to emancipate themselves began to wear clothes which had traditionally been forbidden to them and adopted customs previously reserved for the higher castes, like eating rice and drinking coffee. A similar trend was witnessed in villages in Kerala in the 1990s as the impact of globalisation spread. Here, it was reported that youths from the SC castes were purchasing and wearing cheap imitations of the shirts they had seen film actors wearing, demonstrating their resistance to upper-caste elites. The richer groups among the subalterns purchase consumer durables, even if they do not need them, as a symbol of their raised social status. As many of them are still economically poor, they can only afford cheap imitations of branded commodities without any guarantee of quality. This volume refers to these as "quasi-branded goods". Evidently, the consumption behaviour of the rural masses, rather than being based entirely on an economic rationale, generally reflects their wish to climb the social ladder and tends to be oriented towards "quasi-branded goods". This is my fourth hypothesis.

### The Formation of a National Economy: The Role of Import-Substitution Industrialisation

My fifth hypothesis pertains to the creation of a national economy and the achievements in import-substitution industrialisation between 1950 and 1980. As previously mentioned, it is important to note that the basic conditions for producing goods and services to cater to the expanding demand had formed by around 1980 and enabled the Indian economy to grow after that. As Nayyar (2006) has argued, the import-substitution industrialisation regime, together with the agrarian developments seen above, prepared the ground for further advancements in the 1990s. Protective tariff systems had been partly employed since the 1920s (see Chapter 2). Cain and Hopkins' "Gentlemanly Capitalism" implies that British financial capitalists took the initiative in introducing protective policies to India (Cain and Hopkins 1993), but it is contended here, based on an examination of the Indo-Japan Trade Negotiations in the 1930s, that while the basic aim of British trade policies towards India was to reserve Indian markets for British industries as much as possible, it was the growth of nationalist movements that chiefly forced the colonial government to utilise protective tariffs. This partial introduction of protective policies did support the growth of manufacturing in India, yet it was only under the comprehensive protective tariff system and the state-led industrialisation regime in Independent India that the economy came to develop capital goods in heavy industries. The steel industry alone had grown in the colonial period.

The period between 1950 and 1980 witnessed the establishment of the technological requirements for industrial progress, the growth of entrepreneurs and the materialisation of a large corpus of scientists, engineers and technicians (see Chapter 4). The pharmaceutical and IT industries, which became major exporting industries, also started to grow in the 1970s under government protection. Interestingly, in comparison with other developing countries at a similar stage of development, the Indian economy had a comparative advantage in technologically intensive industries as early as 1980. It was in the period of a closed economy that these foundations for the global developments of the 1990s were laid (Roy 2011). Contemporary economic development, in which the global development of technology-intensive industries plays a leading role, clearly owes much to what was achieved in the formation of a national economy, whose origins can be found in the nationalist movements of the colonial period.

In spite of these achievements, the Indian economy became one of "high-cost, low quality" in the three decades under the Licence Raj, mainly due to a lack of internal and external competition. The Indian share in world trade seriously declined, and low-quality, high-price Indian goods did not have a competitive edge over foreign products. This issue of a "high-cost, low quality" economy was addressed in the process of the pro-market reforms in the 1990s.

## The Growth of Informal Sectors and the Production of "Quasi-Branded Goods"

Sixth is the hypothesis that the development of Indian industries has been affected by the rural and urban poor's preference for "quasi-branded goods".

In terms of employment, the informal sectors have led growth. Though a set of government regulations and policies encouraging the growth of the small-scale and informal sectors were key in this, as Roy has explained (1998), they accounted for the growth only in part. Even in the 1930s, when there were few government regulations on industry and employment, the hosiery industry, which produced a large variety of goods catering in small batches to quickly changing, regionally differentiated markets, was not dominated by large factories based on "the economy of scale" but rather by a large number of small-scale producers (Chapter 3). When the desire for light industrial goods in rural areas swelled in the 1980s, the main producers catering to it were in the latter category. To take an example from the weaving industry, the mill sector, which manufactured branded goods usually for the urban markets, rapidly lost its share in the face of keen competition from the products of small powerloom factories. Chapter 7 finds that in the textile, footwear and plastic recycling industries, the small-scale and informal sectors are chiefly responsible for the output of cheaper varieties of goods. As the units of production are generally small, smaller workshop owners can more efficiently control the manufacturing process, sometimes directly participating in it. Such small-scale and informal sectors can cater to seasonally changing, fragmented markets and benefit from the availability of cheap migrant labourers of low-educational attainment, whose connections with rural areas enable the employers to keep workers' employment conditions low and insecure. They also, crucially, profit from using low-cost inputs, like recycled materials, second-hand machines and imitations of imported machines. In this way, these sectors have a series of systems well adapted to suitably producing quasi-branded goods, that is, cheap goods but with no quality guarantee.

## Rural Demand and the Growth of the Service and Construction Industries

The seventh hypothesis of this volume is that for the service sector and construction industries, the principal markets were rural at least until the end of the 1990s and that small and informal enterprises numerically dominated. The average growth rate of the service sector jumped from 4.5 percent in 1951–1980 to 6.6 percent in 1981–1990 and then 7.5 percent in 1991–2000. This 1 percent acceleration in the 1990s was accounted for by growth in the modern sub-sectors, that is, communication, finance and IT services stimulated by the economic reforms, but the "traditional" sub-sectors like trade and transportation, continuously growing since the

1980s, made up more than 60 percent of the total outturn of the services sector even by the beginning of the 2000s, as mentioned above. Chapter 8 will assert that agrarian development and the subsequent surge in rural demand are likely to have nurtured the growth of "traditional services"; the Green Revolution led to an increase in trade. A survey of tourists conducted around 2003 by NCAER reveals that 75 percent of Indian tourists were from rural households, and they were responsible for more than 60 percent of the total expenditure on tourism. The flourishing of tourism-related industry has been largely dependent upon rural demand. An increasing number of rural people started to migrate to urban and other regions, and even the lower classes started taking part in pilgrimage tours (Chapter 9), which explains the expanding participation in tours by rural people. In construction too, rural areas prove vital, containing about 80 percent of total house construction, in terms of number, and about 60 percent, in terms of cost, at the beginning of the 2000s. The connection between rural socio-economic changes and the growth of the service sector and construction appears to provide a vital key to understanding the rise in their growth rates in the 1980s.

## Growing Connections between Rural Society and Urban Informal Sectors and the Formation of Mass and "Middle-Class" Markets

It is not possible to overlook the interwoven nature of rural society and urban informal sectors over the last three decades. Propelled by an expanding rural demand, urban informal sectors have grown rapidly, attracting a large number of non-elite migrating workers from rural areas, who stay in slums and other peripheral areas in cities. Most of them maintain a strong connection with the rural area. Many have family members in their villages, return there regularly and frequently remit money to their relatives back home. They and their households are very often maintained by income from both rural and urban areas. The rural population and urban informal sector workers have features in common, including their consumption behaviour, with both groups have a preference to quasi-branded goods. Therefore, in terms of goods and services and human resources, multiple varieties of circulation have developed between the two, and a large number of non-elite families live both urban and rural lives. The demands of the rural population and urban informal sector non-elite workers are equivalent to about 70 percent or more of total consumer goods and services, making them the most important mass consumer-market. Furthermore, the owners of informal sector businesses have grown richer and become the core group of the richest 20 percent of Indian households, which are the major purchasers of high-priced consumer durables like cars. If we can categorise the top 20 percent families as "middle class", then we can say that informal sector growth has resulted in the formation of the core portion of the middle-class market.

## A Silent Revolution: The Emergence of New Types of Entrepreneurs and Their Rural Origins

The development of the rural economy and changes in rural society have contributed to Indian economic growth since the 1980s, not only by providing the major market for industrial goods and services, as mentioned above, but also by serving as the breeding ground for a new type of entrepreneur. As Damodaran's work (2000) indicates, though post-Independence industrial growth has mainly been led by the big business houses, most of which originated in trading communities, since the 1970s some from among farmers' communities, like the Kammas from Andhra and the Marathas from Maharashtra, who have gained wealth through the Green Revolution, have founded non-farm businesses in urban areas. Starting from local businesses like sugar production and construction work, they have invested in emerging industries like pharmaceuticals, engineering and electronics and become members of leading business groups. A good number of new capitalists have emerged from the traditional high-caste landlord classes, who had gradually moved to urban areas and started various non-farm businesses. Entrepreneurs with rural origins play vital roles in some industrial cities, for example the knitwear industries of the Gaundars in Tiruppur, the chemical industries of the Naddars in Sivakasi and the engineering industries of the Ramgarhias in Ludhiana.

As some works suggest, these new capitalists, whose appearance has been based on the development of regional economies, are said to be more oriented to technological, as well as global, developments and liberalised policy mixes than the traditional business houses. Pederson (2000) calls this emergence of new capitalists as the leading business groups in newly developing industries a "Silent Revolution" and postulates that it was the social factor which led to the 1991 economic reforms.

## The 1991 Economic Reforms and a New Phase in the Development of Formal Sectors

The period preceding the reforms thus witnessed three major developments in the Indian economy. First, agrarian developments and changes in rural society formed the core historical process in which mass, as well as middle class, markets for non-farm products developed in India. Second, the growth of the agrarian economy birthed new entrepreneurs and business groups, who not only played leading roles in rapidly growing technology-intensive industries like the pharmaceuticals and engineering industries, but also may have prompted the government to start the economic reforms. Third, while the foundation for the further developments was formed in the 30 years of import-substitution industrialisation, the lack of internal and external competition contributed to forming a "high-cost, low quality" Indian economy.

Chapter 10 highlights the historical role of the economic reforms starting in the 1980s and culminating in 1991. It argues that the transformation of a "high-cost, low quality" economy to a more "low-cost, high-quality" one has contributed to combining the core formal-sector industries with the growing markets. As is well known, the liberalisation reforms abolished the Licence Raj, intensified internal and external competition, encouraged the import of machines and technologies from overseas and inspired investment of foreign capital in India. Under this new regime, some important sections of the formal sectors, such as the consumer durables and communication industries, have successfully lowered prices and improved the quality of their products and services so that they meet the demands of the mass and elite markets. Thereby the output of the consumer-durable and communication industries has successfully penetrated the expanding rural and urban markets. This has helped these industries to become the leaders of Indian economic development.

Another aspect the chapter emphasises relates to the in-house system of training and educating employees in technology-intensive industries, like the automobile and IT industries. To take an example of the auto industry, even parts producers catering to auto assemblers have introduced a system of human resource training and education, in which employees are given systematic training so that they may catch up with technological innovations. A system guaranteeing manufacturing at international quality standards has also been widely established under the influence of direct investment from abroad. In this way, these technology-intensive industries have prepared the ground for exporting, exploiting a new field in the world market.

As a whole, this volume asserts that Indian economic growth as witnessed over last three decades is a cumulative result of the experiences of the Indian economy and society since the first half of the twentieth century. Let us look again at the core factors here. Agrarian developments and rural social changes have created both mass and "middle-class" markets and nurtured technology- and global-oriented entrepreneurs to lead newly emerged industries. State-led import-substitution industrialisation established the foundations for further economic growth, though the economy became one of "high-cost, low quality". The economic reforms, which linked the consumer-durable and communication industries with the emerging mass and middle-class markets by lowering prices, have helped technology-intensive industries find new foreign markets through the establishment of a system that guarantees production at an international standard of quality. In other words, we cannot single out only one factor, like a change in government policy, as definitely having determined the trajectories of economic growth. Instead, an accumulation of historical experiences and the connections between them can be identified as resulting in contemporary economic growth.

The importance of examining the relationship between the agricultural, industrial and service sectors has so far not attracted much scholarly attention. In contrast to the generally accepted view that understands the rural economy as a variable dependent on the developments in other sectors, the empirical analyses of this volume, following suggestions by Balakrishnan et al. and other statistical works, stress the impact of agricultural changes on the other sectors. The strengthened complementary connections between urban and rural societies are deemed vital.

The role played by social change, in particular the growth of emancipation movements among subalterns, in economic development has also escaped intense scrutiny so far. The rise in real agricultural wage rates, which contributed to the growth of mass rural markets for non-farm products and services, would have not been realised if the tight control over low-caste labouring classes by the dominant landowning classes had remained unchanged. The consumption behaviour that is oriented to "quasi-branded goods" among the lower classes, which has characterised the mass demand for non-food goods and so aided the growth of informal sectors in India, can be understood only in view of the burgeoning sense of independence among those classes.

## Notes

1 According to Gordon and Gupta (2004), the average annual growth rate of industry declined from 6.8 percent for 1981–1990 to 5.8 per cent for 1991–2000, while the corresponding figure for GDP remained unchanged at 5.8 percent.

2 Nayyar (2012, 64) also suggests that the effect of services export growth on total services growth is still relatively small.

3 In connection with our argument, Kaushik Basu's suggestion relating to understanding the economic growth of India and China is worth attention. According to him, it is simplistic to the point of being flawed to do economic analysis in terms of the size of government (big government is bad or big government is good) or in terms of markets versus the state. He argues that, in addition to markets, trade and incentives, social norms, institutions and the state are also critically important for an economy to prosper (Basu 2009).

4 While the share of the agricultural section in GDP declined after the 1980s, this decline seems to have been compensated for by an increase in non-farm earnings by the rural population. An increasing number of the rural population have been either engaged in non-farm jobs in rural areas or have migrated to urban areas, thus increasing earnings from non-farm sectors. According to Lanjouw and Murgai (2009), in many states in India, non-farm incomes account for nearly half of the total income rural households earn. As Binswanger-Mkhize (2013) reveals, the rural–urban gaps in poverty, per capita income and consumption have not increased sharply over the past 30 years, thanks to increased non-farm earnings by rural households.

# Part I

# Stirrings of Economic Development

## Moves after World War I

When viewing the twentieth century as a whole, the greatest break in economic growth in India occurred around 1950. During the colonial period, the Indian economy was basically under a free trade regime and stagnated, with an annual growth rate averaging less than 1 percent. Following Independence, this jumped to more than 3 percent. Part 1 of this book looks at the colonial period and explores why the economy was stricken with inertia during this time. Under the colonial free trade regime, Indian agricultural production, which was substantial enough to determine the direction of the Indian economy, had been integrated into the global economy. However, with the world agricultural depression and the 1929 Great Depression there was a serious drop in prices, and Indian agriculture fell into stagnation. Yet, despite the sluggishness of the first half of the century, this period nevertheless witnessed stirrings of developments that were further accelerated in the post-Independence period. The potential for growth in agricultural production was already apparent, and movements by village subalterns to emancipate themselves both socially and economically from the village elites sprang into life at this time.

The growth of nationalist movements prompted the partial introduction of a protective tariff system, and this helped some manufacturing industries to grow. The "inward-looking" import-substitution industrialisation (ISI) that was to be implemented after Independence had its beginnings in this period. Industrial expansion encouraged the migration of labourers from rural villages, and the industrial labour market, with its multi-tiered structure closely connected to stratified rural society, can be regarded as the prototype of the post-Independence labour market.

Changing trends in consumption and the competitive environment led to new developments in some traditional industries like handloom weaving, and expansion in lower-class demand multiplied the number of small-scale and marginal enterprises in some regions. Such enterprises, though limited regionally, were to develop significantly within the overall economic growth of the post-Independence period. As the subaltern population sought to raise its status within the hierarchical society, some of its members began to diversify the items they consumed, adopting the consumption patterns of the higher

DOI: 10.4324/9781003341550-2

classes. This was the backdrop against which small-scale and marginal enterprises survived and grew, and the seedbed of the remarkable changes in the consumption pattern of the subaltern population after Independence.

The first half of the twentieth century, then, may have been a time of economic stagnation, but it was also marked by the first stirrings of post-Independence economic and social development.

# 1 Agriculture in the Great Depression

## Agricultural Production and Changes in Rural Society

### Environmental Changes, the Drop in the Prices of Agricultural Products and the Stagnation of Agricultural Production

#### *Changes in Agricultural Production: Expansion of Output and Intensification of Land Use*

In the first half of the twentieth century, when the country remained under colonial rule, the Indian economy grew at a rate of 0.9 percent (as we shall see in Chapter 5). This amounted to barely 0.1 percent per capita and was symptomatic of the lethargic performance of agricultural production. Between 1900/01 and 1946/7 the primary sector grew by only 0.4 percent. However, Indian agriculture itself was by no means stagnant until around 1920. From the nineteenth century, it had seen extensive development of previously uncultivated land and more intensive use of land already under crop. At the beginning of the nineteenth century, only a small portion of land in villages and their environs was put to agricultural use, with the majority being uncultivated "waste" land. Over the century, the latter was rapidly reclaimed. For example, in the dry region of one district in South India, 90 percent of the "waste" land that had previously occupied some 40 percent of the village area was transformed into arable land by 1900 (Yanagisawa 2011a). The extent to which such conversions took place varied from region to region, but in most places there was a fall in unfarmed land. Between the 1860s and the beginning of the 1890s, this vast increase in arable areas stimulated an equally vast increase in agricultural output.

Even in the period between the 1890s and around 1911, agricultural output on the whole improved. Food grains like rice and wheat were produced at a pace that outstripped the growth rate of the population, and there was an even greater rise in the production of non-food grains like cotton and jute. Agricultural production per capita grew significantly. Though exceptionally there was a decrease in Bengal, most regions saw considerable growth, the greatest of which was recorded in the Punjab, followed by Madras and the Central Provinces (Blyn 1966, Tables 5.1, 5.2, 5.6, 5.8). Overall, the per capita increase in the production of both edible and non-edible grains during 1860–1920 was remarkable (Kumar 1983, Chapter II-4).

DOI: 10.4324/9781003341550-3

The conversion of "waste" land – or, in other words, external expansion – was a primary cause of growth in agricultural production. However, in terms of rice and wheat, the rate of increase was in the amount of grain produced per unit area rather than in the area under cultivation; the rise in production owed more to intensive double and triple cropping than to external expansion (Blyn 1966, 130). In many areas, irrigation significantly contributed to the enlarged per acre yield. In the Punjab and the Madras Presidency in particular, the government played an important role in improving and extending the irrigation system, and in the twenty years from 1880, the area under government irrigation grew by 60 percent (Whitcombe 1983, 718). This expansion must have also contributed to the reclamation of "waste" land, though compared with the period before 1880 this process was far slower as a large part of the previously unfarmed areas was now under cultivation. Even more important, however, were private water initiatives, such as wells. These rocketed from the end of the nineteenth century (Whitcombe 1983) and by around 1900, some 60 percent of irrigated land in the country was watered by non-government sources, more than half of which were wells.

### *Decline in Common-Use Land and the Intensification of Agriculture*[1]

From the end of the nineteenth century, farmers and other producers responded to a deterioration in the agrarian environment by developing intensive agriculture. This change can be examined in the context of the Tamil area of South India.

The broad stretches of uncultivated land that existed in the nineteenth century had been used as forest, grazing and quarrying lands, and formed an infrastructure that sustained economic life, providing people with house-building materials, fuelwood, manure and fodder. The rapid shrinkage in their extent from the latter half of the nineteenth century meant a deterioration of this essential infrastructure. In this sense, uncultivated "waste" land was in fact indispensable for sustaining agricultural production in the area. However, the decaying of the agrarian infrastructure was not automatically accompanied by a decline in agricultural productivity in Tamil Nadu, at least until 1930. Rural people not only managed to maintain the yield per acre but in many regions more often successfully raised agricultural productivity by changing their farming practices, moving to more intensive production methods and expanding inter-regional trade in fertilisers and the movement of livestock.

In rice-producing areas under river irrigation, like the Kaveri River basin, uncropped land had shrunk to a large extent as early as the first half of the nineteenth century. A report of the 1880s noted that there was almost no waste land left in the area, due to the continued expansion of arable farming. In Lalgudi, in the neighbouring Trichinopoly (Tiruchirapalli) District, hardly any uncropped land remained in 1865. Because there was no land for pasture in the villages, cattle were fed only straw and were in very poor condition as a result. River-water silt was the only manure available for the rice production, and few farms used any form of fertiliser due to the difficulty of getting hold of it. This meant the land could only be cropped once. Double-cropping was the exception in Lalgudi, and its yield was the lowest of all the districts in Tamil Nadu.

This state of affairs greatly altered towards the end of the nineteenth century. The construction of dams in the upper reaches of the Kaveri reduced the quantity and richness of the silt, and farmers in the area were forced to change their practices. They started penning herds of sheep and goats coming from other districts and using their manure to enrich their fields. Wild indigo (*kolinji*) and other plants were carted in great quantities from the Coimbatore and Salem districts and applied to the fields as green manure.[2] Reports after 1900 note that farmers were aware that it was possible to obtain forms of fertiliser and that its use had become extensive. Moreover, the Kaveri farmers were sending their cattle for grazing to districts with large amounts of pasturage remaining.[3] The general rise in prices for rice and other agricultural products at this time supplied the necessary economic condition that allowed farmers to purchase commercial manure. A 1910 report on the Coimbatore District in the irrigated region states:

> A rise in the price of paddy enables the ryots cultivating lands irrigated by the Kalingarayan channel to increase their expenditure on manure, hence an expansion in the radius within which employment is provided in plucking and carting wild indigo.[4]

Thus, despite the reduction in the availability of river-water silt, farmers not only maintained their paddy yield per acre but increased it considerably. Greater use of manuring allowed double-cropping to become the norm in many villages (Yanagisawa 2011).

In places outside the river-irrigated areas, farming depended on water provided through rainfall, wells and tanks. In the middle of the nineteenth century, there were still large amounts of uncropped common land in such areas, providing farmers with leaf manure and fodder for their cattle. However, here too the environment that supported agriculture deteriorated. As we have already seen, by the end of the century the spread of cultivation into former "waste" land meant that village common land was disappearing. The government's forest reservation policy further exacerbated the situation by limiting the collection of leaf manure from forests, leading to a shortage, and a resultant rise in price, of this fertiliser. Farmers again responded to the altered environment and succeeded in maintaining productivity by adopting more intensive farming practices. They purchased leaf manure, such as wild indigo carted in from forested areas, and also started to grow manure crops in their own fields. As the use of fertiliser increased, so did the number of irrigation wells and the frequency of cropping. The area irrigated by wells in Tamil Nadu rose from 783,000 acres to 1,206,000 acres between 1891/92 and 1922/23 (Season and Crop Reports of the Madras Presidency, various years).

The depletion of common lands and implementation of forest restrictions did not defeat the farmers. Instead, they managed to succeed in preventing a fall in productivity and in some areas even increased it. They did so by seeking access to manure, both purchased and self-grown, and multiplying the number of harvests they could take from the land. In the process, they decreased their dependency on the natural resources of their own locality. A similar situation developed in the dry areas. Rises in the prices of crops such as groundnuts in the dry lands provided the backdrop for the increased use of purchased manures. The 1932 supplement to the *South Arcot District Gazetteer* commented that "[O]wing to the increased profits obtained from groundnut crop grown in dry lands, the manuring of this kind of land has only been lately taken up by the ryots".[5]

### *Drop in Crop Prices and Agricultural Stagnation*

Prior to World War I, agricultural output in India as a whole was on an upward trend, in terms of both area under crop and yield per acre. Food production per capita had risen in all but a few areas. The Great War, however, marked the beginning of stagnation, even regression. Food production came to a virtual standstill, falling significantly from 0.61 percent before the 1910s to 0.03 percent after. At the same time, the population grew by 1.12 percent, a large increase on the preceding period. This meant that food production per head of population fell dramatically (Blyn 1966, 99). Though the production of non-food crops swelled considerably, the growth rate of agrarian output as a whole, including non-food crops, shrank drastically compared with the pre-war period, and was well below the population growth. In the last 20 years of the colonial administration in India, per capita agrarian output was fixed on a downwards trajectory (Blyn 1966, 119).

What caused this stagnation? It is safe to say a major factor was a serious drop in the prices of agricultural products at the time of the world agricultural depression of the 1920s and the 1929 Great Depression that followed. As Figure 1.1 shows, the price of rice in the Madras Presidency rose markedly until 1918, but fell to close to half the figure reached that year in the course of the 1920s, when signs of stagnation and a slump in prices began to be apparent, and the 1930s, when the effects of the Great Depression were being felt.

Indian agricultural production had been increasingly integrated into the global economy since the second half of the nineteenth century. As the global market expanded, price rises for agricultural products stimulated an increase in both the use of fertilisers and the number of wells dug, allowing an upsurge in production. However, once prices began to fall, this process shifted into reverse. A government publication of 1937 pointed out that the low prices then prevailing were preventing the further spread of manuring.[6] This was corroborated by a 1938 survey of a village in South India: "It is said that generally the agriculturist is now content with applying whatever manure he

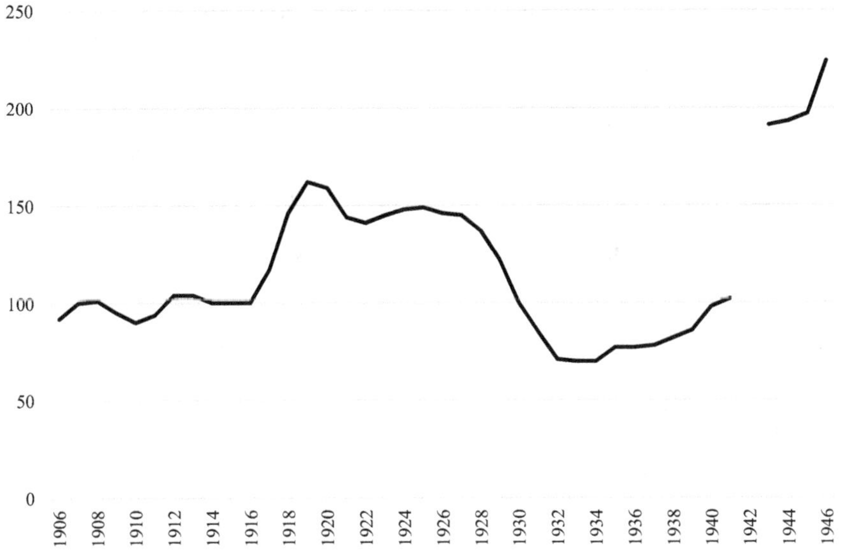


*Figure 1.1* Index number of three-year average of prices of rice in the Madras Presidency (1915–1916 = 100).

himself gathers and is growing more and more reluctant to buy from outside even the necessary cattledung".[7] Further, new wells ceased to be dug. As we shall see in Table 5.3, the area irrigated by wells in the districts making up the present Tamil Nadu grew enormously at the beginning of the twentieth century, then diminished. It was only in the 1950s that the area once again expanded.

The stimulation of Indian agriculture during its integration with the global economy under the free trade regime of the colonial period did not last. From the 1920s, agriculture, and the Indian economy as a whole, began to stagnate and even regress. Global reductions in the prices of agricultural products after the 1920s brought the further use of manure and the expansion of well irrigation to a halt, and affected per capita food production negatively; integration with the global economy under the free trade regime resulted in Indian economic growth remaining at less than 1 percent during the first half of the twentieth century. However, at the same time, we should note that productivity rose in South India down to the 1910s, and in the context of certain conditions, such as better prices for their products, agriculturists actively expanded production by intensifying manure use and well building. This means that Indian agriculture had ample prospects. In the midst of deteriorating environmental conditions – the loss of "waste" (community use) land in the vicinity of villages and the lowering of the nutritional value from river silt – people preserved agrarian productivity and raised it. This demonstrates the latent potential possessed by Indian agriculture from the end of the nineteenth century.

## The Structure of Rural Society: Elites and Subalterns

### *Hierarchical Structure of Village Society*

Examining the social structure of rural villages allows us to investigate not just social developments in the period before Independence but the basis upon which changes in agricultural production occurred at that time. Unlike in early modern Japan, where rural society was centred on small farmers who cultivated their holdings with the labour of family members, that in India was hierarchical and divided into several different castes. Members of higher castes generally dominated the lower castes both economically and socially. In the paddy region of South India in the nineteenth century, those involved in agriculture within a village can broadly be divided into four classes. The first consisted of powerful landowners who possessed comparatively large amounts of land and paid land tax to the government. The second was made up of small farmers, who also paid land tax, but their holdings were on a much-reduced scale. The third comprised tenant farmers who leased land from the large landowners, while the agricultural labourers working for these landowners constituted the fourth.

The first group dominated village society. In the Tamil regions (now Tamil Nadu), most belonged to higher castes, such as Brahmins. Their land was worked either by tenant farmers or by agricultural labourers. In the paddy regions, members of this class tended to own more than half the amount of arable land in the villages, even though they amounted to less than 10 percent of the population there. There were many more small farmers than powerful landowners, but their land was nowhere near the same extent. Though tenant farmers came to make up a large proportion of the population by the end of the nineteenth century, they were not so numerous earlier.

Agricultural labourers were mainly members of low castes or of the Dalit ("Untouchable") class. They owned very little land, if any, and, possessing neither cattle nor implements, could not become tenant farmers or farm managers. Thus, they worked as labourers for the large landowners. The relationship between agricultural labourer and employer was often long term. Many labourers worked their whole lives for a single employer, and often this relationship extended over generations, their subordinate position being reinforced by their being bound by debts owed to employers. Often village elites would lay claim to the title of the land their labourers lived on, while the labourers were dependent on the food and clothing supplied by the employer. These labourers were the principal workforce in the cultivation of village lands. To maintain this body of labour, the village elites effectively excluded them from possessing and cultivating the extensive "waste" land that still remained. From the second half of the nineteenth century, when there was an increasing migration of agricultural labourers to overseas plantations and other places, employers tried to stop workers leaving by threatening to evict their families or on the pretext of reclaiming debts. Though there were some who worked as day labourers, day labour alone could not provide enough money to live on for those without their own or tenant land, given that there were long periods during the off-season when labour was not in great demand.

The existence of this kind of hierarchical society, within which agricultural labourers occupied an important place in the workforce, has been reported from all over India, with regional variations. It was particularly prevalent in those regions where agriculture was rich and advanced. For example, Southern Gujarat had the *hali* system, where bonded labourers were employed by Brahmin landowners (Breman 1974) and the *sepidar* system in the Punjab meant that members of the Dalit Chamar caste provided labour for landowners (Kessinger 1979). In northern India, *bhaiachara* tenure, where land was held in common by landowners, was widespread, but even here there was actually great disparity between the holders of such tenure (Stokes 1983, 64–65).[8] Under the *zamindari* system, practised widely in Bengal, those designated to collect land taxes for the government were *zamindars*, lords of large tracts of land. Among the tenant farmers who paid rent to the *zamindars* was a class of rich peasants called *jotedars*. These were politically and economically powerful locally, and share croppers and agricultural labourers were subordinate to them (Ray and Ray 1973; Ray 1979).

There were also numerous villages, other than those we have seen in the paddy areas with their strong social and economic hierarchical structure, which had a looser class structure. For instance, many villages in the dry field farming areas of South India were inhabited by small farmers, including large numbers of villagers, who held and cultivated a great deal of arable land. In the middle of the nineteenth century, even in dry villages, it was general, however, for Dalits to be excluded from holding land, despite the fact there were no permanent labourers in a strong subordinate relationship as in the paddy areas, and a pattern of day labourers was widespread. In the Deccan, where close to half the population held land and there were not abundant numbers of tenant farmers and agricultural labourers, village society was not strongly hierarchical (Fukazawa 1983, 180).

### *Stirrings of Subaltern Emancipation: Working Away from the Village, Non-Agricultural Employment, Migration to Urban Areas*

Elites may have dominated village society, yet subaltern classes, including the dependent agricultural labourers, began a gradual move towards emancipation. One spur for this was the new opportunities for employment outside the village, particularly for members of the lower classes, on plantations both in India and abroad. From the second half of the nineteenth century, large numbers of workers travelled from all over India to the tea plantations of Sri Lanka and other places. Between 1871 and 1930, migrants from India overseas shot up from an annual average of 240,000 people to 660,000 people. Most of these stayed away from between several months and several years before returning to their villages. Far greater were those employed domestically on the construction of roads and railways, the tea plantations of Assam and the tea and coffee plantations of southern India.

The majority of those working in this way were lower-class members from villages, like agricultural labourers. Occupation outside the village encouraged an increasing emancipation from their subordinate position vis-à-vis their employers within the village, and as we shall see below, people from this group eventually managed to acquire rights to land, however small the amount. In the Punjab, new opportunities among bonded labourers in villages for employment in railway construction, in canal colonies and later in the army propelled a breakdown of traditional patron–client relationships between landowners and labour (Mukherjee 2005, 181). In Bengal and Bihar too, seasonal migration to the Assam tea plantations resulted in the weakening of the relationship between landowners and labourers in the villages and a decrease in those involved in long-term employment (Chaudhuri 1983, 167).[9]

Many members of the higher castes in the villages, including the Brahmins, also looked to cities as the mainstay of their lives, taking up white-collar jobs as civil servants, teachers and lawyers, for example. More of the landowning class chose to move away too, relocating to urban areas to enhance their children's educational prospects and prepare them for better occupations. They then leased their land to tenant farmers, or, increasingly, began selling it. As the village elites progressively moved away, and agricultural labourers found work outside the villages and in non-agricultural employment, important changes occurred in the structure of rural society. These were driven by the intensification and commercialisation of agricultural production. An analysis of the Settlement Registers from what was then the Tamil districts of Southern India throws light on these changes.

In the middle of the nineteenth century, village elites, made up in the main of members of the higher castes, had exclusive possession of most village land in the paddy areas of the Tamil districts. They managed it on a large scale, using subordinate labour. However, when they began moving to the cities from the end of the century, they were no longer directly involved with farm management and leased their holdings to tenant farmers. With the intensification of agriculture, small family-managed farms were able to achieve higher productivity than large ones, and this too encouraged the breakup of large holdings and a reliance on small-scale tenancy. Upper-caste landowners, especially those with large holdings, even began to reduce them. As farm workers moved away in ever greater numbers to work on plantations in India and abroad, bonds with their landlords loosened and they gained greater autonomy. This made it more and more difficult for those with large holdings to use workers as freely as they had in the past, and pressured them to turn the land over to tenants. The Settlement Registers from the Tamil areas show that some farm workers rose to become tenant farmers, while others even bought small parcels of land with the money they had earned working outside the village. By the end of the nineteenth century, the traditional socially fragmented structure consisting of a village elite who held all the land and a large class of workers who cultivated it for them was beginning to collapse, be it ever so slowly.

The patterns of change were not simple, though. Conversely, despite the slow breakdown of the old system and the general diminution of the size of landholdings, there was also a tendency for some large farms to expand even further. This was a result of the commercialisation of agriculture that went hand in hand with the integration of Indian agriculture with overseas markets. In the latter half of the nineteenth century, agriculture in South India, like that elsewhere in the country, gradually increased output to meet the demands of remote markets and farmers entrusted the sale of their produce to merchants. Price fluctuations of produce sold at remote markets were acute, forcing small farmers in particular to run up large debts to merchants or moneylenders. If these could not be repaid, the title to their land passed to the creditors and they could be reduced to tenant farmers or even farm labourers. Therefore, some merchants and moneylenders acquired large amounts of land. Furthermore, the commercialisation of the Indian economy as a whole, as well as railroad and canal construction by the colonial authorities, increased the opportunities for large-scale land acquisition through non-agricultural activities. Much of such land became tenant farms (Yanagisawa 1991).

When we look at landholdings without making distinctions between the social attributes of the landholders, statistically there do not seem to be large changes in their distribution. In reality, however, there was, on the one hand, a decrease in large landholdings of the old type held by members of the upper castes, while on the other there was an increase in large-scale holdings by people who had amassed profits in non-agricultural businesses. Similarly, while the ratio of agricultural labourers among the population engaged in agriculture appears largely static, the constituent members of the class betray prodigious movement; some had risen to become tenant farmers or small landholders, and they had been replaced by those reduced to labouring after having lost the small pieces of land they had previously owned. Contrary to appearances, the actual changes were very great. There were transformations too in agricultural management caused by the reduction in large-scale agriculture, and the tendency for this farmland to be turned into tenant farms. The proportion of land given over to tenant farmers also proliferated as a result of land formerly in the hands of smallholders being transferred to merchants or moneylenders, who then rented it out (Yanagisawa 1991).

Such changes were probably less notable in other areas of India. However, Sumit Guha points out that in western India between 1916 and 1947, the area owned by landholders having less than 15 acres increased rapidly, corresponding with the tendency for a reduction in the scale of management. This may be understood to mean that there was a trend away from large-scale management, as in South India (Raj et al. 1985, 238–240; Kumar 1983, 202). A similar inclination towards smaller holdings and smaller areas managed is also reported from the Punjab (Kessinger 1979, 130). In South Gujarat in the period after 1911, the number of landless labourers declined, partly because of their migration to the cities, and labour shortages occurred (Kumar 1983. 204), and in the 1920s there is evidence that labourers were buying or leasing land (Charlesworth 1985, 224; Pandit 1969). In Bengal too bonded labourers, who had existed there from the beginning of British rule, gained an increased sense of autonomy influenced in part by their going to other areas to work, while many landholders found it more profitable to make loans to share tenants rather than employ bonded labourers who needed to be supervised. The *zamindari* system in Bengal began gradually to break down from the 1920s (Kessinger 1979). In the early period of British rule, most agricultural labourers were mainly domestic servants, belonging to the lowest castes. Their status derived from their indebtedness and to a small extent the loss of land. In the course of British rule, however, there was a steady increase in the ratio of farmers who lost their land to repay debts and went to work as day labourers. There was thus a clear change in the composition of agricultural labourers here, just as in South India (Chaudhuri 1983, 176). In the Punjab, though, the proportion of agricultural labourers was lower. The Chamars, who provided such labour, became less dependent on the landlords as a result of their going to work in the canal colonies.

The powerful landholding class remained socially and economically dominant in village society over most regions of India in the first half of the twentieth century, but the seeds had been planted for the subaltern population to seek emancipation.

## Notes

1 For a detailed examination of this topic, see Yanagisawa 2011.
2 F. R. Hemingway, *Madras District Gazetteers: Trichinopoly*, Madras, Superintendent, Government Press, 1907, p. 141.
3 F. R. Hemingway, *Madras District Gazetteers, Tanjore*, Madras, The Superintendent, Government Press, 1906, p. 102; Government of Madras, Proceedings of Board of Revenue, No. 28, 12 Feb. 1921, p. 49, para. 43.
4 Madras Revenue Proceedings, Government Order, No. 102, Revenue, 10th January 1910, p. 9, para. 28.
5 *Statistical Appendix for South Arcot District*, Madras, Superintendent, Government Press, 1932, p. xvi.
6 K. Ramiah, *Rice in Madras: A Popular Handbook*, Superintendent, Government Press, Madras, 1937, pp. 120, 124.
7 Thomas, P.J. and K.C. Ramakrishnan (eds.). 1940. *Some South Indian Villages: A Resurvey*. University of Madras, Madras, p. 84.
8 For the preventing of the Dalits of northern India and members of other low castes from holding land in order to maintain them as employees, see Siddiqi 1973, 54.
9 For the significance of work outside the village for the survival strategies of the Dalits and other members of the lower castes in India during the colonial period and beyond, see Gidwani and Sivaramakrishnan 2003.

# 2 Growth in the Manufacturing Sector

## Nationalist Movements, Import-Substitution Industrialisation and a Multi-tiered Labour Market

### Indian Nationalist Movements and the Launch of a Discriminating Protective Tariff

#### *Introduction of a Discriminating Protective Tariff System*

Though the interwar period saw the stagnation of agricultural production, as we have seen in the previous chapter, it was also the time when the manufacturing industry experienced an important development. In the first half of the twentieth century, the growth rate of secondary industry was 1.5 percent, in contrast with 0.4 percent for the primary industry. Taking 1913 as 100, the world index of manufacturing activity for 1936–1937 averaged 185, where the index for Britain was 122 and for the United States 167, both below the world average. By comparison, India's index was 230 (or 251), as opposed to Japan's 529 and the Soviet Union's 774 (Morris 1983, 609). The high growth rate was in the large-scale factory sector.

Behind this growth in manufacturing was the partial introduction of a protective tariff system in India. Since 1882, colonial India had been under an almost total free trade regime. The British cotton manufacturing industry centred on Lancashire had pressured the government against setting any protective tariff in India, and even when a very small revenue tariff was imposed, it was offset by setting an excise duty on Indian products. In the period after the Great War, however, economic relations between Britain and India underwent an important change. The Government of India Act of 1919 established a Legislative Council in India and gave India fiscal autonomy, so that if the Government of India and the legislature were in agreement on tariff policy, the Secretary of State for India would not interfere. Subsequently, when preparing legislation regarding tariff policy, the Government of India had to take seriously into account the views of industrialists and other economic interests as expressed through the Legislative Council, as well as the strength of the nationalist movements.

In 1921, the Indian Fiscal Commission recommended the adoption of a discriminating protection policy. A protective tariff was permitted for those industries that met three conditions known as the Triple Formula: That the industry possessed natural advantages, that it would not be able to develop in

DOI: 10.4324/9781003341550-4

a desirable manner without protection and that it would ultimately be able to face international competition without protection. A Tariff Board was set up in 1923 to review applications and report to the government. Between 1929 and 1939, protection was given to nine industries: Iron and steel, cotton textiles, sericulture, paper, sugar, silver thread, magnesium chloride, heavy chemicals and matches. Added to the protective tariffs for these individual industries, across-the-board protection came into being from the 1920s in order to secure fiscal revenue to cope with the strained financial situation.

There were a number of factors behind the adoption of a tariff policy that included the protection of a number of heavy industries, and of a line of policy to develop certain other industries. The first was military in nature. From before World War I, British imperialist strategy had pointed out the necessity of establishing a munitions industry in India, and the Indian Munitions Board was set up in 1917 to develop Indian resources (Dewey 1979, 233). Government protection for the iron and steel industry, as we shall see below, was born of the necessity to cater for the needs of the railways as well as to provide munitions. The second factor was the complications inherent in the competitive relationship surrounding India. During the nineteenth century, Britain was the chief supplier of industrial products to India, but after World War I, the newly emergent industrial nations of Germany and Japan gradually began to penetrate this market. Iron and steel goods from Belgium and Germany in particular increased remarkably after World War I, and the import of cotton piece goods from Japan also accelerated at this time. To protect her Indian market from these imports, Britain put a preferential tariff in place for British products, and in cooperation with Indian capital sought a course that permitted a protective tariff to be set regarding product lines inferior to British products in terms of competitiveness. Both international competitiveness over the Indian market and military needs provided the context for the growth of the iron and steel industry.

### *The Indo-Japanese Trade Negotiations: British Cotton Industry Interests and Nationalist Movements*

In regard to introducing a protective tariff, the cotton industry was one of the greatest areas of concern, and a core factor in its introduction was the rise of nationalist movements in India. At this point, we should give critical consideration to Cain and Hopkins' view on "gentlemanly capitalism". Examining British policies on India, they argue that financial interests in London largely determined these policies, and that the influence of British manufacturers like the Lancashire cotton industry further weakened after World War I. The need to ensure that payments to Britain continued to flow smoothly, and the implementation of fiscal and monetary policies that supported that need, remained central to British policy in India. Therefore, Britain pressed India to follow the doctrine of the balanced budget. It attached greater importance to promoting exports from India to maintain a healthy trade balance than to protecting the market in India for Lancashire products. It also sought to increase revenue by taxing imports and promoting local industries. The protection of markets for Indian exports was of critical importance throughout the trade negotiations of the 1930s (Cain and Hopkins 1993, Chapter 8).

However, an analysis of the Indo-Japanese trade negotiations of the 1930s shows that throughout most of the process, Britain was mainly concerned with promoting the interests of the Lancashire cotton industry in the Indian market. Written communications between the India Office and the Government of India reveal that the two bodies pursued remarkably different aims in the negotiations.[1] Two issues were constantly at the centre of the two rounds of Indo-Japanese trade negotiations of the 1930s: Securing a market for Indian raw cotton and how to protect Lancashire's market in India. The 1934 Protocol linked the amount of Japanese cotton piece goods to be imported annually by India and the amount of Indian raw cotton to be imported by Japan. The point that took the longest time to agree on concerned setting limits on the Japanese cotton piece goods importable into India according to quality and volume. The focus here was how to limit the import into India of Japanese products that had a competitive edge over British cotton piece goods in order to protect Lancashire's Indian market. For example, in the second series of negotiations in 1936–1937, both Lancashire and Japan wanted to secure the Indian market in the area of coloured goods, and printed goods in particular. Here, the views of the Secretary of State for India and the Government of India were markedly different. The Government of India emphasised the importance of maintaining the Japanese market for raw cotton, and agreed with the Japanese proposal to reduce the percentage of plain grey goods and increase the allotment of bleached and coloured goods, as Japanese competition in grey goods had dealt a blow to the Madras handloom industry.

Thomas Ainscough, the Senior Trade Commissioner in India and Ceylon, who sat in on the meetings as an observer to guard British interests, took an opposite view. Since the British cotton industry could not compete with the Indian and Japanese products in the fields of plain greys and bleached goods, the priority was to establish how Britain could maintain a market in India for high-quality products such as coloured goods, and, in particular, prints. As Ainscough himself noted, the share of coloured goods in the category ratios and limits on the proportion of prints both directly affected Lancashire interests. The British government feared that the Government of India would put the security of Indian cotton growers far before the welfare of the Lancashire industry.[2] In a telegram, the Secretary of State for India urged the Viceroy to protect British interests.

This gap between the desires of Britain and those of the colonial government became even more explicit in the trade negotiations between Japan and Burma. With Burma due to separate from India in 1937, the second series of negotiations that began in 1936 included both Indo-Japanese and Burmo-Japanese talks, though both were closely connected. Before starting, the Government of Burma made clear its priorities concerning the Japan-Burma trade. First, it stressed the fact that Japan was not only Burma's most stable market for its raw cotton but also had become an important market for Burmese lead and beans, and so Burma should pursue a policy to expand imports to Japan. Second, it did not favour the maximum quota of piece goods imports and opposed any restriction on imports of cotton piece goods from Japan. "[T]his government is bound, in the interest of the large majority of the population with low purchasing power, to avoid any action likely to raise [the] cost of cheaper forms of piece goods".[3] Third, it was not in Burma's interest to place limits on the import of coloured goods, since it did not produce them itself.

In contrast to these arguments from the Government of Burma, the Board of Trade and the India Office took a completely opposite line. They recommended that the Burmese Government not widen the scope of discussions with Japan beyond the cotton protocol, and took a very strong view about Lancashire's wish to maintain subdivisions by category, seeking to have this reflected in the Japan-Burma negotiations. According to the Board of Trade, the British cotton industry could not compete with the Indian and Japanese markets in the cheaper grades (i.e. grey and bleached goods) and was, therefore, being confined more and more to supplying high-quality goods. For this reason, it was desirable, in the interests of the British cotton industry, that Japanese exports of coloured and printed items should not be stabilised at the high-level obtaining in 1935. Therefore the import of Japanese goods should be divided into categories. Further it wanted to expand the quota to rayon goods together with minimum specific duties.[4] London also warned Burma that

> if, when [the] India Burma Trade Order is discussed, Parliament discovers that this opening for improvement for U.K. interests has already been closed, opposition to the scheme for the Order as a whole … will be renewed.[5]

The Board of Trade stated that if an agreement was reached along the lines proposed by the Government of Burma, this would inevitably create an extremely disadvantageous atmosphere as far as the opening of negotiations between Burma and Britain was concerned. In other words, not only did it strongly urge the safeguarding of Lancashire's market as an issue in the negotiations between Japan and Burma, but it also saw it as one that could affect the upcoming negotiations between Burma and Britain. Thus, unlike the Cain and Hopkins argument, Britain's main concern in its negotiations with Burma was not to protect the market for Burmese products. The India Office conveyed the communication from the Board of Trade to the Government of Burma and left the final decision in its hands.

The correspondence from the British side surrounding the Indo-Japanese trade negotiations reveals a basic difference between the policy of the British government and that of the two colonial governments, India and Burma. The Board of Trade and the India Office were, throughout most of the process, chiefly concerned with promoting Lancashire interests, and showed no apprehension at all about securing or expanding a market for Indian and Burmese products in Japan. It also reveals that unless Burma assisted Lancashire in providing a market for its high-quality goods during the negotiations between the British and Burmese governments to secure a trade agreement prior to Burma's separation from India, Britain was not prepared to make concessions to Burma. Behind the Board of Trade's policy can be discerned the strong influence that Lancashire representatives still maintained in Parliament. Thus the view of Cain and Hopkins that "gentlemanly capitalism" aimed at securing export markets for colonial products and protecting local industry does not hold up sufficiently, at least in the case of India and Burma.[6]

The greatest impetus for the introduction of a protective policy towards the cotton and other industries was not "gentlemanly capitalism" but the strength of the rapidly growing nationalist movements in India. Of those which had been expanding from the early years of the twentieth century, the demands of the Swadeshi (Self-Sufficiency) movement were becoming ever more insistent. As the Indian cotton industry became more competitive with Lancashire in the Indian market, there was greater pressure for the introduction of a protective tariff for Indian industry. The legislative system brought in by the Government of India Act of 1919 became an important mechanism for reflecting nationalist opinion in the formation of Indian government policy. According to Basudev Chatterji, there were many instances where British government opposition to proposals by the Government of India to raise tariffs in order to guarantee fiscal revenue derived from a desire to protect Lancashire interests. The British government proposed in turn securing financial resources through raising excise taxes, among others. However, he concluded that many of the cases where the home government approved the raising of tariffs were the result of fears that not to do so would inflame nationalist movements in India, incite boycotts and therefore cause the market for Lancashire products to shrink even further (Chatterji 1992).[7]

The strength of Indian Nationalist movements, which aimed at the autonomous development of the Indian economy, brought about the introduction of a partial protective tariff system and the beginnings of import-substitution industrialisation. With the achievement of Independence in 1947, the way was fully opened to economic development that looked to economic independence. It was during the interwar period that the basic driving force towards the formation of an independent economy was created and the system that supported it took root.

## The Partial Introduction of Import-Substitution Industrialisation

The partial introduction of a protective tariff policy and of import-substitution industrialisation in the interwar period stimulated the development of manufacturing and promoted the growth of native industries. Export-oriented industries, however, suffered and became sluggish after the Great Depression and the subsequent shrinking of the global economy. This period can be seen as the time when the process that became "inward-looking" import-substitution industrialisation after Independence had its effective beginning. Let us examine the development of, and changes in, India's main factory-based industries.

### *The Cotton Textile Industry: The Development of Import Substitution for a Domestic Mass Market*

Indian investors in Mumbai and Ahmadabad and other places in western India began developing a factory-based cotton industry from the second half of the nineteenth century, based on commercial capital associated with domestic and foreign trade. In Mumbai, Parsi merchants who acted as representatives of British firms in the Far East trade played an important role in setting up spinning mills.

Spinning was at the centre of the cotton industry. Indian spun yarn supplied domestic handloom markets and others abroad, including in China. However, it was not alone. The Japanese spinning industry, which began later than that in India, increased its export of cotton yarn to China from the late nineteenth century, putting pressure on the Indian product. Later, yarn production also developed in China itself and from the beginning of the twentieth century Indian yarn was rapidly driven out of the Chinese market. As a result, the Indian cotton industry, particularly in Mumbai, which had depended heavily on the Chinese market, could no longer just produce spun yarn. Instead, most of the latter was woven into cloth in factories and large quantities were sold in the domestic market as textiles. While the cotton industry had focused on spinning, it had avoided competing directly with Lancashire, but from the beginning of the twentieth century the emergence of large-scale textile production made it an all-out competitor with British textiles in the Indian market.

At the beginning of the century in the Indian market, the share of goods produced in Indian factories was no more than 20 percent, with imported textiles occupying the rest. Yet, this share diligently climbed in the decades to come, reaching over 50 percent by the mid-1920s and over 80 percent by the end of the 1930s. Import substitution had been largely achieved in textile manufacturing. The number of workers in the industry grew from 370,000 in 1925 to 570,000 in 1937,[8] and between 1910 and 1938, the amount of woven cloth produced almost quadrupled, while textile imports declined by around 30 percent. The dwindling of British cotton piece imports can in part be blamed on the acceleration of textile imports from Japan. Britain, India and Japan were enmeshed in a complicated competitive relationship over the Indian cotton market. As far as the Indian industry was concerned, both British and Japanese producers could be considered rivals. However, the protection of the Indian cotton industry that came into force from the end of the 1920s was linked to imperial preference, and cooperation between the cotton industries of India and Lancashire to block the entry of Japanese cotton piece-goods into the Indian market was not surprising.

Regardless of their mutual antipathy towards Japanese producers, the Indian and Lancashire industries could not maintain an equal footing and the Indian cotton industry developed at the expense of Lancashire's market. This was facilitated by the growth of nationalist movements in India and the strengthening of the people's national consciousness. As we have seen, raising tariffs on textiles was to a large extent done with an eye on the desire of those movements for protective tariffs. More viscerally, the sale of Lancashire goods in the Indian market was impacted negatively by the campaign to boycott British products that was an important part of the nationalist movements. The Lancashire cotton industry was rendered unable to compete, not only with India, but also with Japan. Despite imperial preference, it was forced to withdraw from the Indian market.

### *The Iron and Steel Industry: Import Substitution at Government Demand*

Efforts to create a modern iron and steel industry in India began as early as the late eighteenth century. Iron making was attempted using charcoal from South India, but it was a lengthy wait for notable progress on this front. With the spread of railways in the latter half of the nineteenth century, most of pig iron and steel was imported from abroad. In 1889 the Bengal Iron and Steel Company (BISCO) was incorporated. However, they produced mainly pig iron, with very limited success, and their foray into steel manufacturing ended in failure. The company closed down in 1906. The iron and steel industry began in earnest only in 1907 with the establishment of the Tata Iron and Steel Company (TISCO).

The founder of TISCO, J. N. Tata, was a member of a family of merchants involved in international trade, and had already succeeded in setting up cotton mills in Mumbai and Nagpur. He received official help at the planning stage with an agreement that the government would buy a certain amount of steel rails annually and the company, with its capital subscribed to by 8,000 investors, enthusiastic supporters of Swadeshi agitation, was launched with a capacity to produce 100,000 tons of steel. By the late 1930s this had increased to more than 700,000 tons. In 1913–1914, steel for domestic consumption was almost all imported, but by 1926 TISCO's share was 30 percent. This jumped to 66 percent in 1933–1934, as import substitution progressed. The percentage of imported steel dropped further with the addition of steel provided by the Mysore Iron and Steel Works (MISW). In 1938/1939, the domestic product had a share of 73 percent.

The process of import substitution was facilitated by preferential purchase by the state and by the imposition of protective tariffs. With the price of steel falling after World War I, TISCO applied in 1923 for tariff protection in the face of foreign competition and this was granted in 1924, with additional protection later. At the same time, the government introduced a de facto imperial preference system, citing differences in quality between British and continental steel. TISCO, protected from its main rivals on the continent of Europe, was able to increase its share in the Indian market. One factor that led to the state protection of Indian steel was the expansion of imports of steel from Belgium and other countries in Europe. British iron and steel remained supreme in rail and government purchases, but in the private sector the British share of the market in the years 1911–1912 was only 20 percent, and this fell further in the 1920s. Setting a protective tariff that included de facto imperial preference was an attempt to combat imports of continental steel. Also underlying state protection of the industry was the military importance of TISCO as the only British-controlled iron and steel works east of Suez, and, as mentioned earlier, the rise of nationalist movements played its part in encouraging protective policies (Bagchi 1972, 300–303).

Reflecting state policy to foster the iron and steel industry through government purchase, TISCO's chief market was related to these demands – steel rails, munitions, road and bridge construction, etc. There was little demand from the engineering industry, which originally had potentially been its chief market. Though there had been striking developments in the factory textile industry and the jute industry in India, the government did not offer any protection for the production of textile machinery, so there was no expansion in the domestic production of, for example, spinning machines and looms, and manufacturers had to rely on machinery imported from Britain. Therefore, while the capital goods necessary for domestic consumer goods production were imported from the suzerain power, the Indian heavy industry sector did not function as a producer of machine and production goods for the consumer goods industry but was rather connected directly with the rail, military and state needs of the colonial political and economic structure. The pre-Independence Indian economy was characterised by colonial malformation, where the domestic industrial sector was not structurally integrated with the whole. This integration had to wait for the development of a full-scale import-substitution industrialisation policy after Independence.

### *Other Industries*

The sugar-refining and match industries flourished as a result of protection. Whereas the sugar industry received government support in places like Java, there was no such support in India and foreign sugar imports surged from the end of the nineteenth century. The sugar manufacturing industry only developed in India from 1931, as a result of changes in government policy in the course of the Great Depression. A 1929 report had cautioned that unless an Indian sugar refining industry was developed, cultivators would experience a serious blow. This matter was referred to the Indian Tariff Board, at whose recommendation a protective tariff of an ad valorem rate of 185 percent was imposed in 1932. Between 1930–31 and 1933–34 the import of refined sugar rapidly declined and Indian factory refined sugar increased 2.5 times. By 1936–1937, India was a net exporter.

There were attempts to set up matchmaking factories in India from the end of the nineteenth century, when import duties did not exist, but they held little promise. However, revenue duties were gradually raised: In 1922 a high revenue duty was imposed on imports, at an ad valorem rate of 100–200 percent, and in 1928 a protective tariff was applied. This encouraged a large number of local factories to spring up. India was an enormous market for matches, comprising about one tenth of global consumption. More than 60 percent of domestic consumption in 1926 was provided by Indian factories and the remainder was imported. The dominant presence in the match market was the Swedish-controlled Western India Match Company (WIMCO). Before 1922, Sweden had been the largest exporter of matches to India. Following the rise in import duty, the Swedes cannily built factories in India, allowing them to supply about 80 percent of all matches produced in India and maintain their pre-eminence. There were not many local entrepreneurs who could compete with WIMCO. In 1953, the company fulfilled 73 percent of Indian demand, while the remainder was made by a mosaic of 154 small-scale Indian-run businesses.

Import substitution was achieved in the pulp and paper industry as a result of technical improvements and solving supply problems, together with tariff protection. In the nineteenth century, imports of paper from Europe using cheap wood pulp reigned over the market, but as a result of a change in the government's purchase policy in the 1880s that encouraged the use of local paper, a number of European firms built mills in India. After World War I, the government expanded protection of the paper-making industry and local production ratcheted up, but mainly in those varieties of product that were protected. Imports remained large and supplied most of the demand. Suitable sources of wood pulp remained elusive in India at this time, hindering import substitution. It was not until the late 1930s, when improvements in bamboo pulp were well underway, that progress on this front was possible. By around 1940, domestic paper production had managed to more than double compared to a decade earlier and outstripped imports.

Import substitution in the case of cement, which was costly to transport, was achieved relatively early. Between 1910 and 1930 the demand for Portland cement rose as much as 70 percent. Indian factories were already meeting 57 percent of domestic demand at the beginning of the 1920s, and this figure rose to 95 percent in 1936–1937.

### *The Jute Industry*

The jute industry stands in contrast to the above examples of import-substitution industrialisation. It had developed as an export industry and suffered a slump in demand as a result of the decline in the global trade of agricultural products that followed the 1929 Depression, since jute bags, among others, were used for transporting such goods. Exports of jute products halved in value, from Rs 569 million in 1928–1929 to Rs 215 million in 1934–1935. Employees in the industry fell from 340,000 at the end of the 1920s to 260,000 by the middle of the 1930s. To cope with this plummeting demand, the Indian Jute Mills Association tried to prevent over-supply by asking the government to give statutory force to restrictive agreements that limited the hours and days worked. Belated responses such as using jute as a substitute product for paper bags and delays in renewing and improving machinery were further indications of managerial and technical stagnation in the jute industry.

### *Domestic-Market-Orientated Industrialisation and the Road to a Planned Economy*

Foreign trade became strikingly less important in India's post–World War I economy. Instead, there was a strong re-orientation towards the domestic market with the partial introduction of a protective tariff. This period also saw the beginnings of the inward-looking, import-substitution industrialisation that developed in earnest after Independence, as well as a policy that was moving towards a planned economy.

The fading prominence of foreign trade in the interwar Indian economy is easy to observe. The ratio of exports against net domestic production showed a marked downward trend: 11.1 percent in 1925, 8.6 percent in 1930, 6.9 percent in 1934 and 6.8 percent in 1940. Similarly, the ratio of imports was in slow decline: 6.8 percent in 1925, 6.6 percent in 1930, 6.0 percent in 1934 and 5.4 percent in 1940 (Kumar 1983, 839; Sivasubramonian 2000, 366–368). Industries dependent on foreign markets, like the jute industry, fell victim to stagnation and decay within the shrinking global economy of the interwar period, whereas those focusing on daily consumer goods for the domestic market, like cotton textiles and matches, expanded. Certainly the introduction of a discriminatory protective tariff system promoted the growth of industrial import substitution, and we should note that a number of industries achieved a domestic growth that even exceeded the simple import substitution. S. Sivasubramonian suggests that since net domestic production grew by 37 percent between 1920 and 1940, the process of formation of the national economy had proceeded apace, with less dependence on overseas markets and growth centred on the domestic market (Sivasubramonian 2000). The rising tide of nationalist movements and the creation of a national consciousness acted as a formidable catalyst in this process. The construction of the national economy that proceeded in earnest after Independence based on a policy of import-substitution industrialisation was thus already partially underway during the interwar period. However, though import substitution was already well advanced in the consumer goods sector, growth in the production goods sector occurred only in those areas directly related to government demand associated with colonial rule, and real expansion in the production of capital goods like machinery had to wait until after Independence. Yet, we can say that the foundations of post-Independence economic achievement were laid in the interwar period.

Of equal importance to the adoption of a partial import-substitution industrialisation policy were the moves made in the interwar years and at the beginning of World War II towards building a national planned economy led and regulated by the state. The idea that the government should promote economic development through economic planning rather than following a laissez-faire policy had previously been advocated in the early years of the century by Gopal Krishna Gokhale (1866–1915) and others. Yet it was not until the 1930s that it was discussed seriously among senior English officials in the Indian government, at the centre of whom was Sir George Schuster (1881–1982), Finance Member of Council in the Government of India. They began examining various ideas, including setting up an "Advisory Economic Council" that included Indian business leaders. The ideas of John Maynard Keynes and others championing positive government intervention in economic activity hovered in the background, having already begun to influence economic thought and policy change in Britain. The role of the burgeoning nationalist movements was again pivotal, as was the development of farmers' and labourers' movements as the Depression worsened. On one hand, Indian businessmen were strengthening their ties with the Indian National Congress, and on the other, there was a fear that young Indian leaders were beginning to look to the Soviet Union, which had achieved rapid economic development, as a model for a planned economy. Gradually a consensus was reached among senior officials in the colonial government about the need for the government to take the initiative in creating the machinery for economic planning in India (Chattopadhyay 1987, PE-19-29).

When war began, these ideas were swiftly put into being. The Indian National Congress set up the National Planning Committee (NPC) chaired by Jawaharlal Nehru in 1938, while leading Indian entrepreneurs like Sir Purshottamdas Thakurdas (1879–1961) put forward ideas for a planned economy incorporating a proposal to limit the "key industries" for which government regulation was anticipated to the heavy and chemical industries. In tandem, Indian business leaders attempted to build a cooperative relationship with British industrial circles, desiring to import machinery and capital goods, as well as technology, from Britain after the war. Britain too, wanting to protect the Indian market from American advances, leaned towards a policy of positive involvement in and cooperation with post-war Indian industrialisation. At that time, it was quite possible that Britain would accept the plan put forward by Indian businessmen to subject the construction of the economy to state control as a strategy aimed at assisting and promoting rapid industrialisation by the state. With the integration of the Indian economy into the war economy, the government placed production, distribution and import controls on a large number of commodities. The Licence, or Permit, Raj that was a feature of the post-war Indian economy was in many ways a continuation of wartime economic control (Nakazato 2001).

## The Beginnings of a Multi-tiered Labour Market

The growth of large-scale factory-based industry in the colonial period, combined with the development of medium and small businesses, drew large numbers of labourers from agrarian society and rural communities into the non-agricultural sector centred on urban areas. These labourers can be divided broadly into three groups, according to the class and caste they were from, the relationship they maintained between their work in industry and their life in the village, and how these were related to the type of work they did: (1) labourers in the engineering industry, (2) skilled labour in the large cotton mills, and (3) labourers in small and medium-sized businesses manufacturing bidis (cheap cigarettes), workers in the jute industry and mine workers. This section will take up a number of industries, based mainly on the 1944 Report of the Labour Investigation Committee, and examine the structure of the labour market at that time to demonstrate that the multi-tiered nature of that market post-Independence was already in existence.[9]

Factory workers may be divided according to whether or not they were employed by a factory subject to regulation by the Factories Act ("notified factories"). Most of the factories so regulated were large ones. The most representative industries that fell under the Act were the cotton textile industry, the biggest, employing around 500,000 people, the jute industry with around 300,000 people and the engineering industries with around 280,000 people. Industries that escaped its purview included bidi and tobacco manufacturing, mica processing, mat making, shellac manufacturing, carpet weaving, and tanning; of these, bidi and tobacco manufacturing was the largest.

### *Highly Paid Urban-settled Labourers*

Wage labour in the engineering industries was either skilled or unskilled. Unskilled workers like coolies and sweepers were copious compared to skilled workers, but it was the latter who unsurprisingly constituted the core of these industries. Most were male. Engineering was a heavy industry and there were few female workers: Female and juvenile labour occupied only 4.3 percent of the total workforce.

According to the Report,[10]

> [f]rom the earliest years of the [engineering] industry, the initial development of the skilled engineering workers arose entirely as a result of the practical experience of men who entered the factories when they were comparatively young and gained their knowledge of the processes of industry over many years of practical experience.

This informal system of training still existed to a large extent in the 1940s. However,

> the limitations of this system are that the time taken for training is long, the experience of the worker is limited to the machine to which he has been trained and, more than all, the worker obtains no scientific or theoretical technical background.

Therefore, it had gradually become necessary for firms to develop systematic apprenticeship courses and of the 65 concerns investigated by the Labour

Investigation Committee, 39 had an apprenticeship system. All the railway workshops had one, as did most factories in the electrical engineering sector, such as power plants and substations. Apprenticeships lasted anywhere between six months and five years, though most were five years. In this sector, workers aged between 15 and 25 were apprentices.[11] Despite such training courses, it was impossible to meet the mounting demand for skilled workers. The pressure of supply and demand meant that movement of workers between factories was constant. Once the long training period had finished, workers did not necessarily remain in the same factory. Two factories in Madras had trained a total of 70 workers over the previous five years, according to the Report, but only 16 had remained there.

In the context of other branches of industry, wages for trained male workers in the engineering and minerals and metals industries were comparatively high. In Bengal, the daily wage for a skilled worker in those industries averaged around Rs 3, whereas textile workers earned around Rs 2. Since the weekly expenditure of a jute worker in Calcutta with an average family of 4.2 persons was estimated to be around Rs 8, the income of skilled workers in the engineering industry was at least enough to enable labour reproduction at the lowest level. In contrast, coolies earned very low rates and their wages were little different to those earned by unskilled workers in other industries.

Besides the high wage level for skilled workers in the engineering industry, there also existed a system of promotions and wage increments not found in other industries. Each post was divided into a number of grades and a skilled worker gradually rose from the lowest to the highest. For example, in one railway workshop, turners had three grades. A worker entered at the lowest grade, and each year his basic wage would be raised a few annas from the lowest scale within the grade. When a vacancy opened in a higher grade for skilled jobs, "suitable persons [we]re generally selected from among the lower grades and from apprentices". As far as grade promotion was concerned, "the amount of increment usually depend[ed] on their length of service and ability".[12]

Skilled workers in the engineering industry thus earned a high wage sufficient at least to support their families in an urban environment. Whereas the reproduction of labour power for workers in other industries, beginning with the cotton textile industry, more or less included rural society in its scope, skilled workers in the engineering industry reproduced their families in an urban setting through their wage income. According to the Indian Engineering Association, "Sixty percent of workers in Calcutta and Bombay are permanently settled … the remainder are recruited from nearby areas". Further, "Skilled labour is more permanently settled than unskilled". In concerns owned by the government or public bodies in particular, "labour … has been definitely settled in the industrial areas for many years, has no village nexus and is not migratory at all".[13] Settled in the city, skilled workers had no ties with the rural community. They went through an apprenticeship of several years, after which they entered a particular job which was graded internally, and, receiving wage increments each year, rose within each grade and between grades. They were a totally urban-based labour market.

### *Semi-settled Workers from the Rural Cultivator Class*

Morris D. Morris commented on the settled nature of workers in urban areas in his study of labour in the cotton mills of Bombay (Mumbai) before 1947. He maintained that any labour instability was not due to high rates of absenteeism caused by the workers' commitment to the agricultural requirements of their home villages, and that their period of employment in the industry was extremely long, even though they might move from mill to mill (Morris 1965). This overview is backed by the *Labour Investigation Committee Report on an Enquiry into Conditions of Labour in the Cotton Mills of India* (1944), which describes workers becoming increasingly settled and dependent almost entirely on the cotton textile industry for their living.

Workers may have become more rooted in their urban environs, but this did not mean that they severed all connections with their villages of origin. The Report states that workers in the industry continued to preserve their ties to their villages and returned once every year or two for weddings or festivals.[14] This has been further elucidated by Kunj M. Patel in her survey of Ratnagiri textile workers in Mumbai. She found that most of the workers moved to the city between the ages of 15 and 20 and found work in the cotton mills after doing a variety of jobs like hotel porters or waiters. For more than 20 years after that they provided a stable labour force in the industry, not involving themselves in agricultural work at all. Nevertheless, rural society and agriculture played an extremely important role in relation to the generational reproduction of labour power. First, most workers returned to their home villages after retirement, showing that rural society was important as the base for post-retirement life. Second, part of the family continued to live in the village: Each person surveyed had an average of 2.3 dependants living in Bombay and 2.7 dependants living in the home village. Third, the village was a place of security in times of sickness or job loss. In brief, then, cotton textile workers in Mumbai provided a stable urban labour force whose reproduction was entrusted in part to rural society and agriculture.[15]

Workers in the cotton textile industry can be classified according to the wages they received. Most were weavers and commanded the highest rates. In Bengal, their average daily income was 2 rupees 4 annas. Cotton piercers, coolies and so on were regarded as unskilled and received something over one rupee a day. But even weavers, who were considered skilled workers, earned well below their equivalents in the engineering industries, with their income of around Rs 3 a day. Theirs by comparison though was a low level of skill, which they could acquire in one and a half months, and as a result, they were constantly in competition with workers with no skills at all. However, their connections with their home villages meant that they could meet their living expenses regardless of this meagre pay: Since most textile workers incorporated the village into their generational reproduction of labour, their wages had only to support part of their family. Conversely, the low level of wages made it difficult for workers to bring all their family to the city, and so they had to maintain ties with the villages.

Regarding the social composition of Mumbai's textile workforce, a survey made in 1940 by the Bombay Millowners' Association revealed that 51.8 percent were Marathas (who made up 67.4 percent of weavers), a further 13.8 percent were "Bhayyas", while 11.9 percent were scheduled castes (Gokhale 1957, 116).[16] In the Ratnagiri district, Marathas are described as typically being of the landowning class (Patel 1963, 19). Hirokazu Tada asserts that at the end of the nineteenth century the Marathas of Ratnagiri had already begun to break up and some subsistence farmers were engaged as agricultural labourers and as migrant workers. There can be no doubt that the core part of Mumbai mill workers originated from a middle-class farming background. These weavers and textile workers thus occupied a middle position, in comparison to the low-paid labourers from the lowest classes in village society that we will now examine.

### *Workers in the Jute and Bidi Industries from the Agricultural Labourer Classes*

Among the workers of the jute industry, dependence on the rural village for the generational reproduction of labour was widespread. According to a family income and expenditure survey in Bengal in 1943–1944, covering households where the head was a jute worker, 381 households were families and 415 were one-person households. In households made up of a family, an average of 1.6 persons were wage earners and 2.6 persons were dependants. On the other hand, in one-person households, an average of 4.01 dependants lived in the village of origin, and of average weekly earnings of Rs 9–14.4, around Rs 2 were sent to them. A large number of jute workers thus lived alone, leaving their families in the village. When a worker took his family to the city to live, generally the family livelihood was supported by multiple workers from that family.[17] Compared with the 46 percent of dependent family members living in Mumbai shown in the workers' survey there, less than 37 percent of jute workers' dependants were doing so. This reveals the great importance of the rural village as the base of life for dependent families in the jute industry.

The way labour reproduction occurred corresponded to the low level of wages in the jute industry. Weavers earned between Rs 7 and Rs 9 a week and other workers between just Rs 5 and Rs 7. This was a step below the daily earnings of 2 rupees 4 annas of a Bengal cotton weaver. As mentioned above, a worker living alone spent on average around Rs 8 a week; this means that a jute worker received just a single worker's wage. The report on jute justly observes that the living standard of jute workers was lower than that of workers in Bengal's other main industries (*Jute*, 28).[18] It is likely that this gap between textile workers is in part related to their different social origins in rural society. According to a survey of jute workers undertaken in 1948–1949, no more than 41.3 percent owned some kind of land. Of these, 20.1 percent owned between 0.01 and 2 *bigha*, 10.3 percent owned between 2.01 and 5 *bigha*, 5.1 percent owned between 5.01 and 10 *bigha* and 5.2 percent owned between 10.1 and 15 *bigha*. In 1936, the smallest area of land required to support a family was calculated to be 3 acres (about 9 *bigha*). This means that almost no jute workers had enough land to be an independent cultivator, by which we can assume that most came from the lower classes of rural society.[19]

The industry most associated with lower-caste workers from rural villages is *bidi* manufacturing. Distinctively featuring a workforce that consisted mainly of Muslims and members of the scheduled castes, *bidi* production was concentrated in the Central Provinces. The associated report (1946) notes that "formerly bidi making was almost monopolised by the Mahars. Though now Kunbis, Telis and Muslims are coming in, the Mahars still form the large majority".[20] In South India,

> the vast majority of the bidi workers are Muslims who constitute over 80 percent of the total number of workers … The majority of the workers in Calcutta are from Bihar. More than 90 percent in Calcutta are Muslims and the rest are scheduled caste Hindus. At Bankura, the majority of the workers are local people and over 90 percent are drawn from the scheduled castes.
>
> (*Bidi*, pp. 27, 39)

Though the sites of production were different, the core workforce of the *bidi* industry was mainly from the rural labourer class with low social status.

With this group being the main base of supply for the industry, there was a close mutual influence between the wages of *bidi* workers and agricultural labourers. This is highlighted in an interesting episode quoted in the report:

> The rates underwent a change in November 1944, to the detriment of the workers. This was attributed by them to the action of a certain Deputy Commissioner who asked the Bidi Merchants' Association in his district to reduce the rates of wages of bidi makers in rural areas to levels which would not compete with local agricultural rates, or cut down the number employed by 50 percent, as he apprehended that the Grow More Food Campaign was likely to suffer as labourers found it more profitable to make bidis than work in the fields. This action led to considerable agitation among the bidi workers and ultimately the rates were again restored to the June 1944 level.
>
> (*Bidi*, p. 12)

In the Central Provinces, "wage rates for 1,000 bidis in 1940 were … 3 annas 6 pies in village factories" (*Bidi*, p. 12). The previous year, agricultural labourers in the same area had received 4.3 annas a day.[21] The two wages clearly fell within the same scope. The rate for 1000 bidis in the big towns in the Central Provinces was between 6 and 7 annas, but considering the high cost of accommodation and goods there, even this was not actually very different from the rate paid to agricultural labourers. The same can be said about Mumbai. In

1939, the rate for 1000 bidis was 6 to 8 annas outside the city (*Bidi*, p. 19). The agricultural wage here at the same time was 5.4 annas. Again, in light of prices in the city, there was not a great leap between the wage rates for agricultural labourers and for bidi makers.

The presence of a broad class of agricultural worker allowed for a reservoir of ample additional labour and meant that the wages of bidi makers were prescribed by the low wages of the farm worker, and inevitably remained there. Workers were all on piece rates. In Mumbai in 1944, they could earn between Rs. 25 and 35 a month, that is, a little over Rs. 1 a day (*Bidi*, p. 19). Accruing this amount took many hours; the worker was in the factory from 9 am to 6 pm, but before arriving they had to spend around two or three hours preparing wrapper leaves. It should be noted that the earnings of jute workers and bidi makers were almost the same. This adds further fuel to the conjecture that most jute workers were drawn from the lower strata of village society that broadly included agricultural labourers.

It is unsurprising that it was not easy to make a living on such a low wage. Further, with few exceptions, bidi workers did not get any supplementary earnings from farm work. Significantly, a high ratio of women worked in the bidi industry, comprising more than 40 percent of the workforce in the Central Provinces, South India and Bombay province. The report states:

> Due to the laxity of the hours of work, the bidi industry has absorbed many working class women who wish to supplement their husband's income. The source of labour for the industry is generally the working class family. It is not rare to come across a family where both husband and wife and sometimes even their children work in the industry.
>
> (*Bidi*, p. 16)

By adopting such a working pattern, the low wages could be covered.

### *The Three-tiered Labour Market*

The Indian industrial labour market was thus broadly made up of three types of worker. The first were highly paid urban-settled labourers such as skilled workers in the engineering industries, whose wages were sufficient to allow them to settle with their families in the city, maintaining no ties with rural society. They trained in their job for several years and gradually advanced within pay and grade scales. The second were semi-settled workers earning mid-range wages as represented by weavers in cotton mills who were recruited mainly from the rural farmer classes. They preserved links with their villages as places to raise families and retire to.[22] The third were workers in the informal sectors, like bidi makers and many jute workers, who were paid least and recruited from the rural agricultural labourer and petty farmer classes. Moving to the city, they worked in industry for very low wages that were on a level with those of agricultural labourers. It was therefore difficult for them to support their families in the city and so many left them behind in the home village, where they became an important part of the generational reproduction of labour. If they took their families with them to the city, many members of the family worked to increment the income. Other industries unregulated by the Factories Act absorbed their workforce from the same source and low class rural labourers also worked on plantations and as miners, while regulated industries too employed them as coolies.

The lowest stratum of the industrial employment structure was derived from the lower classes of rural society, and therefore, its wage level was basically on a par with that of agricultural labourers; in 1944, skilled workers in the engineering industries and the cotton mills earned two or three times as much. However, while a correlation has been shown to exist between the wage of agricultural labourers and that of the lowest paid workers in industry who had their origins in the same class, the likelihood that there was a similar parallel between the wage levels of cotton mill workers and mid-range wages in the agricultural sector from whence they came remains to be confirmed. It can be said that the industrial labour market as documented in the 1940s had a multi-tiered structure, connected closely with stratified rural society and, therefore, can be regarded as the prototype of the post-Independence labour market, which will be examined in Chapter 11.

## Notes

1 The arguments in this chapter are based on Yanagisawa 2001. For further on the Indo-Japanese trade negotiations, see Yanagisawa 1980 and Kagotani 1996.

2 From T. Ainscough to A. Edgcumbe, 24 August, 1936. E&O 6144/1936. "We fear that Stewart [the Indian representative] may prefer to make some concession with regard to the categories which would be at the expense of the U.K. rather than incur the displeasure of the Indian cotton growers".

3 From Chief Secretary to Government of Burma, Home and Political Departments, to Secretary of State for India, 7 Oct. 1936, E&O 7050/1936.

4 From the Secretary of State for India to the Government of Burma, 17 November, 1936, E&O 7532/1936.

5 From the Secretary of State for India to the Secretary of State, Government of Burma, 24 September 1936, E&O 6531/1936.

6 It has been suggested that even though a protective tariff was set for the Indian iron and steel industry, in fact the interests of British manufacturing were emphasised in a policy that strongly preserved them through the introduction of imperial preference (Wagle 1981).

7 For Indian finances to increase dependence on fiscal revenue was in itself not unconnected with apprehension by the government about the growing Nationalist movement in India. The ratio occupied in fiscal revenue by the land tax, the most important tax in the nineteenth century, declined from the end of the century, as did the ratio it occupied in the amount of agricultural production. After World War I, it would have been possible to combat the financial stringency by levying an additional land tax, but there was the danger this would alienate the landowning class, the social allies of colonial rule, even further. It was hoped that taking a policy that would guarantee fiscal revenue by raising tariffs would bring Indian businessmen to support British rule, since raising excise above the present level would result in a drop in consumption (Dewey 1978, 39).

8 India, Department of Commercial Intelligence and Statistics, *Large Industrial Establishments in India*, for 1924 and 1937.

9 This section is based on Yanagisawa 1975.

10 Labour Investigation Committee, Government of India. *Report on an Enquiry into Conditions of Labour in the Engineering and Minerals and Metals Industries in India*. Manager of Publication, Delhi, 1946, pp. 257–258.

11 Government of India, Labour Investigation Committee, *Report on an Enquiry into Conditions of Labour in the Engineering and Minerals and Metals Industries in India*, Manager of Publication, Delhi, 1946, pp. 257–258, 18–19, 83, 122. The report of each industry surveyed by the Labour Investigation Committee will be referred to below simply as "Cotton", "Jute", etc.

12 Ibid., pp. 125, 258.

13 Ibid., pp. 2, 20.

14 *Cotton*, p. 7.

15 See also Chandavarkar 1994, 151.

16 Almost the same results are shown in a survey of textile workers in Pune in 1957 (Lambert 1963, Appendix B).

17 Government of India, Labour Investigation Committee, *Report on an Enquiry into Conditions of Labour in the Jute Mill Industry in India*, Manager of Publication, Delhi, 1946 (below, "*Jute*"), pp. 27–28.

18 Bagchi understands that the wage differential between the cotton and jute industries was mainly due to that between Bombay and Calcutta (1972, pp. 117–156). However even within Bengal itself there was a clear difference between the two industries.

19 Chattopadhyay 1952, p. 30. For further details about the social class and places of origin of jute workers, see Yanagisawa 1975.

20 Government of India, Labour Investigation Committee, *Report on an Enquiry into Conditions of Labour in the Bidi, Cigar and Cigarette Industries*, The Manager of Publications, New Delhi, 1946 (below, "*Bidi*"), p. 11.

21 Government of India, Ministry of Labour, *Agricultural Labour Enquiry: Report on Intensive Survey of Agricultural Labour*, 1955, Vol. 1, pp. 75–76, Statement 18.

22 It should be recognised that core labourers in India's large-scale cotton industry did not come from the poorest rural labour classes but from classes and castes dominant in village society. It has been argued that policy-dictated restrictions on the growth of the large-scale cotton industry within government-led industrialisation plans from the 1950s inhibited the expansion of the export-oriented and labour-intensive textile industry and prevented any reduction of the poorest classes by absorbing them into industry. However, as the main supply source was not the rural poor it is not wrong to suggest that even if the industry had expanded after Independence, this growth would not have affected any reduction of poverty due to the poor being absorbed by the industry.

# 3 The Growth of Small-Scale Enterprises and Changes in Consumption Patterns

## A Prototype of Post-Independence Informal Sectors

In the 50 years before Independence, traditional industries were faced by growing competition from large-scale factories. Yet in spite of this, some of them – handloom weaving for example – not only survived but adapted. Many small-scale and marginal enterprises also managed to expand and prosper rather than collapse. This phenomenon provides an important key for understanding the post-Independence growth of informal industries, particularly in the 1980s, in defiance of competition from formal sector enterprises.

A number of ingredients came together to produce these developments. First, large-scale industries had the advantage of economies of scale, but these did not work for small-scale enterprises, in terms of demand, the characteristics of the goods produced or the production process itself. Second, simultaneously, efforts among the lower classes in rural society to raise their social status led them to diversify their consumption pattern to imitate that of higher social groups and acquire goods they had previously been unable to consume. Such changes in consumption patterns among both urban and rural lower classes led in turn to a greater demand for various items like rice, cheap edible oil, bidis and cheap hosiery goods, to which small-scale enterprises catered. Third, traditional industries like handloom weaving responded to this new demand structure, adopting technological and organisational innovations, improving machinery, expanding the wholesale system and moving weavers to urban areas, in the process of which a new class of small businessmen, typified by master weavers, was formed. It was this class that was associated with the growth of small-scale and marginal enterprises after Independence.

This chapter will explore the handloom industry, the most representative of the traditional industries, as well as a number of small-scale and marginal enterprises that grew up in South India and other places after World War I, including rice mills, groundnut oil mills, cotton ginning factories and bidi making, as well small hosiery factories, principally appraising why economies of scale did not apply.

DOI: 10.4324/9781003341550-5

## The Survival and Growth of the Handloom Industry and Changes in Consumption Patterns

### *Competition between Machine-made Textiles and the Handloom Industry*

It is generally recognised that though India supplied handspun cotton fabric to the world in the eighteenth century, cheap British machine-made textiles flowed into India following the Industrial Revolution and dealt a severe blow to the domestic industry. Nevertheless, the invasion of inexpensive British cloth did not cause handloom weaving to disappear entirely. English manufactured cotton goods, which chiefly utilised long staple American or Egyptian cotton, used a medium- or high-count fine yarn. Their chief competitors in India were therefore producers of fabrics that the urban middle and upper classes wore on a daily basis, and it was these that were most badly hit by the textile imports. Not directly affected was the market in coarse cloth in the countryside, which used low-count thick yarn, or that in high-quality clothing, like women's wedding garments. Thus many textile workers survived. Weavers of fabrics of medium and high yarn count for the urban market who suffered the most generally turned their hands to coarse cloth production instead. This led to a surfeit, causing prices for low-count weaves to fall, and Indian textile production as a whole was stricken, including areas previously unscathed by English competition (Specker 1996, 175–217; Harnetty 1991).

The profits of the handloom industry had plummeted in the face of domestic machine-made textiles, but a good part of the trade survived. The handspinning industry proved itself less robust. Having formerly provided the raw yarn for weaving, it almost died out in the course of the nineteenth century as weavers, caught in the competition between British machine-made yarn and that produced in large factories in India, turned to buying machine-made yarn in place of the home-spun version made by village women.

The Indian handloom industry persevered through the nineteenth century, responding to intensifying competition from British products mainly by converting its trade to low yarn count products. Yet, by the beginning of the twentieth century new challenges had arisen. It found itself confronted with competition from the developing domestic production of machine-woven textiles for the local market, which had been stimulated by the dislodging of Indian mill-spun yarn from the Chinese market. Deprived of this market abroad, large mills intensified their courting of consumers at home, in rivalry with imports from Britain and with the local handloom industry. Indian factory-made cotton yarn used Indian short-staple raw cotton of a low- to medium-count, producing coarse factory-made cloth that was in direct competition with the handloom products for daily use which were ubiquitous in the rural sector. This struggle was to the detriment of handloom workers, as shown by two surveys of villages in South India undertaken in 1916[1] and 1936,[2] where the number of weavers fell drastically over two decades.

However, the handloom industry did not go into terminal decline. Rather, between 1901 and 1939, handwoven textile production substantially increased, while in the 1930s, small-scale handwoven products occupied more than half the domestic textile market in terms of amount and this ratio improved over the decade.

To what can this be attributed? The response of weavers to the threat from factory-made products varied with locality, but in general took one of two directions. The first was to prioritise producing items that could compete with factory-made goods, such as even finer cotton cloth, non-cotton items like silk or artificial silk commodities, cloth with elaborate bordering or gold thread (*jari*), or high-quality or high-priced articles. Because of the skills and techniques involved, a handicraft industry was more appropriate to produce such items than a factory-based one.[3] The second course was taken by some weavers who determined to survive by specialising in making coarse cloth of even thicker thread than that produced in factories.

The above process was accompanied by changes in how the weavers operated and in their markets. Until this time, handloom weaving had been carried out to meet the call for a variety of everyday items aimed at the local market, but gradually there was a transition to specialised items for distant markets (Yanagisawa 1971–1972; Haynes 1996, 180). Research into the handloom industry in western India indicates that the demand for hand-woven products was specialist, locality-specific and variable. This type of demand, together with the suitability of the handicraft weaving to produce high-quality items, suited small-scale weavers meeting the requirements of a small group of consumers. Mass production by large factories with a strict division of labour, massive capital investment and a fixed technological system could not respond in the same way.

### *Changing Demands: Social Changes and Fluctuations in Consumer Patterns*

There was in fact an overall increase in the consumption of textiles in India. Michael J. Twomey estimates that per capita domestic consumption of cotton textiles was 11 yards in 1880, 15 yards in 1913 and 17 yards in 1930 (Twomey 1983, 47). Brian Tomlinson too supposes that this consumption grew 30 percent between 1920 and 1938 (Tomlinson 1979, 35). This is not surprising when we take the contemporary population increase into account. The production of high-quality and specialised items therefore remained a profitable field for handloom weaving, but its market for everyday items had been taken away by the large-scale factories, and if weavers tried to enter the more specialised market in large numbers, only over-production would result.

From the beginning of the twentieth century, changes in customs regarding clothing lay behind the expansion of demand for those specific products best suited to handloom weaving. In South India, these changes took one of two directions. First was the change to Western modes of dress among males, as the handicrafts market narrowed and demand grew for factory-made products. For example, the use of turbans declined and caps were worn in their place, and the upper garment worn by male Hindus, the *angavastram*, had given place to shirts by the 1920s and 1930s. This adversely affected the weavers, and famous centres of turban production for example had to switch to other varieties of fabric. On the other hand, other changes inspired a growth in demand for hand-woven goods. For example, young women in particular began wearing woven cotton blouses under their saris and the handloom market moved into this area in response.

A further point of note is the loosening of the relationship between social class and dress. As the customs of Brahmins spread to non-Brahmin monied classes, high-quality hand-made goods became more popular. The *Manual of Tanjore District* (1883) had already noted:

> Formerly the use of Kórnádu cloths was almost entirely restricted to the Tanjore Bráhmans; but now the Bráhmanical customs are adopted generally by the higher classes …; these cloths find a market to a greater or less extent all over the south between the latitudes of Madras and Cape Comorin.[4]

Changes were also occurring in the dress of the poorest classes in village society. At the beginning of the twentieth century in Tanjore, it had been understood that the clothing worn by people, even women, of the depressed castes should be above the knee, and that the chest be bared when working.[5] This mode of dress was dictated not only by poverty but also by caste-based restrictions. In Ramnad district, the Kallan caste proclaimed eight prohibitions concerning dress, the disregard of which led to violence against members of the depressed castes, with their huts burned down, their belongings destroyed and their livestock plundered.[6] Such strict restrictions, however, broke down in the first half of the twentieth century. There is evidence that in Thanjavur (formerly Tanjore) in the 1950s, depressed class women were covering their upper bodies with saris while working in the fields in the presence of their Brahmin landlords.

With the relaxing of restrictions on the dress of the lower castes, their members slowly began adopting items of clothing they had never used in the past. Even among the lower classes, there was a growing tendency to purchase clothes for special ceremonies, such as weddings. Women did not, however, buy high-priced silk saris but rather cheap handwoven saris for ceremonial use, made of artificial silk or mercerised yarn. A report of 1929 noted that "the middle and poor classes generally prefer to use artificial silk saris as they are cheaper than silk saris and have the same brightness, gloss and a few other characteristics of silk". A report from the Salem district the same year said,

> The chief reason for the large number of looms engaged in making this [artificial silk] cloth is the cheapness of the material and the large demand it has among the poorer classes. A poor householder who cannot afford to buy a silk sari can buy an imitation of it at a comparatively small cost

> for wear on ceremonial occasions. As every poor housewife would like to have one such cloth, there is ... a large local demand for this cloth.[7]

The mutations in the connection between caste and dress engendered a greater desire for hand-woven goods among the lower classes. Such was the size of their population that even a small increase in their purchase of such items could greatly influence the market. As we have seen in the case of saris, they preferred cheap imitation goods, and this is an important point in common with post-Independence consumer demand among these classes.

Behind these changes in lower class society lay, as we have seen in Chapter 1, transformations in the socio-economic relationship between castes and classes that had been ongoing since the end of the nineteenth century. Labourers from the depressed castes went abroad as migrant workers on plantations, for example, and in so doing gradually gained a sense of emancipation, steadily breaking down the subordinate relationship of the lower castes to the higher castes that prevailed in the middle of the nineteenth century. Daily life could not remain unchanged as a result. As we will examine below, coffee-drinking, which had been a habit of Brahmins, spread to labourers, the lower classes started eating rice instead of millets like *ragi* (*Eleusine coracana*, finger millet) and *jowar* (*Sorghum bicolor*, great millet) and bidi consumption increased. As the feeling of emancipation swelled among the lower classes and they gained a greater voice, the traditional caste system crumbled at the edges, and a new market appeared for handwoven fabrics that became one of the bases for the survival of the handloom industry (Yanagisawa 1993).

### *Technological Innovations and Organisational Changes*

The very substance of the handloom industry evolved in order to secure its survival. The most important technical innovation was the diffusion of the fly shuttle in place of the throw shuttle. The fly shuttle allowed work to be done twice as quickly as before, and what had taken two people to do previously could now be accomplished by one. Further, preparation of the warp, which had until then required a great deal of intensive labour, gradually moved to small-scale specialised factories. These improvements could not negate the clear cost difference in comparison to identical fabrics produced by powerlooms in large factories, but the disadvantage was lessened.

Simultaneously, evolution was evident in the relationship between weavers and merchants. Cotton yarn for handloom weaving, whether imported or manufactured domestically in large spinning mills, was now bought from merchants rather than being spun locally by hand. Also, as we have seen, there was a transition from selling everyday items locally to focusing on specialised items for distant markets. This meant that many weavers came to depend on merchants, both to provide the raw materials needed and to sell the finished products.

A putting-out system developed and spread as merchants increasingly leased looms to weavers, provided the raw materials, took the product, and paid wages to the weavers (Yanagisawa 1971–1972; Haynes 1996). Though the situation varied from place to place, a wealthy class from within the weaving castes usually acted as wholesale merchants (master weavers), and it was they who reaped the largest benefits. The wages of dependent weavers generally either fell or at least did not rise, while it was the master weavers who accumulated capital (Roy 1999). With the reorganisation of the handloom industry, village weavers congregated in urban areas or in the vicinity of small cities. In western and South India, some master weavers started small workshops (*karkhanas*) employing anywhere between a few and dozens of weavers. In the 1920s and 1930s, as electricity supply became more widely available, several workshop owners in Sholapur introduced electric powerlooms. Thirthankar Roy considers that such capital accumulation and the formation of small capitalists were the motive force behind the technological improvements in the handloom industry (Roy 1993, 2002a).

In summary, our examination of the handloom industry during the colonial period has provided a number of insights. First, handspinning and handloom weaving by small scale producers was in competition with factory-produced cotton goods, both English imports and domestic. Whereas handspinning disappeared completely, with the exception of a few centres, the handloom industry largely survived and grew, occupying more than half the market during the period 1920–1930. The economies of scale accruing to factory-produced cotton were given full scope in the production of spun yarn, but they could not drive out the small-scale handicraft production of woven goods, which in fact expanded. Second, the move to the production of goods that fitted the small-scale handicraft industry played an important role in the survival and expansion of handloom weaving. Weavers planned for their survival by moving variously to the production of high-quality items that needed a great amount of handicraft skill, to types of cloth where high levels of variability were needed, either in terms of specialisation or in catering for local markets, and to making coarse cloth of even thicker thread than that produced in factories. Third, the survival and expansion of the handloom industry were supported by an increased demand for products best suited to it. Fourth, an important factor in the latter was changing consumption patterns for clothing, driven by the imitation by members of lower castes of the dress worn by members of higher ones. With the growing social and economic emancipation of the depressed castes and others, social restrictions on their mode of dress weakened. They began buying woven products for weddings and other ceremonial occasions and this was important, given the proportion of the population occupied by these classes. Fifth, of particular note is that what members of the poorest classes demanded was cheap imitation goods, like saris of artificial silk. Sixth, technological innovation was vital for the survival and growth of the handloom industry, as were organisational changes made in response to changes in demand. The industry did not necessarily attempt to maintain traditional forms of production and operation but was able to respond to a changing environment. This generated a large number of entrepreneurs from the weaving castes who were experienced in, and well-informed about, the industry, and so able to respond to the market trends. This class of small businessman was at the heart of the growth of small-scale and marginal enterprises after Independence.[8]

## The Growth of Small-Scale Industries and Changes in Consumption Patterns[9]

### *The Development of Small-Scale Industries in South India in the First Half of the Twentieth Century*

Aspirations toward emancipation changed consumption patterns among the lower castes, sparking new demands that enabled small-scale and marginal industries to continue and even prosper in the first half of the twentieth century. This was not limited to the handloom industry, but included a number of industries based in rural areas in South India, including rice mills, groundnut oil mills, cotton ginning and bidi making. In addition, hosiery production proliferated all over India; large factories could not produce it according to economies of scale because of the special characteristics associated with its demand and production, which were better suited to medium and small firms as intermediate producers.

Let us look at the market characteristics of a number of industries.

### *Rice Mills*

A large number of rice mills were built in South India from the beginning of the twentieth century,[10] partly prompted by rice exports to Sri Lanka and other places. At the end of the 1920s these exports fell drastically, but rice mills still continued to multiply. A look at Thanjavur (Tanjore) district, the most important centre for rice export, in 1933 illustrates matters: While there were 60 large mills mainly preparing rice for export, 503 smaller mills hulled rice to meet local demand.[11]

The chief reason for the massive volume of rice mills in South India was probably the growth in rice consumption among labourers and other members of the lower classes in rural areas, combined with an increased demand from urban markets. In Tamil Nadu, rice was consumed in one of two forms. The first is called "raw rice": After harvesting, the rice is dehulled to produce "brown" rice, which is then refined further to obtain "white" rice. The second is "parboiled rice": Here the grain is first steeped in water for a set time, then boiled and dried. It is then hulled by machine. Both milling methods were in existence in the 1930s. Raw rice was generally the preserve of the well-to-do in Tamil Nadu. Labourers and the poor classes ate only parboiled rice, which was usually cheaper than untreated (raw) rice, and since there was less abrasion of the grain when hulling, it kept better. Rice could be hulled either by machine or by hand. In the Tamil districts, hand-hulled rice was preferred by the wealthier classes. Machine-hulling suited the lower-grade grain consumed by labourers and cost less; the majority of consumers of milled rice were therefore members of the labouring classes. This consumption pattern was not a long-standing one in South India but represents a custom gradually adopted from the beginning of the twentieth century. In the nineteenth century higher-caste members ate rice as a staple food, but except in a few paddy-producing areas, lower-caste people ate various kinds of millet and turned to rice only after the beginning of the twentieth century.

As the urban population swelled in the twentieth century, the market for milled rice did too. Hand-pounding as was done in the villages could not supply urban areas, and rice mills filled the breach, catering for those living in cities and towns. Increased demand was met by cheap types of rice imported from Burma and elsewhere. About half of the imported Burmese rice was of the parboiled variety, and a further 8 percent was the broken rice mainly consumed by people of the lower classes. Imported rice, however, represented only a small proportion of the amount produced in South India. This implies that parboiled and machine-hulled rice from rice mills was becoming ever more popular in the Tamil districts. Thus the growth in the number of rice mills in South India after the 1910s at its core reflects changes in the dietary habits of the lower classes as they depended less on the traditional millet and ate more rice (Yanagisawa 2004, 130–133; Yangisawa 2010).

### *Groundnut Mills*

The cultivation of groundnuts grew rapidly from the end of the nineteenth century in South India, especially in South Arcot district. Most of the crop was exported, mainly to France and other European countries. During World War I, this trade slumped and prices fell. Domestic consumption, however, was encouraged in its place. The sale of groundnuts to Europe recovered after the war, but there was a decline in the share of exports in total groundnut production. Whereas 11 percent of the total crop before the war had been utilised for domestic consumption and crushing, this rose to 40 percent in 1932–1933 and 60 percent by the end of the 1930s.[12] The area under groundnut cultivation swiftly spread. Thus, though the groundnut had been a typical export product before the war, its proliferation after was the result of greater local consumption.

The bulk of consumption, particularly in South India, was in the form of cooking oil. Indian usage of groundnut oil had grown from the end of the 1910s. The most commonly used cooking oil in South India had been gingelly (sesame) oil. The area under sesame cultivation there saw no marked contraction in the three decades after 1905, despite the rise of the groundnut. This suggests that groundnut oil did not profit at the expense of gingelly oil. Instead, it appears that there was a net increase in the total consumption of edible oil in South India.

Information about the family budgets of agricultural labourers gives some clue to which class most increased its consumption of groundnut oil. In 1936, the family of an agricultural labourer in a village in Ramnad district purchased around 445 cc of oil a month, which accounted for 2.1 percent of total food expenditure (Thomas and Ramakrishnan 1940, 41). Twenty years later, the Agricultural Labour Enquiry for 1956–1957 showed that the consumption of cooking oil among families of agricultural labourers in Madras State was about 700 gm per month, or 3.8 percent of food expenditure, indicating that labourers had increased their use of cooking oil over the two decades.[13] The results of a series of nutrition surveys also show a steady climb in the intake of cooking oil among the poorest classes.

There was no shortage of groundnut oil to satisfy this rising demand for edible oils. It was, after all, now the cheapest option. According to the *Trichinopoly District Gazetteer*, both sesame oil and groundnut oil were used for cooking, but "the latter [is used] only by the poorer classes."[14] The concentration of decorticating mills and oil presses in Tamil Nadu can mainly be attributed to this expanding demand for groundnut oil, especially among the lower classes.[15]

### *Bidi Making*

Cheap cigarettes popular in both urban and rural regions of South India, bidis saw a sharp rise in production during the late colonial period. The oldest bidi factory in Tamil Nadu was built in 1887 and until World War I, bidi making was concentrated in Madras City, North Arcot district and the Mukudal area of Tirunelveli district. As the twentieth century progressed, however, it spread throughout Madras Presidency and at the beginning of the 1940s, 90,000 people were employed in the industry there. A survey of 1944 revealed that there was not a single village in the province that did not make bidis.[16]

Bidi smokers were usually from the lower classes. A Madras Presidency report of 1929 noted "the flooding of the country with indigenous beedies [*sic*]" and went on to say that "beedies are mainly consumed locally by poorer classes and also exported to Ceylon and Rangoon",[17] while a "Report of the Madras Youth League" in 1930 estimated that every adult smoked on average 25 bidis a day, based on information obtained from household budgets of poor families.[18] A later report noted that bidis had grown even more common as the habit of smoking spread.[19] The bidi-making boom in the first half of the twentieth century can therefore be attributed largely to their burgeoning popularity among the lower classes.

### *Cotton Ginning Factories*

The case of cotton ginning is somewhat complicated. South India's premier cotton-growing area was the district of Tirunelveli (Tinnevelley), and historically, its cotton had been ginned manually in the villages by the farmers (ryots) themselves. In 1894, the first steam-powered ginning factory was opened in Tirunelveli and by 1913 there were 13 power-driven ginning factories, most of which were owned by large European exporting firms and cotton mill proprietors. This period of large factories was, however, surprisingly short-lived, and soon small ginneries using between 2 and 8 gins started to increase, reaching 49 in number by 1930. Many of the larger factories subsequently either closed down or substantially reduced the number of their gins. Coimbatore, another important cotton-growing district, also experienced a growth of ginning factories: 93 ginning and pressing factories were established by 1930.[20] In Madras Presidency there were 257 factories with 15,000 employees in 1922, 363 factories with 19,000 employees in 1927 and 480 factories with 25,000 employees in 1937.[21]

Before 1930, most of the cotton ginned in these districts was sent to Mumbai or exported overseas, but between the 1920s and the late 1930s, the proportion of cotton sold in Madras Presidency inched up from one third to two thirds. Locally cultivated long-stapled Cambodian varieties of cotton supplied about half of the requirements of the cotton mills in the 1920s, rising to 90 percent in the 1930s (Baker 1984, 274).

As the market for raw cotton changed, the spinning mills in Madras Presidency purchased more of it. Unlike the cotton mills in western India, which after the 1910s churned out larger amounts of woven cloth in competition with the handloom industry, the cotton mills of South India, which were chiefly involved with spinning, found new markets in their local handloom industry. As we have already seen, the South Indian handloom industry responded to the introduction of rival factory products by turning to finer varieties of cloth, woven with artificial silks and mercerised yarn, and goods for export. This change was underpinned, at least in part, by evolving modes of dress among the lower classes. Thus the spread of small ginning factories in South India was, however indirectly, partly based on increasing lower-class consumption of handwoven products.

### *Hosiery Manufacturing and Its Market*

The hosiery industry mushroomed from the 1920s. According to statistics published in the biannual *Large Industrial Establishments in India*, whereas in 1925 there were a mere 12 hosiery factories employing a total of 800 people, in 1946 numbers had grown to 156 factories with 10,492 workers.[22] Following the partition between India and Pakistan, in 1947 there were 139 factories in India with 8,656 workers and in 1949, 256 factories with 10,641 workers. Only factories of a certain size were recorded in the statistics but there was also an immense pool of smaller factories and workshops, and "cottage industries". In Bengal alone there were in 1933–1934 at least ten times more factories producing hosiery goods than the statistics indicate, with 35,000 actual workers compared with the 1,022 that appear on paper.[23] Bengal was at the centre of the hosiery industry, though other areas played their part. The *Preliminary Report on the Survey of Cottage Industries in the East Godavari District* of 1929 tells us that many towns in West Godavari improved their standing by making hosiery goods like banians (shirts), stockings, and gloves. It records that custom came from all classes, including from women of the lowest class. Work in this industry was commended for educated, higher class women. The report also details the role of local merchants, who would buy all the goods and send them to distant markets in the Northern Sarkars.[24]

With the passing of the Indian Tariff (Textile Protection) Amendment Act in 1934, cotton hosiery (undervests, socks, stockings) was given protection, and this was extended to all areas of cotton knitted apparel in 1936 (Second Amendment of the 1934 Act). A 1956 report by the Development Commissioner estimates that factories producing cotton hosiery items had increased from 331 in 1932 to 1,935 in 1956 and that the workforce had multiplied from 6,000 to 25,000 in the same period. Woollen hosiery factories also grew in number, from 332 in 1934 to 912, employing 18,000 people, in 1956. The hosiery industry, including its sewing division, was impossible to overlook by 1956, employing a total of 48,000 people.[25] Yet, import substitution based on tariff protection cannot be seen as the sole agent behind this explosion. Indian imports of cotton hosiery goods fell from 6.5 million lbs in 1926–1927 to 2.1 million lbs in 1936–1937. There were no imports at all in 1956. In the same period, domestic production of cotton hosiery goods rose from 2.9 million lbs in 1926–1927, to 19.5 million lbs in 1936–1937 and to 30 million lbs in 1956. This represents a tripling of the domestic consumption of cotton hosiery between 1926 and 1956, from 9.4 million lbs (imports plus local production) to 30 million lbs.

The manufacture of woollen hosiery goods experienced its own upturn, though without the vigour of their cotton counterparts. Both had their own core customer bases, and this was reflected in their development. Woollen hosiery had its chief market among the wealthier classes. Because the cold is not severe in large parts of India, the demand for woollen outerwear was from only a very small section of the population, the middle and upper classes. In contrast, the ever-expanding urban industrial workers were key consumers of cotton hosiery goods. In Madhya Pradesh and Bombay, they wore coloured cotton banians cloth of coarse yarn,[26] and the use of banians was also spreading in rural areas, as the Development Commissioner noted.[27] The demand for cotton outerwear also came from particular groups: Low-income earners in the eastern part of India, and special categories of consumer such as children and sportsmen.

Despite the looming presence of large producers of hosiery products, small-scale production dominated the sector. In the 1930s, hosiery production took three forms: The cottage industry using hand-powered tools, small producers using power tools and large producers, including combined cotton and spinning mills that had hosiery departments. The 1956 report by the Development Commissioner stated that there had been no increase in the ratio of the amount produced by large units in the previous 20 years. In 1956 there were 32 large-scale units against 1,903 small-scale and cottage units in the cotton hosiery industry. There were 700 units involved with sewing. This represents a percentage between large and small units of 21.5 percent and

78.5 percent respectively. In the woollen hosiery industry there were only 4 large-scale units (woollen mills with hosiery departments) against 908 small-scale units. In eastern areas of India, combined mills fell from 27 to 12 between 1953 and 1956. In the same period, 25 large specialist mills applied for license under the Industrial Licensing Act of 1951. Of these only 20 survived.[28]

The hosiery industry did not prioritise the mechanisation of production methods and processes. According to the 1956 Report, no economies of large-scale organisation applied to the tailoring and finishing processes, which absorbed the majority of labour costs.[29] It was in fact the type of market and consumer preferences that benefitted the small-scale production sector. The hosiery market was seasonal, which meant the qualities changed with season: In winter, heavier qualities were sold, and in summer lighter ones. There was also a demand regarding designs and fashions specific to a local area. Some places preferred a bleached look, others grey; some favoured round necks, others buttoned fronts. The market had to cope with these changing tastes. According to a representation by the Hosiery Manufacturers Association of Bengal,

> if a hosiery department is started in a cotton mill, it cannot work with any special advantage as the department would require different counts and qualities of yarns in small quantities, unless it chooses to manufacture only one quality with the effect of overproduction in a market.[30]

In 1958, the Development Commissioner reported that

> [T]he market for hosiery goods is very festidious [*sic*] and critical about the shapes, designs and colours of products. Mass production of only one shape, design or colour will neither be sound nor a practical business proposition. It is a matter of fundamental importance that each factory should have two or three types of knitting machines fed with yarns of various counts and colours. Also adaptability to new varieties and designs with minimum dislocation of work and organisation is an important criterion of efficiency of hosiery manufacturing units.[31]

Compared with small-scale products, those of the large-scale units had a better reputation in the market because of their comfortable fit and good finish, in terms of the uniform texture of knitting, correct stamping of sizes, low shrinkage and careful cutting and stitching. With coloured goods too, customers preferred the products of the larger producers because of their reputation for fast colours. Quality-conscious well-to-do consumers were the clients of such manufacturers. However, knitted goods of an inferior quality also continued to have a wide market, because they were sold at prices lower than the minimum set by the large producers and relatively well-organised small-scale factories. Price was a major consideration for customers in low-income groups.[32]

This does not mean, however, that low prices were the sole reason for consumers to prefer hosiery goods. As the Development Commissioner's Report indicates, the coefficient of income elasticity was higher for cotton and woollen hosiery than for cotton and woollen clothing, because hosiery fell more in the category of comforts while clothing belonged in the category of necessities. "As incomes increase, there will be some shift from ordinary clothing to items like hosiery".[33]

### *The Background to Changes in Consumption Patterns: The Social Emancipation of the Lower Classes*

To summarise, many of the products we have discussed, like those of the rice mills, cotton ginning factories and groundnut mills, were in the first phase of their development typical export commodities, grown in response to a swelling export market. This suggests that export-orientated commercialisation led to the change in its first phase. Though the two decades following 1920 witnessed a stagnation or decline in the overseas sale of some of these products, their production actually expanded because of increased demand in the domestic market. This expansion was to some extent underpinned by morphing consumption patterns among the lower classes.

Some changes in consumption pattern represented the use of substitutes for certain goods commonly consumed in the past. To some extent, cotton hosiery goods replaced cotton weaves. Though their low prices were a factor in their market expansion, even the poorer classes preferred hosiery goods, not just because of their affordability but because they were "comfortable". The growing popularity of rice among the poor in South India too was at the expense of other cereals. Rice was not a cheaper grain, though its relative price did steadily decline over time, and as nutritionists pointed out, rice was inferior to millet in terms of nutrition.[34] Yet it was substituted all the same. Therefore, this evolution in taste cannot be explained by purely economic factors.

Socio-economic conditions play a major role in taste making. As we have seen in our discussion about the handloom industry, there was a clear difference in nineteenth-century Tamil Nadu in the consumption patterns between upper- and lower-class people. This period saw the gradual emancipation of the rural subaltern population, who started challenging the elite villagers. The consumption patterns of the poorer village groups changed in this context. It is likely that greater emancipation led them to diversify their purchases, sometimes beyond the social restraints placed upon them. Such diversification took a number of forms. One was imitating the lifestyle choices of the upper classes, of which a typical case was drinking coffee. At the end of the nineteenth century, the Brahmins and other high castes would drink coffee every morning and coffee became a marker that distinguished "high" from "low" castes in Tamil culture (Venkatachalaphy 2002). In 1906, the *Tanjore Gazetteer* observed that while it used to be a Brahmin custom to drink coffee every morning, "of recent years however a tendency has become noticeable among Sudras, even of the poorer classes, towards the use of coffee in the early morning in preference to cold rice".[35] The new prevalence of rice among the lower classes was also symptomatic of lifestyle imitation, along with clothing changes. In the handloom industry, as we have seen, non-Brahmins began wearing clothes only Brahmins had previously worn, and there was a great increase in the demand for artificial silk saris by the poorer classes. The growth of cotton ginning in Tamil Nadu was encouraged by the expansion of large cotton mills in Madras Presidency and an important market for their yarns was the handloom industry. In other words, the new demand for handloom products supported not only the handloom industry itself but also indirectly the cotton ginning factories.

Two further types of consumer diversification are exemplified by the bidi and hosiery, respectively. In South India, bidi smoking was not a habit of the upper classes but regarded as a type of behaviour best avoided. Drinking the local palm wine (toddy) also falls in this category. Though there is no conclusive evidence about upward trends, a 1922 report about Tiruchirapalli district mentions, "Toddy is consumed chiefly by working classes, and consumption is increasing", which is suggestive.[36] Increased consumption of hosiery products represents another type of consumer diversification. While their production processes were based on technology developed in the West, their producers in Asia, as in the case of hosiery goods in Japan, succeeded in producing them at very low cost. These goods were purchased and used by a large section of the population in Asia, more concerned with price than quality. In this sense, such products should be called "cheap modern goods". They were preferred as low-cost "luxuries".

The development of small-scale rural industries in the first half of the twentieth century was thus closely related to fluctuations and changes in the socio-economic hierarchy of village society, as illustrated by strengthening moves among the lower classes to emancipate themselves from the dominant class of landowners.

### *The Background to Changes in Consumption Patterns: Changes in Income Levels among the Agricultural Labourer Class*

On what economic basis could this changing consumption among the lower classes have been achieved? Alterations in income levels among agricultural labourers must first be considered. Kamal Kumar Ghose has made an estimate for the average daily wage of agricultural labourers in Madras Presidency for a period after 1916 (Ghose 1969, 182). I have deflated this average wage through the five-year moving average of grain prices, and the result shows a growth in real wage rates in the 1920s and 1930s, with the exception of 1941, when the outbreak of war possibly caused a fluctuation in grain prices (Yangisawa 2010, 66–67).

Landownership among members of the agricultural labourer class evolved and further increased income. As we have seen, a significant number of the previously landless population acquired ownership of small pieces of land from the end of the nineteenth century. Some raised their status from pure employed labourers to tenant farmers. Since the land they obtained was too small in area for them to become independent farmers, most continued working as wage labourers for other farmers. It would have been possible for them spend more on consumer items by combining the money they earned as day labourers with the income from their tiny farms. There were certainly economic possibilities for the labourer classes of Tamil Nadu to expand consumption in the first half of the twentieth century.[37]

This examination of small-scale industries in South India, such as rice mills, cotton ginning factories, groundnut mills and hosiery factories, has allowed an enlightening picture to emerge. These industries were clearly driven by the domestic market, which had as its backbone demand from the non-elite. Furthermore, the evolution of lower-class consumption patterns was key in sustaining the demand for certain products. With increasing emancipation from the village elites, the subaltern population branched out in their purchases, sometimes beyond the social restraints placed on them. One such pattern of diversification was the replication of upper-class consumption patterns, like eating rice. On the other hand, bidi smoking, which was not an upper-class habit, also proliferated. We can say therefore that the growth of these industries and the changes in consumption patterns mirrored broader changes in the socio-economic structure of rural society.[38] As we shall examine in detail in Chapters 6 and 7, though aspirations by the lower classes after Independence to liberate themselves by resisting the upper classes in the village social hierarchy and raising their own status went along with the diversification of consumption and changes in its patterns, we can say that the type of growth experienced in the first half of the twentieth century serves as the prototype of the growth of the post-Independence informal sector.

The example of the hosiery industry has proved particularly fascinating. It shows us that specialisation of demand weakened the economies of scale of the large factories and allowed small-scale enterprises to dominate the industrial structure. These had particularly strong competitive power when producing cheap goods aimed at the poorer classes, whereas the main customers of the high-priced, high-quality goods made by the large factories were the well-to-do classes. It is crucial to realise that it was the small and marginal firms that were most prevalent in many areas of light industry during the period of industrial growth after Independence, when large firms produced branded goods for the urban upper classes and small and marginal firms made cheap commodities for rural villages and the poorer classes. This prototype too can already be seen materialising in the 1930s.

## Notes

1 G. Slater, ed. *Some South Indian Villages*. Oxford: Oxford University Press, 1918.
2 P. J. Thomas and K. C. Ramakrishnan, eds. *Some South Indian Villages: A Resurvey with Analysis and Observations*. Madras: University of Madras, 1940.

3 I am grateful for the insight offered by Dr Haruo Wakimura on this point.
4 *Manual of District of Tanjore in the Madras Presidency*, by T. Venkasami Row, Madras, 1883, pp. 316–317.
5 *Madras District Gazetteers, Tanjore*, by F.R. Hemingway, Madras, 1906, p. 64.
6 Hutton 1977, p. 205. The prohibitions forbade members of the depressed castes from wearing gold and silver ornaments, from trimming their hair, from using other than earthenware tableware in the home, from wearing clothes below the knee and above the hips (males), from wearing coats, shirts or banyans (knitted robes) (males), from using umbrellas or sandals (men), from covering the upper body with clothes or shawls (females) and from using flowers or saffron paste.
7 *Preliminary Report on the Survey of Cottage Industries in the North Arcot District*, Madras, 1929, p. 6; *Preliminary Report on the Survey of Cottage Industries in the Salem District*, Madras, 1929, p. 7.
8 As will be detailed in Chapter 7, the share of the large cotton mills in the textile industry decreased sharply from Independence through the 1980s. The majority share was by small powerloom factories having several automatic looms. An important component of the entrepreneurs engaged in this business were from the textile industry.
9 For details of sources, for example, see Yanagisawa 2004 and Yanagisawa 2010, on which this section is based.
10 *Indian Industrial Commission, Minutes of Evidence, 1916-17, Vol. III, Madras and Bangalore*, Calcutta: Superintendent Government Press, India, 1918, pp. 55, 92.
11 *Madras District Gazetteers, Statistical Appendix, together with a Supplement to the District Gazetteer (1906) for Tanjore District*, Madras: Superintendent Government Press, 1933, pp. 180–81.
12 *Report on the Marketing of Groundnuts in India and Burma*, Delhi: Manager of Publications, 1941, p. 46.
13 Calculated from Government of India, Labour Bureau, Ministry of Labour, Employment and Rehabilitation, *Report on Family Living Survey among Industrial Workers 1958-59, Coimbatore*, Delhi, 1967, p. 62, p. 116.
14 Hemingway, F. R., *Madras District Gazetteers, Trichinopoly*, Madras, 1907, pp. 171–172.
15 In Section 1 of Chapter 1, I pointed out the increased use of fertilisers from the end of the nineteenth century. In this connection, there was a growth in demand for groundnut oil cake to be used as fertiliser.
16 Government of India, *Report of the Court of Enquiry into Labour Conditions in Beedi, Cigar, Snuff, Tobacco-curing and Tanning Industries*, Madras: Superintendent, Government Press, 1947, pp. 5, 8–9.
17 D. Narayana Rao, *Report on the Survey of Cottage Industries in the Madras Presidency*, Madras, 1929, pp. 202, 204.
18 Government of Madras, Government Order No. 1714, Miscellaneous, Development Department, 10 Sept. 1930, "Report of the Madras Youth League", p. 5.
19 Government of India, Ministry of Food and Agriculture, Directorate of Marketing and Inspection, *Report on the Marketing of Tobacco in India*, Second edition, New Delhi, 1953, p. 73.
20 *Statistical Appendix and Supplement to the Revised District Manual (1889) for Coimbatore District*, Madras, 1933, p. 152.
21 *Bombay Cotton Annual*, 1924–25, 1929–30, 1934–35, 1039–40.
22 Department of Commercial Intelligence and Statistics, *Large Industrial Establishments in India*, for 1925 and 1946.
23 "Representation on behalf of the Hosiery Manufacturing Association of Bengal for Protection to the Hosiery Industry", *Indian Tariff Board, 1934*, Vol. 1, Delhi, 1934, p. 182.
24 Rao, D. Narayana, *Preliminary Report on the Survey of Cottage Industries in the East Godavari District*, Madras, printed by the Superintendent, Government Press, 1929, pp. 22–23.

25 Development Commissioner (Small Scale Industries), *Small Scale Industry Analysis and Planning Report, No. 18, Hosiery Industry (All India)*, Ministry of Commerce and Industry, Government of India, New Delhi, 1958, pp. 13–14, pp. 23–24.
26 Development Commissioner, *op. cit.*, p. 38.
27 Ibid., p. 38.
28 Ibid., pp. 45–46.
29 Ibid., p. 45.
30 "Representation on behalf of the Hosiery Manufacturers Association of Bengal for Protection to the Hosiery Industry", *Indian Tariff Board, Vol. 1*, 1934, Delhi, Manager of Publications, p. 177.
31 Development Commissioner, *op. cit.*, pp. 45–46.
32 Ibid., pp. 49–50.
33 Ibid., p. 43.
34 Aykroyd and Krishnan, "Diet Surveys in South Indian Villages," p. 687.
35 *Madras District Gazetteers, Tanjore*, Madras, 1906, p. 65; see also *Madras District Gazetteers, Tinnevelly, Vol. 1, Madras, 1917*, p. 105.
36 Madras Presidency, *Note Book of General Information of the North Trichinopoly Circle*, 1922, Government Press.
37 With the exception of Bengal, Central Provinces and Bihar, other areas in India seem to have witnessed a similar trend towards a rise in the real wage of agricultural labourers. As Ghose points out, this declined in Bombay, the Punjab and United Provinces between 1916 and 1921, but rose substantially between 1921 and 1931. The real wage level declined down to 1936, returning to the 1916 level, but it was higher than 1921. There was a different type of change in Bengal, where the real wage started declining after 1926 and by 1936 was well below even the 1921 level. This is probably due to the fact that the decline of Bengal's jute economy had a far greater and more widespread impact here than in other parts of India (Ghose 1969, Table VII:4 [p. 185]). For increases in compensation for labour in a north Indian village, see Kessinger 1979, pp. 139–146.
38 Morris D. Morris, writing about the period between 1913 and 1936, says that the manufacturing industry in India was constrained by trends from the domestic market rather than from the foreign market. When considering that there was development even in those industries not protected by the discriminating tariff, what was even more important than the tariff policy was the vitality of India's domestic market (Morris 1983). New consumption trends among the lower classes are likely to have contributed in part to this vitality.

# Part II

# The Economic Development in Independent India

## The Formation of a Foundation

After decades of stagnation during the colonial period, the post-Independence economy started to grow at an annual growth rate of 3 percent or more. Part II journeys through the decades from Independence to 1980, when the foundation for post-1980 development was formed.

Under a state-led import-substitution industrialisation strategy, the Indian economy succeeded in establishing an industrial structure, incorporating heavy industry and the manufacture of producer goods. These had been lacking in the colonial period when only light industries existed, with the exception of the iron and steel industry. The production system formed at this time, which was fundamentally self-sufficient, was the foundation of later economic development. Chapter 4 studies this process and draws attention to the simultaneous formation of a "high-cost, low quality" Indian economy.

Agricultural production and the rural economy experienced their own developments from the 1950s. These created a vital base that supported economic growth after the 1980s. Agrarian production, which had stagnated in the pre-Independence period, recovered its dynamism in the 1950, and extended throughout India in the course of the Green Revolution from the mid-1960s. Higher levels of production brought better incomes to most classes of rural society and significantly contributed to rural demand for the industrial and service sectors. Chapter 5 examines the influence of transformations in agricultural production on the environment and explains the role of land reforms in the emancipation of the rural lower classes.

The relationship among the classes in rural society underwent a structural transformation across many regions. The dominance of the landholding classes over the subaltern villagers weakened as the lower classes became more involved in emancipation movements. This helped create the conditions under which the lower classes were able to enjoy the benefits, even if partially, of rising agrarian production in the form of a rise in real wage rates for agricultural labourers. The expansion of non-farm job opportunities for the rural population is a further crucial thread in the fabric of rural change. It not only tightened rural labour markets and so contributed to both the rise in the wage rates of agricultural labourers and to the subalterns' emancipation

DOI: 10.4324/9781003341550-6

movements, but also led to an overall increase in the family income of the rural population. All these transfigurations led to a growth in rural demand for non-farm goods and services. Chapter 6 describes this multi-faceted process and its culmination in the formation of a rural market base which supported economic growth in the three decades after 1980.

# 4 State-led Import-Substitution Industrialisation

## Forming the Foundation for Further Economic Development

### State-led Import-Substitution Industrialisation

After decades of an almost dormant economy under colonial rule, India's GDP found new life in the post-independence period (Table 4.1; Sivasubramonian 2000, 622), and the foundation for post-1980 development was formed.

The growth rate of all sectors rose after 1947, but the highest was in the secondary sector. From this time, industry gradually took centre stage in the Indian economy. Whereas in the periods 1950/51–1964/5 (Period I) and 1980/1–1999/2000 (Period III), secondary industry recorded a high growth rate of 6.8 percent, the 15 years between 1965/6 and 1979/80 (Period II) were a period of low growth. S. Sivasubramonian estimates that total factor productivity (TFP) growth in non-agricultural sectors like manufacturing was 1.21 percent and 2.01 percent in Periods I and III respectively, but only reached 0.07 percent in Period II (Sivasubramonian 2004, 320–321). Not only did India's GDP from industry increase during Period I, but industrial development went hand in hand with a rise in productivity. It can be considered the time when the foundations were laid down for the later expansion of India's economy as a whole.

Between Independence and the new economic policy of 1991, India followed an import-substitution industrialisation strategy based on a state-led model of a planned economy. The period between 1950 and 1964/5 saw this strategy devised and put into action through the initiative of the first prime minister, Jawaharlal Nehru, and P. C. Mahalanobis, of the Indian Statistical Institute. As we saw in Chapter 2, nationalist demands during the colonial era had led to the partial introduction of an import-substitution industrialisation policy by means of a protective tariff, and the interwar period and World War II witnessed a transitional process towards a planned national economy. Even among senior British officials in the Government of India there had been serious discussion about the need for an economic plan to stimulate the national economy rather than relying on a policy of *laissez-faire*. In 1938, the Indian National Congress set up the National Planning Committee chaired by Nehru, and leading industrialists, including Sir Purshottamdas Thakurdas, studied ideas for a planned economy and

DOI: 10.4324/9781003341550-7

*Table 4.1* India's real GDP growth rate by sector (%)

| | *1900/1–1946/7* | *1947/8–1999/2000* | *1950/1–1964/5* | *1965/6–1979/80* | *1980/1–1999/2000* | *Index of growth to 1999/2000 (1947/8=100)* |
|---|---|---|---|---|---|---|
| Primary | 0.4 | 2.5 | 2.6 | 2.7 | 3.2 | 361.7 |
| Secondary | 1.5 | 5.5 | 6.8 | 4.3 | 6.8 | 1,691.9 |
| Tertiary | 1.7 | 5.0 | 4.5 | 4.3 | 6.7 | 1,342.4 |
| Total GDP | 0.9 | 4.1 | 4.0 | 3.6 | 5.6 | 852.0 |
| Per capita GDP | 0.1 | 1.9 | 1.9 | 1.3 | 3.5 | 297.8 |
| Population | 0.8 | 2.0 | 2.0 | 2.3 | 2.0 | 286.4 |

Source: Sivasubramonian, 2000, Tables 9.35, p. 624, Table 9.4, pp. 565–566.

published a set of proposals which envisaged restricting state ownership or control to key industries like engineering and chemicals. Economic planning was an influential concept at that time and the ideas held by business leaders about building the economy through state control as a policy to assist and promote rapid industrialisation were also potentially shared by Britain. Drawn into World War II, the government, in order to secure the supplies needed for the war effort, subjected the Indian economy to import controls and to restrictions on the production and transportation of many goods. The Licence Raj of the post-war Indian economy was in many ways a continuation of wartime economic control (Nakazato 2001).

The central issue of the Nehru–Mahalanobis strategy was to foster growth through the capital goods industry. Mahalanobis wrote, "India's present dependence on ***imports*** of ***capital goods*** is a fundamental structural ***weakness*** which must be corrected as quickly as possible" (Mahalanobis 1985, 116, cited by Majumder 1990). He thought the state should play a leading role in this. First, a number of important industries were reserved by the state. The Industrial Policy Resolution of 1956 scheduled a number of industrial areas that were to be the exclusive responsibility of the state, of which arms and ammunition, atomic energy and railways would be central government monopolies. New industrial units that would be undertaken entirely under government responsibility included mining (coal. iron), manufacturing (iron and steel, heavy plants, heavy electrical equipment, aircraft and ship building, telephones and telegraphs), air transport, and electricity generation and distribution. Other industries, including aluminium, machine tools, ferro-alloys and tool steels, and chemicals, as well as other minerals, road transport and sea transport were scheduled as being open to the private sector, but in a supplementary way, with the state encouraged to develop these as well.

Even where the private sector was permitted to build or expand factories, a government license was needed. Under this system, licenses were issued when establishing factories or expanding production, with the aim of preventing any excess over government targets. Foreign trade was severely regulated through strict foreign exchange controls and even items for which the necessary government import licenses had been granted faced quantity limits and a high rate of customs duties. There were numerous cases where foreign equity participation was permitted to promote the import of technology and avoid a worsening foreign exchange situation, but the government's basic policy was that it would not permit such participation above 51 percent. Government permission was necessary regarding both imports and foreign capital (Itō 1972).[1]

While the government promoted the establishment under state leadership of an independent, heavy-industry economy, there were insufficient efforts either at central or state level to build educational standards to support industrialisation, especially at the primary stage. Pulapre Balakrishnan comments that "it is indeed correct to say that primary education ended up being severely neglected in the Nehru era [1950–1965]". The share of public expenditure given to primary education greatly declined, although that for secondary education sharply increased (Balakrishnan 2010, 89–90). As we shall see below, it was the informal sector, which depended on labour with the absolute lowest education level, that expanded most notably during the post-1980 period of economic growth; this educational weakness of the labour force had its origins in how the education system was constructed after Independence. Nevertheless, the roots of the 1990s IT industry may be found in this emphasis on secondary education.

The state-led import-substitution system underwent some change after 1965, yet its basic framework continued until 1991, and Indian industry certainly made important gains under it. As we have already seen, secondary industry, which had sustained a low growth rate of 1.5 percent between 1900 and 1946, leapt to a rate in the range of 6 percent in the 15 years between 1950 and 1964 with a mean annual rate of 6.8 percent. Though the rate slowed after 1965, secondary industry continued to grow at around 4 percent, a growth trajectory qualitatively different from the colonial period. TFP rose at an annual rate of 1.21 percent between 1950/51 and 1964/65, and it is highly significant that productivity went hand in hand with growth.[2]

In addition, India, which had depended on imports for 55 percent of its capital goods in 1950 (Chandrasekhar 2011, 208), rapidly increased its production rate for heavy industry (Table 4.2). For example, between 1961 and 1965, industrial production grew by an annual average of 9 percent, with the sharpest increase being in the capital goods sector, which reached an annual growth rate of near 20 percent, with basic goods coming next with a growth rate of 10.5 percent (McCartney 2009, 104). As a result, between 1951 and 1980, the proportion of consumer goods in an index of industrial production halved, from 47.6 percent to 23.7 percent, while the proportion of basic and capital goods notably increased (Table 4.3). Rakesh Mohan points out "it is clear that the objective of developing an industrial base has been significantly achieved and the Second Plan heavy industry strategy has been implemented" (Mohan 1992, 102).

*Table 4.2* Index number of industrial production (1950/1 = 100)

| | *1955/56* | *1960/61* |
|---|---|---|
| General index | 139 | 194 |
| Cotton textiles | 128 | 133 |
| Iron and steel | 122 | 238 |
| Machinery (all types) | 192 | 503 |
| Chemicals | 179 | 288 |

Source: McCartney 2009, Table 5.15, p. 104.

Original source: Third F.Y.P., ch. 3:5.

*Table 4.3* Structure of industrial production

| | *Basic goods* | *Capital goods* | *Intermediate goods* | *Consumer goods* | *Consumer Durables* | *Consumer Nondurables* |
|---|---|---|---|---|---|---|
| 1951 | 19.8 | 3.5 | 29 | 47.6 | – | – |
| 1960 | 25.1 | 11.8 | 25.9 | 37.3 | 5.7 | 31.6 |
| 1970 | 32.3 | 15.3 | 21 | 31.5 | 3.4 | 28.1 |
| 1980 | 39.4 | 16.4 | 20.5 | 23.7 | 2.6 | 21.1 |
| 1990 | 38.4 | 23.7 | 17.5 | 30.4 | – | – |

Source: Mohan 1992, Table 3, p. 102.

Original source: Office of the Economic Adviser, Ministry of Industry.

It was import substitution that contributed the most to the development of heavy industry. The existence from 1950/51 of a domestic market that was guaranteed increased trade protection stimulated both public and private investment. Nearly a quarter of economic growth between 1950/51 and 1965/66 came through import substitution. Import substitution was highest in consumer goods until 1957, and then, with the launch of the second Five Year Plan (1956–1961), emphasis was placed on intermediate and investment goods, such as steel, cement and some capital goods (Chandrasekhar 2011, p. 209; McCartney 2009, p. 99). Capital goods, too, of which 55 percent had relied on imports in 1950, reduced this reliance to 44.4 percent in 1959/60 and to 36.4 percent in 1965/66 (Table 4.4). Similar reductions were made with intermediate goods and basic goods as well. This is a measure of the progress of import substitution.

There was important progress too in the formation of the technological basis for industrial production. Sanjay Kathuria (1995, 174) comments that "[a] certain amount of technological change (TC) is inevitable" in the transfer of technology from the more advanced countries:

> This TC includes adaptation of local inputs to manufacturing requirements, changes in production processes to suit scale and skills, and even adaptation of products to cater to local demand conditions.... [S]

*Table 4.4* Rate of import reliance in the industrial sector

| | *1959/60* | *1965/66* |
|---|---|---|
| Total | 18.1 | 14.7 |
| Basic goods | 34.1 | 22.5 |
| Intermediate goods | 21.3 | 10.9 |
| Capital goods | 44.0 | 36.4 |
| Consumer goods | 5.7 | 4.9 |
| Durables | 36.1 | 28.2 |
| Nondurables | 4.0 | 3.0 |
| Total | 18.1 | 14.7 |

Source: Majumder 1990, Table 3 (p. 136).

> tringent local use regulations with regard to components and machinery, as well as raw materials wherever feasible, ensured that a substantial amount of this kind of adaptive TC was undertaken. Apart from this, government policies restricting imports of goods as well as imports of technology, along with fiscal concessions and other incentives for in-house R&D, have resulted in India's leading manufacturing enterprises across a broad range of sectors acquiring a deep and diverse set of technological capabilities.

Matthew McCartney (2009, 106–107) cites Hindustan Machine Tools (HMT) as an example of the indigenisation of technology:

> Hindustan Machine Tools was initially developed through foreign collaborations; this initial agreement was terminated in 1956. A second factory was opened soon after in Bangalore without foreign assistance. Engineers, supervisors and operators moved from the 'mother factory' to set up new offshoots. There are some indications of learning: this second factory was operational in 14 months, while the first took over a decade. More factories were opened in the early 1960s in Pinjore, Kalamassery and Hyderabad. Technology was initially purchased under licence; the production of machine tools was then gradually indigenised. The indigenous content of milling machines increased from 35 percent in 1957/58 to 94 percent 1963/64 … In 1966, HMT made a significant breakthrough and successfully competed for an order of 250 milling machines by the defence ministry. Growth was extensive in nature, acquiring a technology and expanding its use to increase output and indigenise the production process.

As M. R. Bhagavan points out, "by the early 1970s, India had achieved near total self-sufficiency in its capacity to produce most of the standard-modern capital goods required by Indian industry" (Bhagavan 1985, 419). McCartney notes that "[t]he relative price of capital goods remained stable between 1955 and 1965 despite a reduction from 20 percent to 10 percent in the share of capital goods in total imports" (McCartney 2009, 106–107). This means that the more expensive capital goods did not necessarily substitute for imported goods.

However, Kathuria significantly asserts that, in establishing a technological base, India was greatly behind other developing countries in terms of investment in human capital. "For example ... [i]n 1980-82, of ten developing countries ... 73 percent of India's population over the age of 25 had no schooling." This was the lowest figure of the ten. "India [also] had the lowest percentage of the population engaged in vocational education" among ten developing countries. "Similarly, although the number of engineering students was largest in India, amongst the developing countries..., the proportion of engineering students to the population was lower only in Kenya." Kathuria concludes, "It may be said that India's technical education system is structurally flawed. Thus it is probably true ... that vast sections of Indian industry operate with very low skill inputs" (Kathuria 1995, 175–176).[3]

Though the state-led economic development strategy that began in the 1950s carried with it many problems, which we will outline below, it certainly achieved at a fundamental level its principal objective to promote heavy industrialisation and import substitution (Kathuria 1995, 170). The example of the Hindustan Machine Tools Company, which succeeded in indigenising the technology imported from abroad, makes clear that government protection played an important role in the formation of a technological base (Mascarenhas 1982, 201). With the economic liberalisation reforms after 1991, the economy of the formal sector, amid strengthening domestic competition, maintained the growth rate it had attained around 1980, and from the 2000s achieved an even higher level of development. We can confirm, therefore, that the process of import substitution from the 1950s was fundamental in building the foundation for this later positive economic change.

We have already seen that the public sector played a crucial part in post-1950s economic growth. Because units requiring large-scale capital investment and those offering no prospect of short-term profits could not rely fully on private investment, the public sector became a necessity. The state's role in infrastructure was central, and at one time, 60 percent of total production capital, eight of the top ten enterprises and two thirds of operatives fell within the state sector. In the middle of the 1960s, most of the accumulated capital in the public sector was concentrated on industries like iron and steel, machine tools, chemicals, oil, mining and metals. The proportion occupied by the total physical assets held by the public sector in 1950/51 was 2.5 percent; this had increased sharply to 26 percent in 1965/66 (Chandrasekhar 2011, 211).

However, this growth of the public sector did not inhibit private sector investment. Investment by private enterprises grew from 1 percent of GDP in the 1950s to 1.7 percent in the 1960s (Table 4.5). Pulapre Balakrishnan states, "we would on balance imagine the public sector contributing to the expansion of private investment by expanding the market for its goods and at the same supplying the capital goods necessary at a low price" (Balakrishnan 2010, 69).

*Table 4.5* Saving and investment (% GDP)

| | *Private sector industries* | | | *Public sector* | | |
|---|---|---|---|---|---|---|
| | *Saving* | *Investment* | *Saving-Investment* | *Saving* | *Investment* | *Saving-Investment* |
| 1950–55 | 1 | 1.4 | −0.4 | 1.7 | 3.1 | −1.4 |
| 1960–65 | 1.7 | 3.6 | −1.9 | 3 | 7.5 | −4.4 |
| 1989–90 | 2.1 | 3.9 | −1.8 | 1.7 | 10.7 | -9 |

Source: Balakrishnan 2010, Table 2.4, p. 69.

Original source: "National Accounts Statistics, New Delhi: Central Statistical Organisation (CSO).

## The Slowdown in Industrial Growth, Formation of a "High-Cost Economy" and the Development of New Industries

The growth rate of the Indian industrial sector, which leapt in the 1950s, fell in the period 1965–1980. As Table 4.1 shows, the average growth rate of secondary industry declined from 6.8 percent in the period 1950/51–1964/5 to 4.3 percent in the period 1965/6–1979/80. Sivasubramonian's estimate states that the average annual TFP growth rate in the non-agricultural sector fell from 1.21 percent in the period 1950/51–1964/65 to 0.07 percent in the period 1965/66–1979/80 (Sivasubramonian 2000).

### *Background to the Slowdown in Industrial Growth*

According to Isher Judge Ahluwalia, "there was a slowdown in import substitution after the mid-sixties". In 1965/66 the share of imports exceeded 20 percent only in 4 of 20 manufacturing subgroups (petroleum products, basic metals, non-electrical machinery and electrical machinery) and the slowdown in import substitution covered industries accounting for almost 80 percent of total value added between 1965/6 and 1979/80 compared with 1950/51–1964/5 (Ahluwalia 1985, 119–121; see also Chandrasekhar 2011, 214). Yet, scrutinising individual products shows that by commodity there was no negative correlation between import growth and growth of domestic production. Import substitution is only one element of demand growth, and its slowdown only partly explains the stagnation in industrial production after 1965 (McCartney 2009, 120).

The waning of industrial investment was not isolated. Public investment also dwindled from the middle of the 1960s and influenced the industrial sector. Public investment reached 9.6 percent of GDP in 1965/66 but had fallen to 6.3 percent by 1970/71. Pulapre Balakrishnan states that this change "is likely to have impacted manufacturing growth … [as] [p]ublic sector output … was central to private production in the manufacturing sector."

> "With a decline in public investment, profitability in the private sector was struck a blow and excess capacity emerged. As a temporary disincentive now emerged for private investment, it lowered the demand for capital goods produced in the public sector".

This encouraged a certain slowdown, in a cyclic pattern which would continue (Balakrishnan 2010, 129–133).[4]

Industrial stagnation was further encouraged by the structure of demand for industrial products in the 1960s. If such demand was supported by a broad mass market incorporating the rural areas where the majority of the population lived, neither the slowdown in import substitution nor the fall in public investment would have led directly to stagnation. However, as Table 4.6 shows, distribution of income at the time was very much concentrated on the upper classes, with 40 percent of total income earned by the upper 10 percent. This unequal distribution is illustrated in Table 4.7, in the extreme disparity of wealth (property) in rural areas. As we shall see in Chapter 5, land reform was carried out in India from the 1950s, but the unequal pattern of land ownership basically did not change. The majority of the population had virtually no assets such as land and lived in such extreme poverty that their very lives were under threat. Since most of their income went on food, they had little purchasing power for industrial products. The total consumption of non-edible industrial products around 1965 was no more than about 10 percent (Majumder 1990, 143; Chandrasekhar 2011, 215). Thus the narrowness of the domestic market for mass industrial consumer products should also be considered a factor in the industrial inactivity of the time. Important changes to this limited market, as explored in Chapter 6, had to wait until the 1980s.

*Table 4.6* Income distribution by class (% of total income)

| | *1952/53–1956/57* | *1953/54–1956/57* | *1956/57* | *1962 rural villages* | *1962 urban areas* | *1951/52–1959/60* |
|---|---|---|---|---|---|---|
| Upper 10% | 25 | 28 | 37 | 32.8 | 42.4 | 43 |
| Lower 20% | 9 | 8 | 6 | 5.9 | 5.3 | 4 |

Source: A. Vaidyanathan, "Some Aspects of Inequalities in Living Standards in Rural India" in T.N. Srinivasan and P.K. Bardhan eds., Poverty and Income Distribution in India. Calcutta: Statistical Publishing Society, 1974, p. 216 (cited by Majumder 1990, p. 142).

*Table 4.7* Distribution of assets in rural areas (%)

| | *1961* | *1971* |
|---|---|---|
| Lower 10% | 0.1 | 0.1 |
| Lower 30% | 2.5 | 2.0 |
| Upper 30% | 79.0 | 81.9 |
| Upper 10% | 51.4 | 51.0 |

Source: Majumder 1990, Table 12, p. 143.

### *"High-Cost, Low-Quality" Industrial Production*

Demand-related factors were a key element in the slowdown of Indian industry, but the impact of the government's industrial policy cannot be overlooked. It arguably created a high-cost structure and encouraged the spread of monopolistic practices among enterprises. On the one hand, the domestic market had been shielded from competition from foreign imports by the import-substitution policy which had been followed since the 1950s, but on the other, access to new industries by enterprises was severely restricted by the licensing system and this led to domestic competition being extremely limited. The trend of economic policy from around 1965 was complicated, but an approach involving strengthening controls on corporate activities was adopted. For example, managers of private enterprises had to get permission from the state government to close down plants, while the production fields reserved for small-scale enterprises were broadened. Therefore, within a protected market, with fortified restrictions on corporate activities and limits placed on both access and exit, inefficient enterprises could survive in many fields of production. The sluggishness of industrial growth can therefore be blamed on low productivity, high costs, low quality of production and obsolescent technology (Mohan 1992, 100; Ahluwalia 1985).

Among India's private enterprises, business groups resembling the Japanese *zaibatsu* and dating back to the colonial period dominated the industrial sector. Their monopolistic position was in actuality reinforced within the licensing system. According to a 1964 study by the Monopolies Inquiry Commission, 87.7 percent of 1,298 products

> were in the hands of oligopolies with 437 being produced by only one firm, and 229 by two firms each. In fact, excepting for food products, cotton textiles and jute textiles, almost the whole of Indian industry was characterised by monopoly, duopoly and oligopoly.

It is significant that a small number of business groups had a monopoly in most areas through firms under their control, and by means of their financial strength, their performance record and their information-gathering ability they had an edge in obtaining licenses in all areas of industrial activity. They drove up their production capacity in those fields which promised market expansion and where profit margins were high by obtaining the appropriate licenses, but even where markets conditions were slack, they took out licenses as a defensive strategy to prevent the entry of other companies, and continued to hold them without further expenditure on productivity. It was due to such monopolistic corporate behaviour that some commodities, for example cement, remained in short supply (Chandrasekhar 1994, 327–329; Kathuria 1995, 171–172).

Even in the state-owned heavy industrial sector, the former vigorous growth and technical acquisition abated after 1965. McCartney notes that

> a major expansion of the Bhilai steel plant in 1974 required that the major part of detailed design and engineering was done by the Soviets, as was the detailed engineering and technical project work for the construction of the Visahkhapatnam plant in 1979. There was little evidence of indigenisation in plant planning, design and engineering. At Bokaro, the number of Soviet specialists nearly trebled between 1969 and 1983.

McCartney also points out the low level of R&D in the Bharat Aluminium Company (BALCO) and the Hindustan Aluminium Company (HINDALCO). Further,

> [c]apacity utilisation in steel production in Bhilai dropped from 111.8 percent in 1964/65 to 54.1 percent in 1965/66, ... remaining in the range 80–90 percent into the 1980s. Capacity utilisation in steel production in Durgapur dropped from 100.6 percent in 1964/65 to a low of 50.1 percent in 1969 but then fluctuated between 50 and 60 percent until the 1980s... [I]n the late 1970s, India had to import steel despite having unused capacity domestically.
>
> (McCartney 2009, 137)

Though we see here an inclination towards low productivity, high costs and low quality, not all fields of industry were affected to the same extent. According to Kathuria, Indian competitiveness fell down to the mid-1980s, as indicated by the decline in India's share in the export of manufactured goods from the developing nations from 22.1 percent in 1962, to 11 percent in 1970, 4.4 percent in 1980 and 3.4 percent in 1985. Yet, if we consider that the foreign exchange rate of the rupee was set comparatively high and that capital goods were expensive, we can say that production was efficient in much of the manufacturing industry, utilising price competitiveness. It is clear that the high cost of input goods and transportation for iron and steel as well as for metal, plastic and petroleum products was the main constraint on increasing exports.

### *Local Adaptation and Competitiveness*

Kathuria agrees that a large number of inefficient enterprises survived through government policy that restricted both a firm's expansion and its ability to close down a plant, but offers commercial vehicle production (trucks, buses) as a field where competitive enterprises remained going concerns. Two companies, Hindustan Motors and Premier Automobiles, both of which had been established during the colonial period, did not survive competition in the manufacture of commercial vehicles, though they continued to make passenger cars. Two of the five companies producing commercial vehicles built medium-weight vehicles, and three light-weight, maintaining their competitive position in the Indian domestic market. These firms employed technology suited to cope with rough road conditions while keeping their vehicles competitive in price. As a result, even with growing liberalisation after 1980, imports did not penetrate the market for commercial vehicles. One such example was the introduction, and then the withdrawal, of the new Isuzu model. Highly regarded internationally – with excellent traction, gradability, speed, acceleration and fuel efficiency – it had an attractive external appearance and a cab ensuring driver comfort. Hindustan Isuzu introduced it in 1986 as a challenge to the established manufacturers, but problems soon arose over its durability and maintenance costs. These were particularly troubling in the North where the roads are rough and overloading more prevalent. The company was forced to withdraw the model in 1990. Kathuria also speaks of other difficulties the car faced in the Indian market: Its market price was about 12 percent more expensive than its competitors, while the availability of parts, serviceability and familiarity of mechanics affected its resale value. This experience demonstrates why "Indianised" vehicles, with their durability on bad roads, had a market niche in many African countries, even in the face of strong international competition (Kathuria 1996, 153–54).

After 1965, the monopolistic practices of producers grew under the government's policy of import restrictions, leading to high-cost, low-quality industries overall. This said, however, such a tendency did not apply to all fields of industry. Some strengthened their competitiveness because of rivalry among the manufacturers themselves, while others adapted technology to conform to the local usage environment, as exemplified by durable Indian commercial vehicles, and were able to present viable products internationally in countries with similar conditions.

### *Independence from the Domination of Multinationals: Pharmaceuticals and Electronics*

Restrictions on the levels of foreign investment in India from the 1970s and the policy to protect domestic industries fostered the growth of the pharmaceutical and information industries, which developed on an international scale after the reforms of 1991.

India had experience in the manufacture of medicines from the early twentieth century when Indian firms were involved in making pharmaceuticals. After Independence, however, the industry was dominated by multinationals (MNCs) through the 1960s. The Indian Patents and Design Act of 1911, which remained in effect until 1972, awarded patents not only to the pharmaceutical products made by foreign companies but to the processes as well, which meant Indian firms were prevented from manufacturing generic drugs. The government permitted foreign pharmaceutical firms to operate and continued to depend on them for the provision of medicines. A great change was made to this policy in the 1970s. First, the Foreign Exchange Regulation Act (FERA) of 1973 restricted the activities of foreign companies with an equity holding of more than 40 percent (FERA companies). Pharmaceutical firms in this category engaged in producing formulation products or bulk drugs not involving high technology found their activities severely curbed, with many categories of production reserved for domestic firms. This system continued until 1994, when restrictions were abolished (Chaudhuri 2004, 164–165).

The revision of the Patent Act of 1911 was instrumental. This Act had allowed for product patents for drugs and medicines, and virtually all process patents for new drugs and medicines had a term of 16 years. Indian firms were forbidden either to process patented drugs into formulations or to import them. The MNCs holding the patents enjoyed a complete monopoly, and tended to bring in the necessary pharmaceuticals without establishing drug production centres in India. As a result of MNC domination, medicines in India were highly priced and there were delays in introducing essential drugs. The Patent Act of 1970 reduced the term of the patent from 16 to 5 years and allowed only process, not product, patents for drugs and pharmaceuticals; further, a MNC could patent only one process. Indian firms responded quickly to the new act and began developing new and alternative processes to reproduce the most recently launched drugs (Chaudhuri 2004, 166–67). Research units developed by the government, such as the Central Drug Research Institute (CDRI), supported developments by private enterprises. For example, in 1981 Glaxo brought out an antiulcer drug (ranitidine) that it marketed as Zantac; in 1985 the Indian company Ranbaxy was selling it in the Indian market and was soon followed by many other Indian firms, such as Dr Reddy's Laboratories (DRL). The MNCs had, as we have seen, previously controlled the production of bulk drugs in India, preferring to import and assemble them there than to manufacture the final product. From the latter part of the 1970s, however, the manufacture of bulk drugs by Indian firms began to grow, showing rapid expansion in the course of the 1980s (Table 4.8). The share of the MNCs in the Indian pharmaceutical market fell from 68 percent in 1970 to 50 percent in 1980 and 40 percent in 1991. On the other hand, the number of production units in India rose from 2,257 in 1969–1970 to 16,000 in 1989–1990. This growth notably took place before the liberalisation of 1991 (Mazumdar 2013, 43).

The growth in the production of bulk drugs by Indian manufacturers strengthened competition between the MNCs and Indian firms, and as a result, the price of medicines in India plunged, to about 1 percent of that internationally. The Patent Act of 1970 also enhanced the competitiveness of Indian pharmaceutical firms on the international market. Of course, India could not export to countries which recognised the product patent. However, before the expiration of the patent, manufacturers built up their capabilities to produce the drug, which was not under patent protection in India, commercially so that when the patent expired abroad it could penetrate the market very quickly. Indian competitiveness internationally was based on its pharmaceutical firms dominating the domestic market so that they were able to substantially bring down overseas prices (Chaudhuri 2004, 168). Exports after 1991, when the trade in Indian pharmaceuticals was liberalised, proliferated even more remarkably, though as Table 4.8 shows, there was already a striking expansion in the second half of the 1980s.

The Indian pharmaceutical industry thus came to occupy a powerful position in the global market after the economic reforms and trade liberalisation of 1991. It had built on the experience of drug manufacturing acquired during the colonial period, and with restrictions placed on the activities of the MNCs, the revision of the Patent Act and the growth of state R&D units, Indian firms, protected by government policy, were able to make swift progress in production, not only establishing for themselves a dominant position in the domestic market but also a competitive edge internationally.[5]

Like the pharmaceutical industry, the IT industry too, which branched out internationally from the 1990s, had grown up from the 1970s in connection

*Table 4.8* Production of bulk drugs and formulations; value of import and export of drugs and pharmaceuticals (10,000,000 rupees)

| | *Production* | | *Imports and exports* | | |
|---|---|---|---|---|---|
| | *Bulk drugs* | *Formulations* | *Exports* | *Imports* | *Trade balance* |
| May-74 | 90 | 400 | 43.14 | 46.90 | –3.76 |
| Jun-75 | 130 | 560 | 42.27 | 46.02 | –3.75 |
| Jul-76 | 150 | 700 | 54.13 | 54.17 | –0.04 |
| Aug-77 | 164 | 900 | 60.77 | 82.42 | –21.65 |
| Sep-78 | 200 | 1,050 | 69.02 | 95.33 | –26.31 |
| 1979/80 | | | | | |
| Jan-80 | 226 | 1,150 | 71.16 | 120.03 | –48.87 |
| Feb-81 | 240 | 1,200 | 76.18 | 112.81 | –36.63 |
| Mar-82 | 289 | 1,430 | 95.41 | 136.77 | –41.36 |
| Apr-83 | 345 | 1,660 | 111.06 | 148.48 | –37.42 |
| May-84 | 308 | 1,760 | 161.82 | 163.34 | –1.52 |
| Jun-85 | 365 | 1,827 | 217.49 | 215.62 | 1.87 |
| Jul-86 | 409 | 1,945 | 194.37 | 267.40 | –73.03 |
| Aug-87 | 458 | 2,140 | 222.95 | 287.59 | –64.64 |
| Sep-88 | 480 | 2,350 | 289.69 | 349.44 | –59.75 |
| 1989/90 | 550 | 3,150 | 467.60 | 446.91 | 20.69 |
| Jan-90 | 640 | 3,420 | 856.80 | 652.12 | 204.68 |
| Feb-91 | 730 | 3,840 | 962.80 | 604.00 | 358.80 |
| Mar-92 | 900 | 4,800 | 1,502.00 | 807.38 | 694.62 |
| Apr-93 | 1,150 | 6,000 | 1,490.10 | 1,137.38 | 352.72 |
| May-94 | 1,320 | 6,900 | 1,781.40 | 1,440.00 | 341.40 |
| Jun-95 | 1,518 | 7,935 | 2,179.00 | 1,527.00 | 652.00 |

Source: Chaudhuri 2004, Tables 5.1 and 5.2, pp. 148–149.

Original source: (1) Ministry of Chemicals and Fertilisers, Annual Report (various issues); Ministry of Chemicals and Fertilisers, Indian Drugs Statistics (various issues); OPPI 31st Annual Report, 1996–1997; OPPI, A Growth Plan for the Indian Pharmaceutical Industry, 1976. (2) ISMA, Annual Publication (various issues).

with controls of foreign firms. Beginning with the entry of IBM to the Indian computer market in 1964, other foreign firms followed suit. Between 1967 and 1972, IBM and ICL (International Computers Ltd) occupied 85 percent of the Indian market. In this oligopolistic market, the foreign firms imported second-hand computers that had been used in the developed countries for more than five years and rented them out at a high rate. Acting on the recommendations of the Bhabha Committee on Electronics, set up in 1963 to plan for the development of a domestic computer industry, the government directed foreign companies to expand indigenous development and sought the participation of Indian capital in them. IBM was unwilling to comply and was forced to withdraw from the Indian market in 1978. Other foreign firms like ICL and Philips responded to the government's demands and reduced their proportion of equity participation (Joseph 2004, 250). The government's policy placed emphasis on small and medium systems rather than large ones, and recognised the importance of design, assembly, maintenance and, particularly, software development over the manufacture of parts and peripherals. Pulapre Balakrishnan quotes a software industry leader that "the closed economy of India was actually 'a plus'", in that it constrained imports, forcing Indian firms to develop software themselves. Further, computer firms that needed imported inputs were required to earn the necessary foreign exchange, of which the government had a shortage, by exporting software. The government's interventionist policy took an expansionist direction regarding software export and the commitment to training of a broad human resource in the scientific and technological fields as part of the long-term pursuit to establish a science and technology base for an autonomous economy. This resolve helped to establish fertile ground for the later competitiveness of the IT industry before 1991 (Balakrishnan 2006).[6] There is no doubt that the subsequent success of the IT and pharmaceutical industries on the international stage after 1990 was heavily reliant on the policy of autonomous industrial development.

### *The Automobile Components Industry and Automobile Manufacture*

The core of the auto-component manufacturing industry, which supplied the developing automobile industry that grew in tandem after the 1990s, took shape in the 1970s under the government's plan to promote indigenisation of automobile production. Yoshie Shimane identifies Japanese, American and European firms as the premier manufacturers of four-wheeled vehicles on the global stage, and Japanese firms as dominant in the manufacture of two-wheelers, including motorcycles, scooters and mopeds. They tend to be the main source of these products in those developing countries where foreign investment has been liberalised, and it is usual that components are provided by makers operating in concert with them, or through imports. India, by contrast, is characterised by the strong presence of indigenous manufacturers, and the leaders in the growth of automobile production in the 1990s were not foreign-owned enterprises newly entering the market but already-existing Indian firms, including some joint ventures, centring on local industry.

A second characteristic, according to Shimane, was the already present foundation for an Indian domestic auto components industry. Despite the sharp increase in the number of finished vehicles over the 1990s, a pattern of increasing exports and lowering imports continued for components. This growing reliance on domestic components was due both to government policy, which sought a higher rate of import substitution, and to the heightened competitiveness of a cheaper domestic product for finished vehicle producers. Shimane's extremely interesting study identifies the period down to the beginning of the 1980s, when local production was being increasingly enforced within the assembly industry, as the peak time for the establishment of auto components firms through a succession of joint ventures. In other words, the organisational foundation for the production of auto components that underpinned the development of the modern Indian automobile industry can be said to have formed in the period down to the beginning of the 1980s when plans for local production were stepped up (Shimane 2006).

Gokarn and Vaidya, describing the automobile components industry in 1994–1995, identify distinct specialisation patterns across the five main producing states. They point out that Maharashtra and Tamil Nadu have a greater proportion of technology- and skill-intensive industries that manufacture engine parts, drive transmission and steering parts, and suspension braking parts. This was because traditionally the general manufacturing industry was concentrated here.[7] Plants producing less technology- and skill-intensive components are located in the states of Haryana, Delhi and Uttar Pradesh. The prominence of these states in the industry is comparatively recent, due to the presence of major automobile manufacturers in their vicinity (Gokarn and Vaidya 2004, 297). This too is a vital indicator of how the modern automobile industry developed on a technological and economic foundation of machinery manufacturing formed during the time of import-substitution industrialisation.

## Conclusion

When considering how to assess overall in what way the basis for India's industrialisation were formed during the process of import substitution, Sanjaya Lall's evaluation of India's technological development offers some very interesting pointers. Writing in the 1980s, he says that in general technological growth in developing countries occurs in two stages to promote industrialisation. The first is when technology, imported from more advanced countries not just as "know-how" but as "know-why", when the principles behind it are also acquired, is developed independently to suit the needs of the importing country. However, though the developing-country firm may gain the ability reproduce the technology to design and produce goods, it may find that this technology has already become obsolete, given the rapidity of technological change abroad. At this point, newly industrialising countries (NICs) should import more recent, cutting-edge technologies (stage 2). India, says Lall, had "built up an impressive stock 'know-why'" by around 1980, and should now move to "far more advanced technologies than its own capabilities can provide".

Compared with NICs like Brazil, Mexico and South Korea, India was self-reliant in both production and technology, with a high level of manufacturing and a low level of import for production goods as well as a minimal dependence on foreign technology. In particular, Lall draws attention India's broad engagement in "technology export" (TE), compared to the other NICs, particularly of industrial consultancy in the form of feasibility studies for industrial projects, project monitoring and detailed engineering, in Africa, Asia and Latin America. He states that,

> India is able to provide not just the operating knowledge to set up and run industries (the know-how), but also the design and manufacture of plant and equipment, designed specifically for the client (the "know-why"): it is in this latter sense that its TE seems particularly noteworthy in the context of the NICs.

In the course of its industrialisation, with its aim to be self-reliant both in production and in technology, Lall considers that India had developed, over a broad range of fields, "the most diverse and 'deep' (in terms of going into basic design of products and processes) capabilities among the NICs", based on understanding the "know-why" that went beyond the "know-how", and internationally competitive firms had been formed in a number of areas (Lall 1985, 45–76).

Under a state-led import-substitution industrialisation strategy, the Indian economy succeeded in establishing a set of production goods, heavy and chemical industries with an ability to develop basic production technologies and management, and technical human resources. This development strategy created the conditions for the future flourishing of some industries which had their origins in this period. Local technological adaptation of commercial vehicles made them internationally competitive in similar environments in Africa, low-cost formulations, a product of import substitution, that were competitive internationally gave impetus to the pharmaceutical industry, and the core auto-components manufacturing companies, which in the 1990s underpinned the rapid growth of the automobile industry, grew up in the 1970s.

Essential to these industrial and technological developments was the emergence by the end of the 1970s of a pool of cheap, but highly skilled, technical staff, on a scale larger than in any of the other NICs. At the time, 1,800,000 scientists and engineers were employed, while a further 20,000 were out of work. Comparable numbers at the same date were 600,000 in Brazil, 800,000 in South Korea and 400,000 each in Mexico and Argentina. This wealth of human capital owed much to government policies prioritising progress within the sciences and higher level education since the

Nehruvian period. These also contributed to the adaption of technologies to local use, upon which industrial growth relied. Without such policies, technology-intensive industries like IT and pharmaceuticals might not have developed on the international stage after the 1990s. The post-1950s state-led import-substitution industrialisation strategy formed the foundation for the growth of the industrial sector, encouraged the acquisition of technology in the form of "know-how" and adapted it to local requirements. That some of these adaptations became competitive internationally, however, owes much to the creation of a large reserve of scientific and technical personnel.

That said, there remained, as Lall pointed out, the fact that Indian technologies were obsolete by international standards. India needed to import cutting-edge technology from abroad. Its markets for technology export in the developing countries would only shrink in the future. We have seen in this chapter how the lack of both internal and external competition, as well as regulations on corporate investment activities by the government, and the growth of monopolistic practices by firms resulted in many industries being high-cost but low-quality in both product and operations. As we shall see in Chapter 10, a vicious cycle emerged in the electronics industry where a low output pushed up price, prices prevented market expansion and small-scale production was maintained. Whether or not India was at that time entering Lall's Stage 2, by 1980 the situation had been reached where industries and technologies required major reforms. Nevertheless, the fundamental capabilities necessary to achieve new growth under a new policy were already in place in many Indian industries. Kochhar et al., in their study of India's pattern of development, note that in comparison to other developing countries of similar size and so on, India already in 1980 showed a greater development of skill-intensive industries than labour-intensive ones (Kochhar et al. 2006, 14).

This chapter has shown that the economic capabilities that allowed this growth of skill-intensive industries came about as a result of government policy that placed weight on higher education and emphasised the expansion of such industries. These capabilities originated in the 1950s formed the necessary basis for later economic growth, in which technology-intensive industries have played a key role, following the new liberalisation strategy that came into full force in 1991.[8] Further, in connection with post-reform economic development, this chapter has emphasised both sides of the pre-reform period: One forming its foundation and the other creating the problems that needed to be tackled by the reforms.

## Notes

1 Concerning the import of foreign technology, K. J. Joseph notes that we can "discern broadly three phases in India's approach towards technology import": between 1948 and 1965, "marked by a relatively liberal approach towards foreign technology", between 1965 and the early 1980s, "wherein the policy stance was marked by strict controls", and from the early 1980s, when once again "there was a much more liberal approach towards technology import" (Joseph 2004, 265).

2 Mohan calls the 6 percent growth in industrial growth achieved in the 40 years since 1950 "quite an achievement, given the magnitude of distortions built into the system" (Mohan 1992, 102).

3 Kathuria comments that Indian "engineers and other highly skilled technical persons often prefer to remain unemployed than work in hands-on kinds of jobs" (Kathuria 1995, 176).

4 See also McCartney 2009, 133–135.

5 The setting up of public sector plants "created a new climate and confidence that India could also manufacture bulk drugs in a big way". The founders of many of the private sector drug manufacturing firms, including Dr K. Anji Reddy of Dr Reddy's Laboratories, worked at one time in private sector plants and research centres (Chaudhuri 2004, 162).

6 Kochhar et al. too cite the import-substitution strategy to invest in industries such as IT, and comment that "[a] key capability that has been extensively remarked upon in the context of the IT boom is the pool of skilled human capital, built through the technology, management, research institutes, as well as through the public sector, a kind of import substitution effort in skilled human capital development, which was integral to the Nehruvian vision". They point out that "engineers originally employed by the state-owned Computer Maintenance Corporation or Electronic Corporation Ltd (ECIL) provided the backbone for many of the computer firms that started up in Bangalore" (Kochhar et al. 2006, 27). Roy asserts that the expansion of the IT and software industry after the 1990s had its foundation in the achievements of both the IT and pharmaceutical industries during the period of the closed economy, brought about by the growth of technological training and education within state-led capital intensive industrial development (Roy 2011). After the exit of IBM from India, "some ex-IBM employees started small software companies … and several of the major Indian software service companies … emerged during this time" (Upadhya 2004, 5141).

7 For the development of the automobile components industry in Tamil Nadu during the period of import-substitution industrialisation, see Tyabji 2000, Chapter 2.

8 Considering the long-term changes in the Indian economy, Roy too points out that many of the economic successes that supported the globalisation of the IT and other industries from the 1990s were enabled by the achievements during the period of the closed economy from the 1950s (Roy 2011, 315).

# 5 Agrarian Development after Independence

## The Growth of Agrarian Output

### *Before the Green Revolution*

After decades of an economic torpor under colonial rule, India's GDP began to show signs of energetic life in the post-independence period (see Table 4.1; Sivasubramonian 2000, 622). Compared with the time before independence, GDP growth rate in the agricultural sector charted a rise well above that of the industrial sector. Table 4.1 shows a climb in primary industry from a scant 0.4 percent in the period 1900–1946 to 2.5 percent between 1947/8 and 1999. This greatly contributed to the rise in the growth rate of the Indian economy as a whole, and Sivasubramonian considers that the "most significant achievement of the latter half of the [twentieth] century is in the agricultural front" (Sivasubramonian 2000, 626). Without it, the turning point in Indian GDP growth around 1950 may not have been possible.

Whereas in the periods 1950–1964 (Period I) and 1965 and 1979 (Period II) the growth rate was 2.6 percent and 2.7 percent respectively, in Period III (post-1979) it rose to 3.2 percent (Table 4.1). Discussing long-term agricultural expansion in India, Takashi Kurosaki has made estimates for the growth rates of the value added series total output for agriculture and the yield per area under cultivation since 1900 in the regions now comprising India. He draws particular attention to the rise in growth rate in agrarian output between Independence and the beginning of the Green Revolution (Table 5.1) (Kurosaki 2010, 8).[1]

Agrarian growth in Period I can be attributed almost equally to an expansion of the area under cultivation and to an increase in the yield per area. According to Sivasubramonian, with 1950/1–54/5 being considered 100, between 1960/1 and 1964/5, the index of area under crops rose to 116.2 and the yield rate to 118.4. As a result, the index of production rose to 137.1. The per capita availability of good grains improved in this period from 419 grams to 461 grams.[2] Increases in the area under cultivation contributed very little to greater agricultural output after Period II; most was due to enhanced productivity of the land. This was, of course, a consequence of the Green Revolution, which started in the mid-1960s. The introduction of

DOI: 10.4324/9781003341550-8

*Table 5.1* Agricultural growth rates in present-day India (%)

| *Period* | *Total output* | *Output per agricultural labourer* | *Output per area under cultivation* |
|---|---|---|---|
| 1901/02–1910/11 | 1.36 | 0.63 | 0.52 |
| 1911/12–1920/21 | –0.70 | –0.69 | –0.39 |
| 1921/22–1930/31 | 0.09 | 0.08 | –0.22 |
| 1931/32–1940/41 | 0.27 | –0.09 | 0.40 |
| 1941/42–1950/51 | –0.25 | –1.78 | –0.34 |
| 1951/52–1960/61 | 2.99 | 2.02 | 2.77 |
| 1961/62–1970/71 | 2.30 | 0.32 | 2.11 |
| 1971/72–1980/81 | 1.96 | 0.53 | 1.72 |
| 1981/82–1990/91 | 2.08 | 0.68 | 2.04 |
| 1991/92–2000/01 | 2.63 | 1.52 | 2.65 |
| 1901/02–1946/47 | 0.37 | 0.11 | 0.14 |
| 1947/48–2000/01 | 2.28 | 0.81 | 2.15 |

Source: Kurosaki 2010, Table 1.

high-yielding varieties (HYVs), the increased use of fertilisers and the diffusion of irrigation, especially by means of electrified tube wells, began in the agriculturally more developed regions and spread to the whole country. As a result, land productivity improved remarkably and India reached agricultural self-sufficiency and was even able to export some surplus.

It should be noted that this growth in Indian agriculture thanks to increased productivity falls in the period before the Green Revolution. It has generally been believed that the real growth in this sector was sparked by the introduction and diffusion of modern new techniques from abroad, encapsulated under the term the Green Revolution. The fact that it has its origins before this strongly suggests that the potential for growth already existed within Indian agriculture.

### *Long-term Changes in Agriculture in Tamil Nadu: The 1950s*

Studying long-term agricultural trends in the area approximating the modern state of Tamil Nadu is one way of identifying the factors behind the enlargement of agrarian output after the 1950s. The following section explores information concerning land use, irrigation and output in the *Season and Crop Reports* from 1910 to 1994.

Table 5.2 offers us a number of insights concerning long-term changes in land use. First, there was a drastic reduction in the area of "culturable waste" in the 1960s and 1970s, while the "net area sown" increased remarkably. We can take this to mean that much of the culturable waste was developed and converted to arable land. Second, double (or more) cropping became more popular between the late nineteenth century and the 1920s, and showed a further increase and change from around 1950 to around 1970, following a period of stagnation. In short, during the 1950s and 1960s, the total area under cultivation expanded markedly, through the conversion of culturable waste to arable land and by intensifying cropping on single plots.

*Table 5.2* Land use, types and changes in the area equivalent to the present-day Tamil Nadu (acres)

| *Year* | *Total area* | *Forest* | *Wasteland, non-agricultural use* | *Culturable waste* | *Fallow* | *Net area sown* | *Double-cropped* | *Total area under crop* |
|---|---|---|---|---|---|---|---|---|
| 1912 | 3,05,90,612 | 48,38,710 | 62,21,116 | 20,19,775 | 33,74,978 | 1,41,36,033 | 17,54,000 | 1,58,90,033 |
| 1925 | 3,09,68,208 | 45,80,816 | 59,65,700 | 22,35,601 | 46,08,924 | 1,34,48,801 | 20,72,206 | 1,55,21,007 |
| 1930 | 3,15,43,967 | 31,94,886 | 59,46,474 | 28,41,309 | 48,25,142 | 1,32,84,222 | 21,24,650 | 1,54,08,872 |
| 1935 | 3,15,67,629 | 49,76,128 | 56,21,210 | 31,49,752 | 47,96,697 | 1,30,13,842 | 20,33,984 | 1,50,47,826 |
| 1940 | 3,15,89,935 | 50,07,311 | 54,09,521 | 32,81,618 | 44,40,472 | 1,34,51,013 | 25,46,094 | 1,59,97,107 |
| 1945 | 3,14,82,637 | 51,20,187 | 53,03,891 | 36,95,220 | 47,49,071 | 1,26,14,268 | 20,64,277 | 1,46,78,545 |
| 1950 | 3,22,42,960 | 47,93,353 | 55,24,871 | 41,70,271 | 51,01,568 | 1,26,29,415 | 17,04,997 | 1,43,34,402 |
| 1955 | 3,22,42,960 | 48,18,858 | 54,76,946 | 36,15,715 | 41,86,434 | 1,40,75,956 | 27,19,630 | 1,68,28,586 |
| 1962 | 3,20,22,323 | 45,96,710 | 55,45,034 | 32,29,511 | 36,56,751 | 1,50,01,500 | 29,37,838 | 1,79,39,339 |
| 1965 | 3,19,84,633 | 46,92,125 | 54,73,116 | 31,94,983 | 40,66,640 | 1,46,02,683 | 27,85,754 | 1,73,88,437 |
| 1970 | 3,19,84,633 | 49,54,008 | 57,10,878 | 23,72,325 | 37,84,039 | 1,51,82,335 | 29,89,704 | 1,81,72,039 |
| 1975 | 3,19,84,633 | 48,53,072 | 57,19,768 | 19,10,361 | 47,67,794 | 1,47,39,490 | 30,66,423 | 1,78,05,913 |
| 1980 | 3,19,57,064 | 51,33,336 | 57,08,216 | 17,61,680 | 63,49,264 | 1,31,91,093 | 27,30,393 | 1,59,21,486 |
| 1985 | 3,19,61,881 | 50,85,211 | 57,87,927 | 15,57,528 | 55,25,504 | 1,40,71,727 | 27,75,769 | 1,67,81,054 |
| 1992 | 3,20,23,322 | 52,94,024 | 58,53,865 | 16,15,130 | 49,53,425 | 1,43,31,734 | 30,80,375 | 1,73,92,421 |
| 1993 | 3,20,43,852 | 52,76,544 | 59,04,699 | 16,48,863 | 46,10,925 | 1,45,21,596 | 26,62,248 | 1,76,16,980 |
| 1994 | 3,20,03,934 | 52,76,354 | 58,88,742 | 15,91,142 | 49,99,002 | 1,42,48,693 | 30,42,264 | 1,72,90,956 |

Source: Season and Crop Reports.

*Table 5.3* Area under irrigation in the area equivalent to present-day Tamil Nadu (acres)

| *Year* | *Canals (government)* | *Canals (private)* | *Reservoirs* | *Wells* | *Other* | *Total* |
|---|---|---|---|---|---|---|
| 1905 | 13,94,594 | 8,315 | 13,42,646 | 7,85,860 | 89,991 | 36,21,406 |
| 1907 | 14,93,538 | 29,009 | 19,40,661 | 10,42,060 | 1,47,058 | 46,52,326 |
| 1910 | 14,50,669 | 13,671 | 19,04,282 | 9,54,305 | 1,46,099 | 44,69,026 |
| 1915 | 14,02,517 | 18,380 | 17,44,514 | 8,72,904 | 1,12,282 | 41,50,597 |
| 1920 | 14,78,365 | 14,717 | 19,46,441 | 11,82,079 | 1,45,729 | 47,71,838 |
| 1925 | 14,20,157 | 15,565 | 18,72,443 | 10,22,588 | 1,26,700 | 44,50,893 |
| 1930 | 14,56,343 | 18,366 | 19,21,195 | 8,07,958 | 1,08,499 | 43,22,361 |
| 1935 | 15,56,737 | 11,873 | 18,28,065 | 9,91,898 | 1,06,292 | 44,94,865 |
| 1940 | 15,87,098 | 48,621 | 18,92,367 | 10,37,199 | 74,103 | 46,39,408 |
| 1945 | 17,89,236 | 5,542 | 16,13,370 | 11,55,474 | 1,14,095 | 46,77,720 |
| 1950 | 18,89,718 | 4,751 | 13,45,288 | 10,49,222 | 1,26,337 | 44,15,316 |
| 1955 | 19,10,451 | 368 | 19,62,957 | 12,43,381 | 73,494 | 51,90,651 |
| 1962 | 22,17,942 | 3,106 | 23,28,512 | 15,05,322 | 1,07,479 | 61,70,561 |
| 1965 | 19,63,578 | 3,148 | 22,21,163 | 16,09,711 | 92,767 | 59,02,891 |
| 1970 | 21,72,317 | 2,372 | 22,09,789 | 18,59,148 | 87,673 | 63,78,508 |
| 1975 | 22,39,165 | 1,430 | 18,45,327 | 19,86,851 | 86,770 | 63,12,760 |
| 1980 | 21,86,050 | 2,139 | 14,52,362 | 23,50,206 | 58,749 | 63,26,050 |
| 1985 | 19,04,371 | 1,509 | 16,53,113 | 23,17,706 | 61,815 | 61,54,449 |
| 1992 | 20,94,067 | 1,378 | 15,47,551 | 25,26,881 | 41,670 | 66,39,291 |
| 1994 | 20,76,611 | 1,378 | 16,59,442 | 29,15,505 | 37,607 | 71,44,925 |

Source: Season and Crop Reports.

Crucial to the increase of area under crop is changes to the extent of irrigation. Table 5.3 shows that the amount of land irrigated had risen at the beginning of the twentieth century, but after that there was a long plateau until the period 1950–1962 saw an expansion of 1,760,000 acres to a figure well above that at the beginning of the century. To summarise the breakdown of the increases, the land irrigated by government canals rose by 330,000 acres, by reservoirs/tanks by 980,000 acres and by wells by 46,000 acres. If we consider that the area watered by reservoirs decreased a little (temporarily) in 1950, it is obvious that the substantial spread of well irrigation contributed greatly to the total. These figures indicate that, first, the government spent more on irrigation after Independence and we may assume that the reach of government canals and wells grew alongside this, and second, that private investment in well irrigation recovered remarkably in the 1950s and 1960s.

Table 5.4 shows the yield per hectare of rice (after threshing) in Tamil Nadu between 1945 and 1975. A steady rise in yield after 1945 is evident and in keeping with the growth of agriculture in Tamil Nadu in the 1950s. Three factors can be identified as the culprits behind this wider growth: The development of culturable waste land, expanded irrigation and government support through financing and development projects.

It is apparent that part of the increased output was due to the extension of arable land. This was a result of the active development of formerly uncultivated land, the culturable waste, in the 1950s and 1960s. A report by the

*Table 5.4* Yield per hectare of rice (hulled) in the area equivalent to present-day Tamil Nadu (kg): crop estimate by unit area sampling

| *District/year* | *1945–49* | *1955–57* | *1959–60* | *1966–67* | *1975–76* |
|---|---|---|---|---|---|
| Chingleput | 757 | 1,072 | 1,183 | 1,170 | 2,190 |
| North Arcot | 1,061 | 1,645 | 1,459 | 1,320 | 2,116 |
| South Arcot | 1,000 | 1,525 | 1,487 | 1,521 | 2,362 |
| Salem | | 1,725 | 1,799 | 1,809 | 2,442 |
| Dharmapuri | | | | 1,398 | 1,708 |
| Coimbatore | | 1,779 | 1,803 | 1,845 | 2,407 |
| Trichinopoly | 1,176 | 1,474 | 1,320 | 1,557 | 2,016 |
| Pudukottai | | | | | 1,600 |
| Tanjore | 981 | 1,255 | 1,501 | 1,443 | 1,956 |
| Madura | 1,257 | 1,628 | 1,649 | 1,557 | 2,474 |
| Ramnad | 733 | 967 | 869 | 1,093 | 1,155 |
| Tinnevelly | 1,302 | 1,677 | 1,810 | 1,365 | 2,030 |
| Nilgiris | | | 1,666 | 995 | 1,373 |
| Kanyakumari | | | 1,751 | 1,689 | 2,190 |
| Average | 992 | 1,389 | 1,439 | 1,410 | 2,029 |

Source: Season and Crop Reports.

Wastelands Survey and Reclamation Committee published in 1961 concerning Madras State states that "although the total area reported in the revenue records under culturable waste was 2 million acres, a large portion of it has been brought under cultivation by encroachment by landless labourers or cultivators".[3] As we shall see, in South India from the beginning of the twentieth century lower-class agricultural labourers and tenant farmers who were virtually excluded from land ownership began to encroach without government permission on the waste land (village common land) that had hitherto escaped cultivation. The reclamation of waste land in the 1950s and 1960s can probably be seen as a continuation of this kind of occupation by landless labourers.[4]

Also, as we have seen, during the financial climate of the agricultural depression, farmers were reluctant to invest in wells and fertiliser, for example. With the recovery and rise of prices after Independence and increased government expenditure on agriculture, such investment revived, underpinning the growth in output. Well irrigation, which increased in the 1950s, encouraged double-cropping and the irrigation of formerly unirrigated land, improving yield per unit area. The importance of its contribution is undeniable. We can also assume that farmers began using fertilisers again, after the decline during the interwar period and low agricultural prices.[5] Despite the reduction of waste lands, which had traditionally functioned as village common land to provide fertilisers and feed, and their conversion to arable use, the increased use of fertilisers, including chemical fertilisers, and the cultivation of green manure contributed, with expanded irrigation, to the extraordinary rise in productivity. The experience of farmers in South India in the early part of the twentieth century had made them all the more inclined to develop agriculture intensively by building wells and upping fertiliser use. In other words, the potential for growth there already existed.

Concerning this potential, I would like to draw attention to the fact that there was no reason that the ecosystem for river irrigation be limited to favourable areas. In the Salem district of Tamil Nadu, a typical non-irrigated area, the ratio of government canals is low and the main source of water is wells. Between 1950 and 1973, the area irrigated by wells more than doubled, from around 140,000 acres to 380,000 acres, and the ratio between the net sown area and the irrigated area rose from 16 percent to 28 percent.[6] During this time, the composition of the crops cultivated in unirrigated areas also altered, with less millet and more rice being grown. This attests to the dynamism of agriculture in the district. There are certainly restrictions imposed by the ecosystems of the dry districts of India, but the example of Salem shows us that it is not valid to deny the latent potential for the intensive development of Indian agriculture itself based on such restrictions.[7]

The third notable factor in the increased agricultural output of the 1950s and 1960s was the proliferation in government expenditure on agriculture and advances in various projects promoting farming. The colonial Government of India invested very little after World War I on improving arable cultivation through irrigation works, but during and after World War II it spent a great amount on agricultural development. The Grow More Food Campaign that ran between 1943 and 1951 aimed to increase food crops by providing better irrigation, supplying and using fertilisers, and opening up cultivable waste. It set targets to provide finance to purchase tractors and excavate tube wells in 1947 and to achieve self-sufficiency in food by 1952. The First Five Year Plan (1951–1956) focused on expenditure, with a policy of promoting a plan for the intensive development of seeds and fertilisers in those areas best suited to them in terms of rainfall or accessible water. As Dorin and Landy (2009, 8) point out, this plan, whose aims followed the same direction as the later Green Revolution, predated it (Shrinivasan 1965, 10). The increase of large and small irrigation facilities that resulted contributed to extending arable land but also brought about an increased yield per unit.

How typical the results of this analysis of the long-term statistics of Tamil Nadu are for the rest India merits further investigation. However, as we saw in Chapter 1, in many places, including South India, innovative efforts by farmers toward intensive agriculture from the end of the nineteenth century to around 1920 involved well-digging and the application of fertilisers. Though these efforts dwindled with the slump in prices for agricultural products between the wars, there was a recovery thanks to government subsidies and a resurgence of prices in the 1950s. It is probably safe to assume that agrarian growth, including rising productivity, was more or less a feature of Indian agriculture as a whole.[8] The cultivation of common-use land by people including those from the landless classes also played its part to some extent.[9]

It is clear that there is a strong continuity between the period before the Green Revolution and that of the Green Revolution itself. This implies that the latter was not a completely new direction for Indian agriculture. Already there was a strong trend towards a rise in productivity, and the Green Revolution continued this with its spread of HYVs, well irrigation systems and fertilisers. New technologies were diffused to every part of India in the 20 years after the mid-1960s into a ground already prepared for them during the previous period of agrarian growth.

## The Green Revolution

The Green Revolution started in the mid-1960s and was based on three pillars: The introduction of HYVs, the widespread application of chemical fertilisers and irrigation. From the early 1960s, research centres such as the Indian Agricultural Research Institute had begun to introduce HYVs imported from the International ***Maize*** and ***Wheat*** Improvement Center in Mexico. Indian scientists adapted these, creating new varieties to suit India's ecology and meet local demand. The new strains had to be able to flourish in a diverse range of places across India, be high-yielding, have a short growing period and be photoperiod insensitive.[10] Their success was reliant upon large amounts of fertiliser. Nitrogen fertilisers in particular needed an application three to four times greater than that of traditional varieties, and additional phosphate and potassium fertilisers were also required. The amount of chemical fertiliser applied per hectare rose from 5 kg in 1965 to 75 kg 30 years later, and to 112 kg in 2001/02. The highest rate of 173 kg was in the state of Punjab; this was equivalent to that of France. Today India ranks after China and the United States in terms of fertiliser consumption.

The production of chemical fertilisers in India dates back to 1906, when the first factory opened, but it took until after Independence for the industry as a whole to take off. The manufacture of chemical fertiliser has rocketed in India since then. Though potassium fertilisers have to be imported, more than half the current required amount of nitrogen fertiliser is made domestically. The government controls demand, subsidising factories and actively encouraging fertiliser production.

Alongside the spread of HYVs and fertiliser, irrigation also further infiltrated Indian agriculture during the Green Revolution. As Table 5.5 shows, down to 1968, medium- and large-scale canal irrigation and groundwater irrigation had both doubled in extent, fairly equal in terms of rate of growth. After 1968, well irrigation overtook the former and by 1989 it had become the main method of crop watering in India. Most common were open wells, traditionally 8m square. As part of the Green Revolution, the government provided subsidies to deepen wells and install pumps. Tube wells, which can pump water from a deeper level through a tube or pipe, have multiplied since the 1970s in particular. This is not without its resultant problems; the lowering of the groundwater level will be discussed below.

Together with above changes introduced to encourage better crop yields, enhanced agricultural machinery can be included. Though there were regional differences, tractors and other devices – such as power pumps in place of man- and animal-powered pumps – were rolled out across India.

*Table 5.5* Spread of irrigation (million hectares)

| | *Cumulative area of possible irrigation* | | | |
|---|---|---|---|---|
| | *Large- to medium-scale irrigation* | *Large-scale surface water irrigation* | *Groundwater* | *Total* |
| Jan-50 | 8.6 | 7.5 | 6.5 | 22.6 |
| Jan-60 | 13.3 | 7.5 | 8.3 | 29.1 |
| Sep-68 | 17.0 | 7.6 | 12.5 | 37.1 |
| 1979–80 | 25.6 | 9.1 | 22.0 | 56.6 |
| 1989–90 | 31.8 | 12.3 | 34.8 | 79.7 |

Source: Vaidyanathan 1994a, Table 3, p. 69.

Original source: Planning Commission.

The Green Revolution was first carried out in the rice-growing states of Punjab, Haryana and the western part of Uttar Pradesh in North India, and Andhra Pradesh and Tamil Nadu in South India. It spread in the 1980s to what were considered agriculturally backward areas in the eastern part of India. Agrarian output subsequently rose as a whole.[11] As Table 5.6 shows, the ratio of the area under cultivation using HYVs exceeded 70 percent for wheat in 1980, but had not gone beyond 45 percent for rice in the same year. The 1980s saw a higher penetration, which may be due to the spread of the Green Revolution to eastern India. Between 1960 and 2000, the duration of the Green Revolution, the total output of rice and wheat climbed 2.5 times and 6.3 times respectively. India followed China and the United States as a major producing country and even had a surplus for export. Per capita grain output rose from 116.7 kg in 1950/51 and 156.6 kg in 1960/61 to 190.3 kg in 1990/91. Compared with the economic stagnation in sub-Saharan Africa, where attempts to raise the per capita food output ended in failure, there was an important foundation in South Asia for steady economic growth (Fujita 2004; Kurosaki 2010).

The Green Revolution indisputably produced results, in terms of the spread of agriculture and the growth in agrarian output, but it did not represent a policy of agricultural development completely different in character to what India had previously experienced. Instead, the achievements of the Green Revolution show a continuity with what had gone before. The increased use of fertilisers serves as an example. We have already seen that at the beginning of the twentieth century, farmers in South India both purchased fertilisers from distant places and cultivated their own green manure. In addition, the application of chemical fertilisers can be found in the 1920s and 1930s.[12] This use increased further with government subsidies following the Grow More Food Campaign in the 1940s. A village survey conducted in Punjab state showed that chemical fertilisers had been in use since the late 1950s (Ōji 1974). Likewise, irrigation as a whole and groundwater irrigation in particular had grown impressively from the 1950s, as Table 5.5 shows; in other words, farmers were investing in wells before the Green Revolution began.

*Table 5.6* Foodgrains in India: Area under cultivation, yield, ratio of HYVs cultivated, output

| | | *1950/51* | *1960/61* | *1970/71* | *1980/81* | *1990/91* | *2000/01* |
|---|---|---|---|---|---|---|---|
| Area under cultivation (million hectares) | rice | 30.8 | 34.1 | 37.6 | 40.1 | 42.7 | 44.7 |
| | wheat | 9.8 | 12.9 | 18.2 | 22.3 | 24.2 | 25.7 |
| | grains total | 78.2 | 92 | 101.8 | 104.2 | 103.2 | 100.7 |
| | beans | 19.1 | 23.6 | 22.6 | 22.5 | 24.7 | 10.7 |
| | India total | 131.9 | 152.8 | 165.8 | 172.6 | 185.7 | 187.9 |
| Ratio of HYVs cultivated | rice | – | 3% | 15% | 45% | 64% | 74% |
| | wheat | – | 4% | 36% | 72% | 87% | 86% |
| | grains total | – | 2% | 15% | 41% | 63% | 75% |
| | beans | – | – | – | – | – | – |
| Fertiliser (kg. per ha. cultivated) | India | – | 2 | 14 | 32 | 68 | 87 |
| Yield (100 kg per ha. cultivated) | rice | 6.7 | 10.1 | 11.2 | 13.4 | 17.4 | 19 |
| | wheat | 6.6 | 8.5 | 13.1 | 16.3 | 22.8 | 27.1 |
| | grains total | 5.4 | 7.5 | 9.5 | 11.4 | 15.7 | 18.4 |
| | beans | 4.4 | 5.4 | 5.2 | 4.7 | 5.8 | 5.4 |
| Volume of output (million tons) | rice | 20.6 | 34.6 | 42.2 | 53.6 | 74.3 | 85 |
| | wheat | 6.5 | 11 | 23.8 | 36.3 | 55.1 | 69.7 |
| | grains total | 42.4 | 69.3 | 96.6 | 119 | 162.1 | 185.7 |
| | beans | 8.4 | 12.7 | 11.8 | 10.6 | 14.3 | 11.1 |
| Per capita output (kg./yr) | grains | 116.7 | 156.6 | 175.2 | 172.8 | 190.3 | 179.7 |
| | beans | 23.1 | 28.7 | 21.4 | 15.4 | 16.8 | 10.7 |

Source: Dorin and Landy, 2009, Table 1, p. 96.

Original source: Ministry of Agriculture, Fertiliser Association of India, Economic Survey.

The using and improving of HYVs can also be traced to the colonial period, though this was limited geographically. Agricultural research stations have been set up in a number of places since 1871, where work was done on improving farming tools, cultivation methods and varieties. One of the reasons, according to C. Ramasamy, Peter Hazell and P. K. Aiyasamy, in their report on a long-term survey concerning the Green Revolution conducted in North Arcot, Tamil Nadu, that the Green Revolution had not had such a dramatic effect on the district was because of "a long and successful tradition of developing paddy varieties at local research stations, and some of the features of HYVs that account for their higher productivity had already been incorporated into improved local varieties". For example, the rice cultivar TKM6 that was later to become one of the parents of IR20, a HYV closely associated with the Green Revolution, had already been developed by 1952. "This variety is photoperiod insensitive and can be grown all year round. It is also a short-duration variety, with a growing period of only 110–115 days"

(Hazell and Ramasamy 1991, 16). In Punjab state, too, improvement of varieties was being carried out before the Green Revolution. In one village there, yield was increased in the early 1950s by replacing the previous variety with Basmati 370 (Ōji 1974).

Land productivity improved remarkably through the Green Revolution, but it is hard to say that the rate of growth particularly stands out in comparison to the 1950s (see Table 5.1). Earlier government policy to promote agriculture, starting with the Grow More Food campaign, had, as we have seen, many points in common with the Green Revolution's promotion of output. The agriculturally advanced regions of India had already experienced development of the type advocated by the Green Revolution, and this was an important factor in its ability to penetrate into rural villages.[13] All the same, the Green Revolution had one critical difference with what had gone before. New agricultural technology eventually penetrated into areas with a harsh natural environment as well as into agriculturally backward regions, and also among lower class, small-scale farmers in rural society. Of particular importance is the proliferation of tube well irrigation that came in the wake of the Green Revolution. On this topic the views of T. Shah (Shah 2009a, 2009b) are of great interest:

(1) Traditionally irrigation in India centred on canals and tanks (reservoirs), which meant that large areas that could not be so irrigated had to rely on rainfall. The expansion of groundwater irrigation through the use of the tube well has made it possible to water areas that were formerly unsuppliable, and now pump irrigation accounts for over 60 percent of irrigated areas.
(2) Whereas the benefits of canal irrigation were concentrated on privileged groups in the villages, the expansion of groundwater irrigation has offered some irrigation access to a vast majority previously denied it. As tube wells in private ownership increased, a "water market" emerged, with owners renting the surplus water pumped to farmers without wells, so giving them access to irrigation as well. Today one in four farmers in India owns a tube well, and two of the other three buy water from them.
(3) Groundwater irrigation allows farming all year round, not dependent on the monsoon, which means increased demand for labour the whole year.
(4) Especially in dry areas in a scale-neutral format, it has "supported a new drive towards intensive diversification to high-value products such as milk, fruit and vegetables".
(5) It has "demonstrated a strong pro-poor, inclusive bias in irrigated agriculture" (Shah 2009b, 98–105).[14]

The expansion of groundwater irrigation undoubtedly was a core element of the Green Revolution's impact.[15]

What kind of effect did the Green Revolution have on the various classes within Indian society? Many of the early studies on the Green Revolution dating from the 1970s concluded that its benefits were concentrated on the better off and that the poor did not receive their fair share. This was because, they argued, it was mainly the large farmers who adopted the new technology. The Green Revolution brought about lower prices for agricultural products and higher input prices. The larger farmers tried to raise rents, thereby forcing tenants off the land, and increase their own landholdings by buying up smaller farms. Small farmers were forced into landlessness as a consequence. It also encouraged unnecessary mechanisation, reducing rural employment. As a result, "there was a rapid increase in the inequality of income and asset distribution, and a worsening of absolute poverty in areas affected by the [G]reen [R]evolution" (Hazell and Ramasamy 1991, 1).

After 1980, however, evidence was reported contrary to these views. When the technology of the Green Revolution was first introduced, it was adopted mainly by the larger farmers. Yet, it filtered down to small farmers in time and so it was recognised as being in principle scale-neutral. Long-term surveys conducted in the North Arcot district of Tamil Nadu show that the average size of the holding of farmers who adopted HYVs in the 1970s was 2 hectares, compared with 1 hectare for those who did not. Only 15 percent of farmers with less than 0.4 hectares planted HYVs. By the early 1980s, 90 percent of the paddy area was planted with HYVs and operating scale differences had disappeared. In the case of North Arcot, it became easier to acquire farm inputs as a result of increased public funding and government services. This, together with the development of HYVs adapted to the conditions of small farms with a less reliable water supply, led to a greater use of HYVs among small farmers. The differences in yields obtained by large and small farmers in the 1970s had disappeared by the early 1980s (Hazell and Ramasamy 1991, 240).[16]

There is a second question: Did the employment of agricultural labourers grow as agrarian output rose? Under the Green Revolution, there was an increase in the number of croppings, in the application of fertilisers and in labour-intensive crops like rice. An upturn in labour per hectare accompanied this, but was tempered by the introduction of machines like pumps and tractors. Research conducted by Tamil Nadu Agricultural University suggests that for most years the amount of labour required per hectare for HYVs of rice was about 10 percent more than for local improved varieties and so the introduction of HYVs tended to increase labour (Hazell and Ramasamy 1991, Tables 2.4, 2.5 [pp. 19–20]). However, a village survey in North Arcot showed a drop of 4 percent in total employment in crop production between 1973 and 1983. Despite the rise in paddy planted and the labour required for it, this decline reflects a loss in per hectare paddy employment as a result of the increased mechanisation of irrigation pumping and paddy threshing (Hazell and Ramasamy 1991, 240). Fan et al. (1999) have calculated agricultural employment in India to have grown a slight 0.03 percent between 1970 and 1979, declined by 0.78 percent between 1980 and 1989, and risen again by 1.78 percent between 1990 and 1993.

Though opinions are not consistent over the question of employment, most scholars agree on a third issue, concurring that the real wages of agricultural workers rose from the end of the 1970s, when the Green Revolution was in full swing. Surveys in North Arcot reported that real wage rates grew in many, though not all, villages. Agricultural employment earnings virtually doubled for small paddy farms, landless labour and non-agricultural households and went up by 40 percent for non-paddy farm households. "These increases were possible because of a decline in the amount of hired labor supplied by farms operating more than 1 hectare of land and because of competing employment opportunities in dairying and nonfarm activities" (Hazell and Ramasamy 1991, 240–41). For India as a whole, real wages leapt in the 1980s from the perspective of the late 1970s: The average rise between 1970 and 1993 was 2.16 percent (Fan et al. 1999, 18).

A fourth area of interrogation concerns fluctuations in income according to class in rural villages. Family earnings rose somewhat within all classes, including the poorest sections like agricultural workers. It is safe to say that absolute poverty there waned as a result. Real income improved substantially among rural households in North Arcot between 1973/74 and 1983/84, as Hazell and Ramasamy show (Hazell and Ramasamy 1991, 41–42; Table 3.7, Changes in Household Incomes). Of particular note is that landless labourer households more than doubled their income (up 125 percent), followed by small paddy farmers (up 90 percent). The smallest rise was in large paddy farm households (18 percent). Non-paddy farmers and non-agricultural households showed increases of 17 percent and 55 percent respectively. Whereas between 1950 and 1970, rural poverty had swung between 50 and 60 percent, this had dropped to 34 percent in 1989 (Fan et al. 1999, 3).[17]

Fifth, these changes resulted in an increase of household consumption expenditure, including among the rural lower classes, and in improvements to consumer life. In North Arcot, real expenditure among landless labourers tripled in the decade 1973/74–1983/4, and doubled among all other household types, regardless of class (Table 5.7). In the villages here, the intake of foods rich in calories and proteins improved, while the proportion of foodgrains shrank and that of meat and dairy products rose. Expenditure also increased on durables, medical services, transport, entertainment and religious and social functions. The next chapter will examine the expansion of the rural market. What can be said here is that an improvement in income

*Table 5.7* Changes in family expenditures (1973/74, Rs)

| *Type of household* | *1973/74* | | *1983/84* | |
|---|---|---|---|---|
| Small paddy farms | 1,143 | –100 | 3,044 | *–266* |
| Large paddy farms | 2,182 | –100 | 5,105 | –234 |
| Nonpaddy farms | 1,163 | –100 | 2,679 | –230 |
| Landless labourers | 846 | –100 | 2,553 | –302 |
| Non-agricultural households | 1,056 | –100 | 2,191 | –207 |

Note: Figures in parentheses are income indices with 1973/74=100.

Source: Hazell and Ramasamy 1991, Table 3.13, p. 46.

among all rural classes and the rapid growth of rural demand for various services and industrial products mark the Green Revolution as an epochal event in the evolution of the Indian economy.

A number of conclusions can be readily derived from the discussion so far. Foremost is the revelation that land productivity had risen even before the start of the Green Revolution. Though agriculture had suffered a downturn and reversal in the interwar period, it recovered from the early 1950s as the government escalated its expenditure, particularly in terms of irrigation, and expanded well irrigation and fertiliser use by farmers. A number of features considered to characterise the Green Revolution, such as a greater use of fertiliser, expansion of irrigation and variety improvement, were already found in the more advanced agricultural districts. The period before the Green Revolution must therefore be considered the foundation upon which it was built. Furthermore, this preparatory process made it easier for the new technologies of the Green Revolution to penetrate into what had been backward regions of India agriculturally and among various classes, including small farmers. The growth of groundwater irrigation by means of tube wells was potentially an important factor in the broad spread of the Green Revolution both geographically and socially. Subsequently, the per capita agrarian output rose sharply. Also, whether or not there was more demand for agricultural wage labour differs according to region and case study. However, real wages for agricultural labourers clearly rose and there is virtually no doubt that earnings rose among all classes of rural society, including landless labourers and small farmers. The resulting quantitative rise in household consumption led to an expanding demand for non-food products, industrial goods and services in rural areas, among all classes, as we shall investigate in Chapter 6.[18]

## The Growth of Agriculture and Environmental Change

Could this remarkable agricultural growth have been achieved without any severe environmental damage? This section will consider its effect on village commons, water for irrigation including groundwater and forests.

### *Diminishing Village Common Land and Changes in the Governance of Local Resources*

The impact of agricultural growth (through the ongoing cultivation of "waste lands") on village commons and the preservation of local resources is a good starting point. As Chapter 1 laid out, these uncultivated waste lands, which were used communally by villagers according to class to graze their livestock and collect manure, began to diminish greatly as they fell into private hands from the second half of the nineteenth century and were converted to arable. In the process, the governance system for village resources by local elites weakened and there were moves towards a more equal system with the participation of many villagers, including members of the lower classes.

Documents from South India dating from the beginning of the nineteenth century make it clear that the dominant landowners ("mirasidars") had prior rights over the other villagers to graze cattle on the uncultivated land and to collect wood and grass from it. They held these lands as common property and controlled them. Other villagers could use these resources as village common lands as far as was permitted provided the resources were abundant enough. A similar situation applied in Punjab and other places in India, where the dominant group in the village had prior rights over uncultivated land (Yanagisawa 2008b).

The period between the latter half of the nineteenth century and around 1920 witnessed the conversion of extensive remaining stretches of uncultivated land to farmland all over India. The upper-class villagers who already had rights over the wasteland took the lead in privatising it, and government policy also encouraged this occupation. This was reported still to be happening in many places even after Independence.[19] In tandem with this, however, people from the landless classes also started utilising previously uncultivated land. Therefore, as evident in the Tamil area from the beginning of the twentieth century, the system of control of local resources on village common lands by members of the upper castes gradually began to weaken (Nara and Mizushima 1981). According to the *Report on Location and Utilisation of Wastelands in India* (MFA 1961) for Madras state, "although the total area reported in the revenue records under culturable waste was 2 million acres, a large proportion of it had been brought under cultivation by encroachment by landless labourers or cultivators" (MFA 1961, 5). A report from Maharashtra state that Dalits had encroached on the village common lands and were farming them shows that this pattern was continuing well into the second half of the twentieth century (Bokil 1996).

It should be noted that such encroachment was related to the desire among the landless to seek economic and social emancipation. We have seen how, from the latter half of the nineteenth century, increasing numbers of landless agricultural workers from the Tamil districts were going to work on plantations abroad. The possibility of migrant work strengthened the negotiating power of the landless classes who had worked as wage labour for large landowners, and some migrant workers were even able to buy tiny pieces of land with their earnings. Encroaching and farming uncultivated land was a way for the landless to achieve social and economic autonomy in a society dominated by the upper castes. In Maharashtra state, which has a strong tradition of Dalit movements, encroachment was part of their campaign for emancipation. However small the amount of land they acquired, it meant they had become landowners able to manage their own agricultural labour. Such opportunities have been reported in a number of village surveys (Corta and Venkateshwarlu 1999). Surveys of village commons also report the ambition of the landless to acquire even small pieces of land by bringing wasteland (commons) under cultivation (Yanagisawa 2008). These aspirations, driven by the desire to raise their social and economic standing, exemplify the exercising of lower-class rights to common lands that were actually controlled by the large landholders.

In various parts of India, and particularly in South India, dominant sections of the upper castes were able to control common resources, based on their economic and social strength. Yet their influence weakened when they no longer physically lived in the villages and as the spirit of social liberation grew among the lower classes, they were unable to prevent encroachment on local resources. The disturbances caused by these changes to the local resource management system are well illustrated by cases in Tamil Nadu concerning the control of the tank irrigation system. As Mosse makes clear, the maintenance and running of tank irrigation depended on the labour of members of the scheduled castes under the direction of village elites. As the lower castes acquired farmland and their sense of freedom strengthened, the hierarchy of former times was not preserved and this system deteriorated.[20]

While it is obvious that the trend towards a diminishing of common resources continued in areas where the commons were encroached or alienated by ownership, what significance did it have for the long-term protection of local resources? Most studies agree that the creation of a more egalitarian village social structure, where most members own land and animals, makes it easier to reach general agreement about the communal control of village common resources.[21] There are also examples which demonstrate the possibility of voluntary agreements among villagers over the communal management of common resources when there is a certain amount of social and economic equality among them. This has been shown in the case of a village in Rajasthan, where there were no landless living, and where both the upper and lower castes together are involved in community management (Brara 2006). A valuable insight can be arrived at through a study of historical change in Indian village commons: The establishment of a system of community protection of resources relies upon the formation of an egalitarian type society, one where most members of the community possess rights to farmland and common resources.

Speaking generally, the last century has been a time of transition for village commons in Tamil Nadu. Long-term change has seen the waning of the system of common resource control by the dominant classes and a growing independence among the lower classes, which has led to the possibility of a more egalitarian form both of resource management and of village social structure. This may even in turn lead to the formation of a territorial community where households living in an area participate decisively and equally in it. In fact, forest protection committees have been successfully set up on an egalitarian basis in Midnapore in West Bengal (Yanagisawa 2015, 146).

### *Common Resources and Local Economic Reproduction*

Despite the toll wasteland farming has taken on village commons, agrarian output has not suffered. That it was able to grow over the long term was due in part to an evolution in the role that local resources played in agriculture and local economic reproduction. Chapter 1 described how the supply of fertilisers and manures was compromised by the rapid loss of commons and how the supply of river silt, another important form of fertiliser, was reduced by the construction of dams for irrigation. Farmers responded by growing green manure crops in their fields, purchasing fertilisers (including chemical ones), and increasing well irrigation, and by adopting more intensive methods of production, they improved the yield per acre in many districts, not just the output overall due to a wider acreage (Yanagisawa 2011b).

We have already seen that agriculture then stagnated from the late 1920s due to falling prices and reductions in inputs such as wells and fertilisers, recovered after Independence with renewed investment in these inputs and from the end of the 1960s saw a massive expansion in output per unit area based on the diffusion of chemical fertilisers and HYVs. In this new agricultural landscape, the function of village common land as a provider of fertiliser for agriculture was dramatically reduced.[22]

In the paddy regions of South India, the use of common lands as grazing pastures and a source of fodder had already become limited from the end of the nineteenth century. Animals were primarily fed on crop residue such as rice straw, but purchased fodder became widespread after the start of the Green Revolution, including in dry regions (Blaikie et al. 1992). There are also indications that even in farming and pastoral operations in the dry area of Rajasthan there was a shift away from large animals like bullocks and camels, fed by grazing, to more sedentary species like buffaloes, kept on bought fodder and crop residue (Brara 2006). The importance of the common lands diminished in relation to domestic life too. The Green Revolution encouraged the production of plant residue and the spread of *Prosopis juliflora*, a shrub providing fuel-wood that grows on degraded lands, and foraged forest fuel was no longer heavily relied upon.

Local economic reproduction has lessened the need for common land. The fostering of extended well irrigation, however, has created worrying problems. Water levels are falling, and there is a strong possibility that if nothing is done, groundwater resources will run dry. All the same, the increase among the poorest classes of rearing goats and other small domestic animals has created a demand for more grazing ground in common land. In such a situation, community action to regulate the utilisation of locality's resources has an unavoidable significance.

### *The Green Revolution: Technology and the Environment*

Many questions have been raised about the impact of the Green Revolution on the ecosystem. Chiefly, whether or not its technology, centred on HYVs that required the application of chemical fertilisers and pesticides, was ecologically sustainable. Vandana Shiva and others have catalogued a number of concerns. First, HYVs are marked by uniformity and non-renewability; they have done away with traditional plant breeding strategies to ensure genetic diversity. Their large-scale use carries the risk of the spread of diseases and pests, and a higher incidence of crop failures has added to a sense of instability. Also, less straw for fodder is produced. Second, the Green Revolution has reduced soil fertility. Chemical fertilisers and pesticides have increased the noxious chemical substances found in the soil, while HYVs, requiring larger amounts of nutrients, have depleted the soil's micronutrient content. Third, HYVs need heavy water use, and so increased irrigation. Where water from tube wells has been overused, there has been a lowering of the water table and a draining of groundwater. In canal-irrigated areas, over-irrigation has led to salinisation and water logging, causing the deterioration of large areas of land (Shiva 1991).

To a greater or lesser degree, most scholars agree that the drawback of the HYV technology has been the erosion of biodiversity and the reliance on excessive amounts of fertilisers and pesticides (Nadkarni 1988). C. H. Hanumantha Rao, a well-known economist, accepts that the Green Revolution brought about soil deterioration and recognises the harm chemical fertilisers and pesticides have done to the environment and the ecosystem, pointing out that their level of application was at much higher levels than in Western countries. The new technologies, characterised by irrigation, multiple cropping and short-duration HYVs, were essentially "land-augmenting or land-saving". In fact, since the beginning of the Green Revolution in the mid-1960s, the area under cultivation had grown incredibly slowly. Rao finds it reasonable to think that the new technologies contributed to "reducing the pressure for further extension of cultivation ... to the area under forest cover" (Rao 1994, 160–61). Indeed, M. S. Swaminathan, who was one of the first to warn about the dangers of the Green Revolution technologies, has stated that the Green Revolution protected forests (Chopra et al. 1998, 9). Both he and M. V. Nadkarni acknowledge the environmental issues associated with the new agricultural technologies, but do not insist on any wholesale rejection of them and a return to traditional methods, or on the preservation of non-irrigated agriculture. They stress that there should be in the future a combination of leading-edge science and the ecological wisdom of the past, utilising both HYVs and organic fertilisers, incorporating the traditional cropping cycle and creating technologies specific to a locality (Chopra et al. 1998, 12–15).

### *Salinity, Water Logging and Groundwater*

We have seen that irrigation was integral to the spread of the Green Revolution. However, if surface inundation is continued with no consideration of drainage, the water will saturate the soil and the groundwater table will rise. When the water table reaches a specific distance from the surface, groundwater rises, passing through the capillary fringe, and evaporates, leaving salts on the surface, which will continue to build up if the land is left undrained. Similarly, the insufficient removal of surface water caused by over-irrigation can also result in waterlogging.

Writers do not concur even on the fundamental issues of the extent cultivated land has been damaged by salinisation and waterlogging, and whether or not the problems are intensifying. Two fifths of India's irrigation by area is through surface irrigation (canals and tanks), and a report by the Centre for Science and Environment (CSE) says that about half that area is threatened by salinity and waterlogging (CSE 1982, 7). Salinity is estimated to affect 35–36 percent of the total amount of land irrigated. B. D. Dhawan considers that both issues affect about 6 million hectares of the 29 million hectares of canal served land but emphasises that this does mean that all of this land is unsuitable for farming and in fact part of it has the potential to be cultivated. Further, in Maharashtra state and other places, the water table has lowered as a result of well irrigation and the area affected by salinity and waterlogging has decreased (Dhawan 1995a). Karanjot Kaur Brar, who investigated the Green Revolution and environmental change in Punjab state, has denied any connection with the spread of waterlogging, positing that in the state overall between 1966 and 1986, most tube wells experienced a fall in the water table. On the other hand, he comments, a rising water table can be found in areas where the rate of progress of the Green Revolution, which targeted increased cropping in wheat and rice, has been low. Therefore, he denies any connection between the Green Revolution and waterlogging here (Brar 1999). Kanchan Chopra too shows that there was a one third reduction in the waterlogged area in Punjab state between 1965 and 1984 as a result of an increase in pump irrigation (Chopra 1990, 23–36).

There is virtually complete agreement that the problem of groundwater depletion had become acute as a result of the increase in well irrigation in recent years, and a large number of reports show the severity of the reduction in many areas. For example, Marcus H. Moench states that in Gujarat state between the 1970s and the 1990s, the ratio of pump wells rose 40 to 80 percent, and as a result of the falling water table deep wells have to be constructed which are very expensive. He suggests the necessity of user group institutions for groundwater management (Moench 1992a).

It is not easy to appraise the level of exploitation of groundwater. According to B. D. Dhawan, estimates by the Planning Commission and the Central Groundwater Board suggest that no state has reached "disturbing levels" for the state as a whole, but that there is a risk of overuse particularly in certain areas of states like Punjab, Haryana, Rajasthan and Tamil Nadu. Further, 6 percent of blocks (*mandals*) are over-exploited. The level of misuse of groundwater in India has, Dhawan approximates, reached 72 percent of total groundwater resources. In 2005, the Central Groundwater Board thought it probable that nearly one fifth of the 5,700 blocks had reached critical levels of over-exploitation (Vaidyanathan 2006, 23). The introduction into agriculture of more water-efficient technologies like drip irrigation and the establishment of systems to save on the use of water resources are necessary, since without them there will be potentially grave water shortages in a large number of states.

### *Changes to Forest Areas*

The amount of forested area in India and the growth of agriculture are closely entwined. Between Independence and the 1980s, forests disappeared at a fairly rapid pace. Following this time, the decline did not cease but became more moderate (CSE 1982, 33; CSE 1985, 80; CSE 1999, Table 3.1.5, [p. 119]. The loss of forest down to 1980 can largely be blamed on its conversion to farmland (Nadkarni 1987, 368; Ravindranath and Hall 1995, 66). A study of the Western Ghats districts of Karnataka shows that between 1920 and 1990, the area under forest in most districts more than halved. Between 56 percent and 93 percent of this reduction was due to the expansion of farmland (Ecological Economics Unit, Institute for Social and Economic Change, Bangalore 1999), with the exception of one district where tea and coffee plantations were created. Industrial and commercial use is also strongly suspected of laying behind forest degradation, alongside the lesser culprit of firewood gathering by local people (Chambers et al. 1989, 47). A report by the Centre for Science and Environment stressed that the Forestry Department promoted tree felling for commercial and industrial purposes, primarily as a source of revenue (CSE 1982). A possible third factor is directly related to urban demands for fuel. The Forestry Department may say that the demand for local household firewood is damaging, but Ravindranath and Hall, among others, believe that the small-scale gathering of firewood, usually by women and children collecting sticks and small branches, can only account for a minute part of any forest reduction (Ravindranath and Hall 1995). Of much greater impact is the amassing of logs for urban consumption (Nadkarni 1989, 77–81, 94–95).

The alleviation of forest erosion from 1980 has received attention from Ravindranath and Hall, who note that the Forest Conservation Act was passed that year. It banned all unnecessary forest conversion into non-forest, and state governments were required to obtain prior approval from the central government before clearing an area of trees or changing the use of forest land to non-forest purposes. Afforestation programmes also helped halt the tide of destruction. Though natural forest decreased between 1980 and 1990, 14–15 million hectares were planted in that decade under schemes such as Social Forestry (Ravindranath and Hall 1995, 74; CSE 1999, 113–5). In addition, partnerships between the state and local communities to protect and redevelop degraded forests, known as Joint Forest Management, came into being under the India Forest Policy of 1988 and spread through the whole country. Originally conceived of in West Bengal in 1971, this management scheme was very successful and fostered a palpable increase in forest areas (FSI 2000). The role of industry was also addressed; whereas it had previously been able to have an assured supply of timber from government forests at a low or nominal cost, now such subsidies were reduced, encouraging it to use these resources more efficiently. This greater consciousness about forest destruction and its regulation was exemplified and influenced by the environmental movement, starting with the Chipko movement in the 1970s. Public discussion about forest conservation was supported by the press and the judiciary. Finally, the contribution made by the Green Revolution cannot be overlooked. As discussed above, Rao argues the Green Revolution allowed the area under cultivation to grow at a slow pace as new technologies reduced the pressure to extend cultivation. Swaminathan stated that the Green Revolution had actually protected forests.

The growth of agriculture from the end of the nineteenth century and through the Green Revolution gave rise to misgivings concerning, among other matters, the diminishing of village commons, the conversion of forests into farmland and the problems related to irrigation. Taken in conjunction with new trends such as the decline of, and changes in, roles related to agrarian production on village lands, the gradual formation of an egalitarian protection system for local common resources, and moves to stop the further reduction of forests, it is probably also true to say that it led generally to a situation which seriously threatened reproduction. A number of problems certainly remain. In particular, agricultural development cannot be sustained if there is no response to the depletion of groundwater resources.[23]

## Land Reform and Changes in Land Ownership

A study of the post-Independence structure of agriculture must consider the land reforms that were carried out in each state. These fell into three main categories: The abolition of intermediaries, tenancy regulation and placing a ceiling on landholdings. Land reforms were basically carried out under state jurisdiction, and there were considerable differences between states. This hinders any attempt to comprehensively summarise the land reforms, but we will look briefly at their main content.

During the colonial period, the government, broadly speaking, used two methods to collect revenue from the land and its produce. The first was the ryotwari system, where land revenue was collected directly at village level from cultivators (*ryots*), who could number several hundred people. This system was used principally in the Madras and Bombay Presidencies. The second was the zamindari system. Here, the government collected revenue directly from zamindars (literally, "intermediaries"). They were large landowners, many of whom retained the character of feudal lords, who collected ground rents from as many as several dozen cultivators in a village, and controlled the local waste and forest land. The colonial government treated them as landowners and the villagers, who paid ground rents and cultivated the land, as "tenant farmers". In many cases, an intermediate class (or classes) of landlord stood between the zamindar and the "tenant farmer".[24] This system centred on Bengal but was found all over North India, and was also adopted in a few areas of South India where it suited the local conditions. The abolition of intermediaries, which began in the 1950s, did away with landownership by the zamindars and other intermediate classes and granted ownership rights to the "tenant farmers" who had until then paid ground rents. Institutionally, this reform in essence extended the ryotwari system to all of India, with tax being collected at village level directly from the cultivator.

The abolition of intermediaries placed between the government and the "tenant farmers" was accomplished in most places, and 20 million of the latter were recognised as landowners in a direct relationship with the state. All the waste and forest land that had been under the control of intermediaries reverted to government jurisdiction (Haque and Sirohi 1985, Chapter 3). Though many cases were reported where the old zamindar class had substantially preserved their influence in local society even after the reforms, they are generally regarded as having succeeded.

Tenancy regulation has by contrast been evaluated more severely. This reform had as its purpose protecting and raising the status of tenant farmers who had rented land from the landowners and cultivated it under the ryotwari system. With the abolition of intermediaries, there were many sub-tenants in an inferior position to the former "tenant farmers" who had been newly granted rights to their land. These were the object of the reform of the tenancy system. The exact provisions of the reforms varied from state to state, but in general they covered three areas. First was the guarantee of security of tenure for those tenants whose position was uncertain, such as tenants-at-will who could be evicted without notice, and sharecroppers. Landowners would not be allowed to evict tenants from their land. Second, rent should not exceed a certain proportion of the gross produce. Third, in some states the tenancy system was abolished and tenants were given the opportunity to purchase their land. Haque and Sirohi note that "implementation of the enacted laws has been unsatisfactory in large parts of the country, excepting Kerala".[25] Even in states where tenancy has been prohibited, "oral and insecure leases continue" on a broad basis. It has proved difficult to guarantee tenant security because of legal flaws and deficiencies, the absence of proper land records and the inability of poor tenants to resist landlords or to organise themselves to do so (Haque and Sirohi 1985, 66–67).

Concerning rent regulation, most states calculated a figure based on recommendations made under the First Five Year Plan that "a fair rent should normally be within one fourth or one fifth of the produce". However, Haque and Sirohi note that

> our field visits to different parts of the country enable us to believe that the measures remain ineffective in almost every state ... Under sharecropping arrangements, the landlord's share is no less than 50 percent of the produce [and] [i]n case the landlord makes any contribution towards expenses on seeds and manures, this share varies from 60 percent to 75 percent ... The National Commission on Agriculture also observed that the rate of rent at 50 percent of the gross produce prevails almost throughout the country in the case of sharecoppers and unprotected tenants.
>
> (Haque and Sirohi 1985, 76–77)

A number of states – Gujarat, Maharashtra, Karnataka, Kerala, Uttar Pradesh, Madhya Pradesh, and Jammu and Kashmir, as well as part of Andhra Pradesh – banned tenancy cultivation with the view of transferring ownership rights to tenants for the payment of a certain sum. Kerala saw the greatest success here, with around 2.5 million tenants becoming landowners by 1980 as a result of the reform. In Maharashtra, around 870,000 tenants acquired ownership rights over 2.7 million hectares of land. The number of tenants in Gujarat decreased considerably as a result of the legislation. However, the system of oral lease continues to exist. Occupancy rights were offered to 1.38 million tenants; 820,000 proceeded with purchase, but the remaining 550,000 were not able to benefit because of an inability to pay among other reasons. In Manipur, 360,000 tenants acquired land as a result of the reform, as did 130,000 tenants and subtenants in Rajasthan, who obtained 670,000 hectares. In Haryana, 26,000 tenants purchased 650,000 hectares. In Tamil Nadu, there was no legal provision to transfer ownership rights to tenants, but a law conferring ownership rights on agricultural workers and rural artisans resulted in homesteads being granted to around 180,000 people (about 100,000 from the scheduled castes and tribes, about 50,000 from the backward classes, and about 30,000 others) (Haque and Sirohi 1985, 45–66).[26] Haque and Sirohi judge the tenancy reforms as having a varied result overall. In general, the acquisition of ownership rights was deemed beneficial, though this varied from state to state. However, tenancy security and rent regulation have largely been ineffective, except in Kerala.

The success of the reforms that place a ceiling on landholdings has been rated fairly low. In a few states, the ceiling laws were brought in at the same time as those abolishing intermediaries, but in most they were enacted after 1960. The ceiling varied from 4 hectares to 136 hectares, depending on the state. In some the unit of application was the individual and in others the family. Certain categories of land were exempt. The surplus land was to be redistributed to the landless, but there were a large number of cases where nominally the name of the landholder was changed, even to a grandchild. In the 1950s and 1960s, only 820,000 acres were registered as surplus land. The government set guidelines in 1972 to increase the effectiveness of the ceiling laws, as a result of which the ceilings were lowered and the unit of application became the family. Even so, just 2.1 million hectares were registered as surplus in 1984; of this 1.74 million hectares were registered as actual surplus land, and of this, only 850,000 hectares were redistributed. Fifty-two percent of the latter went to the scheduled castes and tribes (Haque and Sirohi 1985, 78–85, 229–229; Hamaguchi 1990, 103). It has been pointed out that the total amount of land redistributed under the ceiling legislation was 1.64 million hectares, no more than 1 percent of the net area under cultivation at the end of the 1970s.[27]

Haque and Siroqi conclude that the abolition of intermediaries completed the early target of doing away with the zamindari system at a basic level, but changes as a result of the tenancy system reforms and the land ceiling legislation were extremely limited and had little impact on the essential structure of Indian agriculture.

In contrast to this negative evaluation is a report from the World Bank. A nationwide panel survey of about 5,000 rural households was conducted in

1982 and 1999. The resultant data were used to assess the effect of land reform legislation on participants over the period. The final report commented that "land reform had a significant and positive impact on educational attainment by households' offspring"; land reform contributed to an increase in income and expenditure, and it "accounted for as much as one third of the growth observed during the period"; and tenancy reform had a greater impact than the ceiling legislation. However, "under the threat of ceiling laws, land owners transferred land mainly to relatives and better-off while tenancy legislation led landlords to keep those with relatively high levels of ability who, even though they were not the poorest, could make more productive use of the land than the original landlord". The report concludes that the land reforms cannot be said to have brought benefits only to the poorest classes (World Bank 2007).

In terms of land ownership, the World Bank team reported, "Overall, land reform constituted a major effort that resulted in the transfer of almost 10 million hectares, 2.5 million hectares under programs to redistribute of ceiling surplus land, and 7.35 million hectares under tenancy legislation". As Table 5.8 shows, the area that changed hands under the tenancy legislation was 5.45 percent of the total land area and it affected 5.35 percent of the population. The land given new ownership under the ceiling legislation was 4.41 percent of the total area, making a total of around 10 percent of arable land that was redistributed and close to 8 percent of the population who benefited. The World Bank stated that "land reform in India was undoubtedly a

*Table 5.8* Households and area affected by land reform in Indian states (%)

| *State* | *Tenancy* | | *Ceiling* | |
|---|---|---|---|---|
| | *Area* | *Population* | *Area* | *Population* |
| Andhra Pradesh | 3.48 | 0.75 | 8.34 | 3.81 |
| Bihar | 0.00 | 0.00 | 4.42 | 4.00 |
| Gujarat | 15.00 | 11.20 | 1.95 | 0.31 |
| Haryana | 0.51 | 0.01 | 1.26 | 0.26 |
| Himachal Pradesh | 0.16 | 3.19 | 0.06 | 0.05 |
| Karnataka | 15.38 | 5.29 | 1.71 | 0.30 |
| Kerala | 8.47 | 12.49 | 1.30 | 1.04 |
| Madhya Pradesh | 2.15 | 0.61 | 2.69 | 0.71 |
| Maharashtra | 27.01 | 10.68 | 7.74 | 1.08 |
| Orissa | 0.15 | 1.43 | 2.24 | 1.28 |
| Punjab | 1.89 | 0.04 | 1.50 | 0.25 |
| Rajasthan | 0.00 | 0.16 | 6.63 | 0.75 |
| Tamil Nadu | 3.65 | 3.23 | 2.47 | 1.24 |
| Uttar Pradesh | 0.00 | 0.00 | 5.81 | 3.68 |
| West Bengal | 6.41 | 10.80 | 14.91 | 19.73 |
| Total | 5.45 | 5.35 | 4.41 | 2.27 |

Source: World Bank 2007.

Original Source: Kaushik 2005.

major historical event, especially if the amount of land distributed under abolition of intermediaries is added to these figures" (World Bank 2007, 39).

Over and above the changes to land ownership as a result of tenancy reforms and ceiling legislation, in 2006 the redistribution of government waste land reached 60.11 million acres.[28] In addition, it is probably safe to say that land transfers through government policy (redistribution by land reforms or of waste land) amount to around 15 percent of cultivated land. Studies such as that undertaken by the World Bank above make it clear that the beneficiaries are not necessarily always the landless or the lowest castes. However, bearing in mind that more than half the land redistributed under the ceiling legislation went to the scheduled castes and tribes, a considerable proportion of the landless and low classes in rural villages must have been able to acquire land or extend it.[29]

Besley and Burgess, using a quantitative methodology to assess the significance of land reform, say that "land reform in general appears to be associated with reductions in rural poverty" (Besley and Burgess 2000, 407). They find "there is robust evidence of a link between poverty reduction and two kinds of land reform legislation – tenancy reform and abolition of intermediaries". Also, "land reform can benefit the landless by raising agricultural wages" since the strengthening of the position of tenants after the tenancy reform caused the labour supply from this class to decrease (Besley and Burgess 2000, 424). They maintain, however, that the reforms hold no influence over raising agrarian output. In West Bengal, in contrast, Banerjee et al. have explored the impact a major change in property rights had on agricultural productivity and drawn a different conclusion. Operation Barga was launched in 1977 to "enforce the tenancy laws that regulated rents and security of tenure of sharecroppers". Tenancy reform gave security of tenure and fortified the bargaining power of tenants; this in turn led to better tenant shares and enhanced productivity. The share of Operation Barga in the rice yield increase was calculated at 28 percent.[30]

The Indian land reforms can be summarised as follows. Excepting the virtual disappearance of zamindars and other intermediaries after the abolition of the intermediary system, the reforms failed to fundamentally change the bipolarised pattern of landownership in the villages. A very small proportion of inhabitants continued to own more than 50 percent of the land. Table 5.9 shows that this situation largely persevered after 1960; the upper 10 percent

*Table 5.9* Distribution of owned and operated area by household size groups (%)

| *Household size groups* | *1961–62* | *1971–72* | *1981–82* | *1991–92* | *2002–03* |
|---|---|---|---|---|---|
| Bottom 60% | 10.8 | 10.8 | 10.5 | 11.0 | 8.3 |
| Middle 30% | 37.7 | 38.2 | 38.5 | 38.0 | 36.5 |
| Top 10% | 51.5 | 51.0 | 51.0 | 51.0 | 55.2 |

Source: Nair and Banerjee 2011, Table 2.3 (p. 53).

of households held over half the land and the bottom 60 percent owned around 10 percent. Even if land redistribution under the ceiling legislation was around 5 percent, as the World Bank survey showed, the basic composition of landowners stayed the same. This marked an essential difference from land reform in East Asia. However, regardless of this limitation, the land reforms plainly still empowered the lower classes in rural villages, and assisted in raising them both economically and socially. A substantial amount of the land redistributed under the ceiling legislation went to landless members of the scheduled castes and tribes, and some tenants obtained land as a result of transfers under the tenancy reform.

The system awarding wasteland in the proximity of villages to the landless classes and scheduled castes is a vital part of the picture. As previously detailed, a broad extent of uncultivated land in Madras state was being encroached upon by the landless in the 1950s. In such cases, after a certain time, the government recognised the cultivators as possessors of the land by issuing them with certificates of land title under fixed conditions. A survey of a North Indian village reveals a sudden drop in the number of landless households there after 1975. This came in the wake of a government scheme to distribute village common land to the landless (or almost landless), thereby facilitating their economic and social independence (Wiser and Wiser 2000, 282).

For those still renting land, their position was further improved by the reform guaranteeing tenancy security, as shown by the research of Besley and Burgess (2000). A large number of village surveys indicate that the legislation gave them more negotiating power (Mencher 1978, 112), and my own fieldwork in South India, to be described below, confirms these findings. Thus tenancy reform too helped propagate the independence of the lower classes and raise their status.[31]

It is possible to take a closer look at some of the threads introduced above. For instance, how did landownership change as a result of land reform? As already mentioned, the extremely unequal pattern, where the top 10 percent owned more than half the land, continued unchanged from the 1960s. The fact that bottom 60 percent only owned around 10 percent – which meant that most households were landless or almost landless – implies that they worked in farming as labourers or tenants. It is crucial when considering India's economy and society as a whole to remember that this social structure, comprising a tiny elite group and a large, virtually landless lower class, had existed quite statically since before Independence. Yet, though the basic structure of landownership in India did not alter, among members of the lower classes some developments occurred; the ratio of those that were landless did shrink in the 40 years after 1960 (Nair and Banerjee 2011, 50). Table 5.10 shows that the proportion of marginal holdings rose in that period, which probably reflects the acquisition of land by the landless. By contrast, East Asian society (including China and Japan) had, over a long period, been defined by small farmers using family labour. The tenancy system there was

*Table 5.10* Size distribution of landholdings (%)

| *Landholdings* | *1961/62 (17th round)* | *1971/2 (26th round)* | *1981/2 (37th round)* | *1991/92 (48th round)* | *2002/03 (59th round)* |
|---|---|---|---|---|---|
| Marginal | 7.6 | 9.8 | 12.2 | 16.9 | 23.1 |
| Small | 12.4 | 14.7 | 16.5 | 18.6 | 20.4 |
| Small-medium | 20.5 | 21.9 | 23.6 | 24.6 | 22.0 |
| Medium | 31.2 | 30.7 | 29.8 | 26.1 | 23.1 |
| Large | 28.2 | 22.9 | 18.1 | 13.8 | 11.6 |
| Total | 100.0 | 100.0 | 100.0 | 100.0 | 100.0 |

Original source: NSS and Livestock Survey, various rounds.

Source: Nair and Banerjee 2011, Table 2.2 (p. 51).

Note: Data for the 59th round is for the Kharif season only.

basically abolished by land reforms in the 1940s and 1950s, and independent farmers working small holdings predominated. This homogenous pattern of a rural society made up of independent farmers is a world away from the Indian experience.

Due to land reforms or encroachment the previously landless ventured into land ownership. Tenants' rights were also reinforced thanks to tenants' movements and tenancy reform. These developments acted socially and economically to usher the poorest members of rural villages towards independence. The relative importance of both the land reforms and the giving of wastelands to the landless will be verified in the next chapter as it investigates long-term social and economic trends among all classes in Indian society.

## Notes

1 Pulapre Balakrishnan, based on Kurosaki's research, draws attention to agricultural growth before the Green Revolution, and referring to the Nehru era, says, "The Green Revolution ought not be seen as episodic but the result of some years of preparation of the seed bed, so to speak" (Balakrishnan 2010, pp. 75, 97).

2 According to one study, about 45 percent of the increase in agrarian output between 1951–54 and 1958–61 was due to an increase in the area under cultivation, and 8 percent was because of changes in cultivation patterns (Vaidyanathan 1994a, 23).

3 Ministry of Food and Agriculture, *Report on Location and Utilisation of Wastelands in India, Part VIII-Madras*, Wastelands Survey and Reclamation Committee, Government of India, 1961, p. 5.

4 Vaidyanathan too identifies the expansion of cultivation as being due to the decrease in fallow land, the clearing of culturable waste and encroachment on forests, pasture land and village common land (Vaidyanathan 1994a, 26). Though he points out the importance of encroachment on common land in the expansion of arable land in India, it is not made clear whether or not this encroachment was made by members of the landless classes. A report on Maharashtra by the Wastelands Survey and Reclamation Committee tells us that in the early 1960s a large portion of the culturable waste there, like in Tamil Nadu, was already being cultivated by members of the Scheduled Castes and other low castes (Ministry of

Food and Agriculture, *Report on Location and Utilisation of Wastelands in India, Part XI-Maharashtra*, Wastelands Survey and Reclamation Committee, Government of India, 1962, p. 5). It is probably safe to say that in a number of key areas in India, encroachment by the landless lower classes was an important part of the extension of arable land.

5 Between 1950/51 and the beginning of the 1970s, the consumption of fertilisers in India grew from below 100,000 tons to close to 2,200,000 tons (Kumar 1983, 960).

6 *Season and Crop Reports for Tamilnadu.*

7 To pursue this argument, we should study the assertion of T. Roy (Roy 2006). He states that the poor quality of natural resources in the South Asia region greatly restricted the potential for agricultural development, and suggests that "investment decisions were constrained by environmental conditions". Raising productivity required "a huge commitment of public money", particularly for irrigation. "Agricultural growth, being intensive in public resources, can be sustained only by drawing money away from other potential uses of public money", depriving non-agricultural areas of investment capacity. However, our long-term study of Tamil Nadu, and the heavy restrictions imposed by the natural conditions of the Salem district, show that the core part of agricultural development and a rise in productivity had been realised through mainly private investment in well irrigation and fertilisers. And certainly the same situation did not apply after Independence, when public investment in industry and its infrastructure grew. For example, though in the First Five Year Plan, 37 percent of the total budget was given to agriculture and irrigation. This declined to 21 percent in the Second (1956–61) and Third (1962–66) Plans, when the focus of expenditure moved to industrialisation, especially heavy industry (Dorin and Landy 2009, 68–69). Given these facts, Roy's argument lacks conviction.

8 Dorin and Landy point out that between 1950/51 and 1964/65, agrarian production grew by 3.2 percent, irrigated areas by 26 percent and the use of fertilisers by 625 times, and that the volume rise in production of grains other than wheat between 1950 and 1965 was about the same as between 1965 and 1990. They remark that agrarian growth had been substantially achieved even before the Green Revolution, contrary to general belief (Dorin and Landy 2009, 68).

9 Encroachment on village commons also undeniably led to ecological problems. We shall examine this point below.

10 Dorin and Landy 2009, 70–72. The description following is also based on this work.

11 See Fujita 2002, 102–103.

12 Satyanarayana 1990, p. 115.

13 Ōji also emphasises that the Green Revolution was not a sudden occurrence in the latter half of the 1960s, but rather it gathered together the various changes that had begun with the start of canal irrigation at the beginning of the twentieth century. He argues with conviction based on his survey of villages in Punjab state that the U.S. contribution to the Green Revolution has been overestimated (Ōji 1974).

14 Drèze, using the example of a North Indian village, says that irrigated land, which had until then been concentrated on wealthy farmers, was extended 50 percent between 1957/58 and 1974/75, and this functioned to even out class differences (Drèze 2002, 214). Roy too points out that the proliferation of "democratic" tube wells and pumps contributed more to the expansion of small-scale farming than to large-scale, and allowed the Green Revolution to spread to very poor farmers in eastern India where conditions for irrigation were adverse (Roy 2011, 308). For the situation in Bangladesh, see Fujita 2005, upon which Shah's argument is based (Shah 2009b).

15 Foster and Rosenzweig, who analysed a sample of 250 villages in various parts of India between 1971 and 1999, found that regions with 60 percent of their lands

irrigated in 1971 showed little change in that ratio in 1999. Where around 18 percent of lands had been irrigated in 1971, the ratio had changed to 50 percent in 1999. This shows that increased irrigation had the greatest impact in dry areas (Foster and Rosenzweig 2004).

16 Singh reports a high yield per area in the case of small scale operations in Punjab state. Further, in the period 1981/2 to 1989/90, the ratio of the area cultivated by large operations fell greatly from 65.26 percent to 40.25 percent. This showed a tendency for operations to be concentrated on areas of between 1 and 6 hectares, not larger. This shows, he says, that poverty and inequality were not increasing in villages in Punjab (Singh 2001, Chapter 6).

17 Donald K. Freebairn reviewed 300 studies on the Green Revolution concerning whether income inequality had increased or not and found that most considered it had. However, most case studies concluded, not that inequality had increased, but that it has either decreased or remained unchanged. In particular, conclusions that it had increased in India and the Philippines were proportionally low (Freebairn 1995).

18 Roy too points out the revolutionary significance of the Green Revolution (Roy 2011, 308).

19 For example, Pathak 1994, 130.

20 The degree to which the aspirations of the landless to acquire land were actually expressed differed according to the how strong was the domination of the elites in the village society and economy. Though there were some districts where the landless encroached widely on uncultivated land, there were others where such land was occupied by the dominant classes. Also, as N. S. Jodha points out, there were not a few areas where land granted to the landless classes later reverted to members of the upper classes. In tank irrigation areas too, in villages where the elites maintained their power, water distribution labour continued as before to be done by members of the scheduled castes (Mosse 2003).

21 See Yanagisawa 2008b for the related sources.

22 Despite the spread of arable into poor land, there was no decrease in average yield, though there is some scope for thinking that there were wide fluctuations year by year. This point needs further empirical research.

23 Another important issue is that the "solution" that substitutes fossil resources, using propane and kerosene for household fuel and chemical fertilisers to lower dependence on green manure from common lands, has been an important factor in preventing the environmental question from becoming more serious. However, a sudden rise among the vast Indian population in a dependence on fossil fuels raises its own problems.

24 For the zamindari system, see the research of Nariaki Nakazato (Nakazato 1994, etc.) and Shinkichi Taniguchi (Taniguchi 1996, etc.).

25 Haque and Siroqi state that in West Bengal, "only about 12.19 lakh [1,219,000] sharecroppers could be recorded up to February 1983" (Haque and Siroqi 1995, 65).

26 Hamaguchi (1990) says that no more than around 3.5 million tenants acquired ownership rights as a result of the reforms and that most were small farmers who were comparatively well off (p. 102).

27 Inoue 2002 reports that until the middle of 1986, 1.31 million hectares had been requisitioned and 920,000 hectares redistributed, and down to March 1995, 26.6 million hectares had been redistributed, 1.5 percent of the total area cultivated.

28 Government of India, Ministry of Rural Development, *Annual Report, 2006–7*, Annexure-XLVIII, Distribution of Government Wastelands, p. 257.

29 In 2006, around 4.9 million acres of land was distributed to 5.4 million individual beneficiaries. Of this, 2.6 million acres (2.96 million beneficiaries) went to members of the scheduled castes and tribes. Government of India, Ministry of Rural Development, *Annual Report, 2006–7*, Annexure-XLVIII, Distribution of Government Wastelands, p. 255.

30 See also Kurosaki 2010.

31 We should also be aware that the land reforms had an impact on industrial growth as well. Because they restricted the expansion of cultivated land by the landowning classes, some of the upper classes in villages began to invest their earnings through agriculture in commerce and industry. Thus was formed an important capitalist class that was a driving force behind the current economic growth (Damodaran 2008, 106–107).

# 6 Changes in Rural Society, the Development of the Rural Economy and the Growth of Rural Markets

## The Structural Transformation of Village Society[1]

Chapter 1 detailed how in the middle of the nineteenth century, particularly in the wet villages of South India, most of the land in the village was in the hands of a very small number of upper-caste landowners. Other villagers, of lower castes, who owned very little land, if any, were employed by them as labourers, or leased land as small tenants. Many members of the depressed (scheduled) castes in particular might work for a single employer their whole lives, and they were often dependent on the food and clothing supplied by him.

This structure began to deteriorate from the end of the nineteenth century. Large numbers of people, especially those from the depressed castes, went overseas to work on plantations and so on. Such opportunities to work away from the village strengthened their bargaining power with landlords over employment conditions, and some labourers even returned from abroad able to buy tiny pieces of land. Lower-caste labourers, who had been in a position of servitude, joined movements to improve their socio-economic standing in an effort to gain independence from the village elites. These movements were connected to the anti-Brahmin and anti-caste movements that started in South India in the 1920s. As large landowners found it increasingly difficult to retain their subordinate labourers, Brahmin landowners were moving in greater numbers to urban areas for education, so that their sons could take up the employment opportunities offered by the colonial government as civil servants, teachers and lawyers. Based in towns and cities, they could not operate their farms easily, so leased some of their land to tenants and, as time went by, sold more and more of it. As we have seen, these changes are clear from an analysis of Settlement Registers dating from the end of the nineteenth and into the twentieth centuries: Landholding was transitioning from the Brahmins and other upper castes to members of the scheduled and backward castes.

The dominance of the upper-caste landowners continued to weaken after Independence, spurred on by the Green Revolution and other events. These changes can be traced and interrogated through a case study of a South Indian village.

DOI: 10.4324/9781003341550-9

### *The Sample Village*

The village I will designate as M. It is located on the banks of the River Kollidam in Tiruchirapalli District in Tamil Nadu. I surveyed it twice, in two phases between 1979 and 1982, and again in 2007–2008. The description that follows is based on the first survey.

The village is some 10 kilometres from Tiruchirapalli city, the district administrative headquarters which is an important industrial hub and an educational centre with a number of universities. Being within easy commuting distance, many of the villagers work there, so besides being a typical wet village, M is also a suburban village of Tiruchirapalli.

As shown in Table 6.1, the village consists of a number of communities divided among the forward castes and the other backward castes (OBC). The Pillais and the Chettiars (forward castes) comprise 58 households, while the majority are Mutturiyans (Mutharaiyar), members of the OBC, with close to 200 households. Next in number are Pallars and Paraiyars, with 111 households. In 1979–1980 the main occupation of villagers was agriculture, in which 57 percent of households were engaged. Nine percent had their main occupation in the urban area, and the remaining 33 percent ran small businesses or worked in non-farm jobs in the village. There were also 38 households of Brahmins and others who did not live in the village but owned a lot of the agricultural land there; their actual residence was Thiruvanaikoil, a village on the way to Tiruchirapalli, where there was an important Hindu temple.

### *Changes in Landownership*

We have seen that, as the hold of Brahmins and other high castes over the wet villages loosened from the end of the nineteenth century, there was a gradual increase in landownership among communities previously excluded from it. This pattern was also to be found in M, and the tendency continued after Independence. First, the area owned by Brahmins decreased from 209 acres

*Table 6.1* Sample households, 1981

| *Community* | *Number of households* |
|---|---|
| Pillai, Chettiar (Chetty) | 58 |
| Muthuraja (Mutharaiyar) | 199 |
| Muslim | 35 |
| Nadar | 19 |
| Asari | 13 |
| Pallar | 93 |
| Paraiyar | 18 |
| Others | 35 |
| Total | 470 |

Source: Author's survey (1979–1981).

(about half the village land) in 1952 to about 170 acres (about 38 percent of the total) in 1979. Second, the land owned by villagers expanded, from just 18 percent in 1952 to 29 percent in 1979. Especially noteworthy is the rise in landownership among the Muthurajas and the scheduled castes (SC). The Muthurajas nearly trebled their landholding from 23 acres in 1952 to 68 acres in 1979, and SC members increased it from 9.1 acres in 1952 to 16.63 acres in 1979. By contrast, there was little change in the size of the holdings of Pillais and Chettiars. Third, despite these increases, villagers owned only 29 percent of the arable land in 1980. To clarify the background to these developments, we will now examine changing trends among each of the main communities after 1952.

### *Pillais and Chettiars*

The Pillai and Chettiar communities had a high percentage of landownership among the villagers, with around half owning land from the time of their fathers or grandfathers. In 1979–1981, two trends were conspicuous in these communities. First, in addition to operating their farms, they tended to start up small businesses like rice mills or match factories in the vicinity. Within the Pillai community, 41 percent were engaged in non-farm activities in the village as their main occupation, and 54 percent among the Chettiar community. Members of these castes ran rice mills, match factories, tea shops and a fertiliser shop, among other concerns. Second, they tended to pursue urban employment in tandem with farm management. About 47 percent of Pillai households and 27 percent of Chettiar households had one or more family members who worked in urban employment, the highest proportion of any community except the Muslim. The percentage was larger in families who operated large farms. Typical employment was as bus drivers and conductors, policemen and skilled workers in a factory manufacturing heavy electrical equipment and in an ordnance factory.

Urban work among members of these communities was related to their educational level, which was high: In 1981, 43.8 percent of Pillai households and 30.8 percent of Chettiar households had members who had passed the Secondary School Leaving Certificate (SSLC) or who had entered Industrial Training Institutes (ITI). Though the majority of village children went to nearby government primary schools and a government high school, many Pillai and Chettiar households sent their children (especially boys) to private schools in towns distant from the village, sometimes even to boarding schools with the additional expenses of tuition and boarding fees and travel costs. To get high-paying non-farm employment, it was necessary to get good marks in the SSLC examination and progress to an ITI, a polytechnic or a university. Though there was a growing tendency within these communities, especially among the larger farmers, towards operating small-scale businesses in the village or engaging in urban work, they were still involved in farm management as of 1979–1981, and holding down dual occupations was common. For example, a Chettiar farmer who was a skilled labourer in Bharat Heavy

Electrical Limited (BHEL) commuted to the factory every day while managing about 5 acres of farmland. He employed a *pannaikaran* (a labourer on a yearly contract) to cultivate the land and took a vacation during busy times such as harvesting to supervise day labourers. This is typical of the pattern of farmer-cum-urban worker found in these communities.

### *Muthurajas*

The Muthuraja community, registered as OBC (Other Backward Class), made up almost half of the villagers. More than 80 percent of the fathers of their households had managed farms and 70 percent cultivated land as tenants. As mentioned above, they extended their landholding from 23 acres to 68 acres between 1950 and 1979 and as of 1979–1981, the total area they operated, either as owners or tenants, was 339 acres out of a total of 452 acres in the village. Since the 1950s, then, the Muthurajas had raised their status as agricultural producers, and by this time occupied a core position as such in the village. Reflecting this is the fact that some 70 percent of the working population of the community and 72 percent of the households were engaged chiefly in agriculture, a figure second only to the scheduled castes. On the other hand, the proportion involved in small businesses was minor, as was that in urban employment, again the second lowest after the scheduled castes. Only a fraction attained the SSLC or had ITI qualifications. By no means, however, had every member of this community raised his status as a farmer. In the first part of the 1950s, before the tenancy laws came into force, many Muthuraja households had either lost their tenancies or had them reduced, forcing them to become farm labourers.

### *The Scheduled Castes and the Agricultural Labour Market*

There were two types of agricultural labourer in this area: Those on a yearly contract (*pannaikaran*) and day labourers (coolies). The *pannaikaran* probably originated in the attached labourers that existed widely in the nineteenth century. A little under two thirds of the respondents among SC households in the village replied that their fathers had been *pannaikaran* or day labourers. Unlike the other communities in the village, SC members had long been employed as agricultural labourers, including *pannaikaran*, as their main job. Their socio-economic position had changed remarkably over the past few decades, however, primarily due to their acquisition of tenancy rights, but also due to an increase in land ownership among them and to changes in the conditions of *pannaikaran* employment.

*Acquisition of tenancy rights*: As mentioned above, an anti-Brahmin and anti-caste movement that included SC members began in the Tamil region in the 1920s. In 1944 a branch of the Dravidar Kazhagam (Dravidian Federation) movement was set up in the village, and in 1956 the Dravida Agricultural Labourers' Association (Dravida Vivasaya Thozhilalar) was established. All of the Pallars (SC) in the village joined it. Soon after its founding, the association began pressuring the Brahmin landlords to give it tenancy rights over a certain amount of land, and subsequently acquired rights over 60 acres of land. These were distributed to the members of the association on the basis of 0.5 acres per household. As a result, SC households, which had until then been completely agricultural labourers, acquired their own holding, however small; most combined tenant farming with work as agricultural labourers. The success of this movement gave lower-class people a sense of solidarity and strengthened their aspirations towards independence from their landlords.

*Increase in landownership*: As we have seen, SC landownership increased from 9.1 acres in 1953 to 16.63 acres (13 households) in 1979. It was very difficult for a SC member to save the money to buy land, but obtaining a tenancy holding was an important stepping stone towards being able to do so. In this sense, the acquisition of tenancy rights as a result of the Dravida Agricultural Labourers' Association's efforts in the 1950s was a key. Previously too, SC members had no way of knowing when a Brahmin landlord wanted to sell land, but after this time they too were informed when this was to happen, according to respondents. Thus as a result of acquiring tenancy holdings and landownership, they emerged from a position of mere labourer to become labourer-tenants, thereby raising their socio-economic status.

*Changes in the conditions of* pannaikaran *employment*: Employment conditions of *pannaikaran* changed in a number of important ways. First, it became extremely difficult for a landowner to recruit *pannaikaran*, since local SC members preferred to be employed as day labourers rather than working for the same person for one year. The survey revealed that 30 people from the scheduled castes had once worked as *pannaikaran*, but only 8 remained in 1980. Second, it was usual in the past for a *pannaikaran*'s contract to be for several years, but around 1980 labourers generally moved on to another employer after one year. Third, *pannaikaran* were demanding higher wages and better working conditions.

These pieces of evidence point to the increasing difficulty local landlords had in getting the long-term services of obedient *pannaikaran* from local SC members. The latter now wished to work as day labourers, a preference underpinned by three developments. The first of these was the strengthening desire for socio-economic independence and a growing sense of self-respect among the SCs. These had been evident from the end of the nineteenth century and were further reinforced by the Dravida Agricultural Labourers' Association in the 1950s. The second development was the acquisition of tenancy rights and land, which formed the economic basis for realising this desire. Without such holdings, many of the SCs would probably have prioritised working in a long-term and stable job as *pannaikaran* instead of having to rely completely on the uncertainty of day labour. With 0.5 acres of tenancy holding however, they could secure at least some of the produce needed for the family's consumption. By cultivating their own land in in addition to working as day labourers, it was possible to get enough income to support the household one way or another. Third, as we shall see below, more days of labour were available in comparison to the past, when slack seasons had reduced demand and therefore income. SC members in the village no longer needed to work as *pannaikaran*.

*Changes in day labour employment*: The most important development was the increase in the number of days that work was required. The expansion of well irrigation following the Green Revolution had enabled greater cultivation of sugar cane and plantain. Paddy alone necessitated very little labour after the end of the second harvest in March until June, whereas sugar cane and plantain started in January and required attention between March and July. Another alteration was found in the effect of an enlarged straw business on the day labour market. Straw left over after harvest was taken to Tiruchirapalli and other centres and sold for cattle fodder. In 1980, this business engaged around 30 percent of SC households. The busiest period was after the harvest in February and March and so provided a valuable work opportunity for farm labourers in what had been the slack season. The migration of labourers to other villages was a further source of change. Increased production brought about by the Green Revolution had augmented the need for labour during harvest. In many districts, there was a gap between labour demand and local supply. To fill it, groups of labourers temporarily migrated, sometimes from remote areas. The village survey revealed that since 1970 two groups of SC workers had been emigrating from the village to designated villages twice a year. In 1980, 40 SC members took part.

To summarise, most SC households that had formerly depended completely on agricultural wage labour (including *pannaikaran*) were now in possession of tiny pieces of tenancy land, allowing them to make a combined livelihood from cultivation and day labour (Table 6.2).

### *Brahmans*

The largest group of non-resident landowners in the village were Brahmins living mainly in Thiruvanaikoil, site of the famous Akilandeswari Temple. Many of them belonged to families with hereditary rights to perform *puja*

*Table 6.2* Distribution of households engaged in agriculture (%), 1981

| | *Owner-cultivator* | *Owner-cum-tenant-cultivator* | *Tenant* | *Tenant-cum-day labourer* | *Day labourer* | *Pannaikaran* | *Total* |
|---|---|---|---|---|---|---|---|
| Pillai | 20.0 | 20.0 | 30.0 | 10.0 | 20.0 | 0.0 | 100.0 |
| Chettiar | 60.0 | 0.0 | 10.0 | 10.0 | 20.0 | 0.0 | 100.0 |
| Muthuraja | 6.3 | 7.6 | 31.9 | 22.2 | 30.6 | 1.4 | 100.0 |
| SCs | 2.2 | 2.2 | 10.0 | 46.7 | 31.1 | 7.8 | 100.0 |

Source: Author's survey (1979–1981).

there, and they derived an income from this, in addition to renting their land in M village and elsewhere.

As previously touched upon, the Brahmins lost around 20 percent of their landholdings between 1952 and 1980. Several factors were involved in this. First, it had become increasingly difficult for Brahmin landlords to collect ground rents as regularly as they would have liked, due to the influence of the movements and activities that tenants and lower-caste people were involved in. This was exacerbated by the passage of the tenancy legislation. Further, white-collar urban employment was becoming ever more popular among Brahmins. This trend, apparent from the end of the nineteenth century, continued unabated after Independence, and in 1980 large numbers of Tamil Brahmins were already living in cities like Madras, Bombay and Delhi, remote from their home villages. Since the city dwellers could not farm their land themselves, they leased it to tenants. The problems of rent collection, however, incited many to sell their holdings, using the money to fund the education of their children, who frequently lived abroad. They therefore became completely dependent on the earnings from their urban employment.

Notwithstanding this inclination towards white-collar work, there were other possibilities open to the households associated with the survey village. One Brahmin household possessed the hereditary right to perform *puja* at the Akilandeswari Temple and derived most of their livelihood from it. They also received tenants' rents, but these had dwindled as land was sold off. However, it is unlikely that households devoted to this form of priestly service were common in the area. Those that had taken up urban employment preferred to have their sons get a university degree rather than perform *puja* services, so they could secure their future with government jobs. Of the 38 Brahmin households surveyed, 14 (37 percent) gave urban employment as their main occupation. In 1979, 16 of the 23 urban employees from this group (a little under 70 percent) were employed in higher-paying jobs earning Rs 500 or more. Most worked in the officer or supervisor class. A third group specialised in farm management. A typical family was one which controlled over 60 acres, held separately by family members (sons, grandsons) and relatives. Part of the land was leased out, but most they cultivated themselves, growing sugar cane and other crops. Six Brahmin families belonged to this category.

### *The Expansion of Non-farm Occupations*

Some traditional occupations, such as pot making, oil crushing, goldsmithing and masonry, could not withstand the pressure of competition of goods from the cities and went into decline. Yet, a number of non-farming economic activities managed to expand, one of which was the synthetic gem polishing industry. It was controlled by merchants, both small and large, in Tiruchirapalli, particularly on the island of Srirangam there, who brought the cut stones to the village to be polished in workers' homes. In 1980, 46 people from 30 households were engaged in this work. This made the industry second only to agriculture in the village. Of the 46, 36 were from families who had neither their own land nor tenancy rights, and most were from the Muthuraja and Muslim communities.

Another product of growing importance was paddy straw. In 1980, 47 villagers had a part in this business. Respondents to the survey had several insights into why the market for paddy straw had become so promising. For instance, people in the region around the city had begun drinking more coffee and tea, and so were consuming more milk than previously. This had led to an increase in the number of families in Tiruchirapalli raising cows for milk, which in turn necessitated a larger supply of straw for fodder. There was also an excess of straw available as a result of the introduction of HYVs and chemical fertilisers. Thanks to the Green Revolution, straw was no longer the manure of choice for the paddies. Landowners could keep the straw for several months after the harvest, allowing the trade to continue throughout the year, even during the slack season, and providing vital employment for members of the lower classes, including the SCs.

Changing consumption patterns among villagers created further employment opportunities in shops and stalls. In 1980 there were seven tea shops; respondents mentioned how very important tea-drinking was to them. They also stated that cycle hire and repair shops had increased from two to five over the past 30 years. More village cycles meant more income from their repair. In addition, there were three "mutton" (goat meat) stalls run by Muslims and a further three owned by villagers in other places. Thus by 1980, non-farm employment opportunities in the village for members of the lower classes had already increased considerably.

### *Findings*

The survey highlighted a number of changes in the village's socio-economic structure:

(1) Brahmin landlord households, dominant in village society from before Independence, had shifted their socio-economic base to urban employment outside the village. Some became full-time priests, though most gradually loosened their ties with the village as a whole, becoming part of an urban elite of white-collar workers, gazetted officers in the civil service, senior civil servants, engineers, lawyers and teachers. In the process, the community reduced its landholdings, and so its economic dominance in the village was reduced. Though there was no change in the basic structure of landownership by groups from the higher castes, a certain amount of arable land in the village moved from them to members of the backward and scheduled castes.

(2) The trend towards independence among lower-caste communities of agricultural labourers, including the scheduled castes, which began in the nineteenth century, accelerated after Independence with their involvement in the anti-caste and other movements, and the seeking of socio-economic independence from the village elites through the

acquisition of tenancy rights. The Green Revolution progressed, and the number of days it was possible to labour increased as the slack season contracted. The negotiating power of farm workers strengthened, and they rejected attached, long-term contracts. These developments, and better opportunities for non-farm employment, contributed to the growing independence of the landless, at least in this village.

(3) The "forward" communities of Pillais and Chettiars were still involved with agriculture in 1980 but were steadily embracing a dual pattern of employment. Their children were gaining educational qualifications at a high school level or higher and were either taking up work as skilled workers in large factories in the city, or as bus drivers and conductors, or they themselves were operating small businesses such as rice mills in the vicinity of the village.

(4) Some members of OBCs, like the Muthurajas, had raised their status as core agricultural producers in the village, as a result of acquiring land through tenancy or purchase. Agricultural improvements associated with the Green Revolution, such as well-digging, also had a positive effect. In 1980, they showed no indication of any move towards urban employment.

(5) Farm workers in long-term contracts fell drastically in number as a result of a growing sense of independence, a preference for day labour that was now available all year around, their acquisition of tenancy rights, and an increase in non-farm employment.

Though the 1980 village survey had begun to reveal the shifts occurring within different communities, there was no fundamental change as of yet. The land remained largely in the hands of Brahmins and temples, and more than half the farmland was operated by large farmers with 5 acres or more. The majority of villagers still had no land at all or only a very small amount, and relied for their livelihood on agricultural wage labour or tenancy.

## The Situation in Other Areas

The changes in M village were similar in many respects to those in other villages, though the speed of advancement varied. The transfer of land from ***Brahmins*** and those of other high castes to people of lower castes is one area of comparison. V. B. Athreya, who conducted a resurvey of Gangaikondan village in Tirunelveli District in 1984, reported that the holdings of Brahmins, who were major landowners in 1916, had been greatly reduced, and in the 1980s the chief landholding castes were Thevars (Maravars), SCs and Konars. He noted that there had also been a sharp decrease in the area of land under tenancy cultivation after 1958–1959, due to the emigration of Brahmins to towns. There had thus been a transition in the village from a Brahmin (and Pillai) landlord system to owner-cultivation by the agricultural castes, including the SCs (Athreya 1985, 9–10, 32, 97–98, 129). The resurvey of Dusi village, where surveys had been made since 1916, also revealed a fall in landownership by non-resident Brahmins and the procurement of land by non-Brahmin caste Hindu villagers. Here too tenancy had decreased. This was related in part to the landlords repossessing tenancy rights following the tenancy legislation and to transfers of land from non-resident Brahmin owners to cultivators living in the village, including former tenants (Guhan and Bharathan 1984, 3, 47, 51, 54, 165). Parallel changes have been observed in other villages.[2]

The experience of M village in regard to the rise in SC and lower-caste status is mirrored in other locations. Tsukasa Mizushima, in his survey of Reddimangudi in Tiruchirapalli District, undertaken at the same time as the M village survey, reported a decrease in landholding by the dominant Reddiar caste as well as a shortage of *pannaiyals* (permanent labourers). He attributes this shortage to a growing self-consciousness among these labourers, but more importantly to an increase in alternative work opportunities like sheep and goat raising, and to a greater demand for agricultural labour in wet areas as a result of the Green Revolution (Mizushima 1983, 173). A survey by Hisashi Nakamura of a dry village in the same Tiruchirapalli District suggests that here too goat-rearing was the basis for the economic independence of SC members. He describes a conflict between the Vellalars, a higher caste, and the Paraiyars, a SC, over the refusal by the latter to perform traditional services for them at funerals, such as beating tom-toms and disposing animal carcasses. The Vellalars then refused to employ the Paraiyars on their farms, so in response, the Paraiyars began to rear goats to support themselves (Nakamura 1982, 56–58). P. B. Mayer has also stressed the difficulties experienced by most landlords over the control of their tenants and labourers (Mayer 1984).[3] A large Pillai landowner in Iruvelpattu in Villupuram District, Tamil Nadu, who still dominated the village around 1980, found it extremely difficult to command labour 30 years later, due to the self-consciousness of the SCs and the proliferation of non-farm employment (Harriss et al. 2010).

A large number of village surveys corroborate the M village shift away from long-term contracts and the preference for day labour among agricultural workers. In Kumbapett village in Thanjavur District, the number of *pannaiyals* fell from 37 percent of male agricultural labourers to 9 percent between 1952 and 1976.[4] In Vadamalaipuram village in Ramnad (Ramanathapuram) District, there were already hardly any left in 1958, and they had disappeared by 1983. Even in 1958, 32 of 42 day labourers who were asked if they wanted to be *pannaiyals* answered in the negative, saying in the main that *pannaiyals* had no freedom and that there was no limit to the hours they had to work. As Athreya pointed out, the growth of non-farm employment in the village factored in their decision. He notes that the availability of casual labour in the local spinning mill and the match factories was much more attractive to workers (Athreya 1984, 94). The development of non-farm labour will be examined below, but it is clear from a large number of village surveys that it had become an increasingly viable option and was instrumental in furthering the independence of the lower castes. Athreya states that in Vadamalaipuram, "the emergence of employment opportunities in manufacturing has been a positive aid to the Thevar households in breaking out of their servitude to Naidu landlords". Greater employment in match factories and other industries led to a relative labour shortage and "this created a situation where the landowners could not muscle the labourers into submission when the Thevar households managed to move out of the cattle-sheds of landlords to huts near the main road" (Athreya 1984, 94, 24, 34–35).

In Tamil Nadu then, broadly speaking, the higher castes have undergone a loss of land and a weakening of their social and economic domination in villages. The lower castes, including the SCs, have conversely experienced an improved socio-economic position through land acquisition and a clearer sense of independence. Whether other states followed this trajectory must be explored next.

The village of Karimpur in western Uttar Pradesh, the subject of many studies since it was first surveyed by William and Charlotte Wiser in the 1920s, despite some differences, displays long-term trends that resemble those in Tamil Nadu. In 1925, Karimpur was under the *zamindari* system and Brahmins possessed 74.3 percent of the land, primarily in the form of tenancy rights. In 1984, following the land reforms, this figure fell to 58.1 percent of cultivated land. The role of agriculture in the village economy had contracted considerably, and many villagers were employed in non-agricultural work. "Many landowning families see shops as a way of employing educated sons while adding a small amount to the family's income".[5] The land lost by Brahmins was transferred to members of lower castes, and poorer, landless villagers looked to outside jobs in large numbers.

> "The number of men whose primary occupation involved labour outside Karimpur has risen dramatically since 1975, from 2 to 84 [in 1984]. These men drive rickshaws, carry bags of grain for mills, load brick kilns, unload trucks, work in construction".

With greater outside employment, the lower classes in the village were able to make a living without having to depend on the landed classes; "The Chamars, who in 1925 were essentially bonded labourers, were freed of their servitude". In an interview, a group of men from a poor background said, "Now we are free, we do not have to work for them [the Brahmins] because we can go outside, we are educated and know our rights". The segment of the population living below the subsistence level had markedly declined since 1975, and Brahmin political superiority was "melting away" (Wadley and Derr 1989, 110, 106, 113, 114).

Palanpur is another village in western Uttar Pradesh which has been surveyed over five decades. Similar changes have occurred there to Karimpur, though they have not been as striking. The village is dominated by the upper-caste Thakurs who are the principal landowners. Their land is slowly being redistributed among other castes, and their economic power is steadily faltering. In their place, the position of the lower-caste Muraos, who had cultivated the land in the past as their tenants, has risen. This is largely due to their skilled farming techniques, their ongoing investment and the benefits they have obtained through the new technology of the Green Revolution. Thus the abolition of the *zamindari* system and the Green Revolution were key to the reversal of position between the Thakurs and the Muraos. Though the socio-economic position of the SC Jatabs and others cannot be said to have improved, their self-confidence has risen and caste discrimination has lessened. For example, the Thakurs can no longer strike Jatabs as they wish or force them to work without wages (Drèze and Sen 2002).[6]

The same situation – defined by the decline of traditional landowners and the rise of the backward castes, increased self-confidence among tenants and labourers and improved wages – can also be found in Bihar, where the strong influence of the old landlords has been noted. According to A. N. Sharma, from colonial times the preeminent landowning castes have been the Bhumiyars, Brahmins, Rajputs and Kayasthas (all designated forward castes) and they control the villages. The *zamindari* system was abolished as part of the land reform after Independence, but the ceiling and tenancy legislation had little effect and the upper-caste landholders continued to overshadow village society.

> "The biggest landholder in the village exercised an unchallenged authority over other villagers and continued to be consulted on issues like determination of local agricultural wages, rights in land and other matters related to the conduct of [the] community's business" .
>
> (Sharma 2005, 963)

However, the agricultural population did not remain static. The land reforms, tenants' movements that were supported by the Communist Party of India (CPI) and the influence of government officials and political workers connected to the agricultural development programmes exposed the poor peasants to what had been happening elsewhere, and "[b]y the mid-1960s, [the peasants] had become aware of their rights, and the circumstances which denied them the same". Significant changes also came about in the course of the Green Revolution. Three upper-middle castes, the Yadav, Koeri and Kurmi (designated OBC), considerably improved their economic position. "These three castes have been the major beneficiaries of the so-called Green Revolution in Bihar.... These sturdy and hardy castes, traditionally engaged in cultivation, have managed to produce more from cultivation than their upper caste counterparts" (Sharma 2005, 964).

Twelve villages in Bihar were surveyed in 1981–1982 and again in 1999–2000. The results largely agree with the trends noted above. As Table 6.3 shows, the percentage of upper-caste households selling land was much greater than those buying it, while the percentage buying land was high among Yadav and lower-caste households. In terms of class, big peasant and landlord households sold much more land than they bought. An analysis of the changes in land ownership according to caste based on a number of surveys of Bihar villages made between 1971 and 2001 confirms that this

*Table 6.3* Percentage of households and average size of selling and buying land, 1999–2000

| | | *Percentage of households selling land* | *Average land sold (acres)* | *Percentage of households purchasing land* | *Average and purchased (acres)* |
|---|---|---|---|---|---|
| Caste | | | | | |
| | Brahmin+Kayastha | 26.51 | 1.22 | 7.83 | 1.34 |
| | Bhumihar+Rajput | 30.68 | 0.93 | 9.09 | 0.85 |
| | Kurmi | 17.86 | 0.24 | 17.86 | 0.76 |
| | Koeri | 10.00 | 0.40 | 3.33 | 0.62 |
| | Yadav | 9.62 | 0.33 | 13.46 | 0.95 |
| | Other backward II | 9.72 | 0.73 | 11.11 | 0.62 |
| | Backward I | 5.16 | 0.53 | 10.97 | 0.64 |
| | Scheduled castes | 1.99 | 0.20 | 4.48 | 0.52 |
| | Muslim | 13.13 | 0.92 | 9.09 | 1.09 |
| Class | | | | | |
| | Agricultural labour | 3.50 | 0.69 | 4.04 | 0.23 |
| | Poor middle peasants | 15.38 | 0.38 | 15.38 | 0.41 |
| | Middle peasants | 17.54 | 0.27 | 17.54 | 0.98 |
| | Big peasants | 24.52 | 1.00 | 13.55 | 1.13 |
| | Landlords | 29.73 | 1.03 | 12.84 | 1.17 |
| | Non-agriculturists | 5.22 | 0.72 | 5.97 | 0.29 |
| Total | | 13.02 | 0.90 | 8.64 | 0.05 |

Source: Sharma 2005, Table 1.

movement from upper to middle and lower castes, including SCs, was happening in many villages (Sinha 2009).

The lives of agricultural labourers were evidently evolving too. One third of them in 1981–1982 were employed on long-term contracts ("attached labour"), but this had fallen to less than 10 percent in 2000, while the percentage of casual workers increased. Real wages rose everywhere, from 50 to 100 percent in various villages (Sharma 2005, 967; Sharma 1995). Sharma considers this rise to be due to worker struggles or migration. He finds that migration occurs among both upper and lower castes; for the latter, it enables them "to break loose of the existing caste taboos". Only 15 percent of migrant workers are employed in agriculture; in the main they work in construction, small manufacturing and brick kilns, or as rickshaw pullers and so on. The survey reported that 40 percent of households had at least one migrant and most received remittances from them. Remittances are an important income source; Sharma notes that they make up nearly one third of the total household income and that the proportion is much higher among the landless and small landholder. He also points out that peasant movements have achieved a rise in wages in areas under their influence and have worked to keep the land reform agenda alive.

> If a substantial portion of the surplus land was acquired in Bihar in the mid-1970s, it was largely due to the pressure generated by the movement launched by poor peasant organisations. It is well documented that the sharecoppers' organised movement ... has done much to give them security of tenure and raise their share of the produce.
>
> (Sharma 2005, 970)

Such movements have also helped eliminate several forms of exploitation in the rural labour market; for example, they have been effective in areas under their influence in reducing forced labour (*begar*) by, and atrocities against, women.

Changes in labour relations are well illustrated by the appearance of upper-caste men ploughing their own land, "which was unheard of some years ago". Sharma comments that

> the upper caste peasants, who have lost their land to the point where the land cannot produce a surplus, find themselves in a dilemma as a member of the upper caste. They cannot meet wage demands nor take to the plough for fear of caste opprobrium. However in recent years a significant trend towards ploughing and other menial agricultural activities on the part of poor upper caste males appears to be emerging.

Educated landowners by contrast generally migrate to urban areas to seek work, rather than attempting to continue running their farms (Sharma 2005, 965).[7]

Reports from rural villages in Gujarat transmit a comparable situation; since the 1970s there has been a reduction in the predominance of the upper castes in landownership and a rise in the standing of medium and lower castes and tribal groups (Streefkerk 2006, 44). Moulik and Moulik traced the changes in the structure of landholding in Gujarat between 1961 and 1981 as follows. In 1961/62, a little over one third of rural households were landless or marginal farmers, controlling a bare 0.47 percent of the cultivable land, while households who operated large and very large farms controlled 48 percent of the cultivable area. After 1970/71, landless and marginal farmers fell to less than a quarter of rural households and their landownership showed a three- to fourfold increase. In the same period, households of small farmers increased to nearly half the total number of households, and the area of their holdings from 8.3 to around 30 percent in 1970/71 and 40 percent in 1980/81. On the other hand, households with large and very large holdings decreased in terms of both their percentage within the total number of households and the percentage of the area owned: Between 1960/61 and 1980/81 landholdings fell dramatically from 48.39 to 9.37 percent. The great structural change in the pattern of landownership in Gujarat over these two decades may be explained in part by the deliberate manipulation of the land registers, but a central role was undeniably played by the Green Revolution technologies and by the land reforms (Moulik and Moulik 1996).

Concerning Maharashtra state, Donald D. Atwood has highlighted long-term changes between the 1920s and 1970s based on a series of surveys of villages in Pune district. In the 1930s, village society was divided into three classes. The lowest consisted of what are now the scheduled castes and middle-status low castes like the handicraft and service castes, below cultivator castes. On average these castes possessed only miniscule plots of land. The middle class were non-elite Marathas and other cultivator castes, and the upper class were elite Marathas and higher castes, who were the major landowners. Later, this structure altered immensely. Large farmers reduced their holdings and land moved to the ownership of the former landless class. The greatest decline was among the higher castes, and even the elite Marathas experienced a slight fall in standing. Other agricultural castes and lesser Maratha households increased their landholdings. The lowest class fell slightly, in terms of the land it held. Some of the educated among the lower castes found non-farm work and some of their members purchased land. Though large numbers of migrant workers flowed into the area, real wages of agricultural labourers rose amid expanding employment both within and without agriculture. The structure of village society could not be considered egalitarian, but opportunities for socio-economic advancement differentiated it from when caste had wholly determined status.

Surveys of two villages in the arid zone of western Rajasthan made in 1963–1966 and 1982–1984 revealed that poor households had gained substantial economic independence from the wealthy landowning class over the period. Though the per capita income rose between the two surveys, when it was deflated some households (around 27 percent) were shown to have suffered a loss in real income. Table 6.4 gives details of these households. Most of them were from the poorest class; therefore, it uses indicators of poverty to show improved economic status. Most households had decreased their reliance on the dominant class over the period, with households with one or more family members working as attached/semi-attached labour falling from 37 to 7 percent, and households residing on the patron's land or in his yard falling from 31 to zero. Like in Tamil Nadu and other states, the lower classes

*Table 6.4* Indicators of declining reliance on patrons (rich people) in villages in western Rajasthan

| | *1963–66* | *1982–84* |
|---|---|---|
| Households with one or more family members working as attached/semi-attached labour | 37 | 7 |
| Households residing on patron's land/yard | 31 | 0 |
| Households resorting to off-season borrowing of foodgrain from patrons | 77 | 26 |
| Households taking seed-loan from patrons | 34 | 9 |
| Households marketing farm produce only through patrons | 86 | 23 |
| Households taking loans from others besides patrons | 13 | 47 |

Source: Jodha 1989, Table III, p. 186.

had become much less dependent on the upper classes as their economic independence grew.

Real income might have fallen in the period between the surveys, but poor households had managed to obtain more stable livelihoods, reducing the amount of income fluctuation over the year, improving their family situation and achieving a rise in their level of consumption. Table 6.5 shows that the same households no longer resorted to low-paying jobs like food, fuel and fodder gathering, and helping with fencing on the same scale.

As Table 6.12 tells us, in the same period increasing numbers of households consumed vegetables and sugar at meals, while those where adults skipped a third meal during summer, when food was in short supply, fell from 86 to 20 percent. Further, the proportion of households where woman and children regularly wore shoes leapt from zero to 86 percent. The living environment also seriously improved. Families living in houses of a *katcha* structure (thatched with mud walls) declined from 91 to 34 percent, those living in houses of a *pucca* structure (tiled roof, brick walls) grew from 9 to 52 percent, and houses with separate provision for people and animals increased from 6 to 52 percent. This is an indicator that economic independence of the poor from the powerful and wealthy class in the village had been achieved accompanied by a significant rise in the quality of life.[8] Jodha suggests that possible ingredients in these changes include the introduction of new varieties, double-cropping, the growth of milk marketing, more off-season employment and institutional reforms that have helped people get land, including house plots, and reduced indebtedness.

*Table 6.5* Economic stability of poor households in villages in western Rajasthan

| | *1963–66* | *1982–84* |
|---|---|---|
| Households engaged in food gathering | 100 | 20 |
| Households engaged in fuel gathering | 100 | 63 |
| Households engaged in fodder gathering | 100 | 23 |
| Households having members engaged in part-time petty jobs like helping with fencing | 100 | 23 |
| Households with members seasonally out-migrating for jobs | 34 | 11 |
| Households withdrawing their children from school to help in busy agricultural periods | 17 | 6 |
| Households selling over 80 percent of their marketed produce during the post-harvest period | 100 | 46 |
| Households retaining up to 25 percent of surplus for sale up to the next rainy season | 0 | 6 |
| Households purchasing key provisions like chillies, onions and oil in bulk | 0 | 6 |
| Households relying on day-to-day petty purchases for key provisions like chillies, onions and oil | 100 | 51 |
| Households making cash purchases during the slack season, festivals, etc. | 6 | 51 |
| Households possessing ready cash up to Rs 200 or more at home during the slack season | 0 | 26 |

Source: Compiled from Jodha 1989, Tables IV and V.

These surveys in Rajasthan are highly significant.[9] They clearly show the close connection between the lower-class march towards social and economic independence from village elites and the enhanced stability and quality of their economic life, as in other states. The instrumental role played by tenancy rights and land acquisition, made possible by land reforms and the policy of granting wasteland to the landless, is again evident, as is the impact of greater opportunities for non-farm employment, including migrant work abroad, upon the self-reliance, economic stability and negotiating power of the lower classes. The rural villages in many of India's most important states therefore share a number of points in common in terms of the direction of social change they have experienced, despite differences in time and degree.

## The Growth of Non-Farm Employment and Rises in the Wages of Agricultural Labourers

The relationship between the growth of non-farm employment opportunities and shifts in village social structure has been touched upon, but it deserves further consideration. Non-farm work expanded rapidly after 1970 for residents of M village, and similar other examples have been widely reported. According to A. Vaidyanathan (1994b, 3152–53), while the decade between the end of the 1970s and the close of the 1980s witnessed stagnation in traditional rural industries like hand spinning, leather and earthenware,

> there have been significant increases in bidi-making, [the] food industry, textile products, and non-metallic mineral products other than earthenware. One of the largest increases has been in repair shops. Estimated employment of rural workers in relatively modern industries, like rubber, plastic, chemical and metal products has also risen, in several cases faster than the total employment in the industry.

Vaidyanathan also reports increases in employment in construction in many areas, and comments,

> No doubt the rapid growth in employment … [in] non-metallic products (probably brick-making) responds to the growth in rural demand, partly from higher incomes and partly shifting customer preferences. The growth of employment in repairs is directly related to the phenomenal increase in the stock of modern mechanical, electrical and electronic equipment used for transport, agriculture and domestic use. With improved transport, it is conceivable that more and more industries … are finding it economical, and even attractive, to locate in rural areas. Part of the increases in the number of rural workers in manufacturing may also reflect a growing tendency for workers in urban industry to commute from their residence in nearby villages
>
> (*op. cit.* 3153)

Vaidyanathan calculates that nearly 70 percent of those in non-farm employment work in the informal sector. P. Hazell and S. Haggblade too state that as of 1991, the non-farm sector in rural villages provided 20 percent of regular employment and one third of income in agricultural areas (Hazell and Haggblade 1991). As a result, the proportion of people working in various occupations in the non-agricultural sector has mounted, even among those resident in rural villages (Unni 1998).

In the 1980s, increases in employment were greater in primary than secondary industry, while those in tertiary industry were even larger. Non-farm employment in rural regions chiefly grew in the manufacturing and service areas of the informal sector, fostering a shift in the male labour force from farming to this type of work. As a result, the female labour force in farm employment has expanded. Peter Lanjouw reports that as of 1993/94, 34 percent of all households in rural villages received income from the non-farm sector. Income from cultivation comprised 55 percent and that from agricultural wages was 8 percent (Lanjouw 1994). Andrew Foster and Mark Rosenzweig state, based on data from 250 villages in different parts of India, that in 1999, 48.1 percent of rural village income derived from non-farm employment (Foster and Rosenzweig 2004). Peter Lanjouw and Rinku Murgai point out that in most states in India, earnings from the non-farm sector provides almost half the income of rural households. Increased female employment in general has also probably inflated the number of wage-earners in each household (Hansda and Ray 2006). It can therefore be said that sectorial linkages between agriculture, manufacturing and the service industry have reached a new stage in that work in the latter industries is now integral in terms of the livelihood of rural households.

In the case of village M, a resurvey in 2007 revealed that 80 percent of Pillai-Chettiar households were mainly in non-farm employment, as were about half of the residents living in Block 1, mostly occupied by Muthurajas. This came to 63 percent if those employed in non-farm work as a sideline are included. In Block 5, where mainly SCs lived, a little under 60 percent of households worked chiefly in non-farm employment; when non-farm work as a sideline is included, the figure comes to close to 70 percent. Since the village is close to the city, the proportion is high compared with other villages, but compared to results of the survey taken in 1980, the importance of non-farm employment is impressive.

Scholars are not necessarily of one opinion concerning the factors influencing the rise in rural non-agricultural employment. A. Vaidyanathan suggests they include the introduction of machinery, changes in consumption patterns of rural households and improved transport and points out that "there is no strong association between growth of foodgrain production and changes in the ratio of non-agricultural to agricultural employment" (Vaidyanathan 1986, A-145). P. Hazell and S. Haggblade assert that agricultural growth has in the first place led to growth in the rural non-farm economy. They estimate the change in non-farm production resulting from a one-rupee rise in agricultural income to be Rs 0.37 in villages and nearby towns. Indirect income growth reaches Rs 0.54 when the feedback effect is added. However, the multipliers are not fixed and go up according to agricultural growth.

> Increased agricultural output stimulates forward production linkages by providing raw materials that require milling, processing and distribution by nonfarm firms. Consumption linkages arise when growing farmer incomes boost demand for basic consumer goods; these typically increase over time as rising per capita income induces diversification of consumption spending into nonfoods.

Further, "the multipliers are bigger for small- to medium-sized farms than for very large farms" (Hazell and Haggblade 1991, 47–48).[10]

According to Ajit Kanitkar, the non-farm sector was growing at a rate of 5.4 percent per annum at the beginning of the 1990s. An empirical study undertaken in 1992 of 86 entrepreneurs belonging to 22 villages from 7 states revealed that they belonged mainly to the middle class of village society and above. When they began, many offered traditional products and services in the local economic environment, like tea shops, paan shops, grocery shops, repair shops and tailoring and hair-cutting shops, but others also moved into areas such as a typewriting class, and brick and clay-tile manufacturing. Seventy percent of them employed non-family members. Such examples tell us that the expansion of non-farm employment in villages took place against a backdrop of the growth and diversification of rural consumption and was closely connected with the development and growth of agricultural production.

Other explanations have been offered for the growth in non-farm employment: The move away from agriculture in villages close to urban centres, the urbanisation of villages and the influence of urban areas;[11] improvements in infrastructure like roads and the extension of education; and the significance of government-led public undertakings. Certainly, though, agricultural expansion following the Green Revolution was a vital prerequisite condition in the growing momentum of non-farm economic activity.[12]

Research has shown that as the rural labour market tightened with the growth in employment and economic activities within the non-farm sector, the real wages of farm labourers improved. The rise in the real wage rate in agriculture and in the average agricultural wage, beginning in the middle of the 1970s, was substantial. Table 6.6 clearly shows the growth in average daily wage income among casual and regular workers in both agricultural and non-agricultural labour. Table 6.7 confirms that this trajectory continued for casual workers from 1983. A survey of the village of Iruvelpattu in Tamil Nadu conducted in 1981 revealed that the rates for "coolie" labour were equivalent to about 3.5 kg of paddy for men and 1.75 kg of paddy for women. A wage level of 3 kg of paddy per day has traditionally been the norm. In 2008, men were receiving an equivalent of 6–8 kg per day, and women 3–3.5 kg. "In real terms agricultural wage rates have roughly doubled, moving well beyond the long-run historic mean" (Harriss et al. 2010, 55).

*Table 6.6* Trends in average daily earnings of different categories of wage labourer (Rs/day at 1960/61 prices)

| | *Adult males* | | | *Adult females* | | |
|---|---|---|---|---|---|---|
| | *1977/78* | *1983* | *1987/88* | *1977/78* | *1983* | *1987/88* |
| Regular | | | | | | |
| Agriculture | | | | | | |
| Rural | 1.21 | 1.44 | 2.24 | 1.22 | 1.83 | 1.64 |
| Non-agriculture | | | | | | |
| Rural | 3.25 | 3.08 | 5.37 | 2.49 | 2.08 | 4.04 |
| Urban | 4.70 | 4.46 | 5.85 | 3.07 | 3.26 | 4.85 |
| Casual | | | | | | |
| Agriculture | | | | | | |
| Rural | 1.18 | 1.38 | 1.73 | 0.82 | 0.94 | 1.14 |
| Non-agriculture | | | | | | |
| Rural | 1.63 | 1.98 | 2.42 | 0.88 | 0.98 | 1.40 |
| Urban | 2.05 | 2.05 | 2.49 | 0.97 | 1.00 | 1.34 |

Source: Vaidyanathan 1994b, Table 7, p. 3,150.

*Table 6.7* Real Wages of Casual Labourers in India (at 1999–2000 prices)

| | | *Wage rate (Rs)* | | | |
|---|---|---|---|---|---|
| | | *1983* | *1987/88* | *1993/94* | *1999/2000* |
| Agriculture | Males | 25.72 | 31.47 | 34.27 | 40.45 |
| | Females | 17.44 | 20.80 | 23.99 | 28.56 |
| Non-agriculture | Males | 38.05 | 44.04 | 47.94 | 59.52 |
| | Females | 18.19 | 25.51 | 27.62 | 37.29 |

Source: Bhalla et al. 2006, Table 3.12, p. 107.

The rise in wage rates of agricultural labourers does not necessarily translate into a better annual income. Mechanisation has eliminated a significant amount of farm employment. It is estimated that in Iruvelpattu in 1981, the average employment for men and women was 180 days a year, while in 2010 it was of the order of 100–120 days. In 1981, the annual income of an agricultural labouring couple would have been around 900 kg paddy. The equivalent in 2010 was estimated at the order of 1,000–1,100 kg. This does not go beyond the poverty line. However, as the doubling of real wages shows, advances in the standard of living have been made over 25 years, due to better employment opportunities for higher wages outside local farms.

Some see a trend towards a rise in real wage rates for Indian agricultural labourers in the 1950s and 1960s (Lal 1976), but other scholars have differing views.[13] The remarkable rise witnessed from the middle of the 1970s has high significance in terms of Indian agricultural growth, since such labourers comprised the bulk of the village population and were moreover the core of the rural poor. Many researchers agree that it contributed greatly to eradicating poverty in villages.[14]

Rises in labour wage rates in a village are connected to the expansion of opportunities in non-farm employment there. The study by Peter Lanjouw and Abusaleh Shariff sees a strong and positive relationship between rising agricultural wage rates and the share of village employment in construction activities (Lanjouw and Shariff 2004, 4443). Whether or not the Green Revolution brought about an increased demand for agricultural labour is unclear, since cases from different regions do not necessarily show consistency. However, there is no doubt that the growth of non-farm employment both within and outside the villages siphoned labourers away from farming and led to a rise in the agricultural wage (Unni 1998; Lanjouw and Shariff 2004; Lanjouw and Murgai 2009; Hansda and Ray 2006). The research also shows a correlation between rising agricultural wages and rising labour productivity in farming, indicating that technological developments in agriculture were also connected to them.

While it can be said that agricultural development following the Green Revolution stimulated economic activity in the non-farm sector, expanding the demand for lower class labour from the agricultural sector, and also brought about a sharp rise in wages through raising labour productivity, such "economic" changes do not convey the full picture. We cannot overlook what lay behind them – changes in the social relationships among the various classes of village society, with the weakening of the village hierarchical structure that had underpinned economic and social life and the growing socio-economic power of the lower classes and their sense of independence.

Chapter 1 outlined how in South India at the beginning of the twentieth century, the landholding upper-caste elites controlled village life economically and socially. Many landless, low-class agricultural labourers were employed as attached workers. Employers dictated working conditions, including wages, in the village, and attempted to stop workers migrating overseas by threats to evict them from their homes. In Bihar too, even after Independence, village elites had the power to set wages (Section 2). However, this hierarchical power has been lost all over India in the past few decades. Lower-class villagers like agricultural labourers and tenants joined movements and found their social consciousness raised, leading to a large reduction in long-term employment and an increase in casual labour. The Chamars of Uttar Pradesh, who had been virtually bonded labourers, were released and were able to go outside to work. Here the movements of lower-class workers played a vital role. In Bihar, the involvement of the lower classes in struggles, and their migration for work, were intrinsic ingredients in the achievement of higher wage levels (Sharma 2005).

The relationship between hierarchy and wage rates is further illuminated by the case of Iruvelpattu, where, despite a rise in real income in terms of kg paddy after 1980, the power of the dominant landholders, the Reddis, still remained strong, making wages here lower than in the neighbouring villages. A man in an adjacent village would receive Rs 5 for his work, but a man from Iruvelpattu only Rs 4. This was because there was a dominant employer in the village who could keep wages down. He managed his workers through five supervisors. When there was talk of a strike, he imported labour from outside the village for the harvest, and he continued to hold to his lower wages (Guhan and Mencher 1983, II, 1068). From around 1980, though, there were greater stirrings for independence among SC members, and one young man organised an Ambedkar Sangham, seeking schools and house sites for the SCs, an adequate drinking water supply, repairs to their temple, a crèche and adult education. These demands were presented to the Collector. The caste village is located on Reddi-owned land but the landowner has stood in the way of giving the SCs houseplots or anything that would make them more self-reliant. In 2008, large landowners complained of labour shortages and labour troubles, which Harriss et al. (2010) ascribe not only to changing attitudes among the SCs but also to wages rising beyond historic levels. In this sense, we should understand that wage rises for agricultural labourers are the result of the long-term daily and non-daily struggles of the lower classes for independence.

## The Development of the Rural Markets

### *Rural Regions as Markets for the Industrial and Service Sectors*

In the process described above, rural society expanded as a market for the industrial and service sectors. Real wage rises for agricultural labourers, the poorest class in rural society, of course, allowed their household income to rise steadily. The work they did in non-farm industries in the locality was largely casual, with low, precarious wages, but as we have seen in the case of M village, it greatly raised the earnings of the village lower classes. A long-term survey of villages in Tamil Nadu between 1973 and 1994 showed that the real income of farm worker households increased 2.8 times in that period (Harriss-White and Janakarajan, 2004). It is questionable whether or not other areas experienced such a rise, but Table 6.8, which studies changes in monthly per capita consumer expenditure according to class for all of India, shows that between 1972/73 and 2004, the lower three classes of the decile groups enlarged their consumer expenditure between 40 and 50 percent, a rate of increase that was a little higher than in classes above them. Landholding classes and others certainly also improved their income with the rise in productivity in the wake of the Green Revolution and from non-farm income (Table 6.8). Foster and Rosenzweig, who analysed data from 250 villages all around India, demonstrate that there was a 70 percent increase in real per capita earnings between 1982 and 1999 (Foster and Rosenzweig 2004). Since the rural population grew 47 percent in this period, this represents a gross income increase of around 2.5 times for rural areas.[15]

The percentage (Engel's coefficient) spent on food in rural households decreased little by little over time: 73 percent in 1972/73, 65 percent in 1983, 63 percent in 1993, 59 percent in 1999/2000 and 55 percent in 2003/04. Expenditure on non-food products and services consequently went up.[16] As

*Table 6.8* Monthly per capita consumer expenditure (at 1972/72 prices) by select decile groups: rural and urban India

| *Decile group* | *1972/73* | *1977/78* | *1983* | *1987/88* | *1993/94* | *1999/00* | *2004/05* | *Increase (%) between 1972/73 and 2004/05* |
|---|---|---|---|---|---|---|---|---|
| | | | | rural India | | | | |
| 0–10 | 16.26 | 16.92 | 19.18 | 22.05 | 22.69 | 26.45 | 25.76 | 58.41 |
| 10–20 | 22.70 | 23.97 | 26.46 | 29.36 | 30.26 | 34.13 | 33.59 | 47.97 |
| 20–30 | 26.90 | 28.89 | 31.47 | 34.39 | 34.69 | 39.32 | 38.65 | 43.68 |
| 30–40 | 30.86 | 31.83 | 34.83 | 38.28 | 39.34 | 44.21 | 43.61 | 41.33 |
| 40–50 | 35.56 | 36.80 | 40.65 | 42.71 | 43.82 | 48.86 | 48.58 | 36.61 |
| 0–100 | 44.17 | 48.90 | 50.67 | 55.09 | 54.98 | 59.69 | 63.08 | 42.80 |
| | | | | urban India | | | | |
| 0–10 | 21.9 | 21.0 | 23.4 | 24.3 | 25.9 | 30.2 | 28.5 | 29.9 |
| 10–20 | 29.9 | 29.8 | 32.0 | 32.9 | 35.8 | 40.6 | 38.8 | 29.7 |
| 20–30 | 36.1 | 35.7 | 38.0 | 38.6 | 42.7 | 48.4 | 46.8 | 29.7 |
| 30–40 | 38.4 | 40.9 | 46.0 | 44.0 | 48.8 | 56.1 | 54.9 | 43.0 |
| 40–50 | 48.5 | 46.8 | 49.0 | 51.1 | 56.3 | 64.7 | 64.4 | 32.7 |
| 0–100 | 63.3 | 65.3 | 68.6 | 71.4 | 77.0 | 89.1 | 92.4 | 46.0 |

Source: M.H. Suryanarayanan, Nutritional Norms for Poverty: Issues and Implications, Concept paper prepared for the Expert Group to Review the Methodology for Estimation of Poverty, Planning Committee, Government of India, New Delhi, 2009 (Table 4.2, p. 29).

Original source: Suryanarayanan 2009 estimates based on corresponding NSS estimates at current prices (GoI, 1979a, 1986a, 1986b, 1991, 1996a, 2001a & 2006b) and deflators implicit in the official poverty lines. Poverty lines from 1977/78 till 2004/05 are GoI estimates and corresponding estimates for 1972/73 are from Tendulkar et al. (2009).

Table 6.9 shows, food expenditure in rural areas increased 2.36 times between 1972 and 2003/04, equalling the rate of growth among the urban population. It is noticeable that the growth rate was particularly high among the poorest rural classes.

Based on the table, we can calculate annual expenditures on non-food items like manufactured products and services in both city and country. Table 6.10 shows the distribution of non-food expenditure in India, comparing rural and urban populations by selected years. Until the beginning of the 1990s, rural areas spent more than 60 percent of gross expenditure on manufactured items and services, though this declined slightly in the course of the 1990s. Non-food expenditure by the top 20 percent group of the urban population, which we may view as representing the urban middle classes, ranged from 18 to 23 per cent, only about half that of the non-elite rural population. Though the former have been considered the major consumer group leading economic growth since the 1980s, the latter have also been pivotal as an important consumer group forming a core market in rural areas for the industrial and service sectors and supporting their high growth.

Research therefore suggests that agriculture and rural society were integral to the growth of the industrial and service sectors. N. Ganesh Kumar's work

*Table 6.9* Monthly per capita expenditure on non-food items according to class, with changes

| | *Non-food expenditure (at 1972/3 prices, Rs)* | | | | | *Non-food expenditure index (1972/73=100)* | | | | |
|---|---|---|---|---|---|---|---|---|---|---|
| | *1972/73* | *1983* | *1993/94* | *1999/00* | *2004/05* | *1972/73* | *1983* | *1993/94* | *1999/00* | *2004/05* |
| | | | rural | | | | | rural | | |
| 0–10 | 2.8 | 4.4 | 6.1 | 8.7 | 8.3 | 100 | 155 | 215 | 307 | 293 |
| 10–20 | 4.0 | 6.4 | 8.2 | 11.6 | 11.3 | 100 | 159 | 204 | 288 | 282 |
| 20–30 | 5.0 | 7.9 | 9.6 | 13.8 | 13.6 | 100 | 159 | 192 | 278 | 274 |
| 30–40 | 5.9 | 9.0 | 11.2 | 15.6 | 15.7 | 100 | 151 | 189 | 263 | 264 |
| 40–50 | 7.3 | 11.0 | 13.0 | 17.7 | 18.0 | 100 | 151 | 178 | 242 | 246 |
| 50–60 | 8.1 | 13.3 | 15.0 | 20.3 | 20.9 | 100 | 165 | 186 | 252 | 260 |
| 60–70 | 10.8 | 15.2 | 18.0 | 23.4 | 24.5 | 100 | 140 | 167 | 216 | 226 |
| 70–80 | 12.5 | 19.8 | 21.9 | 27.6 | 29.9 | 100 | 158 | 175 | 220 | 238 |
| 80–90 | 18.0 | 27.7 | 29.5 | 35.8 | 39.9 | 100 | 154 | 164 | 199 | 222 |
| 90–100 | 45.7 | 60.6 | 70.1 | 67.8 | 101.4 | 100 | 133 | 153 | 149 | 222 |
| Total | 12.0 | 17.5 | 20.3 | 24.2 | 28.4 | 100 | 146 | 169 | 202 | 236 |
| | | | urban | | | | | urban | | |
| 0–10 | 4.4 | 6.4 | 7.6 | 10.9 | 10.3 | 100 | 145 | 173 | 247 | 234 |
| 10–20 | 6.5 | 9.2 | 11.0 | 15.5 | 15.5 | 100 | 142 | 169 | 240 | 240 |
| 20–30 | 8.3 | 11.7 | 13.9 | 19.4 | 20.0 | 100 | 142 | 168 | 234 | 242 |
| 30–40 | 9.0 | 15.2 | 16.6 | 23.9 | 24.5 | 100 | 168 | 184 | 264 | 272 |
| 40–50 | 13.0 | 16.6 | 20.3 | 28.2 | 30.7 | 100 | 128 | 156 | 217 | 236 |
| 50–60 | 14.4 | 20.3 | 24.6 | 34.5 | 37.9 | 100 | 141 | 171 | 240 | 264 |
| 60–70 | 19.8 | 28.3 | 30.5 | 42.3 | 47.7 | 100 | 143 | 154 | 213 | 241 |
| 70–80 | 24.3 | 33.0 | 40.2 | 53.5 | 59.9 | 100 | 136 | 165 | 220 | 246 |
| 80–90 | 36.9 | 48.1 | 55.8 | 73.2 | 84.2 | 100 | 130 | 151 | 198 | 228 |
| 90–100 | 88.3 | 106.7 | 129.0 | 161.3 | 200.7 | 100 | 121 | 146 | 183 | 227 |
| Total | 22.5 | 29.6 | 34.9 | 46.3 | 53.1 | 100 | 131 | 155 | 206 | 236 |

Source: Compiled from Suryanarayanan 2009, Tables 4.1, 4.2, 4.3.

*Table 6.10* Expenditure on non-food consumption (urban and rural) according to class (%)

| *decile* | *1972/73* | *1983* | *1993/94* | *1999/00* | *2004/05* |
|---|---|---|---|---|---|
| | | | rural | | |
| 0–90 | 42.2 | 42.9 | 41.0 | 41.5 | 37.3 |
| 90–100 | 25.9 | 22.7 | 21.7 | 16.1 | 20.8 |
| Total (rural) | 68.1 | 65.6 | 62.6 | 57.6 | 58.1 |
| | | | urban | | |
| 0–80 | 14.1 | 16.4 | 17.6 | 20.9 | 19.4 |
| 80–90 | 5.2 | 5.6 | 6.0 | 6.7 | 6.6 |
| 90–100 | 12.5 | 12.4 | 13.8 | 14.8 | 15.8 |
| Total (urban) | 31.9 | 34.4 | 37.4 | 42.4 | 41.9 |

Source: Calculated from Table 6.10.

Note: Ratio of rural population calculated on the assumption of 80 percent of the 1971 census for 1972/73, 76.3 percent of the 1981 census for 1983, 74.3 percent of the 1991 census for 1993/94 and 72.2 percent of the 2001 census for 1999/00 and 2004/05.

(referred to in the Introduction) revealed as early as 1992 that 1981/82 marked a turning point in the upward trend of the Indian GDP, and that a structural rupture seemed to have been triggered by a break in the growth rate of the primary sector, followed by the secondary and tertiary sectors (Kumar 1992). Balakrishnan and Parameshwaran confirm the role of the agrarian sector in growth acceleration (Balakrishnan et al. 2007), and, again, Ravindra H. Dholakia sees the application of modern agricultural inputs as key to the success of the agrarian sector (Dholakia 2007).

The analysis by Sastry et al. of the linkage of growth among the agricultural, industrial and service sectors of the economy, based on an input-output (I-O) equation and a simultaneous equation framework, exposes how the agricultural sector continued to lead the other sectors, mainly through consumer demand. As an illustration of production linkages between the three sectors, the units from industry necessary to produce one unit of agriculture increased from 0.043 in 1968/69 to 0.140 in 1993/94. On the other hand, for industry to produce one unit, the input requirement from agriculture fell sharply from 0.127 to 0.035 in the same time period. Concerning the impact of rural income on demand for manufactured products (demand linkage), the I-O tables show shifts in demand for manufactured products as a result of higher agrarian output (and associated rises in rural income). In 1968/69, a rise in demand in agriculture by one unit raised demand for manufactured goods by 0.087 units; in 1993/94, this more than trebled to 0.297 units. In the same time period, the demand for manufactured products as a result of industrial growth increased only slightly, from 1.562 to 1.704, while services almost doubled, from 0.237 to 0.457. This indicates the dependence of industry on the agriculture and service sectors was much greater in the 1990s than in the 1970s and 1980s. Sastry et al. then added regression equations to demonstrate three things:

That the linkages between the three sectors were strong, that increased agricultural output caused an increase in demand, in terms of both consumption and investment, for manufactured products, and that the increased production that resulted caused a higher in demand for services. This showed that the ripple effect is more effective in terms of overall economic growth than any direct influence. Specifically, a 1 percent fall in agricultural output brings about a fall in industrial output of 0.52 percent, causing a combined effect of a fall in the industrial sector that leads to a fall in the service sector of 0.24 percent. The drop in all three sectors resulted in a reduction of 0.52 percent in the growth of GDP. Similarly, a 1 percent decrease in industry and exports resulted in drops of 0.34 percent and 0.1 percent respectively.

Sastry et al. conclude their argument as follows. First,

> [d]espite the substantial increase in the share of the services sector in GDPR, the I-O tables suggested that the agricultural sector still plays an important role in determining the overall growth rate of the economy through its linkages to the other sectors. While in the 1960s the linkage was primarily through the production channel, during the 1990s, it translates primarily through the demand channel.

Second,

> though the share of agriculture in GDPR has declined, its contribution in terms of generating demand for the other sectors of the economy, especially the industrial sector, has become more pronounced, as reflected through the I-O Table 1993-94. Even now, the agricultural sector … supports approximately two-third[s] of the population in the country.
>
> (Sastry et al. 2003, p. 2396)

These agriculture-industry linkages that were formed in the 1980s continued into the 1990s.

### *The Rural Market through NCAER Surveys*

The expanded rural market for manufactured products and services was already being reported in large-scale surveys in the 1980s. Surveys of household finances conducted by the National Council of Applied Economic Research (NCAER) in 1985 and 1989 showed that the greatest growth for consumer durables was in the rural market, not the urban. There was a boom in the production and consumption of these products in the latter half of the 1980s and rural consumption, particularly among the low-income classes, swelled substantially. The class demanding consumer durables in rural areas was not the highly educated but those who were not university graduates, according to the surveys. Items in demand centred on wristwatches, bicycles and radios, and these came to permeate rural villages on a broad scale.

Better earnings among all classes there were a factor, but what is especially noteworthy is that consumer durable penetration was related to changing consumption patterns that were not proportionate with rising incomes.[17] The report presumed that there was a strong possibility of changes in consumption among lower-income earners (Rao 1994, 6). Between 1985 and 1989, households owning televisions increased three times, bicycles 1.6 times, radios 1.4 times, pressure cookers around doubled and watches 1.8 times. It commented that income distribution had improved more in rural than in urban areas.

The *Market Information Survey of Households, 1985-1996*, also carried out by NCAER, showed comparable trends. Among rural households, 71.7 percent owned 52.2 percent of consumer durables, with the rural market share greater than the urban and extended further (Natarajan 1998, 2). At the time, 16 percent of rural households owned black-and-white televisions (3 percent had colour televisions), even though only 34 percent of rural households had been electrified. This means that more than 50 percent of households in electrified areas possessed televisions. This reflects the rapid changes in consumption trends in Indian rural areas (ibid., 20). Ramaswamy (2002, 19) attests to the crucial importance of the rural market for consumer durables. Based on NSSO data that estimated the per capita household expenditure on consumer durables in 1993–1994 to be Rs 7.67 in rural areas and Rs 15.17 in urban areas, rural markets consumed 60 percent of the consumer durables (Table 6.11).

The NCAER and other surveys have shown the following:

(1) Rural areas provide the market for more than half of consumer durables and this market has been growing faster than its urban equivalent since the 1980s.
(2) Rural consumption of consumer durables initially centred on cheap items like bicycles, radios and watches, but more expensive items like televisions, fans and motor cycles progressively penetrated rural areas.
(3) Increased earnings in rural areas lie behind this growing consumption, and since the 1980s, income distribution has improved more in rural than urban areas, especially among low-income groups in villages.
(4) Low-income groups, including those who are not university graduates, show the greatest increase of expenditure on consumer durables of all the classes in rural society.
(5) It is assumed they are purchasing consumer durables beyond the bounds of their income.

### *Changing Consumption Patterns: Rajasthan*

N. S. Jodha has studied survey data from two villages in the arid zone of western Rajasthan to assess changes in poverty levels between 1962 and the 1980s. He has shown that great changes occurred in terms of consumption patterns, dwellings and travel, for example. Households with members travelling by paid transport increased, and a higher proportion consumed more

*Table 6.11* The rural market for consumer durables (%)

| *Rural market percentage* | *1989/90* | *1992/93* | *1995/96* | *1998/99* |
|---|---|---|---|---|
| Above 75% | Radio/ transistor radio | Bicycle, radio/ transistor radio | Bicycle, radio/ transistor radio, wristwatch (mechanical) | Bicycles, radio/ transistor radio, wristwatch (mechanical), black-and-white television |
| 50–75% | Bicycles, motor cycle, table fan, sewing machine, wristwatch (mechanical) | Table fan, sewing machines, wristwatch (mechanical), wristwatch (quartz) | Black-and-white television, cassette recorder, pressure cooker, table fan, sewing machine, wristwatch (quartz) | Cassette recorder, pressure cooker, table fan, ceiling fan, sewing machine, wristwatch (quartz), motor cycle |
| 30–50% | Moped, black-and-white television, cassette recorder, pressure cooker, ceiling fan, wrist-watch (quartz) | Moped, motor cycle, black-and-white television, colour television, cassette recorder, pressure cooker, electric iron, ceiling fan | Moped, motor cycle, electric iron | Moped, scooter, colour television, electric iron, mixer |
| 20–30% | Scooter, mixer | Scooter, mixer | Scooter, colour television, VCR/VCP | Refrigerator |
| 10–20% | Colour television, refrigerator | Refrigerator | Refrigerator | Refrigerator |
| 5–10% | Refrigerator | VCR/VCP, refrigerator | – | – |
| Below 5% | VCR/VCP | – | – | VCR/VCP |

Source: National Council of Applied Economic Research, India Market Demographics Report, 2002, Delhi.

and varied meals. Housing conditions onimproved remarkably, more women and children regularly wore shoes, and consumer durables such as radios, bicycles and quilts were slowly making their way into the poorest households (Table 6.12).[18]

*Table 6.12* Travel, consumption and housing among poor households in two villages in western Rajasthan (%)

| | *1963–66* | *1982–84* |
|---|---|---|
| Households with members who travel by paid transport more than twice a year outside the district | 17 | 78 |
| Households occasionally consuming green vegetables during the non-crop season | 0 | 100 |
| Households consuming curries, mainly made from cereals | 100 | 14 |
| Households consuming sugar regularly | 0 | 20 |
| Households consuming rice on non-festive occasions also | 0 | 14 |
| Households with adults skipping the third meal of the day during the summer (scarcity period) | 86 | 20 |
| Households where women and children wear shoes regularly | 0 | 86 |
| Households where maternity feeding to women is provided up to a month of more | 6 | 23 |
| Households having houses with a fully pucca structure | 0 | 14 |
| Households having houses with a partly pucca structure | 9 | 52 |
| Households having houses with only katcha structure | 91 | 34 |
| Households having houses with a gate with doors | 6 | 43 |
| Households having houses with a compound wall/ fence | 13 | 52 |
| Households having houses with separate provisions of stay for humans and animals | 6 | 52 |
| Households having houses with a private place for women (e.g. bathroom) | 0 | 23 |
| Households possessing quilts | 6 | 20 |

Source: Compiled from Jodha 1989, Tables V, VI and VII.

Note: A pukka structure has walls and roof made of brick, stone, cement, concrete, tiles, timber, etc. A katcha structure is made of mud, bamboo, grass, leaves, reeds, thatch, unbaked brick, etc.

### *M Village in 2007: Consumer Durables, Housing, Education, Pilgrimage, Weddings*

M village in Tiruchirapalli District, Tamil Nadu, surveyed in 1980, was resurveyed in 2007. Over the 30 years, much had altered in terms of consumption and in the demand for manufactured products and services. Consumer durables had more or less become an expected part of villagers' lives. As Table 6.13 shows, more than half owned televisions, radios, bicycles, fans, and mobile telephones, and 15 to 30 percent had motorbikes. The NCAER survey confirmed the penetration of consumer durables into rural areas but did not mention connections with the different communities. In the survey of M village, however, it is clear that even in the blocks where the SCs lived, these consumer durables proliferated, with 15 percent owning a motorbike. Significantly, there was no great difference between SC households and other communities in terms of the range of items owned.

Most houses were now brick with a pucca structure and with tiled or concrete roofs. As Table 6.13 shows, the percentage of pucca houses is high, including among the SCs. The government gives grants to SC households to rebuild their houses or build new ones, and such aid is critical in furthering

*Table 6.13* Ownership of consumer durables in M hamlet, Tamil Nadu

| | *Pillai, Chettiar* | *Streets where mainly Mutharaiyars lived* | *Streets where mainly SCs lived* |
|---|---|---|---|
| TV (%) | 67 | 64 | 54 |
| Cable TV (%) | 62 | 53 | 51 |
| Radio (%) | 72 | 50 | 41 |
| Bicycle (%) | 67 | 61 | 28 |
| Table fan (%) | 41 | 35 | 27 |
| Ceiling fan (%) | 109 | 106 | 78 |
| Refrigerator (%) | 12 | 5 | 2 |
| Gas hob (%) | 72 | 27 | 68 |
| Landline (%) | 10 | 9 | 2 |
| Mobile (%) | 78 | 59 | 43 |
| Air conditioner (%) | 0 | 2 | 0 |
| Motorbike (%) | 29 | 24 | 15 |
| Average number of consumer durables (types) | 6.7 | 4.9 | 4.5 |
| Households with tiled-roofed houses (%) | 83 | 85 | 85 |

Source: Author's survey (2007).

this change. Increased household incomes have probably also contributed. In 1980, most of the houses in the two streets where the SCs lived had mud walls and were thatched with plantain leaves. The difference was stark when compared with the streets filled with the mainly pucca houses of the other communities. This visual contrast had almost disappeared in 2007.

As predicted, the educational level had rocketed. The increase in the years of education received by those aged 18 to 39 in comparison to those over 40 was, for males, 32 percent for the SCs, 45 percent for the Muthurajas, and 23 percent for the Pillais and Chettiars. The greatest change was in the duration of female education: 164 percent for the SCs, 132 percent for the Muthurajas and 80 percent for the Pillais and Chettiars. Though there were marked variations among communities, all had a considerable number, including females, who had completed their education to tertiary level. As we shall see in Chapter 11, to get a permanent job in the formal sector (industry, public service, etc.) it was necessary to attain a certain level of education, such as the SSLC. In 1980, the forward castes in the village, like the Pillais and Chettiars, invested in the education of their sons for this purpose, but in 2007 there was a strong desire for education among the Muthurajas and SCs, who previously had not shown much interest in it. Over the past 20 years the educational level required to get a permanent job in the public sector had risen, and this had probably encouraged villagers to aim for a higher level.

As Table 6.14 shows, a relatively high proportion of primary and secondary school children from the hamlet, including SCs and the backward castes, now travelled by bus and other means of transport to schools further away, rather than attending local or nearby schools. This is a good indicator of the demand for education.

*Table 6.14* Distribution of primary and secondary school students' commute

| | *Pillais, Chettiars* | | *Mutharaiyars* | | *SCs* | |
|---|---|---|---|---|---|---|
| | *male* | *female* | *male* | *female* | *male* | *female* |
| Within the village | 23% | 36% | 40% | 34% | 52% | 49% |
| Nearby village | 13% | 8% | 32% | 36% | 11% | 23% |
| Distant village | 10% | 0% | 1% | 2% | 8% | 1% |
| Lalgudi | 23% | 24% | 11% | 11% | 8% | 9% |
| Private school | 13% | 16% | 2% | 7% | 11% | 11% |
| Tiruchirapalli | 13% | 12% | 7% | 5% | 8% | 7% |
| Distant place | 3% | 4% | 6% | 5% | 2% | 0% |
| | 100% | 100% | 100% | 100% | 100% | 100% |

Source: Author's survey (2007).

Other tangible changes concern the evolution of wedding ceremonies and pilgrimage, including among the lower classes. Two large wedding halls were built in the village with very different prices. The cheaper one was used by the SCs, according to an informant. In 1980, most families held wedding ceremonies in their own homes, but there was now a designated space for the occasion that was frequently used by SCs and other communities. Travel for pilgrimage had also become more popular among the SCs and others. In 1980, some people from the wealthy classes among the Pillais, Chettiars and Muthurajas would hire a car and head for pilgrimage sites in Kerala once the harvest was over, and spend several days travelling around other sites on the way. In 2007, some SCs had also begun to take part in such trips. An informant said that from around 2000 they had joined bus tours of several days' length to visit holy sites, mixing with people of other castes. This is a good indication of the steady change in community relations both inside and outside the hamlet, and of the move towards independence among the lower castes.

There has been a great increase in demand not only for consumer durables in the village but also for services like education, religion and wedding ceremonies. This is closely related to aspirations for an improved social and economic life among the lower classes/castes.

### *Changing Social Structure and Consumption Patterns: The Social Meaning of Consumption*

As the above survey shows, income alone cannot dictate demand for manufactured products and services in villages. For villagers who have long lived within a strict socio-economic class structure, consumer behaviour, like being able to purchase consumer durables and clothing and to procure services, has an important social meaning. Osella and Osella (1999) have analysed the process of how people of different classes and castes in a village in Kerala changed their consumption patterns amidst fluctuations in class relations. The poorest members of the SCs and lower castes seek upward mobility and autonomy through fashion – clothing and accessories. The men have a strong interest in new styles and seek out low-cost substitutes. Though cheaper duplicates of Raymonds and Van Heusen shirts are out of their reach, they can have a copy of a film hero's shirt made at a local stitching centre or buy fake designer labels in the cities to be sewn into their clothes. At festivals, young SC women wear saris and blouses in the most up-to-date patterns and the latest fashion in cheap accessories like imitation jewellery. "Bright synthetic shirts, baggy trousers, and cheap trainers are also worn in defiant opposition to the sober white cotton shirt, *mundu* (waist-cloth) and *cerippu* (sandals) of the high caste Hindu" (Osella and Osella 1999, 997). In one village in Tamil Nadu, a local landowner complained about the labour shortage, saying that the members of the SCs in the village preferred to work in construction and other industries in nearby cities. "They parade around in jeans and costly sports shoes", he said, mocking them on their newly acquired dress habits. "Although the dalits are still overtly deferential towards the local elite, their preference for migratory work and consumption of Western attire indicates to landed groups … that the traditional social order is under siege" (Gidwani and Sivaramakrishnan 2003, 200).[19] Underlying this type of consumer behaviour by members of the lower classes in villages and their demand for non-traditional fashion like knitted products, ready-made clothing, imitation jewellery and cheap sports shoes is defiance towards the upper classes and a keen impulse towards upward mobility. This is in contrast to the dressing habits of the upper classes who maintain a preference for white cotton shirts and traditional clothing.

In the Kerala village studied by Osella and Osella, many members of the OBC Izhava community, who were better off than many of the SCs who had remained labourers, expressed their aspirations for social climbing through the purchase of consumer durables. In the middle of the 1990s, one informant reported buying a table fan, a black-and-white television and a marble floor for his front room, while another, a migrant worker, had purchased a colour television and marble flooring imported from Rajasthan. Until the beginning of the twentieth century, the Izhavas, like the SCs, were strictly constrained in terms of clothing, jewellery and dwellings. Such consumer behaviour thus notifies society at large of their freedom from former caste restraints. One family had installed a modern Western kitchen but rarely used it, doing the daily cooking in an adjoining traditional kitchen instead. This purchase is meaningful behaviour (Osella and Osella 1999, 1010–11).

When there is any economic surplus, those desiring to raise their social prestige move their gaze to investing in persons or land and buildings from a long-term point of view. Providing children with education and healthcare is investment in the next generation, helping them towards further upward mobility. All women in the Kerala village register with a doctor as soon as they think they are pregnant, and there are a large number of private schools in the area. Constructing concrete houses and buying up the land of members of the higher castes who have moved to the cities are actions to establish long-term prestige (Osella and Osella 1999, 1012–1014).[20]

Such examples have also been reported from western India. Among the Vankars (SC) of Gujarat,

> whereas older generation Vankars still display deference towards upper-caste groups, younger generation Kankars openly defy the prevalent caste hierarchy. Their attire and demeanor reflect their hostility to caste norms: they are invariably better dressed than their upper-caste counterparts; ... and they place a premium on education as a mark of their difference.

The majority of younger-generation Vankars are schooled outside the village, and their highest educational attainment averages higher than that of upper-caste Patel and Rajput households. One informant "vowed that Vankars and other dalits would one day displace upper-class rule in Gujarat. In his view, education leading to off-farm employment ... was key to this aspiration". With this goal in mind, he sent his daughter to a reputable boarding school in Ahmedabad (Gidwani and Sivaramakrishnan 2003, 197). Higher education thus functions as an expression of SC resistance against the upper castes.

Gidwani and Sivaramakrishnan (2003) argue that even labour migration, an extremely widespread practice among the Indian lower classes, is not a simply economic action but is also associated with the desire to escape village caste hierarchies. For example, in a Gujarat village dominated by Patel landowners, rural workers avoid attached labour on the farms of the higher castes and prefer factory work "because it is free", even though factory wages may be lower. Resistance against the upper castes and a trend towards independence take the form of a migrant worker lifestyle, over and above consumption and education. Considering that as late as 1975, caste restrictions were so strong that Vankars could not walk in the survey village without headgear, aspirations for independence had grown markedly over the previous 30 years.[21]

Chapter 3 studied changing consumption patterns among the lower classes in the period before Independence, showing their diversification within a context of the lower classes furthering their attempts to achieve upward mobility and socio-economic independence. They wore artificial silk saris and drank coffee in imitation of upper-class habits, though in a cheaper form, purchased cheap, "modern" knits and smoked ever greater numbers of the bidis that the upper classes avoided. The cases from Kerala, Tamil Nadu and Gujarat show that the village elites, however much it angered them, could do nothing about the Western clothing worn by the labouring classes as a gesture of detachment from them. The long-term movements towards economic and social independence among lower-class villagers have been touched upon, and it has been shown that this was the basis upon which certain consumption trends have strengthened over the past decades. The NCAER surveys proved that the lower classes continued to amass consumer durables at a rate faster than that of their income increase. Osella and Osella rightly point out that "consumption may be even more important for those at the peripheries of capitalism and modernity than for those at the centre" (Osella and Osella 1999, 1018).

## Conclusion

Three conclusions may be drawn from the above discussion. First, as a result of long-term agrarian expansion, including the Green Revolution, and of heightened independence among the lower classes in rural society, a broad swathe of rural households, including those of agricultural labourers, received a steady increase in wages. Rural areas then developed as the greatest market for the industrial and service sectors. The purchasing power of the rural non-elite for non-food items, which was a little under twice that of the urban middle classes, was undeniably an important factor in the growth of the non-food sector. Village surveys show that consumer nondurables penetrated into SC households as well. Second, rural consumption did not consist of only manufactured products but included services like house construction, education, religious events, travel and wedding ceremonies. Third, this demand was closely linked to aspirations among the lower classes, who had historically lived within a hierarchical social structure, for upward mobility, both social and economic. These reinforced their aspirations as consumers and influenced their consumer decisions.

The next chapter will examine the growth of industry and services from the 1980s in terms of the important rural market.

## Notes

1 For a detailed treatment of this topic, see Yanagisawa 1996a, Chapter 7.
2 Sivakumar and Sivakumar 1979; Athreya et al. 1990, 110; Hazell and Ramasamy 1991, 72.
3 See also Sivertsen 1963, 85–87.
4 Gough 1981, 292, 525. On the other hand, a survey of a village in North Arcot district reports that the number of *padiyals* (hired labourers) had increased (Hazell and Ramasamy 1991, 65). This reminds us that we must consider regional variations.
5 According to Jeffrey and Lerche, in villages in Uttar Pradesh where Jat landowners exert strong control, members of the wealthy landowning class have moved to urban centres in great numbers, taking up work as civil servants, and occupying white-collar jobs in public corporations and elite work in the professions. They are conspicuous in areas such as shopkeeping, businesses engaged in processing agricultural products, educational facilities, transportation and construction. This tendency to move away from agriculture has been continuing for a long time (Jeffrey and Lerche 2000, 96–97).
6 For the strengthening self-confidence and independence among SCs in Uttar Pradesh, and their growing power to stand up to the Thakurs and others from the higher castes, see Jeffrey and Lerche 2000.
7 Kazuya Nakamizo clearly identifies these changes in his study of village surveys in Bihar (Nakamizo 2012, 132–137).
8 Jodha emphasises that although poor households had showed an improvement in their quality of life, the proportion of households in the village below the poverty

line had risen, judged from the fact that the decline in real per capita income terms placed them below the poverty line. Measuring changes in poverty, quality of life and poverty level only through income at one point in time is problematical and "underscores the importance of indepth micro-level investigations in field studies" (Jodha 1989, 193). Pranab Bardhan, who edited the work in which Jodha's essay appears, examines the issue of differences in perception, in areas such as the various evaluations of the supply–demand relationship in the labour market, between micro studies (e.g. village surveys) and research that relies mainly on statistical material (Bardhan 1990, Introduction).

9 The poverty line is set on the basis of per capita income when judging the economic level of Indian villages. The numeric value of income at one point of time does not reflect what the poor classes have gained in the way of rights to acquire small pieces of land, tenancy rights and house plots and houses. Neither does it reflect the year-long stability and economic independence brought about by slack season employment, etc., as reported in surveys of villages in Tamil Nadu. Jodha points out that any judgement about economic level requires per capita income to be combined with the kind of qualitative approach village surveys can provide. There is a need to reconsider post-Independence changes in the rural economic level from this viewpoint.

10 Shukla 1991 also emphasises the strong consumption linkages between the agricultural and non-agricultural sectors.

11 Eapen asserts that the most important factor in non-farm employment in rural villages as a whole is the proximity to an urban centre (Eapen 2001, 67–89). Thus it is clear that linkages with agricultural production are strong for villages remote from cities.

12 Vaidyanathan offers a "residual" theory, that "rural workers who cannot get adequate work in agriculture spill over into rural non-agricultural activities" (Vaidyanathan 1986, A-141). However, as Vaidyanathan himself came to realise, this theory is difficult to sustain, in view of the growth in agricultural wages at the same time as the growth in non-farm employment and the ongoing tightening of the rural labour market (Vaidyanathan 1994b). Biradar 2009 reviews the factors leading to this growth. Foster and Rosenzweig, who studied linkages between yield improvements and rises in non-farm income based on village survey data covering 1971–1999, show that "the expansion of rural industry is not predicated on expansion of local agricultural productivity" (Foster and Rosenzweig 2004, 541). They reject any correlation between agricultural growth and increases in non-farm employment in villages, excepting in those areas where wage levels have risen because of rises in productivity as a result of outside industrial capital. This theory is not, however, very convincing, since there is no evidence that wages are higher in areas with high productivity (mainly dry areas) than in other (irrigated) areas. It also ignores the fact that large numbers of villagers work in or migrate to urban areas and considers, not the spatial movement of the labour force, but only income from employment in village factories.

13 Unni 1988.

14 As we saw in Chapter 5, the estimates of Fan et al. 1999 showed a rise in the agricultural labourer's wage, which was confirmed from the 1970s by Lanjouw and Murgai 2009. For poverty reduction, see Kurosaki 2011, pp. 62–63 and Suryanarayan 2012, pp. 126–129.

15 In Foster and Rosenzweig 2004 most of this rise is from non-farm income.

16 Calculated from Suryanarayana 2009, Tables 4.1, 4.3. In Kumar et al. 2007, percentages for food expenditure fell between 1983 and 1999 from 69.1 percent to 61.5 percent in rural areas and from 59.1 percent to 50.7 percent in urban areas.

17 A higher level of penetration than predicted from low level earnings (Rao 1994, 6).

18 See Chapter 8 for improved housing in villages and increased opportunities for travel.

19 As we shall see in the next chapter, this kind of consumption by the lower classes who do not have the economic power to purchase original brands was largely directed to "fake brands".

20 Douglas Haynes, in his study of the development of small-scale textile production in western India, says weavers developed products to meet "the demand of newly mobile groups for cheaper versions of textiles conveying meanings of prestige and respectability" (Haynes 2012, 308, 312).

21 Around 1980 in Iruvelpattu in Tamil Nadu, members of the SCs were not allowed to wear chappals in the village street or enter the teashop if a caste Hindu was present (Harriss et al. 2010, 58). This also suggests that the lower castes were buying chappals, a type of footwear, in great numbers.

# Part III

# Accelerated Growth and the Structure of the Indian Economy and Society

From the 1980s, India's growth rate climbed to around 6 percent. Part III deals with this acceleration. It views the Indian economy and society as consisting of two tiers: An upper tier, the large-scale enterprise sectors as represented by the consumer-durable and IT industries; and a lower tier, the small-scale and informal sectors, with which the rural economy was closely connected. While tracing the development of each tier, it is argued that the two became increasingly intertwined and though this tighter tie benefitted the large-scale sectors, the two-tier structure has remained basically unchanged.

Chapter 7 explores the growth of industries in the informal sector, as they absorbed large numbers of workers. Expanded demand from rural areas and the lower classes of society provided the market base for the expansion of micro and small-scale industries. These developed production systems very much adapted to this market and its demand for "quasi-branded goods".

The growth of the service and construction industries is examined in Chapter 8. It points out how the new, modern sub-sectors of the service industry remained small-scale until the end of the 1990s and were stimulated by the informal sector. This chapter also posits that the impact of rural socio-economic change on the growth of the service and construction industries has been much larger than has been usually supposed.

Chapter 9 postulates that, following the induction of a large number of temporary and permanent migrant workers from the rural lower classes into urban informal industries, a "rural and urban-informal economies" zone has developed in which both people and commodities circulate.

Chapter 10 studies the development of leading companies against this backdrop of expanding rural markets and informal industries. As regards consumer durables and the communications industry, economic liberalisation and globalisation brought about lower costs, improved quality and increased competitiveness. The rapid expansion of their market into the "rural and urban-informal economies" zone was accompanied by the addition of a new consumer group in the form of a monied class made up of

DOI: 10.4324/9781003341550-10

entrepreneurs in the informal sector, among others. This formed the foundation of the economic growth led by the consumer durables and communications industries.

Though the large-scale enterprise sector has experienced significant growth through growing contacts between the two tiers, Chapter 11 suggests that the two-tiered structure of the Indian economy and society is likely to be maintained and regenerated.

# 7 The Growth of Small-Scale and Informal-Sector Industries and the Production of Low-Cost Goods

## The Growth of Small-Scale Industries

Under the Factories Act of 1948, factories employing ten or more workers with the aid of power (or 20 or more without the aid of power) were required to register. These were called registered factories, and those on a smaller scale unregistered factories or workshops. In India, the latter group is known as the informal (unorganised) sector, and there are difficulties inherent in the statistics concerning them. Factories can avoid registration by counting only full-time workers directly employed by the factory as employees, when actually, if temporary workers and labourers under contractors were included, the total number of people working there would exceed the figure imposed by the Factories Act. However, as such non-compliant businesses are themselves small-scale and marginal, and very different to large-scale enterprises, I will treat "unregistered factories" as belonging to the informal sector, while remaining aware that a certain ambiguity exists. Besides unregistered factories, there are large numbers of small factories with ten or more workers. These micro and small enterprises (MSE) are the main subject of this chapter's discussion (Table 7.1).

India's annual industrial production growth rate increased from 5.3 percent between 1951 and 1980 to 6.8 percent between 1981 and 1990. Over the course of 1991–2000 it slowed down to 5.8 percent. After 1980, the informal sector played an extremely important role in this progression. Table 9.6 in Chapter 9 shows that between 1972 and 1987 employees in manufacturing grew at a rate of 1.5 percent in the organised sector and 4.47 percent in the unorganised sector. In terms of employee numbers, the informal sector was clearly at the forefront (Sundaram 1998, Table 2). Roy (1998) makes the same inference, saying, "In 1991, 70 percent of industrial employment in India took place in units not registered as factories. Between 1977 and 1987, employment in this sector grew at possibly four times the rate at which factory employment did" (907). Table 9.6, outlining changes between 1983 and 2000, demonstrates that the employment rate within the unorganised sector grew at more than four times that of the organised sector.

Marjit and Kar (2012), who studied fixed capital formation in the 1990s, show that investment in the informal sector developed positively at that time. They indicate that whereas capital stock in the formal sector either remained

DOI: 10.4324/9781003341550-11

*Table 7.1* Net domestic product (NDP), employment and productivity growth rates in the organised and unorganised sectors

| | *1983–94* | | | *1994–2000* | | |
|---|---|---|---|---|---|---|
| | *NDP* | *Employment* | *Productivity* | *NDP* | *Employment* | *Productivity* |
| Organised sector | 6.2 | 0.3 | 5.9 | 5.8 | 0.5 | 5.3 |
| Unorganised sector | 4.1 | 2.6 | 1.6 | 7.4 | 2 | 5.4 |

Source: Unni 2003, Figures 5 and 8, pp. 75, 77.

stagnant or dwindled, informal fixed assets flourished. In the textile industry, the ratio of final cloth output to GNP increased in the 1990s and was larger than that of any other industry. However, "[i] t was not just textiles, but the informal sector in textiles, that led to industrial growth" (Roy 2004, 90, 98). The core of India's manufacturing exports after the 1980s was the small industrial sector rather than the traditional large industries (Roy 2011, 312–313).[1]

## Growth Distortion?

Most of the growth in Indian manufacturing has been in the MSE sector, at least in terms of employment. It is commonly held that this has chiefly arisen as a result of government policy placing controls on production by large enterprises and protecting labour. For example, between 1984 and 1985, the government imposed restrictions on composite (spinning and weaving) mills concerning capacity-expansion and product diversification, stipulated the provision of various benefits and social security for workers in the formal sector, forbidding or limiting their dismissal and protecting trade unions, and placed taxes on mill cloth. The argument emphasising government intervention as a cause of growth asserts that it was difficult for large enterprises, bound by such regulations, to oust MSEs from the market through economies of scale. While on the one hand investment in large-scale industries remained static, small-scale industries, especially factories and enterprises not registered under the Factories Act, could employ workers at low wages with no security and could dismiss them at will. Further, they could produce their goods freely, including those lines reserved for them under the product-reservation policy. As a result, they grew at the expense of the large factories. This type of growth is understood as a "distortion" created by government policy.[2]

There is no doubt that the policies to regulate large-scale industry, to protect MSEs and to supervise labour, worked to promote the advancement of MSEs in the post-Independence economy. However, the intervention argument is not convincing when we consider the economic changes that occurred during the colonial period, when very few such laws and regulations existed.

As we saw in Chapter 3, from the end of the nineteenth century, mills developed centred on the spinning industry and moved into weaving too at the beginning of the twentieth century. Nevertheless, the market share of handlooms and powerlooms (small weaving factories) was not easily eroded, and in the 1930s, the products of dispersed MSEs represented more than half the textile market in terms of value. India also expanded its hosiery industry from the 1910s. Though the mill sector produced hosiery goods, it was the MSEs that dominated the industry. Reports by government committees of the time stated that market demand for such products varied with locality and season, and though the mills established hosiery departments, there was little profit in producing small amounts of yarn of different counts and quality. Since more than half the labour costs were in sewing and finishing, economies of scale could not be applied. In South India, cotton ginning was led by the export-oriented large factories at the beginning of the twentieth century, but as the percentage of raw cotton produced for the domestic market increased, small ginneries with two to eight gins came to dominate the industry. This shows that even without government protection MSE businesses could take a commanding position in certain industries without applying economies of scale. A variety of factors brought this situation about, such as technological systems for production, markets and demand, the product's distinctive features and the mobilisation of labour.

A good example of vigorous MSE growth as large enterprises deteriorated after Independence is the relationship between the powerlooms in MSE textile factories and the textile departments of the mills. Most textiles in India immediately after Independence were produced either by handlooms or by mills. Powerlooms, whose products had had only a very small share at that time, multiplied from the 1960s.[3] In 1991, the share in textile production was mills 11 percent, powerlooms 71 percent and handlooms 18 percent. Mills had thus been completely overtaken by powerlooms.[4] Roy (1998), analysing production and costs in both sectors, disputes the argument that the rise of the powerlooms had its origins in government policies of capacity restriction and product reservation. According to the received view, the mills had to pay taxes and provide worker protection which the powerlooms did not, and were subject to production quotas. These regulations reduced the mills' effectiveness in the face of the powerlooms' economies of scale, and gave the latter the competitive edge. Roy does allow that these regulations led to a kind of distortion, but he criticises "the thesis that weaving in the mill was ever capable of being intrinsically more efficient than weaving in the powerloom" as "a result based on a flawed method" (907). First, it is assumed that "mills run on a higher average loom-speed than the powerlooms". However, both systems are able to use looms of the same speed. Second, "the ability to make a wide range of specific cloths with general machinery, [and] to change products quickly" is crucial. On this point, the powerloom owner "supplies certain types of enterprise more cheaply than the mill owner, and is willing to work as owner-manager, unlike the mill owner", and is able to produce cheaper, customised goods. Third, changes in demand create a lucrative situation for powerlooms. When there was an increase in demand for non-cotton yarns like polyester and rayon, mills, which did the spinning in their own factories, could not make the switch to non-cotton cloth, whereas powerlooms could. This facilitated their further growth. Fourth, if we consider that mills also utilise casual labour extensively and that rents in Mumbai are extremely high, the differential between the wage levels of mill workers and powerloom workers is not as great as might be supposed (906).[5] Other ingredients in the growth of powerlooms include the spread of electrification, the increase in numbers of migrant workers from rural areas, a wider demand for textiles in rural areas, and for ready-made goods. Thus the received argument regarding government intervention as propelling the growth of powerlooms may be criticised as insufficient.[6]

Ramaswamy (1994), who studied the share of small industry for the years 1972 to 1987 with reference to employment and added value according to type of product, revealed that in areas like food, drinks, cigarettes, carpentry, leatherwork, paper making, hosiery and ready-made clothing, small industry swiftly extended its share, exceeding even the metallurgical industry. This infers that specialisation is a more important determinant in the success of small industry than protection.

From the research of Roy and others, and the experience of the pre-Independence hosiery industry, it is obvious that the received view concerning the influence of government intervention is inadequate. This chapter, therefore, will attempt to consider the structure of industrial production in India as having developed within a close mutual relationship with various aspects of India's basic socio-economic structure. These include characteristic features of the production process, the structure of demand and changes to it, management, the increase of migrant workers from rural areas and the workings of the labour market, the educational structure and the structure of village society. I will pay particular attention to the significance of the fact that, to a greater or lesser degree, these structures are two-tiered. Of course, small-scale and informal-sector industries fall into many diverse categories, but I would like to focus here on powerlooms, knits (hosiery), textiles (including ready-made clothing), leatherwork and footwear, and the recycled plastic industry as my raw material, relying principally on existing research.

## The Growth of MSEs and the Rural and Low-Income Markets

Let us first consider the growth of MSEs as an important foundation for the rural market and for changing demand within the lower-class market. According to Roy (1998), in 1984,

> "mills dominated the city markets (60 percent in value), but its [*sic*] presence in small towns and rural areas dropped sharply (12–17 per cent). This latter market, which experienced growth especially after the Green Revolution, was captured by the powerlooms".
>
> (Roy 1998, 907, also Table 7.2)

*Table 7.2* Consumption of textile goods by type in urban and rural areas (1984, 1985)

| | *Urban areas* | | *Rural areas* | | *All India* | |
|---|---|---|---|---|---|---|
| | *1984* | *1985* | *1984* | *1985* | *1984* | *1985* |
| | | | Amount (100,000 m.) | | | |
| Mill-made | 624 | 673 | 679 | 950 | 1,303 | 1,623 |
| Powerloom-made | 337 | 380 | 2,098 | 2,318 | 2,435 | 2,698 |
| Handloom-made | 582 | 621 | 2,456 | 2,468 | 3,038 | 3,089 |
| Khadi | 11 | 13 | 55 | 62 | 66 | 75 |
| Hosiery | 119 | 152 | 352 | 472 | 471 | 624 |
| Total | 1,673 | 1,839 | 5,640 | 6,270 | 7,313 | 8,109 |
| | | | Value (Rs 100,000) | | | |
| Mill-made | 8,155 | 9,462 | 7,102 | 10,046 | 15,257 | 19,508 |
| Powerloom-made | 3,943 | 4,547 | 18,312 | 21,255 | 22,255 | 25,802 |
| Handloom-made | 7,712 | 8,859 | 21,392 | 22,543 | 29,104 | 31,402 |
| Khadi | 128 | 159 | 505 | 758 | 633 | 917 |
| Hosiery | 740 | 1,007 | 1,813 | 2,661 | 2,553 | 3,668 |
| Total | 20,678 | 24,034 | 49,124 | 57,263 | 69,802 | 81,297 |
| | | | Value per metre (Rs) | | | |
| Mill-made | 13 | 14 | 10 | 11 | 12 | 12 |
| Powerloom-made | 12 | 12 | 9 | 9 | 9 | 10 |
| Handloom-made | 13 | 14 | 9 | 9 | 10 | 10 |
| Khadi | 12 | 12 | 9 | 12 | 10 | 12 |
| Hosiery | 6 | 7 | 5 | 6 | 5 | 6 |
| Total | 12 | 13 | 9 | 9 | 10 | 10 |

Source: Highlights of Consumer Purchases of Textiles, 1985, Vol. 1, Market Research Wing, Textile Committee, Govt. of India Ministry of Textile, Table No. 22, p. 38.

The growth in demand for non-cotton yarns like polyester and rayon evidently facilitated the expansion of powerlooms, which could convert to their production in a way the composite mills could not. This would not have been possible without changes in the rural market. P. Nayak, director of the Market Research Wing of the Textile Committee within the Ministry of Textiles, tells us that there was no market for artificial synthetic fibres in the 1970s, but at the time of writing (2002), synthetic goods and blended and union fabrics made from synthetic fibres filled the market. Purchasers were the mass consumers of the poor and lower middle classes, which made up 63 percent of the population and who mostly lived in rural or semi-urban areas. Between 1990 and 2000 in rural areas of Andhra Pradesh, the consumption of cotton textiles dropped from 57 percent to 37 percent, while that of blended and union goods rose from 28 percent to 51 percent (Table 7.3) (Nayak and Kopresachari 2002). Interestingly, cotton goods consumption in urban areas increased slightly to 50 percent. Upper-class consumers in cities were maintaining their taste for cotton goods even though they also bought synthetics.

The cotton hosiery industry, another characteristic example of MSE participation in the textile industry, developed primarily on the basis of the rural and poorer class markets. As we saw in Chapter 3, demand from the 1920s for

*Table 7.3* Textile market share by demand, Andhra Pradesh (%)

| | *Urban areas* | | *Rural areas* | | *Rural-urban total* | |
|---|---|---|---|---|---|---|
| | *1990* | *2000* | *1990* | *2000* | *1990* | *2000* |
| Blended, union | 33 | 35 | 28 | 51 | 30 | 46 |
| Artificial fabrics | 13 | 10 | 14 | 10 | 14 | 10 |
| Woollen | 0 | 0 | 1 | 1 | 1 | 0 |
| Pure silk | 5 | 4 | 1 | 1 | 2 | 2 |
| Cotton | 49 | 50 | 57 | 37 | 53 | 42 |
| Total | 100 | 100 | 100 | 100 | 100 | 100 |

Source: Nayak and Kopresachari 2002, p. 7.

its products came chiefly from the urban labouring classes. This later extended to rural areas, in particular as knitwear banians (vests) penetrated the villages, and it was the banian that underlay the success of the knitwear industry in Tiruppur (Singh and Sapra 2007, 77–78; Chari 2004, 246). Table 7.2 shows that as of 1984–1985 rural demand for cotton knits was three times that of urban areas in terms of amount and more than twice in terms of value. In Andhra Pradesh, the market for knits (including woollen ones) in 1990 was greater in rural areas than urban areas when it came to quantity, but its value was slightly better in urban areas (Table 7.4). At this time, the knits purchased in cities cost on average over three times more than those purchased in rural areas (Table 7.5). This probably reflects the acquisition of high-priced items by the urban upper classes. By 2000, the consumption of knits had grown more in rural than in urban areas over India as a whole. In the cities, the value per metre fell from Rs 132 to Rs 53, suggesting that a broad range of people, including the urban poor, were buying cheap knitted goods. It is therefore possible to say that the purchasing of cheap knits by the urban and rural poor was at the centre of the expansion of the hosiery market. Nayak and Kopresachari (2002) report for India as a whole that per capita consumption of banians grew from 0.68 to 0.89 and underwear from 0.11 to 0.29, stating that the desire for hosiery products in the rural sector had crept up as a consequence of a changing rural society.[7]

Small textile companies were also associated with the manufacture of ready-made clothing.[8] In 1990, urban consumption was higher than the rural, but volume later increased by 96 percent in urban areas and by 173 percent in rural areas over India as a whole. Here again, rural consumption led the growth of the market (Table 7.4).

Since both the hosiery and the fabric garment industries rapidly expanded their exports abroad from the 1980s, we cannot ascertain their overall trend directly from those in the domestic market shown above. Calculating the percentage occupied by exports in the total production is tricky, but one estimate suggests 25 percent of ready-made clothing manufactured in India was for export (Singh and Sapra 2007, 44). If this is so, the domestic market occupied three quarters of the total market despite the high export figure. Trends in the domestic market would thus be the main influence on overall trends.[9]

*Table 7.4* Amount of, and changes in, demand for the major textile products, 1990–2000

| | *Urban* | | | | *Rural* | | | | *Urban-rural* | | | |
|---|---|---|---|---|---|---|---|---|---|---|---|---|
| | *Andhra Pradesh* | | | *All India change (%)* | *Andhra Pradesh* | | | *All India change (%)* | *Andhra Pradesh* | | | *All India change (%)* |
| | 1990 | 2000 | Change (%) | | 1990 | 2000 | Change (%) | | 1990 | 2000 | Change (%) | |
| Amount (million metres) | | | | | | | | | | | | |
| Long cloth | 114 | 95 | −16.67 | 6.6 | 206 | 193 | −6.31 | 2.24 | 320 | 288 | −10 | 3.5 |
| Woven ready-made clothing | 76 | 109 | 43.42 | 96.5 | 63 | 156 | 147.62 | 173.43 | 139 | 265 | 90.65 | 137.86 |
| knits | 30 | 43 | 43.33 | 101.54 | 38 | 83 | 118.42 | 112.9 | 68 | 126 | 85.29 | 109.06 |
| All textiles | 422 | 474 | 12.32 | 49.64 | 625 | 917 | 46.72 | 56.96 | 1047 | 1391 | 32.86 | 54.63 |
| Value (million rupees: 1990 values shows according to 2000 values) | | | | | | | | | | | | |
| Long cloth | 13133 | 7946 | −39.5 | −16.17 | 14968 | 11492 | −23.22 | −18.62 | 28101 | 19438 | −30.83 | −17.7 |
| Woven ready-made clothing | 7153 | 10974 | 53.42 | 106.71 | 1704 | 8513 | 117.22 | 141.6 | 11392 | 19487 | 71.06 | 121.59 |
| knits | 3974 | 2270 | −42.88 | 84.68 | 1426 | 2979 | 108.91 | 97.98 | 5400 | 5249 | −2.8 | 92.06 |
| All textiles | 39735 | 37840 | −4.77 | 30.8 | 35639 | 42563 | 19.43 | 27.92 | 75373 | 80403 | 6.67 | 29.17 |

Note: Piece length varieties include long cloth, sheeting, shirting, coating, suiting and women's clothing.

Source: Nayak and Kopresachari 2002, p. 8.

*Table 7.5* Unit cost per metre of textile products, Andhra Pradesh (Rs according to 2000 values)

| | *Urban* | | | *Rural* | | | *Ratio of rural value to urban value* | | |
|---|---|---|---|---|---|---|---|---|---|
| | | | | | | | % | | |
| | *1990* | *2000* | *Change (%)* | *1990* | *2000* | *Change (%)* | *1990* | *2000* | *Change (%)* |
| Long cloth types | 115 | 84 | −27 | 73 | 60 | −18 | 63 | 71 | 13 |
| Woven ready-made clothing | 94 | 101 | 7 | 27 | 55 | 102 | 29 | 54 | 89 |
| Knits | 132 | 53 | −60 | 38 | 36 | −4 | 28 | 68 | 140 |
| All textile products | 94 | 80 | −15 | 57 | 46 | −19 | 61 | 58 | −4 |

Source: Nayak and Kopresachari 2002, p. 8.

The footwear industry has not been left behind and is a core industry of the informal sector. As of 1988, over 1,150,000 producers in the village and household industry sector made up more than 90 percent of workers in it. Workers from the informal and small industry sectors produced 92 percent of the total production (Naidu 2009, 22). India has a number of large footwear markets around the world, and the domestic market is growing at an annual rate of 10 percent (Kollannavar et al., 2010, 135). According to one estimation, 317 million pairs of shoes were produced in 1988–1989 (Naidu 2009, 21–22), while in 1997 demand had risen to 1800 million and was predicted to increase to 2,500 million by 2010 (Kollannavar et al., 2010, 135). These figures include of course exports, but in 2009–2010 exports of leather footwear and leather footwear components remained at 114 million pairs, important, but no more than a small proportion of the 2,500 million pairs comprising domestic demand (Council for Leather Exports 2012, 18).

India's footwear industry initially developed out of leather items like chappals (sandals) but then the demand for non-leather goods soared. Naidu gives weekly production numbers as 1617 pairs of leather shoes, 7,270 pairs of non-leather shoes, 40,815 pairs of leather chappals and sandals, 40,905 pairs of non-leather chappals and sandals, and 71,738 pairs of mixed leather and non-leather chappals and sandals. Non-leather and non-leather mixed items thus occupy the majority of the Indian footwear market. About 25 percent are shoes, and the rest chappals and sandals (Naidu 2009, 22–25).[10] It is significant that although urban dwellers like good quality shoes, people in villages normally prefer cheap and lightweight non-leather shoes. Trends in the Indian footwear industry are thus fundamentally determined by the rural population.[11]

Another prominent industry in the informal sector is plastic recycling. Based around the collection, sorting and recycling of used plastic, this industry spread from the 1970s. One government report in the middle of the 1990s stated that it employed over one million people. Plastic recycling generates a plethora of low-cost, low-quality goods: Cheaper shoes and furniture are made from PVC grain, inferior buckets, mugs and jugs from PP grain, and lower-quality spectacles and pens from acetate. The main final market for these items is again dominated by low-income groups and rural populations.[12]

## Social Change in Rural Society and Consumer Orientation towards "Quasi-Branded" Goods

The primary reason that small-scale and informal industries, making the types of goods outlined above, could find a market in rural areas and among low-income groups was either their initial low cost or later falling prices. Table 7.5 shows that the unit price of the products in demand in rural markets was lower than in the urban market. The price gap among knits and ready-made clothing in the mid-1990s is particularly glaring. The drop in the cost of man-made fibres such as polyester and viscose, and of blends led to a striking infiltration of synthetic products into rural areas, and using recycled rather than pure plastic created especially attractive prices. Low cost was the most important condition for rural market penetration (Nayak and Kopresachari 2002), but it was evidently not the only one. As the research of Osella and Osella and others into changing consumption patterns in South Indian villages has shown (see Chapter 6), members of the lower classes in village society expressed their defiance of class and desire for upward mobility through fashion, clothing and accessories as consumers of non-traditional fashion such as knits, ready-made clothing, imitation jewellery, cheap sports shoes and the like.

Income, though still restricted, gradually increased among the rural lower classes, and facilitated changes in material aspiration all over India. Tirthankar Roy, studying the Indian textile market, found that between the 1980s and 1990s casual wear, like jeans, printed shirts and T-shirts, had become unavoidable. There existed a demand for high-priced branded goods on the one hand, and cheap goods on the other, and it was the latter that grew most rapidly. High-cost goods "combined three features: formal sector fabric makers, global or well-known local brands and … manufacturers … which could invest in advertising". They were sold in outlets most commonly found in the large cities. Higher-demand, low-cost items, however, were produced and marketed through the informal sector, and "consisted of unbranded or what might be called 'quasi-branded' goods. They offered lower prices, but no quality guarantee". In 1997, the ratio between branded and quasi-branded goods in denims was estimated at 30:70 (Roy 2004, 92). What Osella and Osella described as consumer trends among the rural non-elite aspiring to upward mobility is mirrored in the purchasing of quasi-branded goods discussed by Roy. The preference for such goods, with their connotation of socio-economic independence for the economically powerless lower classes, strongly affected market trends for mass consumer goods among rural society and can be understood as an agent influencing industry trends over all India.

Evolving rural consumption must also be appraised in relation to the growing connections of migrant workers from villages with outside society and the India's remarkable socio-economic globalisation from the 1980s. Already from the end of the nineteenth century, opportunities arose for lower-class labourers to work away from the village, particularly abroad, encouraging them to feel independent of the landowning classes in the village. This attitude only solidified from the 1980s. The cash earned through migrant work was put into new clothes or consumer durables, and as the study of a Kerala village by Osella and Osella shows, returning migrant workers brought back commodities from the cities or overseas. Fashion from films and other media outlets influenced the clothing choices of lower-class villagers and by a variety of such agents European tastes provided a model for progress. Further, an increased supply of goods for export meant that domestic prices fell. However, it is not enough to understand changes in mass consumption simply in terms of globalisation.[13] Osella and Osella describe how the appropriation of modern fashion styles from films differs with class within the village. Globalisation has impacted on the village in a number of ways – in social and economic relations both within the village and outside, in life and culture, and in religious awareness. Yet, the direction of changes in rural consumption has largely been defined by shifting relations between classes in the villages, ongoing since the end of the nineteenth century. Globalisation should be understood in this context, as functioning to promote such shifts.

## The MSE System for Producing Cheap Goods

MSEs are principally engaged in producing cheap quasi-branded goods to meet high rural demand. They do this across a range of important industries, including the textile and footwear industries. As Roy pointed out above, the formal sector was responsible for manufacturing and marketing higher-priced branded goods whereas the informal sector was used for the production and marketing of quasi-branded goods.[14]

A case study of the garment industry in Delhi shows that producers are broadly divided into three categories according to scale of production, which is connected to price range. The garment industry is dominated by low-cost goods in the "under $5 category" both for export and for the domestic market. The smallest producers are household-based units which make cheap knitwear and clothing for local evening markets. A large part of production takes place in small workshops (*karkhana*) employing around 20 workers. They use locally made machines "in poorly constructed worksheds which double-up as hostels after work". Large runs of standardised items for export are made in big factories generating economies of scale. They are modern-looking, mechanised and have in-house facilities for cutting, sewing, dry-cleaning and finishing. It should be noted that large factories in the formal sector also contract out the production of the cheapest goods for export to smaller workshops. To summarise, the household-based units supply low-cost goods for the domestic market, the workshops turn out the cheapest goods in the under $5 category for export, and the large factories produce the upper range of goods in the under $5 category (Singh and Sapra 2007, 99, 114–115). Tiruppur, the centre of the garment and cotton knitwear industry in South India, also has a similar differentiation. Whereas the very smallest firms typically make coarse-textured knitted goods which, even if dyed, are of low quality, small to medium-sized and some large firms produce better quality garments for the domestic market. The medium and large firms also manufacture goods for export, where a high degree of quality control is required (Cawthorne 1995, 43–56).

The correspondence between producer scale and product price range is even clearer in the case of the footwear industry of Agra, which chiefly produces cheap shoes and chappals. Here too producers are broadly divided into the informal and formal sectors. The informal sector is made up of several thousand independent businesses each employing around ten workers (including family labour) and run by members of the scheduled castes, with which leatherwork was traditionally associated. The formal sector consists of firms run by white-collar members of the forward castes who employ between ten and several dozen workers from the scheduled castes. Informal-sector producers make extremely low-cost shoes (under Rs 100) and cheap chappals which they take to the main shoe market in Agra. Some also make shoes to order for domestic traders or other agents. These commodities are for the local market; traders buy designs that suit a particular market and then send them off. Several hundred home-based artisans sell their shoes wholesale at roadside markets on the fringes of Agra to non-locals such as people from nearby villages and truck drivers, and at bazaars in the old city catering to low-income consumer demand. They also trade uppers at markets to shoemakers from nearby villages.[15]

In contrast to the informal sector, the products of Agra's formal sector are bought by leading Indian footwear concerns which themselves do not manufacture cheaper varieties, or are exported overseas either directly by the producers themselves or through trading operations. On the whole, Agra produces cheap shoes; units in the formal sector produce comparatively high-priced shoes costing over Rs 100 and there are some that make shoes costing over Rs 250 (Knorringa 1996; Roy 2013, 110–111).

Generally, light industrial producers in the informal sector like the textile and footwear industries manufacture cheap goods satisfying the rural and low-income markets and foreign demand for low-cost products. How is it possible though for MSE producers to produce goods more cheaply than the formal sector, contrary to the logic of economy of scale? MSE producers excel in certain aspects of production, labour and marketing. First, the smallest units of production are both small-scale and efficient, as seen in the knitwear and garment industries. In Tiruppur, the central process is the power table or stitching section, which consists of six to eight stitching machines mounted on a table, all powered by a single motor (Chari 2004, 67–68).[16] In the case of the large-scale factories too, often a large number of small units occupy the same floor, and here there is no fundamental divergence from the dispersed production process. As well, "spatially separate production [processes] … go to make the final commodity" (Cawthorne 1995, 47).

Second, in such small-scale stitching production units, owners take part in the production process on the floor, supervising the labour, and thereby improve efficiency. Former workers in the stitching sections of micro-scale industries in Tiruppur have often themselves become owners. By overseeing employees in such close proximity they are able to strengthen labour intensity. Though machines play a role in the production process, manual labour has remained central and so the input of intensive physical labour is essential. The efficiency of producers is not regulated by machines but through the stronger influence of the personality of supervisors on the floor (Chari 2004, 124, 125, 129). When "garment orders can be so differentiated that there may be as few as tens of a particular size, shape and color", this type of labour supervision and control is particularly effective (Chari 2000, 584).

This has had a large influence on factory growth. Proprietors who do not themselves take part in labour delegate labour intensive processes for small workshops to supervise. Chari states that in Tiruppur the knitwear company that sells the garments may not engage in fabrication at all. Rather, it puts out all the various parts of the process to a great many MSE producers, and so its main activity is organising the assembly of the pieces received from the subcontractors. This form of production greatly weakens any tendency towards the outward expansion of the workshop. A crucial point about the knitwear and garment industry of Tiruppur is that it is a cluster whose core components are an extremely large number of MSEs. In other words, a highly developed network of contractual and trading relationships between an enormous number of businesses undercuts any merit in creating large factories.[17]

As we will see below, larger factories may have multiple units in-house, but employers do not supervise workers directly. Instead they employ "internal contracting", allocating a process to a contractor within the company who uses machines owned by the factory and employs labour at piece-rates (Singh and Sapra 2007, 114, 120).[18] These contractors are also responsible for quality control, ensuring, for example, that the white banians do not get dirty (Cawthorne 1995, 49). In the more substantial footwear workshops in Agra, master artisans are hired for each of the five basic operations it takes to create a full shoe; "they take up responsibility for a full load [and] execute part of the work themselves", using their own apprentices and workers (Knorringa 1996, 86–87).

Third, small units are efficient when there is a demand for a wide spectrum of products. People's preferences in colour, style and fabric for clothes vary hugely according to class, locality and season. The goods produced for such a segmented and changing market are fabricated from an almost infinite combination of various sizes, styles, materials, production methods and ranges of quality. Given this, small-scale production is far more suitable than production methods based on standard products in large lots. For example, in the textile industry, loom speed is not the critical factor in productivity. Of more importance is whether a broad range of cloths can be made and whether items can be adapted quickly. Here, the ability of powerlooms to respond rapidly lends them greater efficiency compared to mills (Roy 1998, 906). The use of the power table as the unit of production in Tiruppur further accommodates this kind of diversification (Chari 2000).[19]

At the beginning of the 1990s, there were 225 shops in the market area of Central Agra occupied by wholesalers buying footwear. These usually dealt in specialised products dictated by the tastes of the region that they or their commission agents were connected to. Demand in footwear, as in clothing, varies with season. In India, demand rises from September and reaches a peak in October and November, when people wear closed shoes because of the colder weather. This is also the time of some major festivals and the main marriage season, for which people wear new clothes and new footwear. MSE footwear producers are able to supply small lot units in response to these fluctuations (Knorringa 1996, 70–71, 88, 91, 107).[20]

The items traded in the plastic recycling industry are also manifold. The Delhi scrap market deals in 450–500 items, ranging from Gillette advertisement hoardings and Saffola cooking oil cans to spectacles and pens (Gill 2010, 131). Depending on their recycling potential, they are categorised by colour and the darkness or lightness of the permanent dye. Seasonality also affects demand in this trade. Waste collection for recycling is slack in summer and during the monsoon. Poorer people wear closed shoes made from recycled plastic in winter and sandals in summer, and this creates a need for plastic in winter. During the Holi festival demand for polypropylene (PP) increases as it is used to make the water-pistols for the festival, and during Diwali more plastics used to make jugs and gift items are required (Gill 2010, 140).

Fourth, producing cheap products requires cheap labour. Informal industry uses an inexpensive, lesser-educated workforce as necessary, recruited from a labour market linked with rural society. The schooling level of the core of workers in the garment industry is low. In Tiruppur, the garment industry has been dominated by the Gounder caste from the region's rural areas, and

> "though 90 percent [of workers] have attended school for at least a year, 60 percent of them have not gone beyond the primary stage. Women and long-distance migrant workers – who account for a growing share of Tiruppur's workforce – constitute a greater section of the lesser-educated segment".
>
> (Vijayabaskar and Jeyaranjan 2011, 146)

Many migrant workers in the Delhi garment industry are from Uttar Pradesh and Bihar. They lodge with men from their village, caste or family who are already employed in Delhi and its environs, and search for work, initially as casual helpers. Women usually migrate after marriage, and most have a family member working in the garment industry. It is normal for workers to maintain a connection with their villages; owners and managers say that they frequently return home for festivals, marriages, funerals and other occasions, going back for four months every year. This information is often accompanied by the criticism that they have no dedication or commitment to their work, yet the survival of the village connection is very convenient for employers. The Delhi garment industry cannot provide work for all 12 months of the year and relies upon the fact that workers can return home when there is none. Employers also use village ties as an excuse not to offer any kind of security for old age or for families in the form of a pension or health benefits.[21]

The employment of lesser-educated migrant workers indicates that most segments of the Indian garment industry that are engaged in the production of cheap quasi-branded goods do not seek highly skilled and knowledgeable employees. To survive and expand in an export market prey to severe fluctuations and a domestic market subject to seasonality, entrepreneurs shift the burden of generational reproduction to rural society and of course to their present workers.[22] There is, however, inherent instability in this set up. Employers and workers do not enjoy a constant relationship and securing a full migrant workforce at the right time can be precarious. In fairly large-scale factories the actual production process is entrusted to contractors who employ their own labour, as described above. This system, which meets the need of small-scale production to have supervisors who have social control over workers, functions to link the rural migrant labour force with the labour demands of the urban informal sector. Contractors routinely employ labour from their own village and caste group (Singh and Sapra 2007, 114; Chari 2004, 60).

While dependence on such a fluid labour market is the basis of the competitiveness of the Indian garment industry (Singh and Sapra 2007, 115), it sets limitations on any plans to improve technology and quality or to move into the finer quality export market. This point will be further discussed below, but according to Vijayabaskar and Jeyaranjan (2011), who have studied the Tiruppur labour market, there is high interfirm mobility among the lesser-educated workers, with most moving on within a year to a higher-grade job. This dynamism makes employers reluctant to provide in-plant training to improve workers' education and skills. By contrast, in the Shandong (China) textile industry, workers generally remain with the same firm for a long period and receive in-plant education, both basic and periodic training to upgrade skills. The educational level here is high, and many workers have attended junior college after completing 12 years of schooling. In addition, the Chinese workers receive social insurance. The technological level of China's textile industry, which is higher than India's, is sustained by long-term employment and in-plant training. In comparison, the fluid labour market and employment relationships in India's textile industry restrict it and make it difficult for it to move beyond the low road scenario of providing goods for the low-cost market by exploiting a cheap labour force.[23]

Despite the fact that even today, a significant number of footwear producers live in rural areas,[24] there has been a steady incursion into urban areas over the past few decades (Naidu 2009, 20). In Agra, most of the workers in the footwear industry are Jatavs, a Chamar sub-caste; at the beginning of 1990 they numbered around 60,000 (Knorringa 1996, 80–81). In the 1961 census, the Jatav population of Agra was just over 70,000. Assuming that one quarter were adult males, we can estimate that there were under 20,000 textile workers at that time (Lynch 1969, 31). It may be supposed therefore that in the 30 years between 1961 and 1990 a very large number of lowest-caste workers relocated to the city from the country. Roy (2013, Chapter 8), who conducted a survey of the Agra footwear industry around 2010, pointed out that 40 percent of Agra's population of 2 million were engaged in the footwear industry, either in production or in sales. If we calculate that one quarter of a household's members are employed and around 10,000 households are engaged in work connected with the footwear industry, then we can estimate that between 100,000 and 200,000 people work in the industry, an enormous number of whom must have migrated from rural areas after 1990.

Not enough is known about the situation of workers in the footwear industry who have migrated to the city from outside. The preservation of village ties is evident in their home visits for festivals and special occasions, which result in the virtual standstill of production (Knorringa 1996). Self-employed persons may go back to the villages to work in agriculture during the sowing and harvesting seasons, showing that the native village often remains a fixture of migrant lives. Roy writes that most workers in the Kolkata footwear cluster are men from Bihar who have left their families there. Workers in Agra, by comparison, are mostly local residents, although many have moved over time to the city from neighbouring districts and states. Workers in the footwear industry are from the lowest socio-economic classes in rural areas, and within the labour market connected with them, they are reproduced as a low-wage labour force (Roy 2013, 45, 50–51, 114).

In the Delhi plastic recycling industry surveyed by Gill, the majority of workers and some of the traders are from the SC Khatiks. They have migrated largely from Rajasthan, with a small number from Uttar Pradesh. Though most have lived in Delhi for more than 20 years, "their 'migrant' standing is sustained at a fundamental level by the illegal status of many of their slum settlements". Many of the traders from the same caste are second-generation, born and bred in Delhi, so they cannot be considered migrants. Nevertheless, they maintain strong links with their native villages. They help men newly arrived in Delhi from the villages in a variety of ways, creating a framework enabling them to enter plastic recycling work (Gill 2010, 158–173).

Fifth, producers in MSEs keep costs down by cheaply procuring the necessary machinery and inputs, like raw material. This approach is readily apparent in the footwear industry. In Agra, while suppliers to one of the large Indian footwear companies like Bata buy their leather from wholesalers specified by the parent company, artisans in MSEs lack working capital and so do not buy proper upper leather and sole material from the main market. Instead, they collect together supplies from the market that deals in left-over and rejected materials from the larger workshops and small-scale factories (Knorringa 1996, 113–114).[25] In addition, India's recycling rate is one of the world's highest at approximately 60–80 percent, and plastic recycling provides PVC grain for making cheap shoes and furniture. Of the total number of products made from recycled plastic, 70 percent are made from PVC. This means that the volume of shoes made from recycled plastic must be rather high.[26]

A study of sandal making in the slums of a large city in South India emphasises the need for cheap raw materials; their cost makes up 95 percent of that of the finished product and so is of decisive importance. Home-based producers use cheap, low-quality materials while most of the larger entrepreneurs use high-grade ones. As a result, there is a large differential in the cost of the constituent parts of sponge sandals, for instance: Around Rs 36 for the large entrepreneur and around Rs 18 for the household-based producer. Thus the cost reduction made through using low-grade materials is considerable (Rani and Galeb 1998).[27]

Highly efficient arrangements for raw materials have developed in the city of Ludhiana in Punjab State, a centre for the hosiery and engineering industries. Unlike in other areas, industry growth here has been led by small- and medium-sized firms. Since the 1970s, the raw materials used by upstream producers have been reused downstream in a series of stages. This has been very important for small and medium firms. For example, a component producer who buys a steel sheet at Rs 10 per length sells the punched sheet on at Rs 6 per length to a downstream producer. The latter takes the material he needs for his own product and in turn sells the rest on to another downstream producer, and so on. The final pieces of scrap are sold by a local scrap dealer to a steel re-rolling mill. This system enables Ludhiana's small component producers (especially of nuts and bolts and other simpler parts) to sell some of their products at prices lower than those paid by producers in other areas, like Mumbai, for the same items (Tewari 1998, 1396).

Saving costs in relation to machinery was also integral to the success of MSEs (Roy 1998, 904; Roy 2004, 108). As will become apparent, MSE producers in an overwhelmingly broad range of industries use a variety of machinery which appears to be mostly second-hand. This is commonly the practice in plastic recycling industry (Gill 2010, 143), and in Tiruppur, an active market for second-hand machinery allowed easier entry for newcomers to the garment industry (Chari 2000, 588). Aggressive powerloom factories acquired the high-performance looms discarded by mills and in turn cast off their old machines, which were then bought by other powerloom factories.

In Ludhiana, trade associations pressure the state government for aid, asking that costly equipment that is too expensive for individual small firms be imported so it can be copied and manufactured locally. The copies of imported machinery can cost as little as one tenth of the original item (Tewari 1998; Tewari 1999). In my study of the knitted garment industry in Ludhiana, I was told that locally manufactured parts were being used even in imported machines. Creating imitation machinery and equipment and new parts for imported machines requires a certain level of existing technological skill. The system whereby MSEs could purchase these items, including access to a second-hand market for them, was underpinned by local developments based on the making and repair of machines. This will be further discussed below.

Sixth, how entrepreneurs themselves worked was crucial in keeping costs down. Roy understands that amid the decline of mills and the rise of powerlooms, mill management determines success or failure. Some mills reacted to changes in demand by improving their products and machines and expanding as producers of branded goods, but many more simply failed. The degree an entrepreneur is engaged in production and sales on the spot is an important factor in competitiveness. The fact that Gounder caste owners in Tiruppur's garment industry tend to work on the shopfloor with members of their family does not only raise labour intensity among the other workers. One reason for Tiruppur's deepening hold over the Indian hosiery market has been its production of "fine banians" using fine counts of thread. This has intensified the need for labour supervision (Chari 2004, 125, 224–25, 229). There is little doubt that entrepreneurs working alongside their workers and simultaneously supervising them has contributed greatly to establishing the position of Tiruppur in the Indian hosiery market.

Many powerloom owners had started out in the weaving industry. They were often members of major weaver castes with direct experience of the craft (Roy 1998, 889, 900). They too worked on the floor and had a good knowledge of the actualities of production. Where it was important to be able to quickly switch between a great variety of fabrics using regular machines, powerloom owners could respond more quickly than the mills, since being able to make swift management decisions would be easier for someone closely involved in on-the-spot production.

In the plastic recycling industry too, detailed knowledge of the local scene is essential for owners, traders and brokers. In Delhi, a worker from a rural area might advance his position incrementally, if he is lucky by dint of hard work on site, and become an entrepreneur or trader. In this industry, which operates and trades in a multi-tiered market made up of a plethora of materials and products, rapid managerial judgements are vital and ideally based on a thorough knowledge of the local situation, derived from experience, and comprehensive information concerning those in the business (Gill 2010,134–141, 162).

Another example where skilled workers have become owners is the engineering industry of Ludhiana. Behind the dynamic growth of the light engineering and metal-working industries can be found skilled workers who are also proprietors of small businesses. They are second- or third-generation descendants of rural blacksmiths from Punjab who gradually moved to the city and engaged in manufacturing bicycle parts. They worked on production themselves but also had the additional ability to make machinery, and so they copied borrowed and second-hand machines, building them on a tight budget. They did not need to pay for skilled labour and were able to establish small businesses to "manufacture" their own machines, having the aptitude to make improvements in design and quality and introduce innovations (Tewari 1999).[28]

In informal industry it is possible to find owners hailing from both skilled worker backgrounds and from merchant backgrounds. In the case of the latter, they possess an in-depth understanding of a diverse and complex market, and their competitiveness derives from this and their useful connections to producers and traders. In the Agra footwear industry, SC Jatav artisans run household-based workshops using family labour, but units on a bigger scale are generally operated by white-collar entrepreneurs from a merchant caste background. They gather information from similarly white-collar traders and suppliers associated with large footwear enterprises with an all-India reach and conduct their business based on mutual trust (Knorringa 1996).

In the Tiruppur garment industry too there is considerable participation by entrepreneurs from a mainly North Indian merchant background, but as we have seen, these rarely engage in domestic production, subcontracting work out to household-based workshops instead. Their competitiveness may be thought to derive from their access to information sources within the Tiruppur cluster and their ties with internal and external markets. However, this remains a matter of speculation.

In any case, within a multi-tiered and complex market structure, where both demand and production are segmented, information gathered from the sites of manufacturing and trade is of particular significance. Knorringa (1996, 77–78) points out that Jatav footwear producers are not in a position to receive market and other intelligence from the white-collar traders, and this is a major impediment to their business expansion, highlighting the importance of knowledge in such a market structure. Graduating from university and becoming "white collar" supplies a substantial advantage, as it allows participation in the information networks.

This section has outlined how MSEs produce low-cost goods whose quality cannot be guaranteed. Their production units are small, and supervision on the floor by owners who are ex-workers is important. In terms of demand, low cost takes precedence over quality. Demand itself is extremely varied and segmented and subject to seasonal fluctuation. They require cheap wages of their labour force rather than labour quality and use low-paid and poorly educated workers obtained through labour markets with links to rural society. Cheap goods are manufactured thanks to a material input consisting of cheap, second-hand machinery and raw materials, such as recycled products. In such an environment – defined by segmented production and the type of labour force used – prompt business decisions represent an efficient use of the system. These are made possible by owners or supervisors of small-scale businesses either being ex-worker entrepreneurs or having merchant backgrounds, enabling access to real experience and information about trading in a complex market. The contrast here with the classic case of the mills, run by an elite managerial class, springs to mind. MSEs prosper thanks to a system based on a series of mutual ties that are mutually complementary.

Related informal sectors have created a system producing cheap goods, linked closely to the circulation of both goods and people (this will be fully explored in Chapter 9). Members of rural society are present throughout. They work themselves in the informal agricultural sector, providing products cheaply to villages and urban areas, and also consume mainly very low-cost manufactured goods with no guarantee of quality. They further contribute to that industry by reproducing cheap labour. Since high educational qualifications are not required for the labour force provided for the informal sectors, the educational fee for reproducing it is minimal. This is a crucial factor in the cost of reproducing cheap labour. Moreover, demand for inexpensive items without guarantee of quality has defined certain characteristics related to the techniques and systems of production: The quality of the machines invested in and the raw materials used, the choice of labour force and the way labour is supervised. In this way reciprocal relationships have come into being.[29]

There can be no doubt that government protection of small-scale industries and the various restrictions placed on the large-scale factories promoted the series of systems for the production of quasi-branded goods. However, even without these restrictions, we may assume that an informal industry with similar characteristics would have developed.

## Globalisation and MSEs

Exports overseas from various Indian industries, including the knitwear, garment and footwear industries exploded from the mid-1980s. In what way was this expansion connected to the growth of MSEs? Tirthankar Roy, for example, understands changes in clothing habits in India to have been the result of the export surplus of ready-made clothing spilling over into local markets (Roy 2004, 92). Even considering that ready-made clothing had a high rate of export within the textile industry, only about 25 percent of its product was actually sold abroad, while the export rate for shoes was extremely low and for the plastics recycling industry miniscule. In terms of quantity, therefore, MSEs were rooted in the domestic market. Also significant, as Roy asserts, was the preference in domestic consumption for cheap quasi-branded garments, which basically determined the direction of production in the industry. This trend cannot be explained without taking into account changes in the consumption patterns of the lower classes, which were connected in turn to social changes in Indian villages, as illustrated in the survey conducted by Osella and Osella. To understand such changes simply as "globalisation" does not take into account market trends for India as a whole, even though it might explain parallel developments among the urban middle and upper classes. Therefore the essential determinant in the growth of informal industries is not exports but altering consumption trends within a broad range of social groups, including the rural and urban lower classes.

It cannot be denied, though, that the expansion of exportable goods exerted a decisive influence on these informal industries. The export share in the final demand for woven cloth and garments accelerated from around 11 percent in the mid-1980s to around 30 percent in 1995 (Roy 2004, Table 3.2, p. 89). Exports of ready-made clothing and knitwear also saw a remarkable rise. The Indian textile industry was energised as a result, and it goes without saying that medium-sized enterprises and MSEs especially benefitted as they took the initiative and entered the export sphere. Less clear is the effect of this area of growth on the organisation of these industries and their production methods. Let us look briefly at a few examples of the influence of exports on the industries examined above in an attempt to elucidate this point.

The textile industry escalated its overseas sales as more opportunities occurred from the 1980s, led not by the mills but by the MSE sector. In 1995–1996, 88 percent of textile exports came directly or indirectly from powerlooms, indicating that the informal sector was more competitive internationally than the mills (Roy 1998, 898). This competitiveness derived primarily from the system developed by the MSEs for the production of low-cost goods. Furthermore, as we will discuss in the next section, local "bottom-up" industrial growth facilitated export expansion.[30] The impact of this growth on the MSEs was multifaceted. Increased exports in Tiruppur, certainly in the early period, appeared to amplify the decentralisation of production rather than bringing about changes in large-scale operations. Between the 1980s, when exports began, and the mid-1990s there was a decrease both in large factories with more than 50 employees and in medium-sized and small factories, while MSE workshops proliferated (Table 7.6).[31]

From the end of the 1970s into the 1980s, the composition of the workforce in the textile industry of Tiruppur evolved. Previously the workforce had consisted mainly of males from the city itself as well as neighbouring villages, but more trading abroad meant a higher demand for labour and the workforce was supplemented by large numbers of SC migrants from various regions of South India and by women. Most of the women were employed in new sections associated with exports, such as checking and finishing, while SC workers were allocated the harshest tasks, like bleaching. From the middle of the 1980s, many female workers were also engaged at lower wages in skilled jobs such as tailoring. The new wave of workers lacked opportunities to become owners, unlike the Gounders, who in the past had started out in banian factories before gaining their independence (Chari 2004, 345–347; Vijayabaskar and Jeyaranjan 2011, 143; Singh and Sapra 2007, 86).

*Table 7.6* Changes in distribution of factories by employment, Tiruppur

| *Factory size* | *1986* | *1996* | *Decadal change* |
|---|---|---|---|
| Less than 10 workers | 0 | 130 | – |
| 10–19 | 0 | 310 | – |
| 29–49 | 151 | 497 | 229% |
| 50–99 | 89 | 37 | –58% |
| 100–499 | 12 | 7 | –42% |
| 500–999 | 20 | 0 | –100% |
| More than 1,000 workers | 0 | 0 | 0 |

Source: Chari 2004, Table 6 (p. 27).

Original source: "Statement III", 1996, at the Office of the Deputy Inspector of Factories, Tiruppur.

Interestingly, the Tiruppur garment industry sought to focus on exports with low prices as it main advantage in meeting foreign demand. For those labourers who bought banians, until then the chief product of the industry, goods intended for export were too expensive. To compete abroad it looked to undercut prices rather than change its technology or improve quality (Chari 2004, 256, 266–267), and pushed towards the lower-priced end of overseas markets based on a cheap, low-quality, fluid workforce. Firms had no incentive to provide training programmes for their insecure migrant workers, and this attitude only strengthened as exports grew. From the 1990s, Tiruppur looked to the middle-range North American market, but contrasted starkly with its competitor, the Chinese textile industry, which had a comparatively higher wage level, a well-educated workforce, including junior college graduates, long-term employment, and investment in technology through in-plant training. Whereas China's share in the global market is swelling, India's has frozen following the phasing out of the Multi-Fibre Agreement in 2005. Tiruppur's future as the site of one of India's most important export textile industries will depend on its ability to rid itself of a mindset that favours a cheap and minimally educated workforce and create a system of technically competent labourers in its place, and whether in the process it can curb its reliance on cheap and low-technology goods (Chari 2004; Vijayabaskar and Jeyaranjan 2011; Roy 2013, 82, 105).

While in Tiruppur, export expansion resulted in the shrinking of production units in the 1980s,[32] in other areas some textile factories increased in size. In the garment industry in Delhi for instance, cotton shirts for the European and North American markets have to be made in a very clean environment, and so cannot be transported in and out of the factory for thread cutting or button stitching; such work has to be done in-house (Singh and Sapra 2007, 115, 120; Roy 2013, 91). The export market for textiles insists on improved product quality and standardisation, and has introduced a new economy of scale. Thus one powerloom firm that wanted to ship its product abroad had to install new machines to weave cloth of a single yarn type in order to exceed the minimum export unit, which needed a very high degree of standardisation (Roy 1998, 903–904). There is nevertheless no uniformity regarding the scale of units. Processes that had previously been outsourced by the large units are now being done on the same premises, and in some cases mass production methods are being applied as a result of fundamental changes in the assembly line. There has, however, been no change, even in Delhi's case, in the labour supply system, centred on cheap fluid labour (Singh and Sapra 2007, 116). This remains, as stated already, the greatest limiting factor for India's future export growth.

As policy slowly adapted in the course of the 1980s towards trade liberalisation, with the 1985 Textile Policy and the 1991 economic reforms, there was an easing of import restrictions on machinery and intermediate goods. This had a great impact on Indian industry. Particularly important among machinery imports from the late 1980s was second-hand textile machinery from East Asia. The Indian textile industry increasingly introduced new automatic looms in place of the older, plain machines. These new models were first utilised by the larger units like mills. The mills then sold on their old looms to progressive powerlooms, which in turn discarded their looms. These were captured by other powerloom centres. In this way, newer technology spread to MSE firms. In some cases, technology was imported as machinery or via collaboration with European and East Asian firms (Roy 1998, 904). In 1994/95, 58 percent of textile machinery available in India was imported (Roy 2004, Table 3.14, p 103). Not unexpectedly, many powerloom owners did not introduce such new machinery. In fact, most probably could not modernise in this way. It should, however, be noted that overall, MSE owners did choose to innovate, including through the introduction of imported machines. As Marjit and Kar have shown, whereas capital stock in the formal sector either remained stagnant or dwindled, fixed assets grew in the informal sector (2012, 254–55, 270). This suggests a connection to the active renewal of machinery. It is probably safe to say that technical improvements by MSEs took place against a backdrop of the increasing importance of both the export and the domestic markets.

## Industrial Growth "from Below"

The enlargement of the rural market was critical for those industries led by MSEs – textiles, footwear, recycled plastics – and rural and local society played a vital role as the seedbed of their workers and owners. Members of the Gounder community, a South Indian agrarian caste, had been leading figures in the development of the textile industry in Tiruppur, site of the largest cluster of MSEs in India. At the beginning of the twentieth century, Tiruppur was located in the centre of a prominent cotton growing area and had an important cotton market. The long-staple cotton farmed there produced a fine yarn that was greatly desired by mills in Madras and Coimbatore.

Gounders played a key role in Tiruppur, as farmers, traders and early industrialists. They cultivated a variety of cash crops in the district and invested their surplus in trade and small industry. After Independence, there was an expansion of village-based industries – stock raising, handlooms, powerlooms, ginning, knits, machinery and so on – and cultivators like the Gounders moved into the Tiruppur knitwear industry as both workers and owners. Gounder labourers from the villages found work in Gounder-run factories, and many gained their independence as petty entrepreneurs with support from the Gounder community (Chari 2000; Chari 2004, Chapters 4 and 5). Agrarian producers, who were used to controlling labour, used their surplus from agriculture to move into industry and ran their businesses according to the same spirit of diligent physical labour (which they call "toil") that they displayed on the land (Chari 2000; Chari 2004). Scholars have accordingly called attention to the "agrarian origins" of the Tiruppur knitwear industry.

Medium and MSE clusters of industries in Ludhiana similarly took shape in close contact with rural society and can also be said to have "agrarian origins". At the beginning of the 1990s, Ludhiana had 40,164 registered small firms and 109 medium/large firms, producing 95 percent of India's woollen hosiery, 85 percent of its sewing machine parts and 60 percent of its cycles and cycle parts. It is particularly significant that up to the early 1980s more than 60 percent of workers in Punjab's small firm sector were skilled. "These skilled workers are not only supervisors/foremen and skilled machinists, but the bulk of them are proprietors of small businesses, job shops and factories in the region's light engineering, metal-working and machine tool industries" (Tewari 1998, 1395). Tewari maintains that these skilled workers had their origins in rural blacksmiths who produced farming implements in the villages during the colonial period. When laying railroads and building canals, the colonial government recruited large numbers of local blacksmiths and other artisans, especially the Ramgarhias. "This exposure to new manufacturing experiences ... enabled these rural craftworkers to upgrade their technological base, diversify their skills and learn how to adapt them to new production tasks and environments" (Tewari 1998, 1397). Some of them accumulated enough capital to set up small metal-working shops in rural areas. They could not achieve upward mobility through the purchase of land, since as "non-agriculturists" they were barred from owning agricultural land under the Punjab Land Alienation Act of 1900. This encouraged them to relocate to urban areas, and many of them collaborated with traders who had knowledge of the markets. As they gained independence they began setting up metal-working shops producing hosiery machines, tools and equipment, as well as foundries. Many of these small metal-based firms diversified into the production of cycles, cycle parts and sewing machines. Ludhiana's small industries are buttressed by a local machine industry that produces cheap equipment, but this industry itself rides on the shoulders of artisans with rural origins. And this is not the only linkage between Ludhiana's industries and agricultural villages. Grain brokers "have played a significant financier-role in Ludhiana's small-firm development" and were a "crucial connection between agricultural surpluses and local industrial investment" (Tewari 1998, 1400). Tewari understands that linkages were weak between Ludhiana's industries and the rural and Punjab urban markets, though we should note that the growth of the Ludhiana cycle industry was led by the rural market (Singh 1990). Reconstruction of old-style dwellings to new buildings with concrete and tile was widely observed in the agriculturally advanced Punjab state during the course of the Green Revolution (A. Singh 2001, 253), which must have pushed the demand greatly for associated construction materials.

The industries of both Tiruppur and Ludhiana, similarly dominated by MSEs, have taken form and grown out of local rural society, and this pattern can be discerned elsewhere. For example, in the handloom industry, weavers from rural areas gradually concentrated in urban areas, and a large number switched from operating handlooms to running powerlooms. Many footwear makers had their origins in village leather workers who had moved to the cities (and who have continued to maintain their village links down to the present). Workers in the Delhi plastic recycling industry too were made up of SC members from rural villages who also continued to maintain close rural ties. The agrarian origins of the informal sector, which led India's industrial growth, and of the industrial sector made up of MSEs were a core factor in their development "from below", in terms of markets, background and, in part, financing.

## Notes

1 Ramaswamy (1994), who studied changes in employment in the manufacturing industry between 1981 and 1991, pointed out a move in relative importance in manufacturing from the large industries to the small ones. The percentage occupied by household industry was falling while in non-household industry, the unorganised sector of small industries grew from 56 percent to 65 percent. Subrahmanya (2004) showed that "the share of small industry in national income increased in the protection period of the 1980s but declined considerably in the transitional period of the 1990s" and that the share of small industry in employment grew significantly in both the 1980s and 1990s. Even in the organised sector between 1956 and 1977, the share of employees in small and medium firms rose rapidly (Kashyap 1988).

2 For example, Mazumdar and Sarkar (2008, 208–209) stress the influence of the small-scale industry reservations policy where the manufacture of a large number of items could be done only by small enterprises. Ishigami (2011) introduces their argument and points out the possibility of critically defeating it. Incorporating the argument of Itō Shōji concerning India's two-tiered low-cost, high-cost economy, he attaches importance to the workings of the Indian consumer market divided into the widespread poor classes, and the wealthy and middle classes. This is an important view, shared by the present author.

3 The total number of powerlooms in the major states was 15,000 in 1942, 146,000 in 1963, 571,000 in 1983 and 1.2 million in 1993 (Roy 1998, Table 2).

4 Indian Institute of Foreign Trade, *Export and Management Capabilities of the Indian Garments Industry*, Market Research Wing, Textile Committee, Ministry

of Textiles, Govt. of India, Mumbai, c. 1999, Table 1.4 (p. 16). From the 1960s, many composite mills fell into financial difficulties and mill production remained static. This was due to the rapid growth of specialist spinning mills in South India. Composite mills, 291 in number in 1956, declined to 281 in 1985. In the same period, specialist spinning mills increased from 121 to 674 (Leadbeater 1993, Table 5.6, 229–230). Post-Independence textile policy imposed a number of restrictions on production by large mills, but according to Leadbeater (1993, Chapter 5), the main reason for the financial troubles faced by composite mills was not the demands of import substitution but their loss of the domestic market to the powerlooms. The specialist spinning mills of South India, the main market of the powerloom sector, underwent great development. Thus Leadbeater, in asking why MSEs grew, seeks out the reasons for the decline of the cotton industry in western India, the greatest of the formal sector industries in independent India.

5 A 1956 report concerning the hosiery industry throws light on the cost structure of the production process of 15 units in South India. The greatest cost was materials (65–90 percent). Labour costs were around 8–10 percent. Of course there were differences according to the scale of production. In large factories, labour costs were around a maximum of 15 percent, while in many small factories they were less than 13 percent and in quite a few less than 10 percent. In household industries labour costs were as high as 19 percent. The report concluded that economising on labour costs through large-scale mechanization in large factories had little effect, and that the size of the labour cost had little decisive bearing on the competitiveness of the product.(Development Commissioner [Small Scale Industries], *Small Scale Industry Analysis and Planning Report, No. 18, Hosiery Industry (All India)*, Ministry of Commerce and Industry, Government of India, New Delhi, 1958, pp. 47–49).

6 As we shall see below, in Tiruppur in Tamil Nadu, the most important centre in India for the manufacture of knits and ready-made clothing, production depends on several thousand MSEs. Singh and Sapra (2007, 67, 87) criticise the argument concerning government regulation as the main factor of growth, pointing out that although government controls regulating entry into this industry were eased after 1991, "there are hardly any signs of a transformation of production organization towards greater centralization, composite production, or FDI".

7 The case of woollen knits made in Ludhiana, a centre of the industry, is thought to be different from that of cotton knits. Whereas the market for cotton knits is the rural and urban poor, that for woollen knits, was, at least until the 1950s, the wealthy classes mainly living in cities (see Chapter 3).

8 According to one estimate, as of 1999–2000, close to 1,745,000 workers were employed in over 780,000 units making ready-made clothing from fabrics or knits. The informal sector accounted for 83 percent of employment and 99 percent of units. Of employees in the formal sector, 5.8 percent were contract workers (Singh and Sapra 2007, 44–45).

9 Ready-made clothing occupies more than half the export market in Indian textiles (Singh and Sapra, 2007, 43).

10 Satyaki Roy, who studied the large footwear cluster in Kolkata that is centred on producing cheap, low-quality goods, pointed out that 32 of the 48 units surveyed had been established after 1980, suggesting that the demand for cheap footwear had increased rapidly at that time. There is a great demand at the lower end of the mass market for non-leather footwear because of its lower cost and durability (Roy 2013, 44, 113).

11 According to a study of informal sector sandal making in a large city, sandals were made either of sponge rubber or of rubber. Those made of sponge rubber targeted the higher-priced urban market and there was competition here from the formal sector. The market for the cheap rubber sandals was much broader with

distant sales, and profits for merchants were large (Rani and Galab 1998). This confirms that high-priced products from the formal sector centre on urban demand and cheap goods serve a broad area, including rural villages.

12 Gill 2010, 15, 17, 133, 161, 170, 248. Gill says that this industry has created a new market for recycled goods among the poorest classes and the rural population.

13 Tirthankar Roy has pointed out the changes in casual clothing that took place in urban areas in the 1980s with the diffusion of jeans, T-shirts, knitted goods, etc. and understands this to have been the result of lower-cost goods becoming available on the domestic market as exports expanded (Roy 2004, 92). Such an understanding that exports led changing consumption patterns is no doubt valid concerning changes in consumption among the urban middle classes in the 1980s, but it is insufficient in that it does not consider the question of changes in rural society in connection with the extensive rural market.

14 The market structure of the metal furniture manufacturing industry is also divided between high-quality, high-cost goods and low-quality, low-cost goods, supplied by the large industry sector and the MSE sector respectively. Around 1990, the prices of branded products such as Godrej, including excise duties and sales taxes, were two or three times higher than the prices of products from the small-scale sector (Guhathakurta 1993, 2040).

15 In Kolkata, shoes for export are produced in larger units employing more than 50 workers, while MSE units produce shoes for the domestic market (Roy 2013, 44).

16 In the case of the Agra footwear industry, "the smallest full-shoe producing units … minimally consist of four male members", who are in charge of one of four processes. A typical small workshop has nine employees (Knorringa 1996, 85).

17 Roy (2013) also points out the importance of cooperative relations among firms in the growth of powerlooms.

18 Many of the contractors "rise from the ranks of workers" (Roy 1998, 909). In Tiruppur, which experienced labour disputes in the past, the use of internal contracts "is often used as a strategy to separate stitching workers from cutting and packing workers who report directly to the boss" (Chari 2004, 125).

19 Roy, speaking of the Delhi garment industry, says that "[t]he size of orders for a specific design to be produced for the domestic market is generally smaller than for exports" (Roy 2013, 86). In the garment industry of Tiruppur, "in the knitting section alone one would require large varieties of machines to cater to different types of fabrics". This is impossible for a single factory, and so many different factories complement one another in the machines they employ (Roy 2013, 100).

20 Around 2010, there were about 600 traders in Agra dealing in footwear for the domestic market. This is a considerable increase over the number at the beginning of the 1990s (Roy 2013, 111). We can infer the possibility that diverse distribution channels were being maintained and extended.

21 Singh and Sapra 2007, 116–117. "The workshops double as hostels after hours" (Singh and Sapra 2007, 107). This too can be said to be a way of securing a cheap workforce. For workers in the Delhi garment industry, see also Roy 2013, 88–89. In Tiruppur, workers generally maintain some ties to the agricultural land in their native villages and go to work in the fields during sowing and harvesting (Roy 2013, 100).

22 Ramaswamy (1994), who compared productivity and wages in the large and small-scale industrial sectors, found that the wage differential was greater than the productivity differential. He explained this as being caused by the high proportion of low wages in small-scale industry.

23 Roy (2004, 109) mentions the "unreliable quality and finish of generic Indian exportable goods" as being a limiting factor to the growth of the Indian textile industry internationally.

24 Half of footwear producers are based in rural areas (Kollannavar et al. 2010, 135).

25 Around 2010, the biggest difference between goods produced for export and those for the domestic market by the Agra footwear industry was in the quality of the leather. As we have already discussed, the domestic market for non-leather shoes has grown greatly. The price of non-leather shoes ranged between Rs 700 and Rs 900, while the cost of leather shoes could not be brought below Rs 1200 (Roy 2013, 117).

26 Gill 2010, 12–13, 133, 148. The relative price ratio between recycled plastics and primary plastic is roughly 0.5–0.75 (Gill 2010, 140). Though they do not publicise the fact, top shoe manufacturers like Bata frequently buy recycled resin at the recycled plastics market and mix it with fresh resin to produce a lower-priced product (ibid., 133).

27 Even in Tiruppur, the centre of the export market for knitwear, a very large number of small and household businesses have grown up, making goods for the domestic market using second-hand machinery and the "waste" that exporting firms, which have to maintain a high quality, have discarded as inferior (M. Vijayabaskar, "Conceptualising Contemporary Formal-Informal Dichotomy: An Explanatory Essay Based on Emerging Evidence from Tamil Nadu, Southern India" presented at the International Conference on "Actualities of Indian Economic Growth at the Rural-Urban Crossroads" held at the University of Tokyo, 15th and 16th December 2012).

28 Between 1980 and 1990, the ceramic ware industry in Gujarat was made up of not only registered factories but also micro enterprises. Many of the registered units produced high-priced goods such as kitchenware and sanitaryware, with Patels owning more than half of them. The Prajapatis, originally a pottery-making caste, owned 28.6 percent of the unregistered units and the scheduled castes 25.7 percent. These units produced cheap goods like cups and toys (Das 2003, 80–81).

29 Haynes (2012, 112), who has made an historical study of the development of small-scale enterprises in the weaving industry of western India, points out that central to the expansion of small-scale enterprises was the ability to produce woven goods using polished, artificial and imitation gold yarns associated with prestige or social identity that were moreover cheap.

30 The woollen knitwear industry of Ludhiana faced a crisis in the early 1990s when the collapse of the Soviet Union deprived it of its most important export market. However, it soon recovered and in a short time had successfully expanded exports abroad, including to Europe. At the same time, the domestic market was crucial. Since the exporting firms also produced goods for the domestic market, it was important not only as a safety valve. From the 1980s knitwear manufacturers had catered for the high-quality and middle-class domestic market, developing better designs and product variety and responding organisationally by improving necessary work processes. Such improvements, which catered to the requirements of the high-quality end of the domestic market, enabled the firms to advance into overseas exports (Tewari 1999). This shows how long-term industrial development based on the domestic market was an important foundation for advancing into the export market.

31 In Table 7.6, only factories registered under the Factories Act appear; those with less than ten employees that do not require registration are basically excluded. As a result, we can suppose that the numerical values appearing in the table represent a significant disparity with the real picture. Thus the table rather represents basic trends in factories with more than ten employees. Satyaki Roy, who conducted an oral survey of the Tiruppur textile industry around 2010, states that "[T]he median size [of units in Tiruppur] in terms of employment are [sic] those employing 50 to 100 workers" (Roy 2013, 95). Table 7.6 shows that in 1996, the most numerous factories were those employing between 29 and 49 workers. Since this figure is based on employee numbers registered under the Factories Act there is little doubt that these numbers were under-reported and were considerably lower

than the real figure. Therefore it is difficult to determine from these figures whether or not factory sizes actually grew in the 15 years since 1996.

32 Singh and Sapra (2007, 97) state that in the Tiruppur textile industry, "a regime of accumulation is being developed which is based on flexibility and deepened control over labour. The highly competitive and fast changing product market makes such control critical for the success of the industry". Producers in Delhi, who depend on the lower-end North American market, also have responded to the fast-changing market by using instable and cheap labour (Singh and Sapra 2007, 118).

# 8 The Growth of the Service Sector and Socio-Economic Changes in Rural Society

## The Development of the Service Industry: The Importance of the Traditional Service Sub-Sectors

Within post-1980 GDP growth rates, the service sector enjoyed a major leap, and it continued to follow this trajectory in the decade after 1991, when the economic reforms were fully adopted. This sits in contrast to the industrial sector, which witnessed a fall in its growth rate of 1 percent. The argument has consequently been put forth that the service sector is responsible for the present growth in Indian GDP.

Rises in the growth rate of the service sector occurred in two stages. The average growth rate jumped from 4.5 percent for 1951–1980 (Stage 1) to 6.6 per cent for 1981–1991 (Stage 2) and rose a further 0.9 percent to 7.5 percent in the 1990s (Table 8.1). Therefore, even down to 1980 the upwards climb was striking. As a result of this growth, the percentage occupied by tertiary industry in the Indian GDP rose from 34.82 percent in 1970–1971 to 43.46 percent in 1996–1997 (Table 8.2), while in the same period, the share of secondary industry went up from 26.78 percent to 33.80 percent. In terms of employee numbers, the share of secondary industry grew between 1970–71 and 1990–91 from 11.2 percent to 12.7 percent, a 13 percent increase, and that of tertiary industry rose in the same period from 16.7 percent to 20.5 percent, a 23 percent increase.[1]

There is a strong conviction among economists (see Introduction) that modern service sub-sectors like IT, communications and finance were stimulated by the 1991 economic reforms and rapid globalisation and became the motivating force behind Indian post-1980 GDP growth. How accurate is this assessment?

The research of Bosworth et al. (2007) into the sources of growth of the Indian economy is of great interest here. Table 8.3 (their Table 5) calculates the growth rates in service-producing industries since the 1960s and their contribution to the growth of the total, and compares "modern services" (communications, finance, business services, and education and medical care) with "traditional services" (trade, transportation and public and personal services). We can extrapolate from this data that there was an acceleration of growth in both modern and traditional services from the 1980s, and

DOI: 10.4324/9781003341550-12

*Table 8.1* Sectoral growth rates (average growth in percent per annum)

| | *1951–1980* | *1981–1990* | *1991–2000* |
|---|---|---|---|
| Agriculture | 2.1 | 4.4 | 3.1 |
| Industry | 5.3 | 6.8 | 5.8 |
| services | 4.5 | 6.6 | 7.5 |
| GDP | 3.5 | 5.8 | 5.8 |

Source: Gordon and Gupta 2004, Table 1, p. 29.

Original source: Own calculations using the Central Statistical Organisation data

*Table 8.2* Sectoral comparison, GDP and workers

| | | *% of GDP* | |
|---|---|---|---|
| | *Primary industry* | *Secondary industry* | *Tertiary industry* |
| 1950–51 | 52.1 | 13.9 | 34.1 |
| 1960–61 | 44.4 | 23.7 | 31.9 |
| 1970–71 | 38.4 | 26.8 | 34.8 |
| 1980–81 | 32.8 | 28.7 | 38.5 |
| 1990–91 | 27.1 | 31.6 | 41.3 |
| 1996–97 | 22.7 | 33.8 | 43.5 |
| | | *% of workers* | |
| | *Primary industry* | *Secondary industry* | *Tertiary industry* |
| 1950–51 | 72.1 | 10.7 | 17.2 |
| 1960–61 | 71.8 | 12.2 | 16.0 |
| 1970–71 | 72.1 | 11.2 | 16.7 |
| 1980–81 | 68.8 | 13.5 | 17.7 |
| 1990–91 | 66.8 | 12.7 | 20.5 |

Source: Madheswaran and Dharmadhikary 2000, Tables 2 and 3, p. 838.

that the growth rate of modern services was higher than that of traditional services. However, it is evident that the proportion of modern services in terms of the gross value added in the service industry as a whole was low and did not exceed 40 percent in 2004, and that as a consequence, the percentage contributed by modern services to the growth rate rise of the service sector in its entirety was lower than that of traditional services. Between 1980 and 1993, the service sector grew by 6.3 percent, but modern services contributed no more than 2 percent to this, less than half of the 4.2 percent of traditional services. Between 1993 and 1999, traditional services occupied 6.2 percent to the 3.9 percent of modern services, but the figures drew closer in the period 1999–2004, with modern services occupying 3.7 percent and traditional services 4.2 percent. These figures indicate that there is a serious drawback to assertions that modern service sub-sectors like IT, communications and finance, which were supposed to have been stimulated by

*Table 8.3* Growth in component service-producing industries, 1980–2004 (%)

| | *Modern services* | | | | | *Traditional services* | | | | |
|---|---|---|---|---|---|---|---|---|---|---|
| *Period* | *Total* | *Communications* | *Finance* | *Business services* | *Education & medical* | *Total* | *Trade* | *Transportation* | *Other services* | *Services less dwellings* |
| Share of total output in services | | | | | | | | | | |
| 1960–61 | 19 | 2 | 6 | 1 | 10 | 81 | 40 | 14 | 27 | 100 |
| 1980–81 | 22 | 3 | 7 | 1 | 11 | 78 | 37 | 16 | 24 | 100 |
| 1993–94 | 31 | 3 | 14 | 2 | 12 | 69 | 34 | 14 | 21 | 100 |
| 1999–2000 | 35 | 6 | 14 | 4 | 12 | 65 | 33 | 12 | 19 | 100 |
| May-04 | 40 | 11 | 12 | 5 | 11 | 61 | 33 | 11 | 16 | 100 |
| Annual percentage rate of change | | | | | | | | | | |
| 1960–80 | 5.7 | 6.9 | 5.9 | 3.4 | 5.5 | 4.6 | 4.5 | 5.6 | 4.3 | 4.9 |
| 1980–93 | 9 | 7.1 | 12.3 | 9.8 | 6.6 | 5.4 | 5.6 | 5.4 | 4.9 | 6.3 |
| 1993–99 | 12.6 | 20.3 | 9.3 | 28 | 10.6 | 8.9 | 9.8 | 7.5 | 8.6 | 10.1 |
| 1999–2004 | 10.5 | 23.8 | 5.7 | 11.4 | 7.1 | 6.5 | 7.9 | 5.7 | 4.3 | 8 |
| Percentage contribution to total services growth | | | | | | | | | | |
| 1960–80 | 1.1 | 0.1 | 0.3 | 0 | 0.5 | 3.8 | 1.8 | 0.8 | 1.2 | 4.9 |
| 1980–93 | 2 | 0.2 | 0.9 | 0.1 | 0.7 | 4.2 | 2.1 | 0.9 | 1.2 | 6.3 |
| 1993–99 | 3.9 | 0.7 | 1.3 | 0.5 | 1.2 | 6.2 | 3.3 | 1.1 | 1.8 | 10.1 |
| 1999–2004 | 3.7 | 1.3 | 0.8 | 0.5 | 0.8 | 4.2 | 2.6 | 0.7 | 0.8 | 8 |

Source: Bosworth et al. 2007, Table 5, p. 21.

Original source: Bosworth et al. calculations from CSO (2006) and previous years.

economic liberalisation, contributed the most to Indian GDP growth between 1980 and 2004. Their input was particularly minor in the period before 2000.[2]

Bardhan (2010, 28–29) too questions any direct linkage between India's GDP growth and the economic reforms. Quoting the above table, which he also reproduced, he wrote:

> A large part of the growth in the service sector ... was in the traditional or "unorganized sector" services, which even in the past decade formed about 60 percent of service-sector output. These services ... are provided by tiny enterprises ... unlikely to have been directly affected substantially by the regulatory or foreign trade policy reforms.

Thus the link between economic reform and growth in the leading service sector is yet to be firmly established.

Analysing the reasons behind growth-rate rises in the service sector from the 1950s, Gordon and Gupta (2004) point out that the climbing of services from 6.6 percent in the 1980s to 7.5 percent in the 1990s can be attributed to the information, communications and finance sectors, which expanded apace due to the economic reforms and increased exports. However, they make scant reference to those factors which led to the rise of the service sector from a level of 4.5 percent in the period before 1980 to 6.6 percent from the 1980s.

This chapter will examine the factors that brought about the growth in the service industry after 1980, considering the problems associated with explanations that emphasise the expansion of modern services as a result of the economic reforms and globalisation.

## The Urban Service Industry: The Importance of the Informal Sector

Let us look first at those factors that led to the post-1980s flourishing of the service industry, taking into account its activity in urban areas where formal modern services may be thought to be found in a higher proportion than in rural areas. Important information on this point has been obtained through a pilot survey of the informal sector in Ahmedabad carried out under the auspices of the Gujarat Institute of Development Research and the Self-Employed Women's Association (the SWA-GIDR survey) (Rani and Unni 2000, etc.).

Table 8.4 shows the totality of employment and income in Ahmedabad. In the service sector, 81 percent of people work in the informal sector and around 40 percent of income is derived from it. If we include the construction industry,[3] the informal sector accounts for 84 percent of all workers and 52 percent of income within the service industry. That is to say, even in the service sector of a city with an urban economy, the informal sector is overwhelmingly large in terms of employment, and even in relation to income, there is little difference from the Indian situation overall where the informal sector accounts for 60 percent of output.

*Table 8.4* Employment, income and productivity in Ahmedabad, 1997–98

| | *Employment* | | | *Income (Rs million)* | | | *Labour productivity* | | |
|---|---|---|---|---|---|---|---|---|---|
| | *Formal* | *Informal* | *Total* | *Formal* | *Informal* | *Total* | *Formal* | *Informal* | *Total* |
| | | | A. Direct output | | | | | | |
| Agriculture | 14,160 | 20,701 | 34,861 | 58 | 324 | 382 | 4,096 | 15,651 | 10,958 |
| Manufacturing | 1,73,785 | 3,59,076 | 5,32,861 | 12,453 | 9,435 | 21,888 | 71,658 | 26,270 | 41,073 |
| Electricity, gas, water supply | 12,472 | 0 | 12,472 | 1,381 | 0 | 1,381 | 1,10,728 | – | 1,10,728 |
| Construction | 0 | 1,39,264 | 1,39,264 | 0 | 2,148 | 2,148 | – | 15,454 | 15,424 |
| Total | 2,00,417 | 5,19,041 | 7,19,458 | 13,892 | 11,907 | 25,799 | | | |
| | | | B. Services | | | | | | |
| Transportation | 16,201 | 1,75,197 | 1,91,398 | 1,369 | 5,654 | 7,023 | 84,501 | 32,272 | 36,693 |
| Storage | 1,422 | 0 | 1,422 | 143 | 0 | 143 | 1,00,563 | – | 1,00,563 |
| Trade, hotels, restaurants | 26,993 | 2,58,573 | 2,85,566 | 4,197 | 7,171 | 11,368 | 1,55,485 | 27,733 | 39,809 |
| Education | 10,579 | 0 | 10,579 | 1,300 | 0 | 1,300 | | | |
| Communications, banking, insurance | 59,365 | 0 | 59,365 | 7,509 | 0 | 7,509 | 1,26,489 | – | 1,26,489 |
| Other services | 35,170 | 2,01,075 | 2,36,245 | 2,267 | 3,416 | 5,683 | 64,454 | 16,989 | 24,056 |
| Total | 1,49,730 | 6,34,845 | 7,84,575 | 16,785 | 16,241 | 33,026 | | | |
| Rentals | 0 | 0 | 0 | 1,307 | 0 | 1,307 | – | – | – |
| Sum total | 3,50,147 | 11,53,886 | 15,04,033 | 31,984 | 28,148 | 60,132 | 91,344 | 24,392 | 39,979 |

Source: Rani and Unni 2000, Table 4.16, p. 46; Unni and Rani 2003, Table 2.5, p 57.

Within the service industry, storage, communications, banking, insurance and education make up the formal sector. Bosworth et al. (2007) delineate traditional services as consisting of trade, transportation and other services (Table 8.3). In trade and transportation, 90 percent of workers not only belong to the informal sector but between 60 and 80 percent of added value is produced by it. In this respect also, the informal sector occupies the greater part of the industry. "Services" for Bosworth et al. include both modern and traditional. Since the vast majority of workers are found in the informal sector, we may presume that a little over half the added value is produced by a small number of modern industries (most likely the IT industry). The construction industry is completely part of the informal sector.

It will be helpful to examine traditional services in more detail according to type. While the transportation industry is overwhelmingly part of the informal sector in light of its worker numbers and income, the SWA-GIDR survey divided it into two categories: Independent owners (taxis, lorries) and drivers of auto and cycle rickshaws. At the time of the survey, there were 62,636 people with an income of Rs 2,541 million in the former category and 112,561 people with an income of Rs 3,113 million in the latter. All transport activity was conducted on the streets, rather than operating out of any fixed premises (Unni and Rani 2003, 50). In terms of their volume and revenue, rickshaw drivers were the most prominent service associated with transportation. The informal sector makes up the greater part of the industry when taxi and lorry drivers are included.[4]

In the service sector of Ahmedabad, the greatest number of people (285,000), generating the largest income, were employed in the category of "trade, hotels and restaurants". More than 90 percent of these were workers in the informal sector, garnering 63 percent of the income. According to the SWA-GIDR survey, these workers mainly acted as street vendors: Hawkers, vegetable sellers, tea sellers and so on (Rani and Unni 2000, 42). Unni and Rani (2003, 50) state that "most of the informal sector trading units (60 percent) and hotels (77 percent) [are] operated on the streets".

The survey also identified 200,000 people employed in "other services" who can be assumed to belong to the informal sector. These include 78,000 domestic servants. In addition, close to 140,000 labourers worked in the construction industry (considered here to belong to the informal sector though classified as a secondary industry statistically).

Autorickshaw drivers, street vendors, domestic servants and construction labourers thus comprise the core workers in Ahmedabad's service industry. Their wages are low compared with the earnings of workers in other sectors, and they are among the city's poorest. If we consider the base as the value-added income for a worker in the informal agricultural sector, estimated at around Rs 16,000, there is not a great difference from the value-added per capita income of domestic servants in "other services" or construction workers. Street vendors and rickshaw drivers may make twice the agricultural income, but no more. The gulf between the earnings of workers in the formal and informal industries is blatant. The per capita value-added income in formal industry is Rs 155,000 in the "trade, hotel and restaurant" category, Rs 126,000 in the "communications, banking and insurance" category, Rs 123,000 in the "education" category and Rs 84,000 in the "transportation" category (Table 8.4). The urban service industry is evidently two-tiered: A high-waged formal industry and a low-waged informal industry. An overwhelming number of workers belong to the latter, which has absorbed a variety of low-income urban classes.

This pattern, where the urban service sector has assimilated the poorest classes, is duplicated in other cities. An analysis of the share of tertiary industry across household quintile ranges based on per capita income (Table 8.5) reveals that in urban areas, the lower the income group, the greater the dependence on the service industry and that in the lowest quintile (5), income from the service industry provides close to 70 percent of the family budget.

The informal sector within the Ahmedabad service industry substantially swelled in the 1980s and 1990s. Table 8.6 gives the results of a survey of workers in the various categories of the industry carried out in the city in 1976–1977. A total of 606,000 people generated an income of Rs 5,784 million. The table divides "manufacturing" and "transportation" into formal (organised) and informal (unorganised) sectors, but as no such division appears for "construction", "trade" and "hotels and restaurants", we can assume them to be informal.[5] As of 1976–1977, of the 288,000 workers generating an income of Rs 2,395 million in the service sector as a whole, 118,000 people making an income of Rs 1,170 million were attached to the informal sector. In the SWA-GIDR survey of 1997–1998, of the 785,000 workers in the service industry (2.7 times the 1976–1977 figure), generating an income of Rs 33,030 million (13.8 times the 1976–1977 figure), 634,000 people (5.4 times the 1976–1977 figure), with an attached income of Rs 16,240 million

*Table 8.5* Share of tertiary sector in different quintiles of household APCE

| | *1983* | *1993* | *1999* |
|---|---|---|---|
| | Rural | | |
| 1 | 8.17 | 7.91 | 10.17 |
| 2 | 10.41 | 10.77 | 12.50 |
| 3 | 11.87 | 14.00 | 14.93 |
| 4 | 13.84 | 17.21 | 18.31 |
| 5 | 20.23 | 25.83 | 27.69 |
| Total | 12.90 | 15.15 | 16.72 |
| | Urban | | |
| 1 | 49.8 | 50.5 | 52.3 |
| 2 | 53.8 | 56.2 | 60.0 |
| 3 | 58.7 | 61.1 | 63.2 |
| 4 | 60.5 | 64.5 | 64.1 |
| 5 | 63.7 | 65.5 | 69.0 |
| Total | 57.3 | 59.5 | 61.6 |

Source: Mazumdar and Sarkar 2007, Table 8, p. 976.

Original source: Estimated from unit level data of several NSS rounds.

*Table 8.6* Sectoral employment and income, Ahmedabad, 1976–77

| | *Workers* | | *Per capita added value* | *Total added value* | |
|---|---|---|---|---|---|
| | *Number* | *%* | *Rs* | *Rs 10 million* | *%* |
| | A. Direct output | | | | |
| 1. Land-based activities: agriculture, mining | 10,614 | 1.8 | 2,712 | 2.9 | 0.5 |
| 2-1. Manufacturing: formal sector | 1,99,123 | 32.9 | 9,843 | 196 | 33.9 |
| 2-2. Manufacturing: informal sector | 82,427 | 13.6 | 7,400 | 61 | 10.5 |
| 3. Electricity, gas, water supply | 6,482 | 1.1 | 12,632 | 8.2 | 1.4 |
| 4. Construction | 20,060 | 3.3 | 12,740 | 25.8 | 4.5 |
| Total (A) | 3,18,706 | 52.5 | 9,225 | 294 | 50.8 |
| | B. Services | | | | |
| 1. Trade | 73,100 | 12 | 11,000 | 80.4 | 13.9 |
| 2. Hotels, restaurants | 15,200 | 2.5 | 8,590 | 13.1 | 2.3 |
| 3. Banking, insurance, real estate | 27,700 | 4.6 | 11,970 | 33.2 | 5.7 |
| 4-1. Transportation: formal sector | 7,900 | 1.3 | 7,975 | 6.3 | 1.1 |
| 4-2. Transportation: other | 29,900 | 4.9 | 7,860 | 23.5 | 4.1 |
| 5. Communications | 2,600 | 0.4 | 7,185 | 1.9 | 0.3 |
| 6. Storage | 3,500 | 0.6 | 9,960 | 3.5 | 0.6 |
| 7. Other services | 1,28,100 | 21.1 | 6,062 | 77.7 | 13.4 |
| Total (B) | 2,88,000 | 47.5 | | 239.5 | 41.4 |
| C. Rentals | | | | 44.9 | 7.8 |
| Sum total (A+B+C) | 6,06,707 | 100 | 9,533 | 578.4 | 100 |

Source: Kashyap et al. 1980, Table 2.18, pp. 93–94.

(13.8 times the 1976–1977 figure), worked in the informal sector. In the 1980s and 1990s, therefore, workers in the informal sector of the service industry increased by 5.4 times, faster than for the industry as a whole, while income rose at the same rate.[6]

Mehta and Kashyap (2002) have made a study of what industries thrived in cities and villages in Gujarat in the 1990s. A number of their observations are of particular importance. (1) The percentage of workers in manufacturing decreased, while that for construction, trade, transportation and communications rose. (2) Overall, there was a considerable increase over the period in the percentage of self-employed people who did not have any regular employees over those employed by firms with more than one worker in regular employment. (3) In urban areas, not only was there a high percentage of self-employed retail workers, but their numbers also went up over the period. (4) Construction workers increased markedly in rural areas.

The above cases in Ahmedabad and Gujarat allow the following conclusions to be drawn about the service industry in urban areas. First, from the 1980s the service sector enjoyed a more accelerated expansion than manufacturing. Second, within the service sector, though there was a growth in modern services like communications, traditional services like trade and transportation occupied the greatest part of the sector in terms of numbers of workers and achieved the most remarkable expansion. Third, at the core of this development were self-employed workers without fixed premises and workers in the micro informal sector, like hawkers, stall keepers, rickshaw pullers and autorickshaw drivers.[7]

Even in Ahmedabad, where modern services are considered relatively advanced, informal sector traditional services have been at the centre of service industry growth since the 1980s. Hawkers, rickshaw pullers and others who do not operate from fixed premises are a prolific and integral part of this. Far from just applying to one locality, however, this analysis of Ahmedabad contains the distinguishing features of the prospering of the service industry in India as a whole.[8] Nayyar (2012, 212–13) divides the Indian service sector into sub-sectors with low educational requirements and sub-sectors with high educational barriers. The former includes the wholesale and retail trade, hotels and restaurants, transport other than the railways, storage, real estate and renting, and other personal, recreational and amusement services; and the latter communication, financial and business services. Between 1993–94 and 2004–05, the low-education subsectors made the greatest contribution to the service industry in terms of the increase in the number of workers. This further suggests that the features apparent in the expansion of the service sector in Ahmedabad are shared over India as a whole.

## The Growth of the Urban Informal Service Industry and the Urban Lower Classes

The ascendancy of the informal service sector in the large cities is rooted in several factors. One way of exploring these is by examining the significance of hawkers and street vendors (including those selling food).[9] These businesses do not have permanent premises but sell their goods on the street, prepare food on temporary stalls, or go from door to door. A special issue of *Seminar* on street vendors published in 2000 reported that there were an estimated 127,000 in Ahmedabad, 60,000 in Patna, 200,000 in Delhi, 200,000 in Mumbai and 191,000 in Calcutta.[10] Estimates of numbers for the various cities vary, but most scholars agree on them being an indispensable part of the urban service industry.[11] Bhowmik (2010, 25) suggests that street vendors make up 2.5 percent of the urban population and there are around ten million throughout India. The National Sample Survey (NSS) of 1999–2000 calculated that there were 16,410,000 workers in the category of trade in the informal sector. It is not clear how the survey reached this figure, but if ten million of these were street vendors, then they are clearly essential to the trading activities of the cities.[12]

Street vendors deal in a wide array of products. Most common are fresh foodstuffs (fruit, vegetables and fish), sundries, kitchenware, toys, clothing, books, magazines and plastic and leather goods. Vendors provide cooked foods, or cook dishes on the spot, while others operate stands selling tea and coffee. Prices are generally cheaper than goods sold in regular shops (Sarkar 2009, 2; Iwatani 2002).

Street vendors are some of the most prominent providers of daily necessities to urban residents, particularly to the lower classes. Their main customers are the poor. "Over half the urban population with lower incomes is totally dependent on them [and] [t]he better-off consumers too buy at least 50% of their needs from them" (Jhabvala 2000).[13] Vendors ply their trade in convenient places like stations, bus stops and near people's homes for the benefit of their poor urban client base. Not only are costs low, but purchases can be made on the way to and from work.

> In general it was found that the economically weaker sections of urban society – the lower middle class and the poor – were the main beneficiaries as they procured their necessities at lower costs from the hawkers.... In Mumbai the richer sections bought fruit and vegetable while the youth purchased clothes from them.
>
> (Bhowmik 2010)[14]

These purveyors offer a form of retailing extremely well adapted to the needs of their core customers, low-waged labourers. While the poorer sections buy grains and suchlike at public distribution shops, they depend on hawkers and vendors for all of their fresh fruit and vegetables, which they cannot preserve.[15] Stalls providing meals also cater for taxi and autorickshaw drivers. Hence, workers in the urban informal sectors are the main users of hawkers and vendors.

The connection between these small street-based businesses and the informal sector is not just a matter of their clientele. Most of the clothing, hosiery, leather goods, plastic products, glassware, kitchenware, toys and imitation goods are produced in small-scale factories and household workshops (Sarkar 2009, 3; Bhowmik 2010). Such producers do not have the power to join the existing distribution networks themselves, and so depend on hawkers and vendors, who function as an important route to distribute goods made in the informal sector. This is how upper-class youth in Mumbai purchase clothing created in the informal sector.

Together with public distribution shops, hawkers and vendors act as a vital channel for goods produced outside the formal sector, including in agriculture, to a consumer base in the informal sector. Much like an inner circulatory system, they link products and consumption. Their multiplication is underpinned by the growth in the number of urban informal sector workers in manufacturing and services and the subsequent rise in demand from them. This confirms just how much the informal economy has developed. Previous chapters discussed the expansion of the informal sector in both manufacturing and services and how this brought great numbers of rural workers to the cities. The development of the informal economy in itself is therefore the first factor in the expansion of hawkers and vendors in the urban service sector.

A second factor is associated with the daily consumption by the urban poor of fresh foodstuffs purchased from hawkers and vendors. In the past, the consumption patterns of the Indian upper and lower classes were keenly divided. However, this has gradually changed over the past decades (see Chapters 3 and 6), as lower-class consumption began to reflect the social aspirations of the poor and alterations in their social and economic standing. Previously, class difference was accompanied by variation in diet. According to a survey of caloric intake conducted in the 1950s, the consumption of fruit and vegetables as well as dairy products was extremely low among the lower classes compared to the upper classes. NSSO surveys from 1983 show adaptations in food intake since then (Table 8.7). Bottom-income groups swiftly come to consume more vegetables, narrowing the gap with the upper-income groups. Fruit consumption also rose, though here a gap remains. Table 8.7 indicates that this is a trend seen across both cities and rural areas.

Vegetables became an essential part of the daily diet of the lower classes, and fruit was also gradually gaining in popularity. Unable to buy fresh foodstuffs at the food distribution shops, they purchased them from hawkers and vendors either on a daily basis or once every two days.[16] Tea and coffee drinking continued to spread too. Chapter 3 described how in South India the custom of drinking coffee, which had been confined to the upper classes in the nineteenth century, caught on among the lower classes, including farm labourers, from the twentieth century. The existence of tea stalls in the cities is testament to the filtering of non-essential "luxury" items into the lower-class market. That households of informal industry workers, a substantial

*Table 8.7* Annual per capita food consumption by different income classes in India, 1983 and 2000 (Kg/person/annum)

| *Commodity* | *Bottom-income group* | | | *Upper-income group* | | |
|---|---|---|---|---|---|---|
| | *1983* | *1999–2000* | *Change (%)* | *1983* | *1999–2000* | *Change (%)* |
| Rice | 66.5 | 75.6 | 13.7 | 94.4 | 85.8 | –9.1 |
| Wheat | 43.6 | 44.9 | 3.0 | 71.0 | 59.9 | –15.5 |
| Coarse cereals | 37.0 | 11.9 | –67.8 | 28.8 | 9.0 | –68.8 |
| Total cereals | 147.1 | 132.4 | –10.0 | 194.3 | 154.6 | –20.4 |
| Pulses | 7.6 | 6.9 | –9.2 | 17.7 | 16.6 | –6.2 |
| Edible oils | 2.6 | 4.6 | 76.9 | 7.3 | 13.7 | 87.7 |
| Vegetables | 36.0 | 53.9 | 49.7 | 65.2 | 90.8 | 39.3 |
| Fruits | 1.6 | 4.2 | 168.8 | 6.4 | 18.2 | 184.4 |
| Milk equivalent | 15.7 | 20.5 | 30.6 | 89.7 | 117.2 | 30.7 |
| Meat, fish, eggs | 1.9 | 3.8 | 100.0 | 4.8 | 10.6 | 122.8 |
| Sugar | 6.4 | 6.6 | 3.1 | 18.7 | 18.8 | 0.5 |

Note: Bottom group – Below poverty line. Upper group – Above 150 percent of poverty line.

Source: Kumar et al. 2007, Table 1, p. 3,568.

Original source: Authors' calculations using data from National Sample Survey Organisation.

section of the urban population, now had the purchasing power to invest in these goods forms the third factor in the expansion of hawkers and vendors. This point will receive more attention in the next chapter.

To summarise, increased numbers of lower-class members, including workers in informal industries in the cities, and changes in their eating habits contributed to the growth of the number of hawkers and vendors at the heart of the urban service industry. They in turn underpinned the development of the service sector. The expanding urban middle classes also played a significant role in the growth of the service industry in the cities. Taxis and autorickshaws appear to have become increasingly present in Ahmedabad from the 1980s. As the main users of these modes of transport were the urban middle classes, formed in the process of economic growth, the responsibility for this proliferation can be laid at their feet. The next section explores this further.

## The Service Industry and Socio-Economic Change in Rural Villages

In tracing the origins of the service industry's development in India, socio-economic and lifestyle changes in villages cannot be overlooked. Agrarian output soared in the course of the Green Revolution, and this led to inevitable adaptations in the marketing process surrounding agriculture, as well as in services. Income had risen for all classes in the rural village, including agricultural labourers, following the surge in productivity, and this led to an increased consumption of services (Chapter 6). As the desire for social mobility grew among all classes, not only did the consumption of manufactured products escalate, but expenditure on education climbed. Great changes occurred in the lifestyle of the poor classes, as they began to take part in religious tours and use wedding halls for marriage ceremonies. The rapid increase in non-farm employment saw many more people moving outside the village or working as migrant labour. This may be assumed to have had the effect of encouraging the growth of the service sector in India. Studying the advancement of various industries within this sector, including the construction industry, and their links with the evolution of rural life will allow for more interrogation on this point.

### *Rise in Output, Changes in Consumption, Expansion of Trade and Commerce*

The Green Revolution transformed agrarian output. Besides increased productivity of the land and the resultant large surpluses, it brought about innovations in crop composition as more market-oriented commercial varieties were sown (Chapter 5). There was an added tendency for a number of specialist crops to be grown in each district. These developments encouraged the inter-regional movement of that most basic commodity, agrarian produce. Sales of surplus agricultural products outside the villages brought in return a vigorous inflow of industrial products, as well as diverse commodities and services. This narrative is perhaps the most definitive one in the story of commercial expansion in India.

Karimpur, near Agra, is famous as the site of a long-term study beginning in 1925 by Charlotte and William Wiser. Susan S. Wadley resurveyed it a number of times after 1960 and published the results in 1984, vividly describing the economic changes that had occurred both within the village and outside as a result of increased productivity. She wrote, "[h]igher crop yields resulting from the green revolution demand a wholesale market for the surplus, and larger incomes are expended on greater quantities of consumer goods". Mainpuri, 13 km north of Karimpur and with a population of around 133,000 in 2011, is the market town for the district, and it is here that the produce from the village land is sent. In the words of Wadley,

> The quantity of goods moving through district markets from the fields and into the hands of rural consumers through commerce has grown immensely. It is this commercial throughput that is now providing jobs to Karimpur men. They are not industrial jobs but rather those of carrying and storing vast quantities of goods, including the grains funnelled into the grain market and the potatoes stored in cold storage plants. With the development of a market for labor and a transportation system that makes Mainpuri a viable work locale, Karimpur men are rapidly shifting from agricultural labor to day labor in the marketplace.
>
> (Wadley 1984, 10–11; Wadley 2000, 286–87)

Mario Rutten, who studied rural areas in Gujarat in the late 1980s following the Green Revolution, has clearly shown that the wealthy classes in many rural villages had begun trading in agricultural products (Rutten 1995, 150). According to Ajit Kanitkar, at the beginning of the 1990s, the rural non-farm sector "was estimated to be growing at the rate of 5.4 per cent per annum" and case studies of 86 entrepreneurs from 22 villages revealed that most of their businesses were in the commercial and service sectors (tea shops, paan shops, grocery shops, tailors, etc.), that 96 percent of their raw material was available locally or within the district, and that 82 percent of their goods and services were marketed locally. More than half of these entrepreneurs had an annual turnover of over Rs 40,000 (Kanitkar 1994, M-25, M-28-29). Considering that in 1989 the monthly wage for workers in the informal sector was around Rs 500 (Ramanujam et al. 1994, 58), there was clearly sufficient demand to generate a certain income for such village businesses. There can be no doubt that this spread of trade and services was born from the expansion of demand in rural society, which in turn had been brought about by improved productivity.

Parmod Kumar (1999) shows that increased agrarian output has led to an ever-greater expansion in the volume of agricultural products being distributed. A survey of the marketed surplus of 400 households in Haryana state in 1993–1994 recorded that "the most outstanding factor in determining marketed surplus is the size of output" (501), that "with the rise in farm size, the proportion of self-consumption part of the farm output falls, which results in proportionately higher production for sale at a higher output level"

(516), and that oilseeds and cotton were highly commercial crops (515). It is likely that the growth of output beyond the subsistence level during the Green Revolution caused a rise in marketable surplus at a rate exceeding that of increase of output. Further, since the Green Revolution promoted cash crops and regional crop specialisation, marketing on both a regional and a national level evolved rapidly.[17]

Statistical analyses concerning rural non-farm economic activity show that increased production and market growth promoted the prospering and proliferation of local trade and services. Shukla (1991) demonstrates that there are significant positive correlates with the percentage of rural employment in the wholesale and retail trade, restaurants and hotels.[18]

The local and national circulation of foodstuffs, where surplus agricultural products are moved out of villages and various commodities brought in, was promoted by the changes in people's eating habits discussed above. Between 1983 and 1999, an overwhelmingly large number of people, including members of the poorest classes, more than doubled their consumption of fruit and "meat, fish and eggs", and greatly increased that of edible oils, vegetables and milk products. Eggs for instance, are transported in large quantities from production sites to distant markets, so such consumption pattern changes have certainly had an impact on the volume of agricultural produce, among others, that is being marketed domestically.[19]

The thriving of the trade and commerce sector in rural villages and adjacent urban areas has ushered villagers towards the cities to work in this sector, driving up the employment figures for non-farm occupations. In the process, physical linkages between the villages and nearby cities have been fortified. In the case of Karimpur, mentioned above, by 1984 there was a regular bus service to Mainpuri, and horse-drawn carriages (tongas) and cycle rickshaws were also available for the journey. Wadley adds, "The majority of households have at least one bicycle, used by schoolboys or their brothers and fathers. Only the poor regularly walk to town" (Wadley 1984, 10). Villagers not only worked in the Mainpuri market but six ran businesses there, repairing radios and bicycles and selling bangles. A further 16 were engaged in collecting milk from Karimpur and nearby villages and taking it to sell in Mainpuri. As villagers became more economically active in towns, they also strengthened their connection with them, travelling to them for schooling, using the hospital for serious illnesses, and going to the cinema or attending festivals. Arni, a town of 60,000 people in Tamil Nadu, developed between the 1970s and 1990s as a hub for the shipment of local agricultural produce both within and outside the state and for the transit of goods and commodities to rural districts. With between 40 and 50 percent of the town's full-time workers commuting from adjacent villages from the 1980s, the town and village society were intertwined (Basile 2013, Chapter 6). Trade and commerce thus grew in the region, while close links with the local economy and society were preserved.

Rural–urban trade links sprang up in various segments of the service sector, such as education, amusements and transportation, and proved key in the formation of the urban economy, and the growth of the informal sector in particular. In many regional cities, the collection of agricultural products from the local rural area and trade with it became a defining feature.[20] Figure 8.1 shows the rapid progression of family-run trading business activity, both rural and urban, in the informal sector in the 1980s, as goods increasingly circulated between villages and the cities. The pace by which the numbers of both businesses and employees grew in both urban and rural areas was initially much the same, but then rural businesses took the lead. This strongly suggests the possibility that trading activity in the informal urban sector expanded under the influence of the boom in rural trade.

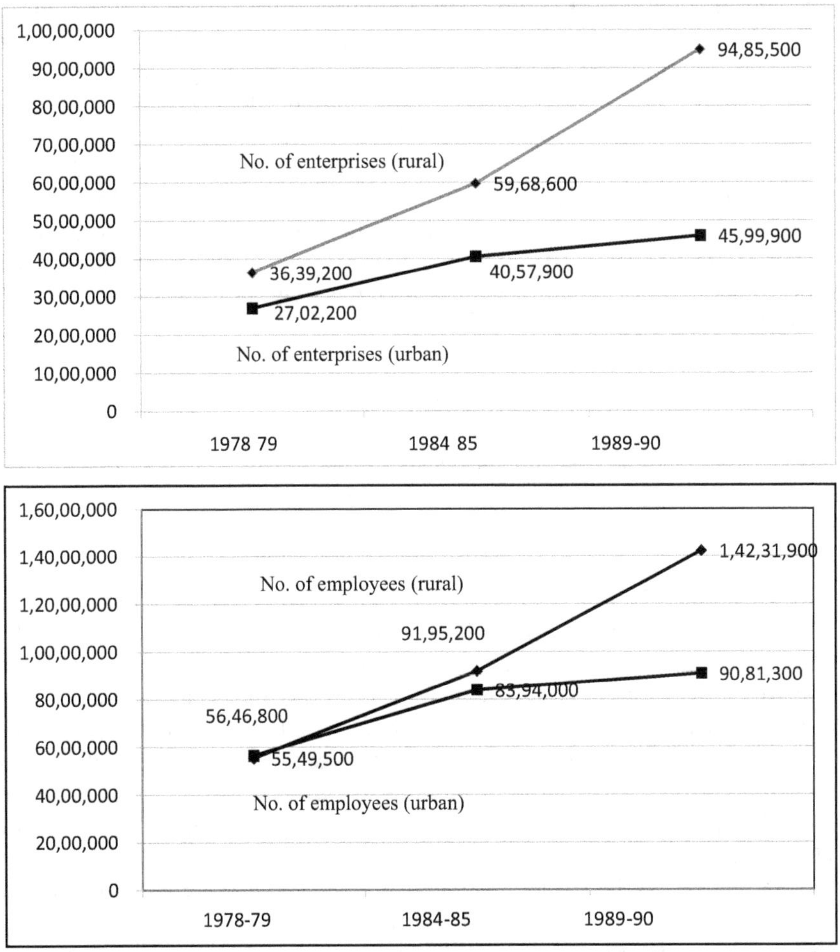


*Figure 8.1* Number of trading concerns in the informal sector and changes in employee numbers.

Source: Kulshereshtha and Singh 1998, Table 5, p. 59.

### *Increased Travellers from Rural Areas and Participation in Religious Trips: Growth of the Tourist Industry*

The tourist and travel industry occupies a pivotal place in the Indian service industry, and spans a number of segments, including transportation, the food and drink industry, and restaurant and hotels. Few realise, however, that most tourists and travellers are people living in rural areas.

In the words of Saundarjya Borbora (1998, 113), "direct employment figures [generated by tourism] rose to 6.96 million in 1992-93". In addition, "the huge pilgrim movement, both seasonal and regular, contributes to large-scale employment generation in many parts of India", for example, Sabarimala in Kerala and Tirupati in Andhra Pradesh. Borbora estimated that "total employment generation due to tourism will be more than 6.41 million, accounting for about 5 percent of the total workforce". A government report a few years later stated, "Tourism is estimated to contribute 5.83 per cent to the GDP and 8.27 per cent to employment in the country; the employment generated by tourism is estimated at 51.1 million in 2006-07".[21] The *Economic Survey, 2010-11*, noting that "In 2007-08, the contribution of tourism ... to total jobs (direct and indirect) in the country was estimated at ... 9.24 per cent", commented that tourism was one of the major engines of India's economic growth.[22] By comparison, in 2007–2008, the contribution of IT-BPO industries to India's GDP was 4 percent, and they created two million jobs. This is indicative of the importance of tourism within the service sector.

As Borbora writes,

> There has been an impressive growth in domestic tourist traffic also over the years. While the total domestic tourist visits during 1987 were about 34.8 million, the same increased to 81 million by 1992 registering an average annual growth rate of about 18.4 percent.
>
> (Borbora 1998, 112)

The Domestic Tourism Survey conducted in 2002–2003 by the National Council of Applied Economic Research (NCAER) reported that in 2002 there had been 229.4 million trips taken (excluding day trips) by 549.4 million tourists. This represents an increase of 2.8 times in the decade since 1992. In 2009, domestic tourists numbered around 670 million, showing that the increase was continuing into the twenty-first century.[23] Numbers of foreign tourists rose from 1.87 million in 1993 to 5.28 million in 2008, but even though this represents a considerable gain, there is no comparison with the size and importance of domestic tourism.

Can we ascribe this growth to the business classes whose activities gained momentum as a result of economic liberalisation and to the newly wealthy urban middle classes? The above NCAER survey, looking at tourist activity by household, makes it clear that this was not the case. Of the 230 million trips taken by domestic tourists in 2002, 73 percent were by rural inhabitants (NCAER 2002-03, 13).[24] Also, 75 percent of Indian households as a whole who took part in domestic trips were rural. Calculating the total expenditure on domestic tourism from the NCAER survey, rural households spent Rs 197,300 million against Rs 124,500 million by urban households. Thus in terms of expenditure, as well as numbers, rural households were at the centre of domestic tourism. Over India as a whole, 40 percent of urban households produced tourists in 2002, while 46 percent of rural households did so.

Among these rural households, the majority of tourists were surprisingly not from the wealthy classes: 26.4 percent were from the scheduled castes or tribes (SC/ST) and 34 percent from the "other backward classes" (OBC), totalling 60 percent. Further, 39 percent of the rural tourist households were landless and 34 percent were marginal or small farmers, and if categorised by their earnings, 23.2 percent had the "least income" (under Rs 22,500) and 32.1 percent had a "low income" (Rs 22,500–45,000) (NCAER 9, 11). The lowest socio-economic rural classes were therefore the most prevalent participants in domestic tourism.[25] More than 70 percent of domestic travel was by bus.

The most popular reason for travel was "social" (58.9 percent) – visiting friends and family, travelling for births and deaths, and marriages – with 61 percent of such trips being made by rural inhabitants (NCAER, i, 13–14). The marked increase in non-farm employment in rural areas mostly took the form of work in the urban informal sector undertaken by migrant workers. Those employed in this fashion probably maintained strong socio-economic ties with their home villages. These bonds and increased wages allowed large numbers of people, including the poor, to take trips of one overnight or more.

The second most common motivation for travel was "religious/pilgrimage". This comprised 13.8 percent of journeys. Then came "business/trade" (7.7 percent) and "leisure/holiday" (6.0 percent).[26] Rural inhabitants took a little under 70 percent of trips having a "religious/pilgrimage" purpose (NCAER, 13). As Fuller (1992, 205) has asserted, even when pilgrimage has primarily a religious purpose, people usually combine it with visits to tourist spots like monuments, museums, coastal areas and sightseeing locations. The sacred and the secular cannot easily be separated. The extension of the railways initially facilitated pilgrimage, but in the past 30 years pilgrimage by bus has become the norm and rural lower-class pilgrims have proliferated. A small number of members of the wealthy urban middle class fly or use private cars. In 1980, it was the wealthy middle-caste residents of M village in Tamil Nadu who went on pilgrimage; a number hired cars and took a pilgrimage trip of several days to a famous Hindu temple in Kerala, visiting several other temples on the way. Since 2000, however, SC members have been taking part in bus pilgrimage trips, reflecting their raised social status and better economic base in rural society. Sumie Nakatani has conducted a groundbreaking survey of recent changes among various castes in a Rajasthan village (2009). The Holi festival was held there annually until the 1990s. It had upheld the traditional status quo of the village hierarchy among the various castes, but it ceased to be performed once the social structure with the former landed elite at the pinnacle was no longer accepted. In its place, the Ramdev cult, previously associated with the low castes, grew in popularity and members of both high and low castes now take part in pilgrimage to Ramdev's grave in western Rajasthan. Alterations in the village social order have given rise to an increase in pilgrim numbers and to a widening class participation. The research of Yoshio Sugimoto into religious facilities in South India shows that there has been an enormous growth in the number of pilgrims visiting certain temples, including Christian churches. He connects this escalation with the higher volume of village-level pilgrims (Sugimoto 2010).

We have focused on social travel and pilgrimages by rural inhabitants, but the importance of business and leisure travel by the urban middle and upper classes should not be ignored. According to the NCAER survey, "business/trade" was responsible for 13.8 percent of domestic travel, and, calculating from average daily expenditure, it is estimated to be worth a little under 20 percent of total domestic tourist expenditure (NCAER, 26). It is thus an imperative part of the Indian domestic tourist industry. The "high income groups" identified in the survey, those with an annual income of Rs 160,000, are estimated to comprise around 20 percent of urban households.[27] They took no more than around 11 percent of the total number of trips taken in India. However, their expenditure at Rs 5,263 on one trip was around four times the average across all income groups, gauged to be around 42 percent of the total amount spent on domestic tourism across India (NCAER, 28). This means that the "high income groups" engage in an entirely different form of tourism compared to the vast majority of Indian tourists, making them a driving force behind the formal tourist industry.[28]

The NCAER survey provided an analysis of domestic tourism in India as it appeared in 2002 rather than looking for changes that had occurred. However, the data it supplies makes it very difficult to explain the explosion of tourists experienced by the industry in the previous 20 years chiefly as being propelled by the urban middle classes and business people. Instead, the key factor in the soaring of domestic tourist numbers was the wide participation in tourism by a huge number of rural households, including the lower classes, whose income had improved considerably. Behind this lay the closer relations between villages and urban areas that existed as a result of migrant labour and the relocation of many across a broad sweep of classes, and the increase in the number of lower class pilgrims due to changes in village society.[29] It is easy to imagine that this underlay the growth of tourism-related industries in the ever-expanding informal sector.[30] At the same time, the recently wealthy middle and business classes had begun to engage in tourism, and their expenditure probably created a foundation for the rapid development of the formal tourist industry in India.

### *Rural House-building and the Construction Industry*

The construction industry provides employment for 5.6 percent of India's workforce (Raju 1994) and is critical in rural areas, as exemplified by villages in South India. Housing renovation and new builds can be found in all areas of India. Between 1983 and 2008–09, *katcha* houses became less prevalent, falling from 51 percent to 17 percent of housing in rural areas (Table 8.8).[31] An analysis of data from 250 villages from all over India shows that between 1982 and 1999, the value of the house as an asset grew five times (Foster and Rosenzweig 2004, 520). This suggests that house construction in the villages thrived in this period. The creation of a large demand for building in rural areas brought about a significant growth in the number of construction workers.[32]

It should be noted that most housing construction occurred in the countryside, as shown by a National Sample Survey (NSS) of 2002 (Table 8.9).

*Table 8.8* Housing in rural and urban area of India (%)

| | *1983* | *1987–88* | *1993–94* | *2002* | *2008–09* |
|---|---|---|---|---|---|
| | | | rural | | |
| *katcha* | 51 | 49 | 33 | 21 | 17 |
| semi-*pucca* | 32 | 32 | 38 | 43 | 28 |
| *pucca* | 17 | 19 | 29 | 36 | 55 |
| | | | urban | | |
| *katcha* | 16 | 18 | 10 | 3 | 2 |
| semi-*pucca* | 26 | 24 | 20 | 20 | 6 |
| *pucca* | 57 | 58 | 70 | 77 | 92 |

Note: Katcha: houses with walls and roofs made of mud, bamboo, grass or leaves, reeds, thatch or unbaked brick. Pucca: houses with walls and roofs made of baked brick, stone, cement, concrete, tiles or timber. Semi-pucca: houses whose walls or roofs are not of pucca construction.

Source: National Sample Survey Organisation, Government of India, Dwellings in India: NSS 50th Round (July 1993–June 1994), Fifth Quinquennial Survey on Consumer Expenditure, March 1997, 18; National Sample Survey Organisation, Government of India, Housing Condition in India, Housing Stock and Constructions, NSS 58th Round (July 2002–December 2002); Housing Conditions and Amenities in India, 2008–09, NSS 65th Round (July 2008–June 2009), National Sample Survey Office, Government of India, 2010.

*Table 8.9* New builds and construction costs of residential housing in rural and urban areas (2002)

| | *Rural* | *Urban* | |
|---|---|---|---|
| | | *Slum areas* | *Non-slum areas* |
| Cost per new build *pucca* house (Rs 1,000) | 113 | 80 | 263 |
| Estimated number of buildings completed in the past five years | 3,63,94,951 | 12,14,164 | 69,87,943 |
| Estimated construction costs (Rs 1,000) | 4,11,26,29,463 | 9,71,33,120 | 1,83,78,29,009 |

Note: "Estimated construction costs" are calculated on the assumption that all new builds are pucca constructions.

Source: Housing Condition in India: Housing Stock and Constructions: NSS 58th Round (July 2002–December 2002), Report No. 488, H-3, Table 75.

Estimates indicated that 82 percent of new builds and 68 percent of construction costs were based in rural areas. This expansion of rural construction greatly affected the demand for finance. From the 1980s to the end of the 1990s, more than 45 percent of housing loans in India were taken out in rural areas, and even after this time the figure remained at more than 42 percent. Both rural housing construction and the need for finance occupied an important position within India as a whole.[33]

The rural building industry also leaps ahead of its urban counterpart when it comes to estimates of the number of construction workers in Gujarat. According to Mehta and Kashyap (2002, 126), between 1990 and 1998 the number of construction workers in Gujarat state increased 7.1 times in rural areas, from 4,424 to 35,963 and 2.6 times in urban areas, from 9,248 to 33,535. The net increase is particularly striking because Ahmedabad, one of the largest cities in India, is in Gujarat, yet even so the proportional increase of workers in the construction industry was higher in rural areas than urban. Though there were some differences in how the statistics were taken, it is clear that the construction industry was experiencing rapid growth in all areas, making it an essential element within India's post-1980 economic growth. Nagaraj (2003), in an investigation of those sectors leading India's economic growth since 2003, states that it was the household sector rather than the private corporate sector that was "the engine in the recent economic boom" and that "the construction-led boom in private housing" played a leading role here (p. 61). Building work in rural areas, centring on renovation and new builds, was clearly a central component of economic expansion.

### *Growth and Diversification of Education in Rural Areas*

Rural areas were at the forefront of growth in industries connected to construction, trade and tourism, but they also provided fertile ground, far more than urban areas, for the development of education, an essential part of the service industry.

Rural socio-economic growth and change that had been accelerated by the Green Revolution not only affected trade and commerce but also fuelled the demand for education. Foster and Rosenzweig (1996), analysing the relationship between schooling and the technical changes of the Green Revolution, showed that educated farming households were able to use the new technology appropriately and that schooling returns increased. The two scholars (2002) used data on 240 rural villages spread throughout India covering the period between the 1960s and 1999 to study the relationship between secondary school building and crop productivity. Table 8.10 shows that significant numbers of both public and private secondary schools were built during this time. Foster and Rosenzweig (349) maintain that there is a clear correlation

*Table 8.10* Per-village secondary schools built in the subsequent decade

| | *1971–81* | *1982–92* | *1990–99* |
|---|---|---|---|
| Public | 0.059 | 0.117 | 0.061 |
| Private | 0.098 | 0.053 | 0.076 |
| Total | 0.157 | 0.17 | 0.137 |

Source: Foster and Rosenzweig 2002, Table 8.1, p. 344.

between secondary school building/enrolment rates and expected future increases in yields:

> Increases in the productivity of land increase the opportunity cost of attending school for those children used in farm production, but expected increases in yield rates, expected growth, raise the gross returns to investments in skills, skills that have enhanced payoffs in a dynamic environment.

When productivity visibly rises, people come to accept and expect the benefits gained through investment in education and the skills it fosters. An increased demand for, and expenditure on, education inevitably follows, which leads to more schools being built and greater investment. Rural economic development, which is premised on increased output, promotes education.[34]

The promotion of education thanks to rural socio-economic growth is confirmed in numerous village surveys. One of the most remarkable changes in village society from the 1980s was, as exemplified by M village in Tamil Nadu, diversification and sophistication in village people's demand for education. In 1980 there was a close correlation between educational standards and socio-economic position and class status in the village, but this evolved in the succeeding years. Whereas members of the lowest social class had tended to send their children only to the public primary schools in the village or to the nearby secondary school, by 2007 there were a number of people from the lowest social classes who had attained graduate and postgraduate degrees. A considerable number of children from these classes travelled by bus to schools in the city and local towns, including private schools and English-medium schools (Table 6.14). The education level of girls also rose significantly. Villager aspirations towards higher education had not only increased but had become broader. In response to this trend, more new schools, both public and private, were built within and outside the village.

From the first half of the twentieth century, many caste and local social groups had begun to pour their efforts into educational facilities with the purpose of raising the socio-economic position of their members. In western

India, a new class of capitalists from the Maratha and other communities were key figures in the development of the sugar industry there. Warananagar in Kolhapur, for example, is an industrial complex centring on a sugar mill, but it also contains, in response to community and local demands for education, an education complex "comprising both Marathi and English-medium pre-primary to high schools; an arts, science and commerce college; an industrial training institute; a pharmacy college and an engineering college" (Damodaran 2008, 248).

The desire for higher and more diverse education accompanied ambitions for socio-economic advancement. In the rural regions of South India, higher classes like Brahmins had by 1980 already formed an elite group; having left university at either graduate or postgraduate level, they were working in stable and high-paying jobs in public companies, large enterprises or the civil service. After this time, non-Brahmin classes began putting great efforts into raising the educational level of their children to elevate them from the agricultural classes. Indian society, however, raises high barriers to achieving this, and these must be surmounted. As Chapter 11 describes in detail, the labour market for Indian firms is extremely socially stratified. In Japan during its high growth period, firms employed high school graduates and trained them on the job to be multi-skilled workers, many of whom retired at the management level. In contrast to this system, which prioritised the firm's internal labour market, most large Indian enterprises employ unskilled workers, skilled workers, managers and administrators directly from the external labour market, with strict requirements concerning educational attainment for each type of job. Academic qualifications, such as a master's degree or doctorate, or a diploma from a polytechnic or an Industrial Training Institute (ITT), are usually required for a regular white-collar position or a high-paying skilled job in a firm. It is virtually impossible to get regular work in the formal sector without the SSLC. If further education is undertaken beyond this, the scope for the type of work available broadens, with the promise of a good income in the future.

If the purpose of schooling is first and foremost to get such qualifications in order to guarantee future income, then the necessary educational expenses become an investment in the future. At the same time, in order to obtain the high marks in the SSLC required to continue on to higher education, it is first imperative to attend a suitable primary and secondary school. Since it is very difficult for those taught at village primary schools or local high schools to enter this route, the chosen school – non-local, private or English-medium – has to be selected from the first grade. There is consequently a large and growing demand for educational institutions other than the local public schools that will ensure students get the appropriate qualifications for entering higher education. These educational preoccupations have emerged in India as an important "industry".

Increasing diversity of demand for education as a function of aspirations for socio-economic advancement is reflected in the figures for the field "education and medical" in Table 8.3.[35] As this table shows, "education" as service-producing industry exhibited constant growth from the 1960s, having begun its expansion in the previous decades.[36] This trend was only fed by Indian economic growth and globalisation after the reforms of 1991. Greater expenditure on education may have been particularly striking in urban households, but it is possible to ascertain that even rural areas saw a broadening in demand for education (see Chapter 11).

### *The Popularisation of Wedding Halls*

The wedding industry too, first embraced in urban areas, spread within rural society. Before the advent of wedding halls, marriage ceremonies had been held in the homes of the bride and the groom by the family and the community, usually presided over by senior family members. The practice of holding weddings in purpose-built halls or hotels swiftly caught on among the urban upper and middle classes, and wedding hall management became the core of the newly emerged events industry.[37] According to the *Sunday Tribune*, in 2004 the wedding business was worth Rs 500 billion (Rs 50,000 crore) and was growing at 25 percent annually, which meant that India spent more on weddings than any other country.[38] Two wedding halls were built in M village in Tamil Nadu (see Chapter 6), marking the infiltration of the new wedding custom into rural areas, and more people (including members of the SCs) began utilising these specialised spaces.[39] As Patricia Uberoi (2008) points out, weddings are an important site, for both upwardly mobile classes and the lower classes competing with them to assert their desired socio-economic position while expressing their modern lifestyle.

This section has followed the growth of various service industries, paying attention to their links with socio-economic structural change in Indian society, including in rural areas. A combination of contributors to this growth have been underscored: Increased agrarian output with the Green Revolution, increased agricultural surpluses, higher wages and changing consumption among the agricultural classes, growing aspirations within hierarchical village society for upward socio-economic mobility and the consequent changes in consumption patterns and lifestyle. The development of the village economy played a leading role in commerce and trade, the travel industry and the construction industry among others, while the education and wedding industries, ushered into being by the urban middle classes, expanded throughout Indian society as social change took root.

## Economic Reform and the Growth of the Modern Service Sector

There is no doubt that post-1991 economic liberalisation and the ensuing globalisation of the Indian economy brought a new dimension to the expansion of the service sector. Chapter 10 will look more closely at the significance of economic reforms of the 1990s; therefore, this section will limit itself to a brief overview of the formal service sector whose growth is considered to have been stimulated by them.

### *Communications*

In the communications industry, the telephone business has indisputably experienced the most growth in the period since economic liberalisation. In 1991, India had only 5 million telephone subscribers, but by 2007 this number had rocketed to 233 million, an annual growth rate of 27 percent. The contribution of the communications sector to India's growth performance rose from 1.6 percent in 1999–2000 to 4 percent in 2005–2006 (Mani 2008, 38).[40] Despite this, down to 1999 its percentage contribution to total services growth remained lower than transportation in the traditional services. This contribution increased, however, after the beginning of the twenty-first century (Table 8.3). As we shall see in Chapter 10, deregulation and liberalisation, the introduction of mobile phones and fierce competition among public and private companies, including foreign ones, lowered charges and contributed to the rapid spread of telephones.

We should note that telephones must have quickly found their way beyond the urban upper and middle classes to workers in the informal sector and to rural areas. Teledensity, the number of telephones per 100 of the population, which had been 7 percent in 2004, had climbed to 73.3 percent by December 2012. Urban teledensity had reached saturation point at 149.5 percent, while rural teledensity, which had been 1.6 percent in 2004 now reached 39.9 percent. The rural share in the total number of telephones rose from 16 percent in 2004 to 36.9 percent in December 2012. The rural telephone growth rate in 2010–2011 was 29.41 percent, and the urban growth was 25.43 percent. The key to the future expansion of the communications industry is the rural market, where there is ample room for the further proliferation of telephones.[41]

This book's Introduction referenced the report that in one village in the poor state of Bihar more than 60 percent of households owned a mobile phone (Tsujita and Oda 2012, Table 2, p. 28). Another survey in Uttar Pradesh claimed that, as of 2007, ownership of mobile phones was around 30 percent, even among the SCs (Kapur et al. 2010, 42). According to the 2011 census, more than 50 percent of rural households had a telephone.[42] This penetration is indicative of rural socio-economic change, which, as we saw in Chapter 6, occurred against a backdrop of increased income among all rural classes, the growth of migrant labour and changes in labour relations within the village. For example, Bihar sends a large number of migrant workers to Punjab state. Rodges and Rodgers (2011) recount that "since virtually all migrants have or have access to mobile phones, it has become common for farmers in Punjab to call villagers in Bihar directly when they need labour for harvesting" (46). A recent phenomenon is the migration of young boys between the ages of 10 and 14 from Bihar to work in factories in Moradabad, Delhi or Firozabad. One correspondent relayed that her son called home regularly using a mobile phone (47).

While the communications industry started out in response to demands from the urban middle classes, it maintained its high growth in the same way that television did, by expanding to non-middle-class urban inhabitants, and then into the rural market, where it swiftly mushroomed as a result of migrant labour and the availability of non-farm work.

### *IT and IT-related Industries*

The Indian IT industry and related industries such as BPO (business process outsourcing) have grown rapidly since the reforms of the 1990s, and with increased globalisation, it has become India's representative export industry. As we saw in Chapter 4, higher education progressed at the expense of primary and secondary schooling as India built its economy following Independence. Many of the upper classes, including those living in rural villages, received their higher education in English and so India developed as a country having highly educated human resources. The government gave special attention to training scientists and technicians, and created a technological base in the process of its policy of import-substitution industrialisation. It also developed IT-related industries under a protective system by imposing controls on foreign investment by firms such as IBM. However, real development occurred only after the economic liberalisation policy was introduced in 1991.

The IT-BPO sector occupied no more than around 1 percent of GDP in 1997–98, but this figure had risen to 4 percent in 2007–2008. If IT hardware is added, there was a leap from 1.8 percent to 5.5 percent in the same period. Employees in the industry increased from 230,000 in 1998–1999 to nearly 2 million in 2007–2008.[43] In 2012–2013, when 230,000 extra jobs were added, the industry directly employed 2.8 million, and provided indirect employment for 8.9 million. It then occupied 7.5 percent of GDP. Unlike the communications industry, the IT-BPO sector is an export-oriented industry, with two thirds of its market overseas, and rapid development has made it India's most visible export industry. Its share in total exports (goods and services) shot up from less than 4 percent in 1998 to around 25 percent in 2012.[44]

Although the IT industry had been energised by the globalisation that followed the economic reforms and by the ending of government monopolies in telecommunications, it was still only small-scale in the 1990s and hardly contributed to the growth of the service sector. Verma (2012, 278–279) concludes that "although trade was growing in [the service] sector, it accounted for a small proportion of services value added. Hence, an export-led growth hypothesis for the Indian service sector is difficult to support". Even in Ahmedabad, employees in "business services" were only 2.1 percent of the total workforce in 1999 (Unni 2000, Table 4.4). The impact of this sector on the economy as a whole was thus limited.[45] Since the end of the twentieth century, however, it has been in the vanguard of the service industry, with a substantial influence over the economy as a whole.

### *Banking and Finance*

The financial services sector (banking, insurance, real estate, etc.) has also swollen as a result of the changes since economic liberalisation.[46] The share of "banking and insurance" in the service sector rose from 6.5 percent in 1981 to 10.2 percent in 1991 and 11.3 percent in 2006.[47] It is significant that housing loans were increasingly important in the growth of banking and finances from the 1990s. The largest borrower from India's commercial banks is the industrial sector. The annual average growth rate of loans to the industrial sector in the 1990s and in the period 2000–01 to 2004–05 was 15 percent, while in the same periods the growth rates of personal loans were 23 percent and 38 percent respectively, the highest in the field. As a result, the share of personal loans in total bank credit amounted to 22.2 percent in 2005. Housing loans accounted for a little over half of the personal loans.[48] Thus personal housing loans became a more integral part of borrowing. As mentioned before, between the 1990s and the beginning of the twenty-first century, housing loans in rural villages occupied 42–45 percent of all housing loans throughout India, and so their escalating popularity gave them a prominent position in the financial growth of India as a whole. A very large share of consumer credit not spent on housing went on consumer durables (Nagaraj 2008, 59). It has been thought that non-bank and other consumer loans had been focused on an urban demand for cars and similar items, but an NCAER survey on Indian consumer markets showed that the growth rate of cases where consumer credit was used to buy high-priced consumer durables like motor bikes, colour televisions and refrigerators was greater in rural areas than in urban, and that consumer credit ballooned in the rural sector from the latter half of the 1990s.[49] We should therefore note the impact of considerable rural capital demand on the field of finance.

The fields of communications, IT and IT-related industries, and finance underwent profound growth, as Table 8.3 shows, yet in terms of their involvement in the growth of the service sector as a whole, the figure for the three combined was only 2.5 percent in 1993–1999, less than the 3.3 percent of "trade" in the traditional sector. Even in the period 1999–2004, their combined contribution rate did not exceed that of "trade". The question of the importance of these "new" services needs to be re-examined.

### *Outsourcing and Subcontracting*

Some scholars place great emphasis on the move towards subcontracting to smaller firms (for services like computing, cleaning and security) that occurred as manufacturing companies restructured following the deregulation that came in the wake of the economic reforms and greater competition between enterprises.[50] Gordon and Gupta (2004, 12), however, discussing how crucial splintering has been, conclude that "splintering may have added about ½ percentage point to annual services growth during the 1980s" and about ¼ percentage point in the 1990s.

### *Employment in the Public Sector*

In the period since the economic reform of 1991, employment in the public sector was at the forefront of the formal segment of the service sector. In the words of Mazumdar and Sarkar (2007, 973–74), "the formal sector accounts for a quarter of tertiary employment in rural areas and more than a third in the urban economy. It also accounts for 30 per cent of all tertiary sector employment". Further, "[public sector employment] accounts for more than half of formal tertiary employment in urban areas and more than two-thirds in rural areas". Employment in the public sector may have declined in the post-reform period, but its value within the service sector as a whole endures, particularly in rural areas.

### *The Service Industry and the Growth of the Urban Middle Class*

Members of rural elites, those who had steadily migrated to the cities after the end of the nineteenth century, had been part of the long-term formation of urban society since Independence. They were employed in specialist occupations as public servants, lawyers and teachers, in white-collar work or in the management of firms. As the next chapter will show, in the 1980s and 1990s, the urban middle classes predominated in these occupations and enjoyed an elevated status in parallel with the flourishing of the urban informal industry. New entrants to the middle classes emerged through the growth of fields like finance, IT and IT-related industries, and communications in the post-reform period.

As the middle class multiplied, they were responsible for an increase in the number of autorickshaws and taxis, their chief means of transport in the cities. In addition, our examination of expenditure on domestic tourism revealed that the high-income households spent 42 percent of the Indian total. This suggests that the urban middle classes were vital in the growth of service industries centring on the formal sector. It was probably also the middle classes that led housing construction in urban and suburban areas. Yet it was in education that the importance of their demand was most marked. For the urban middle classes, who wanted to remove themselves from the village and agriculture, receiving a high level of education and thereby obtaining well-paid and stable urban employment was virtually the only way to survive in the future. While education had a vast hinterland in the countryside, it was in the cities that it expanded the most, led by middle-class demand.

## Summary

Six conclusions have been reached through the above discussion.

(1) Rises in the growth rate of the service sector fundamentally appeared in the 1980s, before the economic reforms of 1991.

(2) Throughout the 1980s and 1990s, it was the expansion of the traditional sector that most contributed to the growth of the service sector. Even in the large cities, the informal sector occupied a very great proportion of the service industry. The modern service industries like IT and IT-related industries, the communications industry and finance and banking, which received a great impetus through the economic reforms, were small-scale up to the end of the 1990s and did not add much to the growth of the service industry as a whole. We need to re-examine whether the economic reforms that began in 1991 alone can explain the fast rise in the growth rate of the service industry from 6.6 percent to 7.5 percent in the 1990s.

(3) Structural changes that progressed in rural areas, like improvements in the agrarian and rural economies through the Green Revolution (for example, changes to the structure of village society, lifestyle change and improved wages), were the most important driving force behind the promotion of the traditional service sector and the construction industry. The rise in agrarian output, and the increase and diversification of consumption in rural villages led to the rapid increase of trade, including in urban areas. Those travelling from rural areas, associated with the movement of people from the villages and the participation by the lower classes in religious trips, were overwhelmingly greater in number than those from urban areas, and this engendered rapid growth in that part of the service sector connected with travel and tourism. There was much more housing construction in rural areas than in urban, and demand also grew there in industries usually considered to be led by urban middle-class demand, like education and weddings, resulting in their swift proliferation through India as a whole. The communications industry, the typical modern service industry, which had its beginnings in the cities, swelled after 2000 among the poor rural classes, and rural demand was integral to its explosive growth.

(4) The development of the urban service sector was centred on the traditional industries of the informal sector. Underpinning its growth were changes in the eating habits of the increasingly numerous lower-class inhabitants who worked in the urban informal sector. Many of these employees had been migrating to the cities from the village lower classes – temporarily or permanently – since the 1980s. The advancement of the urban service sector was accelerated by this movement of people from country to city.

(5) Urban upper and middle classes grew with the gradual increase in the number of households of village elites who had moved away from farming to live in residential districts in the cities and work at management level in the informal industry or as white-collar workers. The growth of these classes promoted the expansion of the service sector, centred on education, the formal sector tourist industry and the informal sector transport industry (e.g. autorickshaws).

(6) After 2000, the modern service sector (IT and IT-related industries, the communications industry and finance and banking, etc.) increasingly

became a leading industry influencing India's GDP. Chapter 10 will consider how these industries changed after the 1991 reforms and established links with markets both at home and abroad.

## Notes

1 Expenditure on services within consumer spending as a whole grew from 10.45 percent in 1970–1971 to 12.35 percent in 1980–1981. Growth thereafter was rapid, and reached 19.29 percent in 1996–1997. Consumer spending on services and goods grew 7.65 percent and 2.95 percent respectively in the 1970s, 4.98 percent and 3.42 percent respectively in the 1980s, and 8.02 percent and 4.04 percent respectively in 1990–1996. Expenditure on services grew at a high rate in all cases (Madheswaran and Dharmadhikary 2000, Tables 7 and 8).

2 Bosworth et al (2007) point out, concerning their conclusion regarding the substantial contribution of traditional services, that "[a] n alternative explanation is that increases in the price of services are being underestimated, leading to an overstatement of real growth". They themselves however state that "this hypothesis is difficult to verify" (p. 22). Unni and Rani (2003), whom we shall consider below, show that the number of workers in the informal sector in Ahmedabad increased fivefold between 1976 and 1997. Workers in the service industry, comprising a significant proportion of the informal sector, increased several times in the same period. It is undeniable that the service sector must have grown rapidly in India as a whole. Concerning the question whether or not the growth rate of traditional services over modern services has been overestimated, Nagaraj (2008) points out the possibility that the growth of IT and IT enabled services, the backbone of the modern service industry, has itself been overestimated. These are "almost entirely export-related industries" and "data on the foreign exchange earnings of these services" are supplied by NASSCOM, the industry association. "Value added in this sector is arrived at by subtracting the rupee value of intermediate inputs from the value of the exports.... If these services were to be values [*sic*] at domestic prices, then the growth rates would probably get reduced to one-fourth or one-fifth of the reported numbers" (58). A variety of views exist concerning methods of calculating growth rates, but here we will operate on the premise that Table 8.3, constructed from the calculations of Bosworth et al. (2007) approximately reflects trends within the service industry.

3 India regards the building industry statistically as a secondary industry, but internationally it is usual to include it within tertiary industry. Unless otherwise noted, it will be considered part of the service industry in the following discussion.

4 Rani and Unni 2000, 39.

5 This understanding concerning the informal sector agrees for the most part with Unni and Rani (2003, 56).

6 In Mumbai too the informal sector grew at an extremely fast rate. Numbers employed in the sector grew from 805,000 in 1961, to 1,087,000 in 1971, 1,628,000 in 1981 and 2,317,000 in 1991 (close to a threefold increase). The ratio to employment in the city as a whole was 47.7 percent in 1961, 49.5 percent in 1971, 56.1 percent in 1981 and 66.2 percent in 1991 (Sharma and Sita 2008, 342).

7 In Gujarat state, as of 1990, the number of workers in the non-farm sector in rural villages was less than half that in cities, and half the number worked in service industries in the villages compared with the cities. The most remarkable growth in worker numbers in the 1990s was in the retail trade and construction (Mehta and Kashyap, 2002).

8 In the retail business, there has been a remarkable growth since 2000 of the organised sector, with the opening of supermarkets and malls. Nevertheless, as

of 2006, their share in the organised retail sector has not gone beyond 4 percent (*Report of High Level Group on Services Sector*, Government of India, Planning Commission, New Delhi, March 2008, pp. 27, 139). The proportion occupied by domestic trade in the Indian GDP rose from 13 percent in 1999–2000 to 15.2 percent in 2006–2007. Retail trade comprised 11–12 percent of this. There were 30 million workers in the retail trade in 2004–2005, equally divided between urban and rural areas.

9 From a survey of street vendors in New Delhi, Dasgupta (2003, 51–80) also points out that they are the largest and most important component of the informal service sector. Ramanujam et al. (1994, 22), who surveyed the informal sector in six towns, state that 22 percent of workers in the informal sector are engaged in activities with no fixed premises, like hawkers, stall keepers and rickshaw pullers.

10 *Seminar* 491, July 2000, p. 58.

11 Sharma and Sita (2008, 344) give the total number of hawkers in Greater Mumbai as 102,401. Though domestic servants make up the largest category of the informal sector, "hawkers constitute another important category and this segment appears to be increasing in number" (341). Jhabvala (2000) estimates street vendor numbers to be 200,000 in Delhi, 250,000 in Mumbai, 100,000 in Ahmedabad and 50,000 in Patna and writes "Estimates show that about 15% of the urban informal sector workforce are street vendors". Shah and Mandava (2005, 61) estimate the figure in Mumbai to between 100,000 and 110,000 persons.

12 Government of India, National Sample Survey Organisation. *Informal Sector in India, 1999–2000, Salient Features*. NSS 55th round (July 1999–June 2000), p. 25, Statement 4.1.

13 According to a questionnaire-based survey conducted by Joseph and Soundararajan (2009, 152–153), customers of push-cart fruit and vegetable hawkers are centred on the low-income classes. They do not shop at all in retail shops in the formal sector like the supermarkets that have sprung up all over India since the beginning of the twenty-first century and so make up a consumer class different from the upper-income groups. Fruit and vegetable hawkers have thus been little affected by new and modern forms of retailing (p. 133). A similar report can be found in *Report of High Level Group on Services Sector*, Government of India, Planning Commission, New Delhi, March 2008, pp. 142–143.

14 According to Sharma (2000), "Mumbai annually consumes vegetables and fruits worth Rs. 750 crore [7,500 million] in the wholesale market. The retail price is 25 to 40% higher than the wholesale price. Most of these are sold to the customer by hawkers and vendors". Bhowmik (2000) notes, "The survey in Calcutta showed that 82% of the consumers bought vegetables daily, or more than three times a week, from hawkers". They also buy paan (made from betel leaves), cigarettes, tea, biscuits and other food, fruit juice and sherbet, clothing, toys, electrical goods, newspapers, magazines, lottery tickets, cosmetics, imitation ornaments, cassettes and recorders, leather and rubber shoes, sandals and chappals, and kitchenware (Sarkar 2009, 8).

15 Customers believe that what they buy from hawkers and vendors is fresh because it is bought early the same morning. One in four customers in Ahmedabad reported they buy from hawkers because "What they sell tastes good" (Sarkar 2009, 5).

16 In Calcutta, 82 percent of consumers bought vegetables daily, or more than three times a week, from hawkers (Bhowmik 2000).

17 Harriss (2006, 127–128) states, from a survey of Arni in North Arcot, Tamil Nadu, that at the time of the Green Revolution, when production of staple crops in surrounding villages grew by 50 percent, the products marketed in Arni grew by 400 percent, calculated in terms of constant price. He points out that the rise in agrarian production expanded trade and made an important contribution to the growth of the town's economy.

18 Shukla (1991) further shows that increased rural income led to a greater frequency of migration and travel by local people and to an increase in the number of people working in areas connected to transportation.
19 Increased consumption of milk and milk products has been called the "white revolution" and is known to have greatly affected the structure of distribution.
20 Ramanujam et al. (1994) selected as subjects for their study of employment in the informal sector six towns at the level of district administrative centre. In four of these, industries related to agriculture (e.g. markets) occupy a particular important place in the urban economy.
21 *Report of High Level Group on Services Sector*, Government of India, Planning Commission, New Delhi, March 2008, pp. 9, 68 (http://planningcommission.nic.in/reports/genrep/rep_ser.pdf).
22 *Economic Survey, 2010–11*, p. 246 (http://indiabudget.nic.in/budget2011-2012/es2010-11/echap-10.pdf).
23 *India Tourism Statistics at a Glance 2010*, Ministry of Tourism and Culture, Department of Tourism, Government of India, c. 2011. (Web version), p. 10.
24 The NSS survey, *Travel and Use of Mass Media and Financial Services by Indian Households, NSS 54th Round (Jan-June 1998)*, Report, No. 450, Statement 8, also makes it clear that 70 percent of domestic trips of one overnight or more were undertaken by rural households.
25 "The fact that low-income households are a majority has important policy implications. It would suggest that building of tourism infrastructure, its upgradation and provision of related facilities must also target this section of the tourists. This would affect, for instance, the relative focus on building say low-cost hotel accommodation and *dharamshalas* as opposed to expensive luxury hotel accommodation" (NCAER 2002-03, 11). Jodha (1989) reports the increase in travel among the lower classes in the villages. According to village surveys in Rajasthan, while only 17 percent of poor households took paid journeys outside the district in 1963–1966, this had risen to 78 percent in 1982–1984. Social classes taking trips had expanded rapidly.
26 Surjit Singh (2001) puts the rise in domestic tourism down to two factors: trips to places of religious interest and the mobility of the middle classes.
27 According to the National Survey of Household Income and Expenditure (NCAER 2005), as of 2001–2002, 17 percent of urban households earned more than Rs 180,000.
28 A 1995 article in the weekly *Sunday* predicted a demand for three and four star hotels in the face of a massive growth in the number of business travellers ("Hotel Full", *Sunday*, 19–25 March, 1995, pp. 52–57).
29 Mazumdar (1995) too says that tourism, which used to be the preserve of the wealthy, had grown rapidly in recent decades through the participation of lower classes.
30 According to the *Indian Tourism Statistics 2004* (Market Research Division, Ministry of Tourism and Culture, Department of Tourism, Government of India), the number of hotel rooms in India as a whole was 1.2 million. Only 7 percent of these were in starred (approved) hotels, with the vast majority of hotels being in the informal sector. Surjit Singh (2000) stated that tourist trends were extremely important for the great number of restaurants in the informal sector (they employed 3.79 million people in 1993).
31 The change from *katcha* to *pucca* in rural villages began comparatively early. A village survey in Rajasthan reported that 91 percent of poor households had *katcha* houses in 1963–1966 and that this had decreased to 34 percent in 1982–1984 (Jodha 1989, 191).
32 Shukla (1991, 2591), speaking of the 1970s, suggests that rising incomes in rural areas had led to an increased demand for residential housing there.

33 Satō, Takahiro, "Indo no fudōsan ichiba to shisan kakaku baburu" (Real estate markets and asset price bubbles in India). INDAS Working Paper No. 4, March 2011, p. 4.

34 The existence of a strong demand for education can also be elicited from Kingdon (1996). In 1994, 27 percent of children attending school in the rural areas of Uttar Pradesh were enrolled in fee-paying private primary schools.

35 The numeric values in the field "education and medical" in Table 8.3 are shown as "community services". Of "community services", education and health services comprised 70 percent and 23 percent of value added respectively (Gordon and Gupta 2004, 10).

36 A household survey of students in Mumbai investigated schooling choices and income to determine to what level income rose later when students were enrolled in English-medium schools. It showed that the beneficiaries of English-medium education in terms of wage outcomes were girls. Wage rises were highest in the 1980s but fell off in the 1990s. The study showed that English-medium education being reflected in higher income was a phenomenon that predated the economic reforms of 1991 (Munshi and Rosenzweig 2006).

37 Uberoi 2008.

38 Trehan 2004, "The Big Fat Indian Wedding", *Tribune*, Spectrum, August 29, 2004. http://www.tribuneindia.com/2004/20040829/spectrum/main1.htm. *India Today*, however, reported that in 2002 the business was worth Rs 50 billion (Rs 5,000 crore) "The Great Wedding Bazaar", December 10, 2002. http://www.indiatoday.intoday.in/story/multi-crore-indian-wedding-industry-on-flamboyant-high-as-it-continues-to-reinvent-itself/1/232029.html (accessed August 11, 2016).

39 According to a NSS survey in 1994, household expenditure on the wedding ceremony, for example, over a 30-day period passed Rs 4,458 in rural areas and Rs 3,342 in urban areas. Considering that the average monthly expenditure per capita was Rs 281 in rural areas and Rs 458 in the cities, the amount spent on weddings in rural areas comprised an extremely large part of the household budget (*Wages in Kind, Exchange of Gifts and Expenditure on Ceremonies & Insurance in India, 1993-94, 5th quinquennial survey of consumer expenditure, NSS 50th Round, July 1993-June 1994*, Report No. 428, p. 18).

40 The share of the communication sector in the service sector rose sharply from 1.7 percent in 1991 to 7.5 percent in 2006–2007 (Government of India, Planning Commission. *Report of High Level Group on Services Sector*. New Delhi, March 2008, p. 31).

41 *Annual Report 2010–11, 2012–13*. Department of Telecommunications, Ministry of Communications and IT, Government of India, New Delhi.

42 *Census of India, 2011, Houses, Household Amenities and Assets, Figures at a Glance*, Government of India, 2012.

43 *Report of High Level Group on Services Sector*, Government of India, Planning Commission, New Delhi, March 2008, pp. 34, 51.

44 National Association of Software and Services Companies (NASSCOM) website: http://www.nasscom.org/indian-itbpo-industry (accessed August 11, 2016).

45 Gordon and Gupta (2004, 9) too say the contribution of IT to GDP growth was "quite modest" in the 1990s.

46 Bishwa Nath Singh (2000) points out that there was a demand for new services with the changes brought about by economic reform, that there was a need to expand the capital market out of the need to raise private capital and that new financial services were necessary with the inflow of foreign capital.

47 *Report of High Level Group on Services Sector* 2008, p. 31.

48 Reserve Bank of India, *Reports on Currency and Finance: Special Edition, Vol. III, 2005-06*, dated 31 May 2007, "IV. Credit Market", n.p. https://www.rbi.org.in/Scripts/PublicationReportDetails.aspx?ID=502. Accessed August 11, 2016.

49 National Council of Applied Economic Research, *India Market Demographics Report 2002*, Delhi, 2003, Table 6.2, p. 42.

50 Unni 2003, 73. The *Report of High Level Group on Services Sector* 2008 (p. 34) too states, quoting Dr Pronab Sen: "Economic analysts should keep in mind the fact that several Indian manufacturing and service companies have started outsourcing the non-core activities, resulting in high growth of services".

# 9 A Growing Connection between Rural Society and the Urban Informal Economy

Chapter 8 detailed how the growth of the manufacturing and service industries hinged upon the flourishing of the informal sector. This chapter will focus on the links between the urban informal sector and rural society, within the context of Indian socio-economic change.

## The Formation and Growth of the Urban Informal Stratum

A survey and study of the city of Ahmedabad has shown that 81 percent of service sector workers were employed in the informal sector. Table 9.1 gives the informal employment situation in the city regarding the entirety of the non-farm sector, including manufacturing. Close to 65 percent of male workers and 82 percent of female workers were engaged in the informal (unregistered) sector. If we add the figures for workers in registered enterprises without security of employment or contracts, the total of those with links to informal employment rises from 70 to 87 percent for men and from 75 to 91 percent for women (Unni 2000). Some 80 percent of households in Ahmedabad were employed in the informal sector, and we may assume more were connected with it through casual employment in registered enterprises.

The "self-employed", who made up around 30 percent of informal sector workers, can be roughly divided into two groups, based on whether or not they had their own premises. Around 60 percent of workers in the categories of "trade" and "restaurants" (which account for a prodigious part of the urban service sector) did not have their own premises. The other 40 percent, entrepreneurs who owned the sites for their businesses, belong to a different socio-economic class to other informal sector workers. In this study, I refer to workers in the informal sector and casual workers in the formal sector collectively as the "informal stratum" and separate them into those entrepreneurs with their own commercial properties ("upper tier") and the rest ("lower tier"). If around 15 percent of workers in the informal sector in Ahmedabad are estimated to be in the upper tier,[1] it can be assumed that some 70 percent of total number of households in the city belonged to the lower tier. Unni, who made a household ***survey*** of informal activities in ***Ahmedabad*** in 1998, also enquired into the types of houses the respondents lived in, and found that 30.4 percent had *pucca* houses with walls and roofs made of brick,

DOI: 10.4324/9781003341550-13

*Table 9.1* Informal sector workers and informal employment, Ahmedabad

| | *Proportion of non-farm workers (%)* | | |
|---|---|---|---|
| | *Men* | *Women* | *Total* |
| A. Informal sector workers | | | |
| Self-employed | 28.9 | 34.5 | 30.2 |
| (owners of small enterprises) | 2.7 | 0.1 | 2.1 |
| (own account workers) | 26.2 | 34.4 | 28.1 |
| Unpaid family helpers | 5.3 | 24.1 | 9.9 |
| Employees in unregistered enterprises | 30.6 | 23.1 | 30.1 |
| Total | 64.8 | 81.7 | 70.2 |
| B. Informal workers | | | |
| Informal sector workers | 64.8 | 81.7 | 70.2 |
| Workers in registered enterprises with no security of employment | 5.4<br>–21.7 | 3.5<br>–17.4 | 5.1<br>–21 |
| Total | 70.2<br>–86.5 | 85.2<br>–99.1 | 75.3<br>–91.2 |

Note: The figures in brackets show the percentage when workers with security of employment in registered enterprises, but without a contract, are included.

Source: Unni 2000, Table 7.3, p. 60.

concrete, tiles, etc., and the remainder had *katcha* houses (Unni 2000, Table 3.1. p. 16). This too suggests that 70 percent of Ahmedabad households belonged to the lower tier, whose members could not get permanent employment in the formal sector and whose work was low-paid and unstable. In terms of wage levels and stability of employment, above these lower-tier workers in the informal stratum there existed what might be called a middle and an upper class. The middle class included entrepreneurs who owned their own premises, in the upper tier of the informal stratum, as well as public servants, teachers, the middle management of firms and skilled technicians. The upper class was economically very well off.

According to Unni (2000), the average wage in Ahmedabad's informal sector was Rs 46.8, below Rs 52 that was the poverty line there in 1998. While there are a number of arguments about what constitutes the poverty line, the wages of informal sector workers certainly did not greatly exceed the wage level of the poor. There was a clear distinction between the low-income class with an instable economic base and the middle and upper classes. Since it still remains to be seen whether Ahmedabad can be considered typical of Indian cities in relation to the proportion of its population belonging to the bottom level of the informal stratum, the discussion can be advanced by considering those characteristics held in common in Indian cities with similarly high low-tier populations.

Migrants, both permanent and temporary, had been moving to the cities from rural villages since the end of the nineteenth century. In South India, under English rule, village elites, including Brahmins, gradually relocated to urban areas in order to educate their sons, facilitating their prospective careers in city administration or as public servants, teachers, lawyers and so on. Increasing numbers from the village landholding classes too found work in cotton mills and other large-scale factories. This movement continued after Independence (Pothana 1994). The majority of the migrating upper and middle classes probably moved into the urban formal sector as public servants or through involvement with public works, or into urban business life as self-employed entrepreneurs.

Between the 1970s and the 1980s, workers from a broad swathe of the village lower classes also began to surge into urban centres, inflating the urban informal stratum. The share of agriculture in the workforce in India declined between 1971 and 1981, falling from 69.7 to 66.5 percent (Bhattacharya 1998, 1255), and rural-to-urban migration encouraged this tendency.[2] Migration was not forced on the rural population due to inadequate support from agricultural work; this was the period when agricultural wages had begun to rise as the Green Revolution progressed. Rather, the growth of agrarian output gave rise to a great variety of non-farm opportunities, in markets, trading and transport, and stimulated trade in urban areas (Chapter 6). Bhattacharya concluded that "the informal sector … was a dynamic and productive sector, attracting and sustaining labour" (Bhattacharya 1998, 1260).

A study of six regional towns in India revealed that between 1980 and 1989 the total number of employees of small businesses in the informal sector grew annually from 14 to 27 percent. Over India as a whole, the annual growth rate of the informal sector in small cities of the same size almost doubled from 6.68 to 12.81 percent. The multiplication of the number of workers employed per business in these six towns over this period is indicative of continuing economic vitality (Ramanujam et al. 1994, 36–47). The urban informal sector, dynamically expanding in the 1980s, was absorbing its necessary labour force from rural villages.

## The Urban Informal Stratum and Village Society

In the course of the 1980s and 1990s, a good deal of field surveys was undertaken concerning the urban informal stratum. It is rather difficult to reach a coherent conclusion from them, as they were diverse in methodology, location and choice of respondent, while there were also great differences according to the city. However, as a whole they reflect the absorption of large numbers of the rural non-elite and show that it was possible to discern a commonality and continuity between the urban informal stratum (in particular its lower tier, which was in the majority) and the lower stratum of village society. At the same time, it is evident that the groups comprising owners of small enterprises and suchlike had characteristics that were quite distinct from the lower classes in the urban informal sector.

First, the educational level of workers in the urban informal sector was, generally speaking, low. Many were illiterate and most workers had at best received just a primary education. According to R. S. Tiwari, who made a survey of workers in the informal sector in Agra and Kanpur (Uttar Pradesh) and in Puri (Orissa) through random sampling, the educational level of workers in the three cities combined was as follows: Illiterate, 30 percent; primary (up to grade 5), 17 percent; up to grade 8, 16 percent; up to grade 10, 20 percent; up to grade 12, 10 percent; graduate, 6 percent; postgraduate, 1 percent; and a vocational diploma, 0.5 percent (Tiwari 2005, 160). This shows that more than 60 percent of workers had not received the SSLC, taken in grade 10. While the educational level in the manufacturing industry is high, that in the service and construction industries is quite low, with 36 percent of workers illiterate (60 percent of whom are under the age of 35).[3] A 1999 survey by Arup Mitra of slum dwellers in Delhi mostly working in the informal sector showed that 39.5 percent of respondents could not read or write, and only 18.2 percent had received a secondary education or above (Mitra 2003, 42). It seems clear that the majority of workers in the informal sector would find that their educational background made it challenging for them to find employment in large public or private enterprises in the formal sector.

There are differences too in education level between entrepreneurs with fixed premises in the informal sector, their workers and entrepreneurs without fixed premises. The study of six regional towns in 1989 showed that 65 percent of the first group (who comprised 25 percent of workers in the informal sector) had attained the SSLC or above. Only 34 percent of members of second group (64 percent of informal sector workers) and 16 percent of members of the third (22 percent of informal sector workers) had received the SSLC, while 17 percent of the former and 34 percent of the latter were illiterate. The contrast between the groups is marked (Ramanujam et al. 1994, 106, 115).

The proportion of members of the SCs and OBCs is high in the urban informal sector. In Kanpur, STs and SCs made up 73 percent of informal sector workers, and in Puri and Agra, 40 percent and 26 percent respectively (Tiwari 2005, 109–127). Though the proportion is particularly high in the construction industry, neither is it low in the service industry. Nevertheless, it should be noted that other castes, including the upper, are important in real estate, business services and the wholesale trade. Thus, though the educational level of most workers in the informal sector from the lower castes is fairly limited, many of the entrepreneurs in the sector with fixed premises are from the higher castes, with a high level of education. Here too we find two different social groups: The upper and lower tiers of the informal stratum.

The volume of workers in the urban informal sector who are migrants from rural areas reflects several decades of assimilation of the rural population. The 1989 study of six towns showed that 39 percent of employed workers and 30 percent of entrepreneurs (with and without fixed premises) were migrants (Ramanujam et al. 1994, 107). While capital was required when starting out in business in the informal sector, even for self-employment,[4] hardly any was needed to find work as a labourer. Migrants tended to first find work in the construction industry when coming to the city. In Visakhapatnam, one of India's fastest-growing cities, 66 percent of construction workers were migrants (Raju 1994, 21).[5] A 1991 survey of informal sector workers in Ongole (Andhra Pradesh) disclosed that 60.4 percent of households were migrants; two thirds were casual labourers and four fifths were from rural villages (M. Koteswara Rao and K. Gangadhara Rao, 1994a, 89, 91; M. Koteswara Rao and K. Gangadhara Rao, 1994b, 28). Ludhiana in northern India is also a rapidly growing industrial city, and between 1981 and 1991, its population increased 59 percent, due to migration (Bhashin 2004, 157).[6]

The bulk of workers in the informal sector, including those who had migrated from rural areas, lived with their families in the city. The Visakhapatnam survey reported that 84 percent of such workers were married. In Ongole too, there were 1.42 workers per household, with only 2.4 percent single (Sreeramamurty 1986, 70; M. Koteswara Rao and K. Gangadhara Rao, 1994b, 39). In Vijayawada, the average age of migrant workers was 24, and at the time 46 percent were married (M. Koteswara Rao and M. Prasada Rao 1994, 109). A survey of migrants in Ludhiana related that the average family size of migrants was 5.28 members, and here there was virtually no difference between migrants and non-migrants (Bhashin 2004, 159). Many single male migrants probably worked in jobs such as rickshaw pullers and do not represent the typical migrant.

Those relocating from rural areas did not usually return to their village after just a short stay in the city. In Visakhapatnam in 1990, 41 percent of workers in the construction industry were migrants who had started work within the last year. In general, one quarter of migrant workers, including those in other industries, worked for a year or less, 18 percent worked for more than five years, while the majority were residents who worked between one and five years (M. Koteswara Rao and M. Prasada Rao 1994, 110). The 1999 survey in the Delhi slums indicated long residence, even among migrants. Of the respondents, 26.6 percent were non-migrants, 36.8 percent were migrants who had lived there more than 16 years and 17.9 percent were migrants who had lived there between 11 and 15 years (Mitra 2003, 45–46).

Though most migrants from rural areas working in the informal sector remained in the cities with their families long term, they did not sever their ties with their villages and centre their lives completely in an urban environment. A sizeable portion of them maintained their familial connections and regularly sent money back to their place of origin. At the time of the 1990 survey of Visakhapatnam, 76 percent of migrant workers sent remittances home, 25.6 percent of them sending between Rs 150–200 a month and 7.37 percent more than Rs 250, when 55 percent of workers in the informal sector were earning below Rs 700 per month. The amounts sent were not negligible. Much of the dispatched money (65.3 percent) was to repay loans that their parents had borrowed from relatives; other purposes included the education of children left behind in the village (11.6 percent) and medical costs (9.5 percent) (M. Koteswara Rao and M. Prasada Rao, 1994, 112–113). In the 1991 Ongole survey, 33.6 percent of the migrant population (60 percent of respondents) sent remittances, mostly to rural villages. Most were of the order of Rs 50–150 per month and were for schooling and weddings, and to repay loans (M. Koteswara Rao and K. Gangadhara Rao 1994a, 98–102).

According to Duraisamy and Narasimhan (2000), who conducted a survey of migrant workers in the informal sector in Chennai, the money remitted amounted to 18 percent of the average income. Most migrants had come as couples, with 34 percent of them leaving their children in the village to be educated. As many as 51 percent expressed a wish to return to the place of origin, and 42 percent still had family land there. The survey plainly showed that people wanted to return and that remittances were high from migrant households who had left their children behind.

The case of Delhi slum dwellers surveyed in 1999 is of great interest. As mentioned above, the survey centred on migrants who had lived in Delhi for a long time. Table 9.2 shows that 84 percent of migrant households sent money to their parents living in the place of origin. Another 14 percent sent money to their children, and payments were also sent to siblings and to the spouse's relatives. More than half the households remitted over Rs 1,000. Conversely, the proportion of remittances received from those to whom money had been sent is extremely high. According to the survey, there was also a great deal on non-monetary inter-household transfer, such as giving clothing and other items, helping with child care, giving emotional support, and assisting with finding jobs. Table 9.3 tells us that more than half those who sent money had land in their place of origin, while most had a house there and visited regularly. Thus, even long-duration migrants kept their land and houses in their former homes and provided monetary and non-monetary help to the parents, children and relatives remaining. The relationship between the migrants and their static family, and between life in the city and

*Table 9.2* Monetary transfers by residents of Delhi slums

| | *Remittances sent to* | | *Remittances received from* | |
|---|---|---|---|---|
| | *Proportion of households sending money to total respondents* | *Proportion of households sending more than Rs 1,000 to total number of households sending money* | *Proportion of households receiving money to total respondents* | *Proportion of households receiving more than Rs 1,000 to total number of households receiving money* |
| Parents | 84.4 | 51.9 | 60.9 | 57.1 |
| Children | 14.1 | 59.3 | 0.0 | – |
| Siblings | 7.5 | 50.0 | 13.6 | 66.7 |
| Spouse's relatives | 1.6 | 50.0 | 18.2 | 50.0 |
| Member of the same caste group | 0.4 | 0.0 | 4.5 | 100.0 |
| Co-villagers | 0.8 | 50.0 | 4.5 | 100.0 |
| Others | 0.8 | 50.0 | 9.1 | 50.0 |

Source: Mitra 2003, Table 6.2, p. 110.

*Table 9.3* Remittances by residents of Delhi slums and their contacts

| *Remittances sent to* | *Among those remitting* | | |
|---|---|---|---|
| | *% of households with cultivable land at the place of origin* | *% of households with house at the place of origin* | *% of households visiting the place of origin* |
| Parents | 57.0 | 83.9 | 99.1 |
| Children | 70.4 | 92.6 | 96.3 |
| Siblings | 64.3 | 85.7 | 100.0 |
| Spouse's relatives | 50.0 | 100.0 | 75.0 |
| Member of the same caste group | 0.0 | 100.0 | 100.0 |
| Co-villagers | 50.0 | 50.0 | 50.0 |
| Others | 100.0 | 100.0 | 100.0 |
| Parents | 57.0 | 83.9 | 99.1 |

Source: Mitra 2003, Table 6.4, p. 111.

life in the place of origin, should be understood as being one of mutual complementarity.[7]

Despite the constant inflow of people from the rural non-elites into the urban informal sector, migrants' lives were not divorced completely from their places of origin. A case study in Rajasthan reports that "migrant households have significantly higher income levels than nonmigrant households" and that income from migrant labour accounts "for almost 60% of their total annual income" (Gidwani and Sivaramakrishnan 2003, 196). Those who make their living from the urban informal sector not only share points in common with the rural non-elite, in terms of social status and educational level, but the lives led by the migrants and others in the cities who make up the majority of the informal stratum are connected in a continuous fashion with the life of the village. This is a very important point, for it means that a much of the urban informal stratum has a semi-rural character. A much deeper interrogation of the linkages between the urban informal stratum and rural villages is needed.

## The Urban Informal Sector, Rural Society and Material Circulation

The movement of a migrant labour force between rural society and the urban informal stratum, especially its lower tier, made for commonality and continuity between the two. Commodities too circulated between the informal sector and the village economy.

India's commodities and services and its consumption structure can be broadly separated into two. Products and services in the formal sector were tied closely to their purchasing power with other industries in the formal sector and with the urban middle and upper classes. In contrast, those in the

*Table 9.4* Proportion of black-and-white televisions among all televisions owned (black and white and colour) (2001–02, %)

| *Income groups (annual income, Rs)* | *Urban* | | *Rural* | |
|---|---|---|---|---|
| | *Proportion of inhabitants (%)* | *Proportion of black-and-white televisions (%)* | *Proportion of inhabitants (%)* | *Proportion of black-and-white televisions (%)* |
| Up to Rs 45.000 | 14 | 89 | 43 | 92 |
| Rs 45,000–90,000 | 32 | 74 | 40 | 86 |
| Rs 90,000–135,000 | 24 | 41 | 10 | 68 |
| Rs 135,000–180,000 | 14 | 16 | 4 | 42 |
| Above Rs 180,000 | 17 | 10 | 4 | 26 |
| Total | 100 | 45 | 100 | 74 |

Note 1: "All televisions owned (black and white and colour)" is the sum of small black-and-white televisions and standard colour televisions.

Note 2: The income classes are based on the price level of 2001–2002.

Source: Compiled from NCAER 2005.

informal sector were bound up with demand from other informal industries, the urban poor classes and rural villages.

To pursue this point, let us first explore common characteristics in the consumer behaviour of rural inhabitants and of people in the lower tier of the urban informal stratum. Rural consumers placed great emphasis on low prices when buying commodities (Chapters 6 and 7), as did the lower tier of the urban informal stratum. It is of interest here that when buying a television, the lower half of urban inhabitants (in terms of annual income) and 90 percent of rural inhabitants exhibited the same consumer behaviour, compared with the higher half in terms of income. As Table 9.4 shows, the half of urban dwellers earning more than Rs 90,000 per annum preferred to buy colour televisions, while the half earning under that amount and 90 percent of rural inhabitants, even those earning more Rs 90,000, had a strong preference for black and white. Thus rural dwellers, as well as the less affluent half of urban dwellers, attached greater importance to price than to function when buying a television. The market for the plastic recycling industry and other informal industries too was similarly shared by these two groups, another example that rural demand is characterised by a commonality of interest with the urban poor classes.

For the rural lower classes, what they chose to spend their money on was an expression both of resistance against the upper classes and of a desire to be free of the oppressive class structure of the village (Chapter 6). Urban textile workers had a similar consciousness concerning their consumption. For mill workers in the cotton industry in Coimbatore (Tamil Nadu),

> conspicuous consumption is part of [the] response [to the low social status associated with their condition]. [They] are keen to match, if not outdo, their more prosperous kin and white-collar office-goers when it

> comes to dressing expensively and spending lavishly on weddings and imitations. This is their way of showing they are inferior to none even though they are of a wage-earning class.
>
> (Ramaswamy 1983, 143–44)

Munshi (2012), who investigated consumer consciousness among employees in the Delhi beauty industry originating from rural areas, reported that they bought imitation branded jeans for Rs 50, displaying their social mobility through their consumer behaviour.

As T. S. Papola, the noted labour economist pointed out, the informal sector provides low-cost products to markets beyond the reach of its formal equivalent (Wishwakarma 1993). These cheaper goods and services were often of poor quality, and their greatest market was in rural areas and among the urban poor (Chapter 7). The plastic recycling industry, for example, relied upon this market (Gill 2010, 133, 170, 249), and the expansion of powerloom production in the informal sector was based upon the large, post–Green Revolution rural market and the purchasing power of the lower tier of the urban informal stratum. Powerloom production grew to become the core of India's textile industry, vying with the large mills. Roy (1998, 907) points out that "[m]ore recently, there has been an extremely rapid development of street retailing of cloth in the cities" and suggests that this was due to the penetration of powerloom-made goods into the urban market. The formal sector of the Indian textile industry in comparison had as its main customers the urban upper classes. Cheap powerloom goods were often sold by street vendors, as were other manufactured products from the informal sector. In Delhi, vendors sold a variety of products, such as clothing, cheap rubber and plastic footwear (slippers, sandals), bed sheets, kitchenware and furniture to low-income groups at prices far lower than those in shops with fixed premises. Many of these items were made in small-scale or family-based workshops in the city and other towns (Bhowmik 2010, 52–55).

The informal retail industry of street vendors has hardly been impacted by the expeditious enlargement of modern retailing since the end of the twentieth century (Joseph and Soundararajan, 2009). This further suggests the existence of a two-tiered market consisting of the formal sector catering to the urban middle and upper classes and the informal sector tailored to the lower classes. As a fascinating study outlined in Chapter 7 has shown, the Agra footwear industry, for instance, has separate distribution routes for each tier. Footwear produced in the informal sector is sent to regional markets and local markets patronised by the poor, whereas that from the formal sector is circulated in a variety of ways. Some, cheaper products not made in their own factories, are bought in by large Indian manufacturing and sales companies; others, manufactured by the producers themselves in Agra, are directly exported; and another portion is traded abroad through agents.

Entrepreneurs in the informal sector, in both manufacturing and services, largely buy in their input goods from comparable informal businesses, not the formal sector. For example, the street vendors who are the representative face of the informal service industry predominantly deal in items produced by household industries in the same sector. The study of six regional towns carried out in 1989 illustrates this modus operandi; here, the entrepreneurs, whose scale of production and income were both low, without exception purchased the small amount of inputs they needed for the day from the overwhelmingly large number of informal sector markets (Ramanujam et al. 1994, 37, 63, 91).

It is the same with industries connected with travel and tourism. Hotels, laundry and cleaning services, and relevant goods manufacturers in the hospitality industry of the informal sector enjoy a reciprocal relationship, and most workers are procured from the informal labour market. Their employment is casual and unstable, and there is a high turnover. Most do not receive any sort of proper training for the tourist industry. These non-starred hotels are in turn linked to informal transport facilities. Taxis, autorickshaws and cycle-rickshaws transport hotel guests and take them on guided tours, and their drivers receive commissions for escorting their customers to souvenir shops and restaurants, also in the informal sector (Surjit Singh 2001). A large number of guests come from rural areas and so are an important consumer group for the informal industries tied to the tourism industry.

It would, however, be inaccurate to assume that the currents of circulation linking the formal sector with its urban middle- and upper-class clientele, and the informal sector with the lower tier of the urban informal stratum and rural customers are completely segregated. The expanding urban middle classes, for one, are important users of the informal transportation industry in the form of autorickshaws and the like. The kite-making industry of Ahmedabad, which belongs to the informal sector, also engages with the urban middle classes, as does hand-weaving. On the other hand, rural inhabitants and the lower tier of the urban informal stratum buy consumer durables and services from the formal sector. Vital too in recent times are the close linkages between the two sectors in subcontracting and outsourcing. It should be noted, however, that these connections were previously weak, particularly in the period before 1990, and circulation could more or less have been characterised as strictly two-tiered in the past. The two currents initially increased contact from the middle of the 1980s, when wealthy rural households emerged as purchasers of consumer durables of the formal sector, such as watches and bicycles (see Chapter 10). This trend accelerated in the post-reform period.

## The Structure of the "Rural and Urban-Informal Economies" Zone

Obvious streams of both people and commodities pass between the urban and rural informal sectors. The sphere of their movement can be referred to as the "rural and urban-informal economies" zone, and it is integral to understanding the modern Indian socio-economic structure. The roots of this sphere may be found in a number of historical developments. First, from the Mughal period down through British rule to independent India, the city was the locus of government, and as such, the place of residence of bureaucrats, government officials and the upper classes and the location of educational institutions. It therefore attracted a great variety of informal sector workers like traders, handcraftsmen, servants and so on. Second, the existence of important temples was a fundamental factor in urban formation. The demand generated by the temples and the people who visited them drew in various types of craftsmen and traders. Third, from the second half of the nineteenth century, large cotton mills were set up, centring on Bombay and Ahmedabad. Other industries developed from the 1920s, bringing large numbers of factory workers to the cities. This trend continued after Independence and escalated under the government-led policy to develop heavy industry, when large public and private enterprises appeared in many cities. The demand generated by the factories and the vast number of workers encouraged the establishment of a large variety of informal sector enterprises.

Fourth, the core workers of a number of traditional handicraft industries moved from the country to the city from the end of the nineteenth century into the first half of the twentieth, becoming an intrinsic part of the urban informal economy. Handweaving is a typical example. While there were some textile workers in the cities in the nineteenth century, producing goods for the courts and the ruling classes and for long-distance markets, the large majority of weavers made goods within the village to meet the demands of the extensive local population, using the yarn spun by local farmers as a side business. From the latter half of the 1800s, however, spinning mills were built in the bigger cities and village weavers turned to machine-made yarn. The mills began weaving cloth, as well as spinning yarn, for the market in the 1900s. Many village weavers then started specialising in distinctive products in order to survive the competition from the mills. In the process, an extremely large number of weavers moved from the villages to urban areas, living in enclaves on their outskirts (Yanagisawa 1971b, 1972). These handloom centres made unique fabrics which were sold in distant markets through networks of master weavers and traders. The primary market for the goods of weavers who had moved to the cities was in rural areas with a high population. During the twentieth century, social changes in rural society fostered a demand among the lower classes for new handwoven products such as saris made of artificial silk (Chapter 3) and the handloom industry in South India and other places reached new heights from the 1920s. Following Independence, the handloom industry preserved its former structure, while part of it introduced powerlooms using second-hand automatic looms discarded by the mills. In time, the powerlooms deprived the mills of their market base in the countryside. The Indian handloom industry, while moving its base of production from country to city, maintained strong linkages with rural villages, which were its prime market. With the expansion of powerlooms it occupied most of India's textile production. This can be understood as a process where an industry with its roots in the village extended into urban areas and where the village economy developed and grew by incorporating the urban.[8]

Albeit in a different context, the leather and sandal-making industry followed a similar trajectory. Originally based in rural villages prior to Independence, it went on to find fruitful footholds within the urban informal sector. The changes that emerged in the consumption patterns of the rural lower classes, connected with their growing sense of independence, encouraged this growth and led to the emergence of small and micro-industries such as rice milling, the groundnut oil industry, bidi manufacturing and cotton ginning (Chapter 3). These too can be seen as expanding from rural to urban areas.

The evolution of the economy and society in rural areas after Independence, especially in the course of the Green Revolution, not only gave rise to new, non-farm activities but also fuelled trade and manufacturing in the cities (Chapter 8). As the case studies from Karimpur in northern India and Arni in Tamil Nadu reveal, after the Green Revolution, surplus agricultural products were sent to the towns and manufactured goods flowed back to the villages. This enabled vigorous economic activity between rural areas and nearby urban centres in service industries such as trading, transportation and storage.

In four of the six towns studied by Ramanujam et al., the main industries were connected with agricultural products. The informal sector grew rapidly in all six towns in the 1980s, particularly trading (from 14.46 to 26.82 percent), but excepting one town where Hindustan Machine Tools (HMT) was set up, this growth can be explained in terms of changes in the production and consumption of rural societies, such as increased agrarian output as a result of the Green Revolution, the specialisation of produce and the diversification of consumption patterns regarding agricultural products.[9] Interestingly, the study of the six towns introduced cases where, within the informal sector, the growth of tertiary industry encouraged the development of secondary industry. For example, traders in cloth began to be involved in the sewing business and dealers in medicinal herbs began processing them. Trading had given the entrepreneurs the technical skills and market know-how needed to engage in manufacturing. The informal sector had the capability of self-development through the enrichment of content. In fact, in the six towns the percentage of those employed in manufacturing and repairs among the total employed in the informal sector rose sharply from 24 percent in 1980 to 28 percent in 1989 (Ramanujam et al. 1994, 37, 39, 65).

We have seen above how agricultural changes, such as the rise in agrarian output, and changes in the village social structure led to an expansion in the demand for services, with an increased participation by village people in education, travel and hospital use. In many cases this brought about a growth and diversification of the service sector within the urban informal sector.

The regional manufacturing industry too experienced a large growth in rural demand, as raised agricultural output levels and the expansion of non-farm employment improved incomes. The results of the NCAER survey of household consumption, conducted in 1992–1993, indicate a boom in both the making and buying of manufactured consumer goods. Rural households and the low-waged classes had become voracious consumers of a great many basic consumer goods as well as a number of durable items, a previously unthinkable situation. Goods for which the rural market exceeded 70 percent included radios, bicycles, wristwatches (mechanical) and cigarettes and for which it exceeded 60 percent, laundry detergent, footwear (casual and PVC), toothpaste and edible oils. It also occupied between 50 and 60 percent for table fans, sewing machines, motor cycles, kerosene stoves, ghee, vanaspati, footwear (leather), tea and toilet soap (Rao S. L. ed. 1994, 1, 9, 13). A vast array of daily consumer items, both durables and nondurables, had begun to penetrate rural society, including the lower classes. Manufacturing in both the formal and urban informal sectors was encouraged to become more diverse and prolific as a result and many commodities developed as informal industries, including powerloom products, synthetic goods, cotton knits and cheap footwear (Chapter 7). Rural society also took centre stage in the emergence of MSEs in urban manufacturing. Handweaving and powerlooms have already been discussed in this context. The garment industry of Tiruppur and the engineering industry of Ludhiana too had rural origins, in that they were developed by entrepreneurs of very important MSEs with historical connections to rural society.

To summarise, from the end of the nineteenth century, the rural economy experienced a process of expansion, diversification and urbanisation, stimulating the formation, development and growth of services and manufacturing within the urban informal sector. The growth of agrarian output as a result of the Green Revolution and changes within rural society acted as catalysts. Many entrepreneurs in the urban informal sector had rural origins, and a significant part of that sector today owes its existence to the development of the rural economy. Both people and commodities circulated within the "rural and urban-informal economies" zone, which shared many points of commonality, and a large (perhaps the largest) part of the urban informal sector was in reality an extension of the rural economy.

It need hardly be said that just as the rural and the urban informal economies were tightly bound together, the latter also had ties with the urban formal sector. However, as the example of Ahmedabad shows, the percentage of workers in this quarter was by no means high, and so demand from them was limited. In terms of the service sector, the trend by companies to outsource services like computing, cleaning and security as a result of restructuring and for small companies to be subcontracted is given emphasis by some, but estimates of growth rates of the services sector through splintering from other sectors showed a scant 0.25 percent rise in the 1990s. Ramaswamy (1999, 365–66) states that production subcontracting takes place widely in Indian firms, but the benefit of this delegation in 1992–1993 was only 4.5 percent value-added. It was "qualitatively insignificant" if the garment and fabricated metal industries were excluded. Further study is required here, but it seems that the informal sector does not have particularly strong linkages with the formal sector, especially the large manufacturing sector, through subcontracting.

Figure 8.1 showed the mushrooming in the 1980s of trading activities between rural and urban areas. Figure 9.1 demonstrates changes in informal sector manufacturing concerns that developed after 1978 in rural and urban areas. There is a similar pattern of movement between both, suggesting that they shared common factors propelling the development of manufacturing. Pulapre Balakrishnan (2010, 147–152), Ganesh Kumar and others have seen the stimulus given to secondary and tertiary industry by the growth of the agricultural sector in the post–Green Revolution period as the most significant juncture for the Indian economic growth that began around 1980 (see Introduction and Chapter 6). This process, however, was actualised through the formation of the "rural and urban-informal economies" zone, where rural economic development stimulated that of the urban informal sector. In this sense, the development of such a zone was in itself the strongest foundation for the post-1980s growth of the Indian economy. This view is consistent

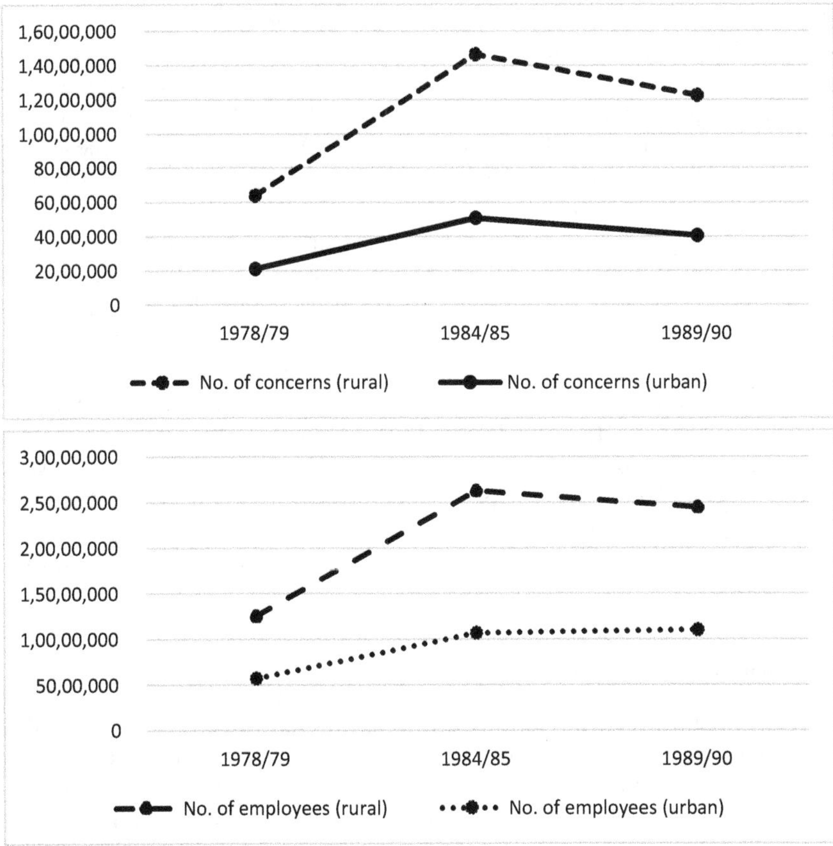


*Figure 9.1* Number of manufacturing concerns in the informal sector and employee numbers.

Source: Kulshereshtha and Singh 1998, Table 4, p. 58.

*Table 9.5* Annual growth rate of sectoral employment, 1972–73 to 1987–88

| | *Organised sector* | *Unorganised sector* | *Total* |
|---|---|---|---|
| Mining and quarrying | 1.87 | 12.42 | 5.68 |
| Manufacturing | 1.25 | 4.47 | 3.72 |
| Electricity, gas, water | 4.78 | NA | 4.78 |
| Construction | 0.12 | 8.55 | 7.03 |
| Trade, hotels, restaurants | 2.38 | 5.1 | 4.47 |
| Transportation, storage, communications | 1.33 | 8.82 | 4.98 |
| Other services | 3.94 | 3.03 | 3.4 |
| Total | 2.51 | 4.96 | 4.2 |

Source: Sundaram 1998, Table 2.

with the analysis of Ravallion and Datt (1996) in their work concerning the share of India's poor in the country's sectoral economic growth. They state that "[b]oth the urban and the rural poor gained from rural sector growth. By contrast, urban growth had adverse distributional effects within urban areas, which militated against the gains to the urban poor". Their conclusion, that "it is the dog (the rural economy) that wags the tail (the urban sector), not the other way around" (Ravallion and Datt 1996, 19), amply suggests the leading role played by rural areas in the formative process of the "rural and urban-informal economies" zone.[10]

Table 9.5, giving the sectoral growth of employment numbers in non-farm industries between 1972–73 and 1987–88, illustrates that the employment growth rate in the informal sector was almost double that of the formal sector. According to Unni's calculations, between 1983 and 1994, the growth rate in informal sector employment, excluding agriculture, was 3.9 percent, far outstripping the 1.2 percent of the formal sector.[11] Between 1994 and 2000 too, the growth rate in the informal sector was 3.2 percent, to a mere 0.4 percent in the formal sector (Unni 2003). Further, between 1999–2000 and 2004–05, the percentage of non-farm workers in the informal sector rose from 60 to 72 percent.[12] This too is an indication of the centrality of the dynamic growth of the informal sector to India's economy as a whole.

## The Emergence of the Upper Tier in the Urban Informal Sector

A variety of workers in the urban informal sector have been mentioned so far, including entrepreneurs with fixed premises, other businessmen, and the self-employed, all usually with a high level of education and often from the upper castes. From the 1970s, the development of the informal sector took place in concert with a surge in the activities of business proprietors, entrepreneurs of small-scale factories, and financiers.

Another look at the footwear industry in Agra at the beginning of the 1990s illustrates how the upper tier of the informal stratum operates. About

60,000 SC workers (members of one of the traditional leather working castes) were engaged in footwear production in Agra, and there were between 675 and 700 footwear-related shops in the central market, Hing ki Mandi, around 450–475 of these supplied the manufacturers with the necessary materials, while around 225 shops were run by wholesalers who bought the finished footwear (Knorringa 1996, 88). The suppliers and wholesalers were not members of the SCs who actually made the footwear, but "forward-caste Hindus with Punjabi or Sindhi background, Sikhs and well-to-do Muslims". They are "white collar" workers and are reported to go around the houses of the SC producers by motor bike, pressing for delivery. In the 1980s, some forward caste Hindus set up small-scale factories employing SC workers. An increasing number of SC women began doing piece-rate work at home or working in registered small-scale factories, and by the beginning of the 1990s, there were several hundred small workshops that employed ten or more workers (Knorringa, 73, 80). Some of the small-scale factories run by non-SC entrepreneurs produced goods to order for local markets, while ones with more than ten employees, as we have seen, manufactured footwear on behalf of the large India-wide footwear firms or for export. In the case of the Agra footwear industry, trading and manufacturing were developed by members of the upper tier of the informal stratum, some of whom went beyond the informal sector. This was made possible by the growth of the export market. The same social group was also vital in the development of the domestic market. The structure of the footwear industry in Agra thus comprised management by an economically well-off class in the small- to middle-range field of the informal sector and a low-waged labour force from the lower tier of the informal stratum.

It is significant that the development of the informal sector went hand in hand with the growth of the upper tier of the informal stratum. Sengupta et al. (2008) have worked on data sets from surveys of the National Sample Survey Organisation (NSSO), classifying each sample household according to income. In 2004–2005, 23.3 percent of India's population fell into the middle- and high-income range, and of these, 80.1 percent worked in the informal sector (Table 9.6). These had a high educational level, and 71.4 percent of them were either employers or self-employed. Most, 40.4 percent, were from the forward castes, with OBCs coming next at 35.6 percent. The Sengupta et al. study included agriculture in the informal sector. According to NCAER estimates, in 2005–2006, of the 18.7 percent of India's households that had an annual income of over Rs 135,000, 7.2 percent were in rural areas and 11.5 percent were in urban areas. Therefore, more than 60 percent of what Sengupta et al. refer to as the middle- and high-income groups of the informal sector are what we call here the upper tier of the informal stratum. As Table 9.7 shows, among informal sector enterprises, trade and repair services are the most numerous, followed by manufacturing; these two fields comprise as much as 70 percent of the total. The middle- and high-income groups in the informal sector may be seen as the entrepreneurial class in trade and manufacturing.

*Table 9.6* Percentage distribution of unorganised workers of different income levels by social group

| | *Total workers (in millions)* | *Unorganised workers (in millions)* | *Share of unorganised workers to total workers (%)* |
|---|---|---|---|
| Poor and vulnerable | 345.1 | 332.6 | 96.4 |
| Middle and high income | 112.4 | 90 | 80.1 |
| Total | 457.5 | 422.6 | 92.4 |

Source: Sengupta et al. 2008, Table 7, p. 53.

*Table 9.7* Sectoral distribution by industry of informal sector enterprises (1999–2000)

| | *Enterprises (1,000)* | | |
|---|---|---|---|
| | *Rural* | *Urban* | *Total* |
| Manufacturing | 9,614 | 4,656 | 14,270 |
| Construction | 1,181 | 673 | 1,854 |
| Trade and repair services | 8,578 | 8,794 | 17,372 |
| Hotels and restaurants | 848 | 928 | 1,776 |
| Transport, storage and communications | 2,012 | 1,924 | 3,936 |
| Financial intermediation | 42 | 119 | 160 |
| Real estate, renting and business activities | 200 | 572 | 773 |
| Education | 232 | 348 | 580 |
| Health and social work | 455 | 331 | 786 |
| Other community, social and personal services (excluding domestic services) | 1,906 | 1,000 | 2,906 |
| Total | 25,068 | 19,344 | 44,412 |

Source: Informal Sector in India, 1999–2000, Salient Features. NSS 55th round (July 1999–June 2000), National Sample Survey Organisation, Government of India, May 2001.

It is frequently said that the expanding "middle classes" lead consumption in the Indian economy. There is a basic flaw in this understanding that will be returned to below. The facts relayed above show that the MSE entrepreneurial class in trade and manufacturing in the informal sector, formed with the expansion of the urban informal sector, comprises, at least in terms of numbers, the core of the "middle classes" (the middle- and high-income groups).

## The "Rural and Urban-Informal Economies" Zone as a Consumer Market

The "rural and urban-informal economies" zone constituted the largest ultimate consumer market for the Indian manufacturing and service industries, underpinning them all. Sengupta et al. (2008) divided Indian households into "poor and vulnerable" and "middle and high income" as a standard for per capita expenditure based on the per capita annual income of the various classes (Table 9.8). Households with a consumption expenditure more than twice the poverty line are classed as "middle and high income", and those below twice the poverty line are classed as "poor and vulnerable". They calculate that "middle and high income" constituted 19.3 percent of the Indian population in 1999–2000 and 23.3 percent in 2004–2005.

Table 9.8 indicates that between 50 and 60 percent of total Indian consumption expenditure was by the "poor and vulnerable". Excluding "food and beverages", expenditure on "essential non-food items" such as clothing, footwear and bedding was several times the scale of "durable goods". Here can be seen the overwhelming importance of the "poor and vulnerable" market, and it means that the non-elite classes in the "rural and urban-informal economies" zone were the most important group of consumers for daily consumer items excluding durables, education and suchlike. As we have seen, these classes were the most significant market for the cheap goods and services provided by the informal sector. The flow of goods produced and consumed within the "rural and urban-informal economies" zone forms a key part of the economic circulation of Indian consumer goods.[13]

Table 9.8 also shows that the "middle and high income" groups occupied twice the market volume for durable goods compared with the "poor and vulnerable". Such goods were typical products of the formal sector. It is, however, critical to note here the difference in the situation between high-cost durables such as cars and low-cost durables such as fans, bicycles, radios and televisions. Table 9.9 gives distribution figures based on income, according to NCAER, for the ownership of televisions, both black and white and colour, in 2005–06. The two wealthiest groups (18.7 percent of all households) owned only 35.7 percent of all televisions, meaning that most televisions were owned by the low-income groups. Low-cost durables included a broad range of goods – bicycles, radios, fan, cookers and so on. By comparison, 96 percent of cars, extremely high-cost durables, were owned by the two wealthiest groups, an extremely high percentage of ownership concentration. Motorbikes and motorised bicycles fell into the intermediate range.

In terms of the end market for consumer durables, relatively cheap mass-produced goods, typically televisions, had as their main market the "poor and vulnerable" classes in the "rural and urban-informal economies" zone, while extremely expensive items such as cars were concentrated on the upper-income groups, amounting to between 10 and 20 percent of the Indian population. We should note here that 80 percent of the "middle and high income" groups, the upper 20 percent of the population, worked in the informal sector. Extremely small-scale traders and wholesalers, manufacturers and service providers were without doubt the core of the car-buying group. The Indian consumer durable manufacturing industry may thus be said to have relied heavily on the purchasing power of the "rural and urban-informal economies" zone.

*Table 9.8* Annual consumption expenditure according to class (Rs 1,000 million)

| | *−1* | *−2* | *−3* | *−4* | *−5* | *−6* | *−7* |
|---|---|---|---|---|---|---|---|
| | *Food and beverages* | *Essential non-food items** | *Education* | *Medical* | *Other non-food items* | *Durable goods* | *Total* |
| 1999–2000 | | | | | | | |
| Poor and vulnerable | 2,537 | 638 | 77 | 183 | 461 | 64 | 3,961 |
| Middle and high income | 1,250 | 362 | 105 | 186 | 538 | 125 | 2,566 |
| Total | 3,787 | 1,000 | 182 | 369 | 999 | 190 | 6,527 |
| 2004–05 | | | | | | | |
| Poor and vulnerable | 2,937 | 912 | 141 | 225 | 613 | 114 | 4,944 |
| Middle and high income | 1,771 | 633 | 298 | 316 | 985 | 275 | 4,278 |
| Total | 4,709 | 1,545 | 439 | 541 | 1,598 | 389 | 9,221 |

Source: Sengupta et al. 2008, Table 18, p. 57.

Original source: Computed from NSS 55th and 61st round survey on Employment-Unemployment, 1999–2000 and 2004–2005.

* These include heating and lighting, clothing, bedding and footwear.

*Table 9.9* Ownership of televisions, motor bikes and cars according to income group, 2005–06

| *Annual income (Rs at 2001–02 prices)* | *Percentage of households* | *Numbers owned* | | |
|---|---|---|---|---|
| | | *Televisions* | *Motorbikes, motorised bicycles* | *Passenger cars* |
| Below Rs 45,000 | 25.8 | 7.2 | 2.8 | 0.0 |
| Rs 45,000–90,000 | 39.0 | 32.5 | 17.6 | 0.0 |
| Rs 90,000–135,000 | 16.6 | 25.1 | 24.6 | 5.9 |
| Rs 135,000–180,000 | 8.0 | 15.0 | 21.3 | 16.6 |
| Above Rs 180,000 | 10.7 | 20.3 | 33.7 | 77.6 |
| Total | 100.0 | 100.0 | 100.0 | 100.0 |

Source: NCAER 2005.

## Convection within the Urban Informal Sector and Limitations on Increases

Workers in the urban informal sector evidently did not form a single consumer group. Investigating the range of social classes and mobility within the sector will flesh out this interpretation.

The wages and income of the lowest class of urban worker were slightly higher than those of agricultural workers. At the time of the village surveys I conducted around 1980, the daily rate for an agricultural labourer was Rs 10, which was not greatly different to the monthly wage of an urban worker of less than Rs 300 (Yanagisawa 1991, 376–377). The same relationship between rural and urban wages was found to exist in the resurvey of 2007. The annual income of a male agricultural labourer in the village was Rs 2,400–3,000 and that of a male working in construction or security in the cities was Rs 2,800–3,000. Table 6.6 (average daily earnings of wage labourers) shows rural non-farm and urban wages to have increased more or less in parallel, above those of farm workers.

The analysis of the structure of non-farm employment around 1944 (found in Chapter 2, Section 3) suggested that the lower classes in the non-farm labour market – workers in bidi manufacturing and unskilled workers in the coal mining and jute industries – were mainly SC members with rural origins and that their wage level was set according to the wage level of agricultural labourers. This relationship between rural and lower-class urban wage levels basically continued to be maintained. In a labour market where employers were not looking for educational or technical skills in their workers, it is unsurprising that the urban wage level should be near that of agricultural labourers, given that most of the workers in the urban labour market were most likely migrants from rural areas. As Ravallion and Datt (1996) pointed out, rural economic growth improved the income of the urban poor thanks to ties between the two labour markets.

According to the research of Amita Shah concerning the influence of employment in an industrial complex in Gujarat on local villages, because many of the employees in the complex were engaged on an informal basis, work here was not very attractive to land-owning households and only 38.6 percent of the workers in the complex were from such families; the majority (64.5 percent) were from the landless class. This clearly shows the linkages between the informal labour market, the landless classes and agricultural workers classes.

Even though the wage rates of workers in the urban informal sector were set according to those of agricultural labourers, the income of urban workers tended to be marginally better than that attainable in the village. In a survey of workers in the informal sector in Delhi, Mitra (2003, 36) found that it was widely recognised that the income gained as a result of moving from the country to the city enabled upward social mobility. Dasgupta (2003, 64), who surveyed the informal sector in Delhi centring on street vendors, reported that "68.7 percent of migrants answered that the income they were earning in the city was higher than what they had earned, or could expect to earn in the villages".

The *National Survey of Household Income and Expenditure* (*NCAER* 2005) showed that of poor households with an annual income of less than Rs 45,000, 43 percent were in rural villages and only 14 percent were in urban areas (Table 9.10). Since, of course, there are differences between urban and rural living costs, it is not possible to provide an index of poverty directly through income. However, most scholars agree that the percentage of poor households in the cities is much smaller than in rural areas, even in their debate about the poverty line.[14]

As well as urban lower class wages being slightly superior than those for rural labourers, the percentage of other family members like wives working appears to be higher in the cities (Mitra 2003, 24, 39). Dasgupta (2003, 60) states that "it has been estimated that women constitute about 22.7 percent of informal sector employment in India in 1993". It is however "possible that other kinds of informal activities, such as home-work (production of *bidis*, incense sticks and food products from home) ... are dominated by women, so that their total representation in informal employment is higher". Dasgupta posits that the findings of the survey corroborate this. "Most of the spouses of the men interviewed worked in the informal service sector as domestic helps". Since though the percentage of female workers from the agricultural labourer class in rural areas is also considerable, a more careful comparison is required to confirm whether or not there is a higher rate of multiple family members at work in urban areas over rural.

Attaining higher wages in the urban informal sector is chiefly achieved by finding a better job or status within the sector. In the Delhi street vendor survey, "of those involved in intra informal sector shifts, approximately 60.0 percent reported an *increase* in income because of the change" (Dasgupta 2003, 64). The survey of Delhi's slums too revealed that there was considerable mobility within the sector. "long-duration migrants are less likely to be in

*Table 9.10* Distribution of household income in rural and urban areas, 2001–02 (%)

| *Annual income (Rs)* | *Urban* | *Rural* |
|---|---|---|
| Below Rs 45,000 | 14 | 43 |
| Rs 45,000–90,000 | 32 | 40 |
| Rs 90,000–135,000 | 24 | 10 |
| Rs 135,000–180,000 | 14 | 4 |
| Above Rs 180,000 | 17 | 4 |
| Total | 100 | 100 |

Source: NCAER 2005.

casual employment – with an increase in the ditation of their stay, they manage to acquire for information regarding the job market" and "with an increase of income the possibility of sending remittances increases" (Mitra 2003, 56, 115). Newly arrived migrants were restricted to low-status jobs, but the longer they remained the more opportunity there was for advancement within the informal sector.

It has been highlighted, however, that there are important class differences in advancement within the informal sector. According to a survey of Delhi's poor (Hayami 2005), workers in the waste collection industry were of several types: Waste pickers, waste collectors, dealers, wholesalers and those in recycling plants. The bulk of waste pickers were illiterate migrants from Bihar and West Bengal whose earnings were below the poverty line. They lived in squalid temporary shelters made of mud and tin, and did not have the opportunity to move up to the rank of collectors and experience the better conditions prevailing there. Many of the waste collectors in comparison were sons of migrants from Uttar Pradesh; they lived in permanent houses made of brick and cement and took home an income more or less above the poverty line. Since the higher-level jobs like dealers and wholesalers were occupied by men with origins in Uttar Pradesh, communal ties, mutual trust and network connections allowed collectors who were of the same origin to advance to these higher-grade jobs. This avenue of promotion was not open for the waste pickers from Bihar and West Bengal.

Knorringa's study of the Agra shoe industry also draws attention to the close relationship between community/class and advancement within the informal sector. In Agra, it is the Jatavs, a Chamar (SC) sub-caste, who are actively involved in making footwear, while forward caste Hindus from Sindh or Punjab operate either as traders, selling the footwear Jatavs produce, or as employers of Jatav labour in small workshops or factories. The study found that there was a strong mutual distrust between the Jatav artisans and the traders, that necessary information concerning improvements in production was not communicated between them and that there was no inclination within either of the groups to improve production. A great gap existed in bargaining power between the Jatavs, dispersed in their homes or workshops, and the traders, who determined prices favourable to themselves. Very little profit remained in the hands of the Jatavs. While there were exporters' and traders' associations in Agra, there was no organisation representing Jatav interests, and there were no cases of Jatav producers rising from the lowest class to become traders or the like (Knorringa 1996, 73–74; 96–98).

Workers in the informal sector are, as we have seen, two-tiered; there are the lower classes made up of people from low castes with a poor standard of education, and the upper classes, many of whom are comparatively highly educated members of the forward castes. The analysis of NSS data (which combine urban and rural figures) carried out by Sengupta et al. (2008) infers that some 40 percent of informal sector workers in the middle- and high-income groups, which correspond to the top 20 percent of India's income bracket, are categorised as "others", not of the scheduled castes or tribes (SC/ST) or the other backward castes (OBC). This implies they are from the forward castes and have a high level of education (Table 9.11). Table 9.12 shows the composition of the various income groups in the informal sector according to social class. The forward castes ("others") constitute 41.2 percent of the middle- and high-income groups, while the other groups are all less the 20 percent. Thus the forward castes are extremely well represented among the high-income earners. Table 9.13 gives a comparison of the education level of the total population over the age of 15. Since 80 percent of the middle- and high-income group work in the informal sector, it may be assumed that graduates within the informal sector had a strong possibility of entering the middle- and high-income group, while that prospect was unlikely for those below middle school level.

*Table 9.11* Percentage distribution of informal sector workers according to income by social groups, 2004–05

| | | *SC/ST* | *OBC* | *Muslim* | *Others* | *Total* |
|---|---|---|---|---|---|---|
| 1 | Extremely poor and poor | 44.9 | 33.6 | 12.9 | 8.6 | 100.0 |
| 2 | Marginal and vulnerable | 30.5 | 40.6 | 10.8 | 18.1 | 100.0 |
| 3 | Poor and vulnerable (1+2) | 34.3 | 38.7 | 11.3 | 15.6 | 100.0 |
| 4 | Middle and high income | 16.4 | 35.6 | 7.6 | 40.4 | 100.0 |
| 5 | Total (3+4) | 30.5 | 38.0 | 10.5 | 20.9 | 100.0 |

Source: Sengupta et al. (2008). Table 7, p. 53.

*Table 9.12* Income distribution of informal sector workers according to income by social groups (%)

| | | *SC/ST* | *OBC* | *Muslim* | *Others* | *Total* |
|---|---|---|---|---|---|---|
| 1 | Extremely poor and poor | 30.6 | 18.4 | 25.6 | 8.6 | 20.8 |
| 2 | Marginal and vulnerable | 65.1 | 59 | 62.3 | 43.2 | 57.8 |
| 3 | Poor and vulnerable (1+2) | 88.5 | 80.1 | 84.7 | 58.7 | 78.6 |
| 4 | Middle and high income | 11.5 | 20 | 15.4 | 41.2 | 21.3 |
| 5 | Total (3+4) | 100 | 100 | 100 | 100 | 100 |

Source: Sengupta et al. (2008). Compiled from Tables 5 and 7, pp. 52, 53.

*Table 9.13* Percentage distribution of population (age 15+) in different educational status according to income, 2004–05

| | *Illiterate* | *Up to primary* | *Middle* | *Secondary and above but below graduate* | *Graduate or higher* | *Total* |
|---|---|---|---|---|---|---|
| Poor and vulnerable | 86.1 | 83.3 | 71.2 | 52.4 | 29.7 | 72.6 |
| Middle and high income | 13.9 | 16.7 | 28.8 | 47.6 | 70.3 | 27.4 |
| Total | 100 | 100 | 100 | 100 | 100 | 100 |

Source: Sengupta et al. (2008), Table 8, p. 53.

More empirical proof is needed, but it seems that though members of the lower classes from the low castes with a low level of education can achieve a higher wage level to some extent, the route to the middle- and high-income group is littered with obstacles.

## Notes

1 Sengupta et al. (2008) estimate that as of 1993, 18 percent of workers in the informal sector, both urban and rural, were in the middle- and high-income groups.

2 According to Yoshifumi Usami, male population movement in India soared in the 1990s ("Indo ni okeru kinnen no jinkō idō – pataan, jŭgyō jōtai henka, sōkin keizai" (Recent population movement in India – patterns, changes in the employment situation, the remittance economy). Unpublished paper given at the workshop "Indo nōson chōki hendō" (Long term changes in Indian villages), September 28–29, 2011 at the University of Tokyo.

3 A survey of residents in a district of Ongole (Andhra Pradesh), where many migrants live, reported the number of years workers in the informal sector had spent in education as 4.81 for migrants and 6.12 for non-migrants, with an average of 5.68 years. Of these, 29 percent had not received any education at all, 32 percent had completed primary education and 30 percent had gone on to secondary education, However, only 7 percent had completed the SSLC, and 2 percent had received technical qualifications from specialist institutions (M. Koteswara Rao and K. Gangadhara Rao 1994b). In the case of construction workers in Visakhapatnam (Andhra Pradesh), 95 percent were members of the backward or scheduled castes, and 84 percent had received hardly any formal education, having dropped out at the primary stage (Raju 1994). Another survey in Visakhapatnam conducted at the beginning of the 1980s also indicated that the educational level of informal sector workers was low; 22 percent of workers in the formal sector and 51 percent in the informal sector were illiterate (Sreeramamurty 1986, 68).

4 As of 1989, the average fixed capital needed to set up a business with fixed premises in the informal sector was Rs 3,649, and without fixed premises, Rs 1,450. The monthly wage for employed workers in the informal sector at the time was in the order of Rs 500. To set up any kind of business would require three months' wages (Ramanujam et al. 1994, 58, 118).

5 At the beginning of the 1980s, 74 percent of workers in Visakhapatnam's informal sector were migrants (Sreeramamurty 1986, 75). A survey of informal workers here in 1990 gave a figure of 59.5 percent (M. Koteswara Rao and M. Prasada Rao 1994, 108–9).

6 In the decade 1971–1981, the proportion of non-migrants to migrants in the city of Delhi was 5 to 15 percent higher (Mitra 1994, 127–133).

7 According to Yoshifumi Usami (forthcoming), who has analysed national sample surveys and others, in 2001 the population of male migrant workers was 93.3 million, 17.5 percent of the total population. Between 60 and 90 percent of men migrating from Bihar, Punjab and Tamil Nadu sent remittances to their places of origin. One in four households in these three states had a member who was a migrant worker and virtually all received remittances.

8 Chowdhury (2001, 230), while accepting that powerlooms were extremely numerous in urban areas, points out that they had characteristics of a village industry.

9 An important product of HMT was watches. Sales increased rapidly in the middle of the 1980s with the boom in consumer durables, and rural customers were the most important market. In this channel too rural markets acted as a strong stimulus to the growth of urban industries and services, both formal and informal.

10 The degree the growth of the urban economy contributed to both urban and rural poverty reduction increased after 1991. Datt and Ravallion (2010) report that the urban informal economy, which used unskilled labour, had seen higher employment growth since 1991. This shows the continuity of the lower classes labour market within the "rural and urban-informal economies" zone.

11 Raj (1984) states, "while the number and range of activities of [unregistered] non-household enterprises are known to have increased phenomenally since 1970–1971, there has been serious under reporting in regard to them and the methods used for estimating changes in the gross value added by them preclude to a significant degree their true dimensions being captured" (p. 1802).

12 National Commission for Enterprises in the Unorganised Sector, *The Challenge of Employment in India: An Informal Economy Perspective*, Vol. 1, The Main Report, New Delhi: Government of India, 2009, p. 13. Concerning the period since 1990, whereas employment in the informal sector has increased, that in the formal sector has come to a standstill. Jordan's paradox of "growth without employment" is well known. Wages grew in the informal and formal sectors between 1983 and 1994 by 5.7 percent and 7.2 percent respectively, and between 1994 and 2000 by 7.2 and 8.4 percent respectively. This makes it appear that while the informal sector continued to show vigorous growth, the formal sector grew even faster. Since informal sector growth was probably greater, care needs to be taken with these figures. Kulshershtha and Singh (1998; 1999) showed that between 1985–86 and 1996–97 the informal sector share of the Indian GDP fell. The authors, who belong to the Central Statistical Organisation in New Delhi, both understand the reason for this fall to be inadequacies in how the data was collected from the informal sector (underreporting by entrepreneurs, for example), since it depended on self-assessment by the entrepreneur. There is thus also the possibility that wage growth rates in the informal sector were underreported.

13 Table 9.8 shows that between 1999 and 2005 that the "middle and high income" groups increased their consumption share compared with the other groups. This increase in fact strongly reflects the increase in the share of this group within the total Indian population, from 19.3 percent to 23.3 percent during this time. In 1999, the expenditure growth rate for this group, that is, the 19.3 percent constituting the upper class, only just exceeded that of the "poor and vulnerable" groups.

14 Government of India, Planning Commission, *Report of the Expert Group to Review the Methodology for Estimation of Poverty*, 2009, p. 7.

# 10 Economic Reforms and the Development of the Large-Scale Formal Sector

The state-led import-substitution policy that began in the 1950s created the foundation for post-1991 industrial development, moulding the previously import-dependent capital goods sector into a fundamentally India-centric one (see Chapter 4). It brought basic foreign technology into Indian industry, and created the under structure that gave a competitive edge internationally to those Indian industries like pharmaceuticals that leapt into the global market in the post-reform period. Some industries developed products and technologies that met the needs of developing countries, while a state-of the-art auto parts industry flourished. At the same time, the government kept competition, both domestic and foreign, under control and imposed restrictions on the investment activities of large-scale enterprises. In many areas of Indian industry there was a growing tendency towards the production of high-cost, low-quality goods using obsolete machinery. Stagnation in both industrial output and productivity from the mid-1960s was closely connected to the high-cost Indian economy. For a great many formal sector industries, both manufacturing and service, it was necessary to shake off this high-cost economic constitution in order to look to the future.

Signs of change in India's economic policy gradually appeared from the 1970s. Though restrictions on the import of capital goods were eased, together with a partial alleviation of the Licence Raj system, as well as the introduction of a policy that was in part more open to foreign participation – permitting more foreign investment, for example – fundamental change had to wait until 1991. The ensuing economic liberalisation then did away with the Licence Raj, encouraged the participation of foreign capital, liberalised trade, permitted enterprises freedom of economic activity and strengthened market competition both internationally and domestically. It was a landmark decision that clearly expressed a change in direction towards the globalisation of the economy.

Much excellent research has already appeared detailing the fine points of the reform. Therefore this chapter will concentrate on investigating not the reform itself but how the framework for the development of the Indian manufacturing and service industries altered in response to the reform. It will look mainly at the formal sector, particularly industry in the large corporate sector.

DOI: 10.4324/9781003341550-14

At the beginning of the 1990s, a leading article where the general manager of the Godrej group, a leading Indian conglomerate, queried whether it was possible for Indian industry to survive in competition with multinational companies, brought to the fore perhaps the most basic and critical question confronting Indian industry at the time. The author emphasised the necessity, for the survival of Indian conglomerates, to reform how management was carried out (by members of the founding family, for example) and the decisive importance for the product sector, unlike the materials sector (cement and steel, etc.) where price was the only consideration, to secure its market in a sustainable way by producing goods aimed at mass market consumers. In developing countries, such goods had first of all to be low-cost (for example, half the price of goods sold to advanced countries) and of low specification. Research and development was necessary for this, as was a work culture and managerial system different from the present. Only one or two Indian companies would survive in each segment, able to provide goods to the all-important masses and operating under better management, he stated.[1]

Whether or not existing Indian conglomerates had built a base from which sustainable development through penetration of goods among the "all-important masses" was possible, the development performance of the large corporate sector in India after 1991 was phenomenal. As we have seen, from the 1990s, consumer durables like televisions, mobile phones and motorbikes rapidly penetrated the mass market, including the rural non-elite. Consumer durables were the fastest-growing section of the manufacturing industry (Chandrasekhar 2011, 223) and since 2003, when the growth rate rose, motorbikes, passenger cars, communications and private housing construction, which have been led by the vast household sector, have played an important role, together with the overseas market leader IT, in propelling the Indian economy (Nagaraj 2008).

This chapter explores how these industries, the driving force behind post-1991 Indian economic growth, were able to access domestic mass consumers and foreign markets, and how the R&D and "work culture" that made this possible were formed. It also considers the historical significance of globalisation and of the Indian economic reforms that began in the 1980s and reached full development after 1991. These are thought to have played a decisive role in opening up the mass market and in promoting R&D systems inside firms.

Section 1 looks at the construction of the mass- and middle-class-markets that absorbed the consumer durables down to the 1990s. Section 2 then identifies the emergence in the period after the 1960s of a new group of entrepreneurs, the "new capitalists", from communities other than those which had produced the traditional big business houses, as playing an important role in newly developing industries and backing the progress of the economic reforms. Against this historical backdrop, Section 3 argues that economic liberalisation led to a significant lowering in real prices of high-cost consumer-durables and services like telephone charges, which, from the 1990s, has enabled products and services to penetrate the emerging mass markets of the "rural and urban-informal economies" zone as well as the middle-class markets. Together these form a decisively important market for the core section of the large corporate sector. Section 4 shows that mechanisms to ensure quality and standards to an international level have begun to be implemented in a number of Indian industries, most notably the auto parts and IT software industries, and technology-intensive industries at an international level have been set up. Section 5 discusses how the Indian economy integrated foreign markets on the basis of the growth of these technology-intensive industries and others.

## The "Rural and Urban-Informal Economies" Zone and the Formation of a Middle-Class Market

In the course of the 1980s, consumer durables like bicycles, watches and radios penetrated the "rural and urban-informal economies" zone, and it became a defining market for them. Electrical goods, like fans and black-and-white televisions, followed suit in the 1990s. In 1989–1990, between 30 and 50 percent of rural households owned a black-and-white television; this rose to above 75 percent in 1998–1999 (Table 6.11). By 2005, an important market for comparatively cheap mass-produced consumer durables, as typified by televisions, was the "poor and vulnerable" group in the "rural and urban-informal economies" zone. One of the factors behind the growth in the market for consumer durables was, as we have seen, the expansion of the urban informal sector. The flow of rural migrants to the cities swelled as the sector expanded and mass consumer demand grew as a result of the mutual social and economic links between migrants and rural households in their places of origin. A characteristic of consumer demand here was for cheap industrial products, and their ready availability contributed to their infiltration of the market.

On the other hand, as we have seen, passenger cars were, under the circumstances, virtually limited to the urban high-income groups. In 2004–2005, 80.1 percent of the "middle and high income" groups, comprising 23.3 percent of India's population, worked in the formal sector. Owners of MSEs in the segments of trade and manufacturing in the urban informal sector were at the core of the "middle classes", at least in terms of numbers (Chapter 9). This understanding, that owners of MSEs were at the centre of those that purchased high-cost consumer durables, is shared by E. Sridharan (2008) in his study on the composition of the "middle class". In 2005–2006, about 6 percent of the population consisted of the "elite middle class", of whom some 30 percent were in public employment, an estimated 14 percent were private sector employees in the formal sector and the rest, around 56 percent, were self-employed, "small and medium enterprise owners, including in small and medium manufacturing, real estate and particularly wholesale and retail trade" (p. 18). Sridharan shows that after 1998–1999 there was a large drop in the percentage of public employees and publicly subsidised farmers. While it is very difficult to estimate accurately the composition of the middle class (p. 16), it can be said confidently that the majority in terms of number are enterprise owners in the informal sector and that the number of households in the higher-income bracket of the informal sector is swiftly rising. While it is true that groups like IT engineers earn a high income far above the national average, the growth rate of employment in the private, organised (formal) sector is low, and even in 2005 was less than half the number of public sector employees (Table 10.1). Sridharan's estimate that no more than 14 percent of all middle-class households are those of private sector employees in the formal sector indicates that the percentage of middle-class technicians and management groups in these new private enterprises is by no means large. Rather, the key factor supporting the growth of the middle class is the expansion of the informal sector.

Thus, it is patent that the foundation for the two-tiered market, the mass and the middle class, that underpinned the production of both cheap and expensive consumer durables can be found in the expansion of the "rural and urban-informal economies" zone.

*Table 10.1* Employment in the organised sector (100,000 people)

| | *Public* | *Private* | *Total* |
|---|---|---|---|
| 1971 | 107.31 | 67.42 | 174.73 |
| 1981 | 154.84 | 73.95 | 228.79 |
| 1986 | 176.84 | 73.74 | 250.58 |
| 1987 | 180.24 | 73.64 | 253.88 |
| 1988 | 183.20 | 73.92 | 257.12 |
| 1989 | 185.09 | 74.53 | 259.62 |
| 1990 | 187.72 | 75.82 | 263.54 |
| 1991 | 190.57 | 76.76 | 267.33 |
| 1992 | 192.10 | 78.46 | 270.56 |
| 1993 | 193.26 | 78.51 | 271.77 |
| 1994 | 194.45 | 79.30 | 273.75 |
| 1995 | 194.66 | 80.59 | 275.25 |
| 1996 | 194.29 | 85.12 | 279.41 |
| 1997 | 195.59 | 86.86 | 282.45 |
| 1998 | 194.18 | 87.48 | 281.66 |
| 1999 | 194.15 | 86.98 | 281.13 |
| 2000 | 193.14 | 86.46 | 279.60 |
| 2001 | 191.38 | 86.52 | 277.89 |
| 2002 | 187.73 | 84.32 | 272.06 |
| 2003 | 185.80 | 84.21 | 270.00 |
| 2004 | 181.97 | 82.46 | 264.43 |
| 2005 | 180.06 | 84.52 | 264.58 |

Source: Sridharan 2008, Table 18, p. 28.

Original source: Directorate General of Employment and Training, Employment Review for various years, cited in Institute of Applied Manpower Research, India Year Book 2008: Manpower Profile, 2008, Table 3.2.21, p. 198.

## India's New Capitalists and Economic Reform

The domestic market for services and manufactured goods, including consumer durables, was therefore fostered by rural socio-economic developments and the concurrent and connected swelling of the urban informal sector. A crucial change also occurred among those who owned enterprises through the 1970s and 1980s, as a new group of capitalists emerged out of rural society. They went on to play an important role in areas like the pharmaceutical, auto parts and IT industries that flourished particularly after economic liberalisation. Pedersen (2000) expressed this as the "'quiet revolution' within Indian industry".

We have already spoken of the agrarian origins of MSE entrepreneurs (Chapter 7) and the development of the urban informal sector in close relationship with agriculture and rural society (Chapter 9). New entrepreneurs also emerged from leading Indian corporations in the formal sector. Industrial growth, beginning with the cotton industry, had taken place from the middle of the nineteenth century using Indian capital (Chapter 2), and the core of these industrial capitalists had their historical origins in long-distance trading by the old merchant castes and also the Parsis. Particularly significant here were the Marwaris, to which the Birlas, holders of a large family business, belonged. Also prominent were the Banias of Gujarat. Men from these communities were at the centre of the Federation of Indian Chambers of Commerce and Industry (FICCI), set up in 1927. In the post-Independence period of state-led industrialisation, these traditional merchant communities invested their capital to expand into a broad range of industry, and many of their businesses grew into conglomerates. They maintained close links with the government as it forwarded its import-substitution industrialisation policy to establish a domestic manufacturing industry, spreading throughout India. Sanjaya Baru (2000, 210) and others call these business houses "national capitalists". In the course of post-Independence economic development, some of these, like Tata, have managed to remain influential, while others have fractured or almost disappeared. Some, like the Bania conglomerate the Reliance group, have surged ahead.[2]

While the India-wide conglomerates run by members of the old merchant communities dominated post-Independence industrialisation, during the 1970s and the 1980s a new group of capitalists from communities that had hitherto not produced industrialists – upper-castes like Brahmins, agricultural castes, and the backward and scheduled castes, etc. – emerged in the segments of manufacturing and services. Some of these prospered and became large-scale entrepreneurs. Since many of them expanded their businesses in tandem with local rural economic development, they have been termed "regional capitalists".

According to Harish Damodaran (2008), high (scribal) castes like Brahmins, Khatris and Kayasthas previously contained some moneylenders or members involved in other financial activities, but compared with the Banias they could not have been labelled a business class (50):

> The entry of Khatris and Brahmins into corporate industry in phenomenal proportions, as against sporadic or isolated ingressions, is largely a post-Independence feature. Even the 1965 Monopolies Inquiry Commission's list of 75 premier industrial houses had only two Khatris and five Brahmins. Since then the two communities have made long strides to a position where they today account for the country's leading entities in pharmaceuticals (Ranbaxy), bicycles and two-wheelers (Hero group), tractors (Mahindra), beer and spirits (United Breweries), and paper (Ballarpur Industries), besides the No. 2 software exporter (Infosys), well-known tyre maker (Apollo Tyres) and internationally established hotelier.
>
> (the Oberoi chain)

Brahmin enterprise grew remarkably in Gujarat and Maharashtra in western India, in Tamil Nadu, and in other places in the south. While Khatris who originated in Punjab and the north, the Mahindra brothers for instance, were an integral part of a prominent new group of entrepreneurs in the automobile parts and IT industries.

Other caste groups were no less important. The Kammas and Reddis, agricultural castes of Andhra Pradesh, were particularly active. Carol Upadhya's research into the farmer-capitalists of coastal Andhra Pradesh (1988) focuses on these two powerful, landowning groups, revealing the manner in which they ventured into trade and manufacturing in the course of the Green Revolution, when a capitalistic type of agriculture developed in rural areas due to high productivity and increased surpluses. Increasing numbers in the Kamma community, having become wealthy through agriculture, have diversified into a wide variety of non-farm businesses, including construction (sub-contracting for public works), the agro-industry (sugar, food processing, etc.), the machine industry, cement manufacture and cinemas. It is interesting to note that a major impetus for the rural wealthy to invest in non-farm businesses has been the difficulty, as a result of the land reform that limited land ownership, of using accumulated capital to buy more agricultural land. Damodaran (2008) remarks that "pharmaceuticals is a sector that has produced an avalanche of new-generation Kamma entrepreneurs from the 1980s" (110). These entrepreneurs have an extremely high level of education, many with master's degrees and doctorates in pharmacy, and many have built their business after working with pharmaceutical firms abroad. These companies mainly manufacture and export generic drugs. Linked to drugs are hospitals, and a number of them are owned by the Kammas. A member of the same community runs Amara Raja, India's second largest car battery producer.

In addition, the Reddis of Andhra Pradesh have founded major businesses, including the now international pharmaceutical company Dr Reddy's

Laboratories (DRL) and Apollo Hospitals Enterprise Limited, based in Chennai, which owns and manages 38 hospitals, making it Asia's largest health carer. The Rajus, also from coastal Andhra, have advanced into a variety of areas, such as Satyam Computer Services Limited.

In Tamil Nadu, the Naidus and Gounders, who were primarily farmers, were the source of a substantial number of industrialists. The Naidus had been involved in setting up cotton ginning factories even before Independence, and they established a number of textile mills in Coimbatore. These were essentially spinning factories, providing yarn to the handloom weavers of the Tamil region, and so their development was tightly intertwined with the local economy (Damodaran 2008, 144). An engineering industry grew up beside the textile industry in Coimbatore after Independence, and today the region is the centre of a large machine industry. There are around some 600 foundries there. These started out in close relation to agriculture as workshops repairing machinery in the cotton and sugar mills and manufacturing ploughs and other farm equipment before blossoming into a national centre for the manufacture of pumps, motors and spinning machines (Damodaran 2008, 147). Naidu firms produce 60 percent of India's spinning machines and half of its pumps, and have become a global force in the manufacture of textile machinery. The Gounders predominate among the entrepreneurs in Tiruppur, India's foremost export hub for knitwear and ready-made garments (Chapter 7).

Also in South India, the Nadars, a backward caste whose traditional work was making and selling toddy, set up a match factory in Sivakasi, and the Ezhavars, a caste with a similar background to the Nadars, produced coir matting. A member of the Ezhavars was one of the cofounders of a "Brahmin institution" called Infosys Technologies.

The emergence of business founders from communities with strong connections with farming and a base in rural economic growth is conspicuous in South India. In western India too many came from two farming castes: the Patidars and the Marathas. Here, cooperatives appear to have been a popular form of enterprise, and many entrepreneurs disengaged themselves from their base in dairy and sugar cooperatives, which are essentially family affairs, to move into industries such as chemicals, pharmaceuticals, textiles and the manufacture of products like soap, watches and turbans. Their advance into education, including the establishing of colleges, is striking (Damodaran 2008, Chapter 7; Attwood 1992).

Mario Rutten, who made a field study of the mindset of rural industrialists in central Gujarat from May 1986 to May 1987, vividly describes the materialisation of the new class of rural capitalists against a backdrop of agricultural growth. "[N]o less than 50 of the 75 large farming families have economic activities outside the agricultural sector, i.e. in trade or industry, in non-farm businesses, in trade or manufacturing". Four of them had invested in "setting up agro-processing enterprises such as a rice mill, a tobacco processing factory and two cold storage buildings" (157). His study of 59 industrial enterprises between the two survey villages showed that most of them had been founded in or after the 1970s. They were engaged in a wide range of businesses, including cold storage, agro-processing, sawmills, brickyards, tile factories, cement pipe factories, cement article factories and engineering companies. In 20 of the 59, production was associated with agriculture (180–81). Thirty-nine of the firms employed ten or fewer persons, while two each engaged 250. In terms of the total number of workers, the share of firms employing ten or fewer workers was no more than 20 percent. One quarter of workers were permanent employees, like foremen and night watchmen, who came from nearby villages. The others were paid on a piecework basis and almost all were migrants from tribal areas (185–88). Most of the entrepreneurs had not been previously employed in the kind of business they later started but worked in farming or trading activities in rural areas. Ninety percent of them had their origins in a rural village, and two thirds of them were born and raised in or near the two survey villages. Rutten says that the establishment of these industrial enterprises was the result of the investment of agricultural surpluses in the non-farm sector by capitalist farmers following the rise in agrarian output.

The ascendancy of the new capitalists has a number of distinguishing features. First, an extremely large portion of them came from communities or classes connected with farming in rural districts. Communities such as the Kammas, Reddis, Patidars and Marathas both operated their own farms and were large-scale landowners in the village. Many Brahmins similarly belonged to the dominant landowning class in the village. With the exception of the traditional merchant communities, however, it took until after Independence for remarkable numbers of these communities to begin engaging in business. Some of the largest firms in India arose at that time. Damodaran understands the rise of the new capitalists, especially in southern and western India, as "the democratisation of capital", with the easing of the stranglehold on capital by the traditional mercantile and banking communities.

Second, the growth of agrarian output, typified by the Green Revolution, allowed powerful agriculturists in the villages to move into the non-farm sector. In many cases the new capitalists moved first into businesses processing agricultural products, like sugar, with a strong base in the local economy, and then into a variety of other segments. The growth of the local economy, based on the expansion of the agricultural economy and of rural society, may be regarded as the most important foundation for such industrial investment.[3] Pre-Independence agricultural growth and changes in rural society not only formed a market for non-farm goods and services but also prepared the way for the emergence of those entrepreneurs who would play a role in the new industrial developments from the 1980s. Prominent economic centres developed in a number of regions. Baru (2000) says that states like Punjab, Haryana, Gujarat, Maharashtra, Tamil Nadu, Andhra Pradesh and Karnataka had emerged as regional economies from the end of the 1970s.

Third, movements aimed at the social advancement of agricultural communities were a key motivation. A typical example is the bank established by the Nadars "to promote commercial and industrial enterprise among the members" (Damodaran 2008, 183). Cooperative relationships among caste and family played a very important role in securing capital.[4] Caste advancement movements are thought to have been particularly significant in raising education levels, and higher education, at universities for example, has been a central factor in the proliferation of non-farm businesses among agricultural communities. Entrepreneurs have paid close attention to education, as seen from the educational complexes, including colleges, they have built in rural areas in western India.

The influence of caste advancement movements was not limited to agricultural communities. In southern and western India where the presence of anti-Brahmin movements was strong, there were firm barriers against the entry of Brahmins and members of other high castes to government jobs, and this resulted in them moving into the business world. While in the south and the west of India the reservation policy is an accepted reality and gave birth to the "democratisation of capital", in northern India the traditional mercantile communities monopolised business. This made it very difficult for the Jats, mainly agriculturists, to make the transition into business even when they had become prosperous farmers (Damodaran 2008, Chapter 10). Ashutosh Varshney (2012, 226) maintains that it is the erosion of caste stratification in the south that has led to its surging economy, as caste and occupation are no longer so rigidly connected, allowing a variety of castes to enter into trade and business.

Fourth, these new capitalists have developed under the protection of various government policies. A major factor in the entry of the Khatris and others into the two-wheeler and auto parts industries was the restriction on imports, and the government's manufacturing protection policies facilitated the movement of the Naidus of South India into industry. Many entrepreneurs were also supported through subcontracting for public works undertaken by the government. A crucial policy was that designed to protect small-scale industries; regional new capitalists realised growth by asking the central government to protect small-scale industries via the state government.[5] In 1973, the government reserved match production, dominated by the Nadars, for the small-scale sector and simultaneously constrained the capacity of the Western Indian Match Company Limited (WIMCO), a subsidiary of a Swedish firm and at the time India's largest match supplier. As a result, Sivakasi now produces four fifths of India's match consumption (Damodaran 2008, 185).

Concerning the penetration of the new capitalists into Indian business circles, Baru (2000) estimates that "nearly a quarter of the top one hundred private companies in India today is owned by first-generation businessmen" (214). These operate in various industries – textiles, cement, sugar, chemicals, fertilisers, pharmaceuticals, electronics, and steel and engineering goods (215). In the IT industry too, many of the leading companies (as of 2000) there did not emerge out of the old economy but were started as small ventures. "Wipro and Tata Consultancy Services, both of which grew out of old economy companies ... remain in the minority" (Upadhya 2004, 5142, 5149).

It would be of great interest to know how central these new capitalists were in industries like pharmaceuticals, electronics and IT software, which expanded remarkably from the 1990s and extended their exports.

A number of studies have shown that the new capitalists, compared with the old, nationally based conglomerates, had a strong technological orientation and wanted the liberalisation of regulations so they could introduce foreign technology. For example, a case study concerning a large industrial estate near the town of Vapi in south Gujarat looked at small- and medium-sized entrepreneurs. The group investigated included not only Banias but also Brahmins and members of artisan and lower castes. Some of the enterprises on the estate had moved from the domestic to the export market, while others engaged in technical collaboration with foreign firms. The entrepreneurs stressed their technical orientation and asserted that they were different from those in large firms who pursue short-term profit and engage in rent-seeking. They acknowledged that they had benefitted from state aid in the past, but they considered their success not due to that but to their technical expertise and superior management. Protectionism was no longer necessary, they insisted, and the regulation of imports and the license system simply fettered development (Gorter 1997).

In 1974, the Association of Indian Engineering Industry (AIEI) emerged from a fusion of two organisations representing foreign and Indian engineering companies. This became the Confederation of Indian Industry (CII) in 1992. According to Jøgen Dige Pedersen (2000, 270), more than 75 percent of its members were medium and small companies with fewer than 500 employees. They had "a stronger than average orientation toward the use of modern technologies, indicated by the almost universal presence of technological collaboration agreements with foreign companies". In 1990, Stanley A. Kochanek (1996b, 531, 545) relayed that 33 percent of CII's members came from the South and 29 percent came from the West. CII tended to "represent newer sunrise industries including electronics, software and computer technology", and was "very active in promoting Indian exports and in building an extensive network of overseas contacts". It sought the globalisation of the Indian economy and the abolition of reservations, controls and licenses in all segments of industry. Kochanek writes, "many high-level government officials in India see FICCI and Assocham as 'aging dowagers whose best days are behind them' and the CII as composed of dynamic, efficient and forward-looking 'yuppies' who deliver the goods".[6]

Multiple investigations have asserted that the economic reforms of 1991, which fundamentally changed policy in the direction of liberalisation and greater foreign investment, deeply affected the formation of the new capitalists. The power of influence of this group, many of whom operated small-scale businesses, can be seen in the broadened reservation policy of the 1970s, when entrepreneurs in the matchmaking industry of Sivakasi appealed for reserved status through the state government.[7] Policy changes in the 1970s resulted in a massive leap in the production of bulk drugs by Indian firms (Chapter 4), and Damodaran (2008, 72) comments: "it is rumoured that the

Hathi Committee report of 1975, which gave a huge boost to the domestic pharma industry was drafted in was Bhai Mohan's office" (Bhai Mohan was a Khatri entrepreneur who controlled Ranbaxy). Kochanek (1996b, 546) notes how CII developed a close working relationship with the bureaucracy and "systematically established deep roots in each of the major economic ministries".[8]

Pedersen (2000), exploring changes within the state elites and economic pressures from abroad, such as the economic crisis and the IMF, as causes behind the reform process of 1991, says it was the "quiet revolution" among industrial capitalists, that is, the formation of the new capitalists, that was the key to the social changes that brought the reform about. "The change to a new economic policy in 1991 may be interpreted as a political reflection of these changes within the Indian society" (271).[9] As Pedersen himself states, his arguments regarding the correlation between the 1991 policy change and the materialisation of the new capitalists are "of a preliminary nature and … can best be viewed as hypotheses subject to further inquiry" from a variety of angles: The process of the policy decision, the industries the national conglomerates of the time were involved in, and changes in economic policies. The "democratisation of capital", however, formed the social and economic backdrop that stimulated the policy shift. This had important historical significance for changes in India's economic structure.[10]

Expanding agricultural output, changes in rural society and caste advancement movements drove the rise of the new capitalists, but beneath all these lay the development of the local economy (including the rural). Long-term changes in agricultural output and village society laid the groundwork for a prospering domestic market for non-farm goods and facilitated the emergence of a new group of entrepreneurs. These business owners helped set the direction of the 1991 reform and led industrial innovations, having been given a leg up by the state responses of the 1970s and 1980s, such as the small-scale industry reservation policy.

## The Penetration of Manufactured Goods and Services into the Domestic Market

### *Economic Reform and the Fall in Relative Price and Quality Improvement of Consumer Durables*

The penetration of consumer durables like bicycles, watches and radios into the two-tiered domestic market was well underway in the 1980s. From the 1990s, more expensive products such as televisions, other electrical appliances and the costly passenger car joined them. This influx is thought to have played a decisive and vital role in the policy shift towards the liberalisation and globalisation of the Indian economy from the 1980s into the 1990s.

The rise of the television provides a telling example. Until the 1970s, the government's strategy towards electronic consumer goods was centred on technological self-reliance and small-scale domination. The formal sector was allowed to manufacture televisions through licensing, but capacity restrictions were imposed. During the 1970s, the small-scale sector was the main producer. Market concentration was low, with the share of the top four producers at only 46 percent. Whereas in the same period, firms in Japan, South Korea and the United States were operating on a scale of several million sets annually, the leading Indian firms were producing several thousand annually. As a result, the cost of components in India was 2.6 times higher than that abroad, the cost of assembling, marketing, etc. was four times higher, and the cost of a typical 51 cm set was more than three times higher than international prices (Joseph 2004, 252–56).[11]

This high-cost structure changed with the easing of regulations from the 1980s. Policy liberalisation during that period permitted all sectors of industry, including joint ventures with up to 40 percent equity, to participate, and removed the ceiling on capacity, though foreign companies were excluded. As a result, whereas in 1976 the top ten manufacturers of black-and-white televisions had all been small-scale firms, all but one had become large-scale in 1988. The 1991 reform removed entry barriers to foreign firms, and Sony, Akai, Samsung, Goldstar and Thomson entered the Indian market by setting up fully owned subsidiaries (Joseph 2004, 260). K. J. Joseph (2004, 264) comments that

> [p]rice competition has been observed in almost all the [electronic] products. In the TV industry, firms offer different models with significant differences in the basic features. It is important to note that the advertisements for most of the products clearly state their prices along with product characteristics. This is indeed a new trend in the Indian industry.

From around 1991, the relative price of consumer durables showed clear signs of falling, moving away from the price trend of consumer nondurables (Figure 10.1). The relative price of durables fell overall between the mid-1980s and 1998–1999. The fall in the cost of "radios and televisions" is especially striking (Figure 10.2). It should also be noted that within the fall in the relative price of televisions, there was a marked improvement in function (Joseph 2004, 264). The relative price of consumer durables fell again after 2000. The wholesale price index for "all commodities", where the base 1993–1994 = 100, rose 242.9 percent in 2009–2010 but the index for "electrical apparatus and appliances" dropped to 76.5 in the same period. This means the relative cost of "electrical apparatus and appliances" plummeted to under one third during this time.[12]

As we have seen, black-and-white televisions had infiltrated more than half the rural market in 1990–1999. In 2005, they reached the "poor and vulnerable" market within the "rural and urban-informal economies" zone, which preferred relatively cheap, mass-produced and marketed consumer durables. Such penetration could not have been achieved without the fundamental shift in economic policy which allowed the participation of foreign capital and large-scale industries.[13]

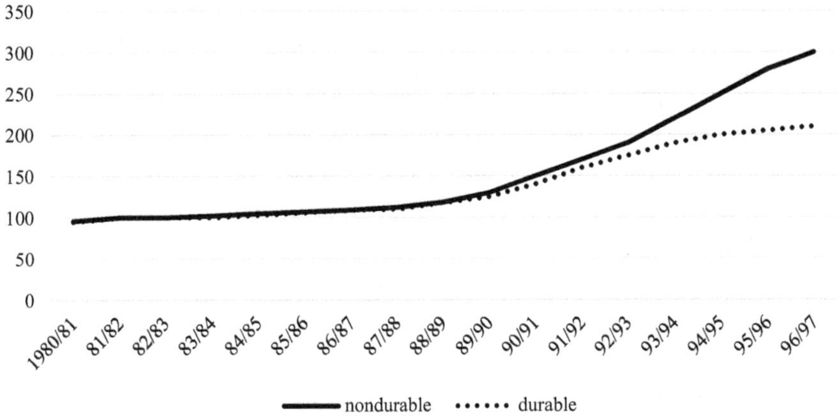


*Figure 10.1* Price trends of consumer durables and nondurables.

Source: Roy, Tirthankar. "Consumer Non-Durable Goods Industries: Growing Market and Increasing Competition". In Shuji Uchikawa ed., Economic Reforms and Industrial Structure in India, New Delhi: Manohar, 2002: Figure 5, p. 100.

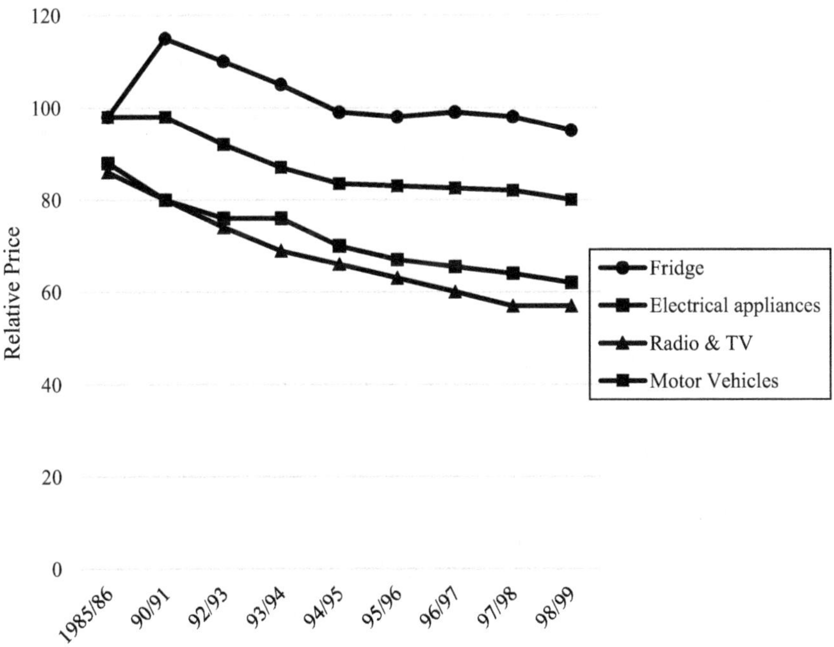


*Figure 10.2* Price trends of main durables.

Source: Ramaswamy, K. V. "Economic Reforms, Industrial Structure and Performance: The Case of Consumer Durable Goods Industry in India". In Shuji Uchikawa ed., Economic Reforms and Industrial Structure in India, New Delhi: Manohar, 2002: Figure 1, p. 131.

Passenger cars too probably would not have spread throughout the domestic market without the restructuring of the industry that occurred from the beginning of the 1980s as a result of the entry of Maruti Udyog Limited (MUL), a joint venture between Suzuki Motors and the Government of India. Following the introduction of an import ban on completely built vehicles in 1949, the automobile industry had operated under severe restrictions. In 1975, an automatic capacity expansion of 25 percent every five years was declared acceptable, but it did not include passenger cars. Moves towards liberalisation in this segment began in the period 1977–1980:

> The state loosened its tight grip in favor of increased competition at home and greater participation of foreign capital. This was achieved by relaxing regulations governing production licenses [and] foreign collaboration … [and] to reap the benefits of scale, the policies aimed to do away with limits on capacity.
>
> (D'Costa 1995, 487)

The government also relaxed entry regulations for domestic business houses and foreign companies, allowing them to produce a range of related products, like two-wheelers and four-wheelers. All the same, the liberalisation of the 1980s was not unrestricted and it continued under government control.

Down to the beginning of the 1980s, a number of manufacturers of commercial vehicles had cornered the Indian market and retained their competitive force internationally (Chapter 4), but already by 1980 the production of passenger cars was not meeting middle-class demand. The vehicles produced by Hindustan Motors (HM) and Premier Automobiles (PAL), the leading manufacturers, were 1950s models and very expensive (Table 10.2).[14]

According to Anthony P. D'Costa (1995, 490–91), the government thought that restructuring Hindustan Motors, which was owned by the "old capitalist" Birla group and "relied on obsolete technology in a sheltered market", would be an arduous task. It looked therefore to produce a competitive fuel-efficient passenger car by utilising economies of scale and setting up a joint venture between its Maruti Udyog Limited and Suzuki. Table 10.2 shows that Maruti's basic car was highly economical in terms of both price and quality, giving it an advantage in the domestic and the low-price international markets. Maruti's entry into the industry invigorated Indian passenger car production and enabled the absorption of rising middle-class demand.

The telephone industry too saw high rates of growth following the post-1991 economic reforms, with rapid cost reduction and an expanding market. The National Telecom Policy of 1994 legalised the entry of private firms into the industry, including mobile phone businesses; the addition of mobile phones to fixed phone lines heralded the creation of an extremely competitive environment. The Telecom Regulatory Authority of India (TRAI), set up in 1996, broadened telephone access and began monitoring the industry to ensure low prices and the quality of service. Numerous service providers in each region competed with one another and a large number of foreign

*Table 10.2* International competitiveness of Indian vehicles

| *Indian vehicles* | *Price in India* | *Comparable foreign vehicles and price abroad* |
|---|---|---|
| Maruti (800 cc) | $3,567 (1985) | Yugo $4,000 (1986, US) |
| Maruti (800 cc) | $3,992 (1990) | Citroen AX-10E $8,664 (1990, France)<br>Austin Mini $7,739 (1990, France)<br>SEAT Marbella $6,600 (1990, France) |
| Maruti-Zen (993 cc) | $7,161 (1993) | Nissan-March (997 cc) $7,284 (1993, Japan) |
| HM-Ambassador (1,489 cc) | $4,329–5,733 | Obsolete vehicle with no international competitors |
| HM-Contessa | $5,468–7,026 | Obsolete vehicle with no international competitors |
| PAL-Padmini (1,089 cc) | $4,200–5,510 | |
| TELCO – 16.6-ton truck | $15,000 (1986) | Fiat Iveco – 13.3-ton truck – $23,000 (1986) |
| Ashok-Leyland – 15.2-ton truck | $11,850 (1985) | |

Source: D'Costa 1995, Table 5, p. 497

Original Source: World Bank (1987), p. 18; Kathuria (1996). Table 3; Nissan Motor Co., Ltd. (1993), personal communication; SEAT (1994), personal communication.

companies began manufacturing mobile phones. Before the easing of restrictions and the introduction of mobile phones, telephone charges were periodically raised, but now, since all the providers were new, they competed in terms of price and conditions of sale, causing telephone fees to nosedive. Between 1994 and the beginning of the 2000s, charges per unit of call time on mobiles fell by one eighth.[15]

This swift reduction in price led to a dramatic increase in the number of subscribers. In December 2011, Indian teledensity (the number of telephone connections per hundred people in an area) reached 76.86 percent (urban 167.46 percent; rural 37.52 percent), which made India the second largest country in the world in terms of telephones. As previously mentioned, the 2007 survey of a village in Tamil Nadu revealed that 43 percent of SCs had mobile phones and that in Uttar Pradesh too their diffusion among the SCs was above 30 percent. Even in rural villages in Bihar, considered to be a deprived area, a 2011 survey reported that 63 percent of households had mobile phones (Tsujita and Oda 2012, Table 2, p. 28). This reveals a penetration pattern of mobile phones moving from the upper to the lower classes in the cities, and then into rural villages and spreading even among low-income groups.[16] As the 2011 Annual Report of the Indian Department of Telecommunications revealed, urban teledensity had reached saturation point and so private firms were looking to rural areas to extend their reach, with the result that the growth rate was greater in these areas (Chapter 8). Thus the lowering of costs following the easing of regulations after 1991 allowed the telephone industry to access a market on a national scale, including the lower classes.

The real price of construction has also fallen. According to R. Nagaraj (2003, 3710), the gradual decontrol of the cement industry after 1982 led to increased capacity creation, the entry of new firms and technological upgrading, which brought down the price of cement. Supply constraints on steel were also relaxed, prompting accelerated growth in the construction industry.

### *The Consumer Durables, Communication and Construction Industries at the Core of the Growth in Manufacturing and Services*

Consumer goods contributed greatly to the expansion of manufacturing (see Table 10.3). Their contribution ratio may have been small, but their growth rate was high (Chandrasekhar 2011, 223). Ramaswamy (2002) too judged that consumer durables grew through domestic-market-orientation as a result of liberalisation, seeing their most vigorous growth rate in the virtuous circle of liberalisation, large investment, output increase, cost reduction and diversification of products and structural change.

The communication industry saw rapid growth from the end of the 1990s to great effect. Between 2000 and 2005, this sector grew 24.02 percent, more than any other in the economy, making it the highest contributor to the growth of India's overall GDP. Of total spending on information and communications technology (ICT), some 63 percent was in communications. It can thus be said that the communications industry occupies a greater position that the information sector, and that the telecom industry is more important than the IT industry in India's economic growth. The telecom industry derives its income from both services and equipment manufacturing, the former being several times greater in amount than the latter. At the same time, the dramatic diffusion of telephones has made India the world's second biggest market for mobile phones and the equipment sector, centred on foreign investment, has markedly swelled (Mani 2008).

In view of the fact that the growth rate of the Indian economy after 2002–2003 reached 8.7 percent per annum, R. Nagaraj (2008) interrogated whether

*Table 10.3* Manufacturing growth rate, 1994–94 to 2004–05

| | *Growth rate (%)* | *Contribution margin ratio (%)* |
|---|---|---|
| Basic goods | 4.49 | 1.59 |
| Capital goods | 6.92 | 0.67 |
| Intermediate goods | 6.39 | 1.69 |
| Consumer goods | 6.45 | 1.83 |
| Durables | 9.16 | 0.47 |
| Non-durables | 5.65 | 1.31 |
| General | 5.83 | 5.83 |

Source: Chandrasekhar 2011, Table 9.2, p. 223.

Original source: Computed from figures on the Index of Industrial Production obtained from the Central Statistical Organisation, as available at www.mospi.nic.in, accessed January 2009.

the private corporate sector could be considered the engine behind it. He indicated that it was instead the household sector that accounted for the sharp rise in domestic savings and investment and emphasised the centrality of the communication industry domestically and business services abroad, together with the two- and four-wheeler manufacturing industry and the home construction industry. Chapter 8 also pointed out the importance of the construction of private homes in rural areas, which had spread after the reduction of real construction costs following economic reforms. With the exception of the IT industry, which depended on the foreign market (to be discussed below), the core of modern Indian high economic growth were those industries that had been brought about by the coupling of the mass and middle-class markets, which had expanded thanks to the flourishing of the informal sector. Industries in the formal sector that had developed in the course of import-substitution industrialisation had partially succeeded in accessing the rural market through bicycles and radios, but their main markets generally consisted of the state sector and consumers in the very upper levels of society. Economic liberalisation, however, allowed the formal industrial sector to broaden, engaging informal sector entrepreneurs and reaching into the "rural and urban-informal economies" zone and the middle-class market. This dramatic expansion of the industrial base is of historical significance.

## Technological Growth, the Expansion of Skills and Training Systems, and the Proliferation of Technology-Intensive Industries

In the course of the shift to economic liberalisation and globalisation from the 1980s, many new technologies were inevitably introduced into a range of industries and machines and production processes were modernised. However, the introduction of innovative practices did not guarantee the immediate production of high quality goods that met global standards and were competitively priced. This depended on the relevant workers, supervisors and senior staff being enterprising and capable enough to employ the new and different technologies to full effect.

Aya Okada (2004) conducted a case study, interviewing the two leading auto assemblers, Maruti Udyog Ltd (MUL) and the Tata Engineering and Motor Company Ltd (TELCO), and 50 first-tier suppliers to them between 1996 and 1998. Among her findings were a number of significant changes that had occurred in one section of Indian industry. As workers and firms responded to changing technology, systems for training and skills development were put in place, suppliers provided quality assurance and new linkages between firms grew up.

According to Okada, the component industry grew by 21 percent annually in the 1990s but with increased competition, component producers came under growing pressure to raise their technological level.

> Many auto component suppliers in Faridabad, an old industrial district in the state of Haryana, started out as suppliers of tractors components

> in the 1970s, and moved to auto parts when MUL started operation in the mid-1980s… Until the mid 1990s, employment practices for production workers, typically with little education, had been mixed. Some firms, paying low wages, saw frequent job turnover, whereas in other firms production workers remained for over 20 years, becoming highly skilled. (1271)

However, there was a new direction from the mid-1990s. First, even small firms began demanding production workers who had received post-secondary vocational training, especially at Industrial Training Institutes (ITIs). This was because, with increased automation and computerisation, workers required new basic technical knowledge. Second, in the past, some firms employed high proportions of casual workers in production, recruiting them without asking for qualifications, but now firms began favouring long-term employment practices. Because customers required better product quality, firms could not rely on casual workers who would need time-consuming and costly retraining. Casual workers also could not be expected to possess the level of responsibility and commitment needed. Third, MUL had adopted some Japanese work organisation practices and modelled their implementation. The practices included QC circles, suggestion schemes, multiskilling/rotation and ISO 9000 certification, and these spread widely among component producers, such as those supplying TELCO. A majority of the firms sampled had introduced regular training programmes after 1993. These involved annual training plans for each employee and induction training for new entrants.[17] The relations between firms also changed. To reach a global standard in terms of price and quality, TELCO supported suppliers in raising their technical standards and sent out engineers to help them if they ran into difficulties. Such relations strengthened the mutual promotion of technical training in particular. In addition, quality assurance methods changed from post-production checks to pre-production precaution through process controls.

Overall, it is safe to say that a system that assured product quality within the production process began to permeate the auto components industry. This was the result of the employment of an educated workforce, serious consideration of a regular skills-development process within the firm based on a system of long-term employment, and the building up of worker commitment. This was a critical turnaround from the pre-reform system whose competitiveness was founded on a cheap, short-term labour force of less-educated workers.[18]

The same evolution can also be seen in the case of the Indian software industry. Here too we find in-house education and training systems being developed, plans being made for a constant rise in technical skills and technological levels, worker commitment fostered through long-term employment and the intention to assure and raise product quality thereby.

From around the end of the 1980s, there was a rapid increase abroad in the demand for computer professionals. At that time, there was little demand domestically for technicians involved in software services. The Indian software industry employed this large stock of unemployed engineers, trained them in software techniques as they worked and so was able to profit hugely through their response to overseas demand. In the early period, its use of human capital was extravagant and this negatively influenced the supply of technicians to other industries (Athreya 2005). This glut had disappeared by the mid-1990s, leading both to a scarcity of engineers and to rising wage levels. It was estimated that there were 160,000 engineering graduates every year in various fields, but in 1998, 250,000 employees were required by the software industry. Given the situation, a number of firms began utilising mechanisms to train non-engineers in software programming. It is said that Indian software firms were able to raise graduates with three years' experience to the same level as those in Europe with ten years' experience. They introduced employee stock options as a way of retaining their interest and loyalty and charted management career paths for technical personnel. Various managerial methods were applied to share knowledge among employees by easing hierarchical class divisions and encouraging teamwork. In the process, firms built up the organisational ability to supervise and manage large-scale human resources, allowing them to deliver high-quality outsourcing services in a timely manner by a trained and well-placed workforce. Athreya (2005) says

> [d]ynamic capabilities are central to understanding the evolution of the Indian software industry. Export success, initially as a result of favourable factor endowments (availability of cheap, skilled software programmers, became a "created" comparative advantage in outsourcing resting on the organizational capabilities of a few large software service firms.
>
> (415)

The labour shortage and the expanded market contributed to the formation of this "comparative advantage". The offshore model is said to be one third of the cost of the on-site model. Through outsourcing, Indian firms acquired the ability and reputation to provide a product in a timely manner, at low cost and with quality assured. With the brand "Made in India" established, there was a spillover effect into other services, such as electronic customer management, medical transcription, financial data analysis and call centres.

Vijayabaskar's (2005) analysis of changes in the work environment as a result of the introduction of ICTs into the Indian automobile industry is pertinent here. The first development was the decrease in blue collar work:

> "The deployment of CNCs (computer numeric controls) and robots has led to a reduction in the number of operators required on the one hand, and a shift in job type from that of an operator to that of a machine tender".
>
> (398)

Among white-collar jobs, there has been a reduction in routine clerical work like documentation, inter-departmental communication and data processing, leading to a smaller body of staff. The introduction of CNCs to the workplace has devalued operating skills and placed the emphasis on machine monitoring. Now, the ability to solve cognitive problems and to identify and rectify a malfunctioning machine is prioritised. Further, in order to respond to a flexible product market, management seeks multi-skilled workers who can be trained in specialised fields different from their present one. Workers with higher academic qualifications than those held by traditional skilled workers are therefore looked for, and the absorption of trainees from industrial training institutes has dropped "due to the declining need for a blue-collar workforce" (405).

Connected with this evolution in the type of worker sought is the increased weight placed on product quality assurance. This has led firms who were unsure of the quality levels of their suppliers to retain operations themselves. Yet, the introduction of ICTs has not led to changes in the levels in outsourcing, nor has it led to a reduction in firm size. The need to reduce costs encourages a firm to subcontract certain tasks, but the need to raise quality pushes it to avoid this and to guarantee stable employment for its workers.[19] All the industries considered above have made the pursuit of quality their prime goal, and since the 1990s have sought not workers who have undertaken vocational education with the aim of becoming proficient in a particular skill but people with a higher level of education, a high cognitive knowledge and the ability to undertake on-the-job training. They encourage and guarantee long-term employment of their workers and, by means of in-company training and education, seek to create workers with high levels of commitment to the job and workplace and the flexibility to respond to a daily changing technological environment.

Kaliappa Kalirajan and Shashanka Bhide (2005) examined post-reform competitiveness within India's manufacturing sector. They assessed the impact of firm-specific technical efficiency measures on export intensity, raw-material import intensity, technology import intensity, research and development (R&D) intensity, advertising intensity and foreign collaboration in the three manufacturing sectors of chemical products, electrical machinery and transport. Their findings highlighted "the importance of R&D, including training of workers, to improving firms' competitiveness" (148). The fact that the contribution of electrical-machinery import intensity was extremely low in the electronics industry may be attributed to an insufficiency of workers able to use the new machinery. This suggests the pivotal importance of worker training systems that enable technological expansion in the creation of competitiveness in Indian manufacturing. Attaining world-level product quality assurance, as promoted by these changes, was a monumental achievement in terms of the competitiveness of technology-intensive industries, and was of epoch-making significance in the history of Indian industry.

That this shift occurred as a result of the globalisation of industry from 1980s is glaringly evident. It has already been adequately shown that the economic reforms that began at that time brought technologically advanced machinery and equipment into India. Nor is this all. The globalisation of the 1980s and 1990s arguably provided the genesis of a profound socio-economic transformation that went beyond technological change in the narrowest sense and encompassed social relations, including those between workers and management in firms, broader labour relations and inter-firm relations.[20] It may therefore be said that the economic reforms led to the appearance in certain comparatively advantaged Indian industries of technology-intensive industries. Chapter 4 introduced the argument of Kochhar et al. (2006) that the process of import-substitution industrialisation from the time of Nehru created the basic capabilities necessary for the growth of technology-intensive industries in India. Building upon the foundation established prior to 1980, these industries were able to confirm their leading position as they attained a new standard in international quality assurance in the wake of the globalisation of the Indian economy.[21]

However, the trend towards planning to raise product quality through guaranteeing worker employment and setting up in-house training schemes by no means prevails throughout all industries in India. Many industries have become more dependent on casual labour to decrease costs, and there is a growing tendency towards outsourcing. A report by the National Commission for Enterprises in the Unorganised Sector points out that even in the organised sector, "any employment increase consists of regular workers without social security benefits and casual or contract workers again without the benefits that should accrue to formal workers" (14).[22] An increase in non-regular workers has also been reported in the automobile industry, and, as we saw in Chapter 7, in the MSE-heavy export-oriented textile industry, workers with low levels of education frequently move between factories that have no training schemes and many "large firms" outsource most of the production process.

To summarise, the prominence of technology-intensive industries in the Indian economy has risen greatly since 1980, and international standards of product quality have been prioritised by means of employment guarantees and in-house training schemes. By contrast, labour-intensive industries have pursued a direction of cost reduction by depending on a low-waged, low-quality, insecure workforce and on outsourcing. There is much here that must await future study.

## Changes in the Structure of Exports

Export markets took on a new importance with the growth of the Indian economy, and many of the trends explored above were reflected in them. As Table 10.4 shows, India's share of world exports declined sharply from 1.39 percent in the 1950s to 0.9 percent in the 1960s. Growth occurred in the 1970s due to the depreciation of the real effective exchange rate (REER) of Indian currency and the adoption of export promotion policies in the form of subsidies. However, world exports grew even more at this time and India's share fell to 0.5 percent. From the latter half of the 1980s this rose again with the

*Table 10.4* Indicators of India's export growth, 1950–2005 (US $ millions)

| *Period* | *Average annual growth rates* | | | | *India's share in world exports, averages* | | *India's exports of goods and services (percent of GDP), averages* |
|---|---|---|---|---|---|---|---|
| | *Goods* | | *Services* | | *Goods* | *Services* | |
| | *India* | *World* | *India* | *World* | | | |
| 1950–59 | 0.22 | 6.30 | 3.78 | NA | 1.39 | NA | NA |
| 1960–69 | 3.58 | 8.77 | 1.78 | NA | 0.90 | NA | 4.21 |
| 1970–79 | 17.97 | 20.41 | 26.61 | NA | 0.54 | NA | 5.20 |
| 1980–85 | 2.39 | –0.86 | 3.79 | 0.36 | 0.47 | 0.81 | 6.05 |
| 1986–90 | 17.76 | 12.36 | 10.47 | 14.14 | 0.48 | 0.63 | 6.29 |
| 1993–97 | 13.30 | 10.56 | 14.10 | 9.22 | 0.60 | 0.59 | 10.50 |
| 1999–2001 | 10.26 | 4.09 | 9.52 | 3.07 | 0.66 | 1.07 | 12.52 |
| 2002–05 | 25.29 | 17.58 | 45.36 | 15.16 | 0.81 | 1.64 | 17.19 |

Source: Veeramani 2007, Table 1, p. 2,420.

Original source: Data on merchandise exports (for 1950–2005) and services exports (from 1980–2005) have been accessed from the WTO website; India's services exports for 1950–1979 are from the RBI; Exports of goods and services (percent of GDP) are taken from the World Development Indicators database, World Bank.

assistance of the easing of industrial regulations and a number of measures towards liberalisation regarding the import of capital goods. The across-the-board reforms of 1991 introduced a brief period (until 2002) when the export growth rate for goods actually fell before rallying in parallel with a healthy rise in India's share in world exports. The latter was considerable compared with the growth spurt of the late 1980s. The export of services grew enormously from the end of the 1990s, and its world share similarly swelled (Table 10.5). The share of exports in India's GDP increased remarkably from 7.13 percent in 1990 to 23.48 percent in 2008 (Mukherjee and Mukherjee 2012, 7).

*Table 10.5* India's services exports across sectors, average annual growth rates

| *Sector* | *1993–97* | *1999–2001* | *2002–05* |
|---|---|---|---|
| Travel | 7.67 | 1.65 | 33.25 |
| Transportation | 6.57 | 12.51 | 36.40 |
| Insurance | 18.26 | 11.66 | 47.22 |
| Miscellaneous | 25.99 | 4.26 | 49.81 |
| Software | NA | 7.27* | 35.29 |
| Total commercial services | 13.96 | 4.83 | 45.59 |

Note: Value of software for the year 1999 was estimated based on the share of software in miscellaneous in 2000 (RBI has been reporting separate data on software exports from the year 2000 onwards).

Source: Veeramani 2007, Table 3, p. 2,421.

Original source: Reserve Bank of India.

According to C. Veeramani (2007), a country's export growth is determined by the "world trade effect" (the growth of world demand), the "commodity composition effect" (commodities for which world demand was growing higher than average), the "market distribution effect" (growth of the share of fast-growing regions/markets) and the "competitiveness effect" (raising the level of competitiveness). Table 10.6 calculates the composition of these effects in different time-periods. Before 1991, the competitiveness effect was generally negative, but a shift occurred after that year and the improvement in competitiveness made an important contribution to the growth of Indian exports. After 2002, the contribution of the competitiveness effect showed a decline. However, Veeramani contends that "despite the possible erosion of price competitiveness [in this period], … as reflected in the appreciation of the REER, the competitiveness residual may well remain positive if there have been improvements in the non-price factors" (2424).

In terms of export composition, Chandrasekhar (2011) notes, "[i]n recent years, the share of India's traditional manufactured exports such as textiles, gems and jewellery and leather in the total exports of manufactures has declined, while that of chemicals and engineering goods has gone up significantly" (227). In 2008, top ranking manufactured exports included, as well as the traditional gems and jewellery and textiles, electrical goods, machines, iron and steel, railway-related products, medicaments and ships and boats. Also important were mobile phones and small passenger cars (Ishigami and Satō 2011, 106–09; Mukherjee and Mukherjee 2012).[23] Whereas the relative proportion of exports from traditionally labour-intensive industries fell, that of technology-intensive goods rose radically. There was also a rapid increase in IT-related exports. In 2008, software services and business services reached

*Table 10.6* Growth decomposition of India's merchandise exports

| *Period* | *World trade effect (%)* | *Commodity composition effect (%)* | *Market distribution effect (%)* | *Competitiveness effect (%)* | *Total (%)* | *Actual change in India's exports (US$ millions)* |
|---|---|---|---|---|---|---|
| 1962–70 | 339 | −102 | 39 | −176 | 100 | 625 |
| 1970–80 | 187 | −48 | 48 | −87 | 100 | 5,495 |
| 1980–86 | 15 | 49 | 25 | 11 | 100 | 2,245 |
| 1986–90 | 97 | −6 | 12 | −3 | 100 | 7,820 |
| 1993–2005 | 57 | −12 | 6 | 49 | 100 | 80,493 |
| 1993–2000 | 73 | −22 | 3 | 46 | 100 | 22,380 |
| 1993–2001 | 71 | −19 | 3 | 45 | 100 | 21,142 |
| 1993–1997 | 90 | −10 | 0.1 | 20 | 100 | 12,210 |
| 1997–2000 | 56 | −39 | 10 | 73 | 100 | 10,170 |
| 1997–2001 | 47 | −34 | 10 | 77 | 100 | 8,933 |
| 1997–2002 | 32 | −14 | 5 | 76 | 100 | 17,152 |
| 2002–2005 | 78 | −5 | 12 | 15 | 100 | 51,131 |
| 2000–2005 | 59 | −2 | 11 | 32 | 100 | 58,112 |

Source: Veeramani 2007, Tables 4, 5, p. 2,423.

a figure equivalent to 36.1 percent of goods exported (Ishigami and Satō 2011, 113). Considering the growth in IT service exports, it may be safe to say that technology-intensive industries have become the core of Indian trading abroad.

In the process of post-1980s economic reforms and globalisation, as the cost of consumer durables fell and their quality improved, the middle-class market of the "rural and urban-informal economies" zone and the informal sector merged with the market for consumer durables and the telecommunications and construction industries. This gave the technology-intensive segment, as well as the traditional labour-intensive segment, the capability of advancing into the export market. The formation of systems to assure quality in these industries was a vital part of the heightened competitiveness that drove Indian exports after 1991. As Table 10.4 shows, India's exports as a percentage of GDP quickly climbed. Export markets provide a key base for further economic development, and in this case they catered for IT-related products, the textile industry, chemical and pharmaceutical goods, and auto components.[24] The entrepreneurial activities of the new capitalists who evolved out of local economies, including the rural, in the 1970s and 1980s were integral in the shaping of these new progressive areas of business.

This new developing economy featured a significant constraint, however, that will be discussed in the next chapter.

## Notes

1 Sanjay Bhargava, "Indian Business Houses in the 1990s", *The Economic Times, Midweek Review*, June 17, 1993, p. 13.
2 For trends in these conglomerates, see Ishigami and Satō (2011, Chapter 10).
3 The rise of capitalists in India's rural villages is premised on the expansion of agrarian output, but I do not think we can understand this as a typical example of capitalistic growth in the rural economy. Powerful classes like the Kammas, the Reddis, the Patidars and the Marathas from which these capitalists emerged were historically large landholders in the villages. They generally operated part of their land using a bonded workforce and leased out part to tenant farmers, and even in the period after Independence it is difficult to call this a typical capitalistic kind of operation. Also, we should note that owning a large extent of land was an important part of those operations, together with the profits accrued from them, was an extremely important foundation for their emergence into the non-farm sector. It would therefore not be accurate to understand that emergence as a consequence of typical agricultural capitalistic development. Upadhya (1988) illustrates this point well through case studies.
4 For the connection between the cooperative movement that was the basis for the rise of Maratha entrepreneurs in western India and the non-Brahmin movement, see Damodaran 2008, pp. 224–25.
5 Roy (2011, 304) points out, "[p] rotection offered to small firms, and capital accumulation in the green revolution regions, led … to industrial entrepreneurship … involving new communities that had made their money in land". These promoted the small-scale industry sector that was at the centre of manufacturing exports from the 1980s. Tyabji (1989) and Gorter (1997) see the concern for small industry as a legacy of Gandhian philosophy, but point out that the small industries policy

is directed at the modern capitalist sector using modern technology. Subhrajit Guhathakurta (1993), who investigated the metal furniture manufacturing industry in India in 1990, reported that the regulations aimed at protecting the small-scale sector, while contributing to the growth and expansion of small-scale industries, also hinder the further development of small and medium industries. The Industrial Policy Statement of 1977 that expanded protection of cottage and small-scale industries has been seen as a policy for poverty alleviation and to promote the new "backward" regions, but an extremely interesting topic is under what political and social conditions were the various policies formed (Inoue 1992, 85–89).

6 FICCI opposed trade liberalisation at the beginning of the 1980s, and Tata and Birla also expressed opposition (Kohli 2012, 105). Most industrialists and industrial associations welcomed the abolition of controls and the liberalising of the domestic private sector, but not globalisation in terms of lowering tariffs and opening to foreign investment. There was also criticism from elite business groups (Kochanek 1996a, 1996b). Upadhya (2004) points out that software company entrepreneurs are not from existing old economy companies but rather have come out of working in small-scale companies. They wholly support globalisation and liberalisation, and in this regard are different from the old-style capitalist class.

7 Match producers in Sivakasi who had been able to corner the domestic market as a result of matchmaking being made a reserved industry later mechanised. They spoke of the necessity of freeing themselves from the policy: "Small scale reservation helped us initially. But now it is time to modify the policy and raise investment limits in plant and machinery" (Damodaran 2008, 188). Black-and-white television production came under the small scale reservation policy in 1976; nine of the top ten manufacturers which had been small scale in 1976 had become large-scale by 1998 (Joseph 2004, 258). Thus enterprises that had been facilitated through the small-scale policy that later grew in size regarded the policy to be a hindrance to expansion. It is necessary to consider the connection between changes in the policy and changes in the actual condition of the group of new capitalists.

8 For the close working relationship between CII's predecessor AIEI and Rajiv Gandhi, see Ganguly and Mukherji 2011, 86–86.

9 Pedersen (2000) says that the economic crisis of 1990–1991 is not sufficiently convincing as a basic factor bringing about the reform: "it is an important explanation of the timing of the new policy measures" but "[i] t is much harder, however, to explain the continuation of reforms in the period when the immediate external balance-of-payment problems were resolved" (271). Indian economy and society had been connected with overseas trade and distant markets from before the nineteenth century, and in this can be said to have been open. The discussion that old capital originating in "open" trading activities being converted to industrial capital was less open than the new capitalists with their close links with the rural economy and society and their mindset towards technological expertise raises interesting questions about "openness" and those who seek it. There may be a crucial discontinuity between the "openness" of nineteenth-century India and that exemplified in the 1991 reform in terms of direction and the character of the actors. In the nineteenth-century open economy, there was always the possibility that commercial capital, whose aim was profit from business, would be disposed towards controlling the flow of capital. There may be some connection here therefore with the activities and characteristics of present large conglomerate-type firms criticised by entrepreneurs of small and medium firms as pursuing short-term profit and engaging in rent-seeking. On the other hand, the "openness" sought by the new capitalists, with their base in agriculture and the local economy and society, their opposition to the large firms and their monopolistic domination and pursuit of profit, was that associated with the possibility of reaching a global

technological level. This in itself may be considered at the core of the modern Indian conception of "openness". These points remain within the realms of conjecture but are ripe for future discussion. In studying "openness" in the economy and society, we should take the historical context into account when considering the actors, their direction and their nature. Roy (2011, 312–15) severely criticises views that see post-1990 globalisation as a return to nineteenth-century globalisation. In the "closed" period from 1950 to the 1980s, "protection nurtured domestic business to strength, and saw a convergence of government and capital-intensive manufacturing that spawned a regime of technical training and education with huge potential spillover". This was the foundation for the later growth of the knowledge-intensive industries. Roy points out that many of the post-1990s successes were the result of the restructuring during the "closed" period and suggests that modern Indian globalisation could not have been achieved without experiencing the economic and social development that took place in the several decades of the "closed" period.

10 Baru (1995, 132) points out the confrontation over licenses between the traditionally dominant business houses and the new capitalists. The economic reform of 1991 may be seen as the government's response to the demands of the latter. The old capitalists, as represented by FICCI, were forced to compromise with the new capitalists and foreign capital. Baru's argument is interesting, but further empirical study is required. Kohli (2012, 58–59) recognises the existence of surface differences between FICCI and CII over policy regarding foreign capital but asserts that these differences cannot be overestimated.

11 In 1990, the small-scale protection policy made it difficult for new entrepreneurs to enter the metal furniture manufacturing industry and compete with the large-scale manufacturers who dominated the high-cost market. As a result, these manufacturers were able to maintain very high prices (Guhathakurta 1993).

12 *Statistical Yearbook India, 2011*, Government of India, Ministry of Statistics and Programme Implementation, Central Statistical Office, 2011. (Accessed September 1, 2016.)

13 An article titled "Rustic Tactics" in *Business India* (February 23–March 8, 1998, pp. 125–27) introduced the development and sales tactics for household appliances, including cheap colour televisions with minimal functions, aimed at the Indian rural market by Korean firms like Samsung and LG. In 2006, these two firms had acquired a leading position in the Indian appliance market, with LG in first place and Samsung in second in the colour television, washing machine and air conditioner markets. In all cases they gave particular attention to the rural market, and we should note the important role they played in the penetration of electrical appliances here. Park (2016), who has studied Korean firms in India, notes that a factor in their success has been the investment in low-cost models and what powerfully underlies their lead in the consumer market is low-cost consumer goods centred on the masses.

14 In 1970, Hindustan Motors and Premier Automobiles occupied 51 percent and 26 percent of the market respectively. "In 1984–85, the price of a popular scooter represented roughly 25% of the annual salary of a public sector employee … and cars cost 10–15 times more than scooters" (D'Costa 1995, 487).

15 Parikh and Radhakrishna eds. 2005, p. 133.

16 Ganguly and Mukherji (2011, 93) state that telephones have penetrated rural as well as urban areas and that the poor as well as the wealthy have taken part in the telephone connection boom. Those who have benefitted from the telephone revolution include construction workers, farmers, vegetable sellers and taxi drivers.

17 Okada (2004) correctly points out that many firms introduced QC circles for managers and staff, not for workers, and that in-house training schemes were for the management class alone. Thus there were limitations imposed according to the

stratified company structure. For the experience of Maruti-Suzuki, see Kiyokawa 2002.

18 Tata Steel has introduced a Japanese-style management approach that actively involves workers in manufacture on the line. They are educated in product quality and customer-oriented thinking, and have the authority to stop the line if something untoward happens during manufacture (Ishigami 2008). Suzuki and Shintaku (2010) cite a number of cases of representative firms within the Indian machine industry where Japanese methods like pokayoke and kaizen have been introduced, workers' multi-skill development is ongoing and the employee turnover rate has been greatly reduced. For the creation of a worker training system, incorporating ITIs, at Maruti and Tata Motors, see Okada 2006.

19 Large firms in Bangalore's software industry too do not outsource to smaller firms but have rather increased the number of in-house workers (Okada 2008).

20 In the 1970s and 1980s, when the Indian pharmaceutical industry grew centred on the domestic market, technological backwardness and a lack of innovative products were evident. The economic liberalisation of 1991 steered firms to create capabilities to enable them to advance on the large global generic markets (Chaturvedi and Chataway 2009, 146–47).

21 Kochar et al. 2005 say that while there has been no proportional increase in labour-intensive industries in the post-1980s Indian economy, fast-growing Indian states are moving towards skill-intensive services (5).

22 National Commission for Enterprises in the Unorganised Sector, *The Challenge of Employment in India: An Informal Economy Perspective*, Vol. 1, The Main Report, New Delhi: Government of India, 2009. http://nceuis.nic.in/The_Challenge_of_Employment_in_India.pdf (accessed September 20, 2016)

23 In 2009, medicaments, telecommunications equipment, and motor cars and vehicles occupied respectively 4.0 percent, 3.6 percent and 2.6 percent of India's manufactured exports (Mukherjee and Mukherjee 2012, 23).

24 "Automobile exports grew at an annual average of 35 percent for six years between 2000–01 and 2005–06, with the industry exporting about 18 and 16 per cent of its domestic production of three wheelers and passenger cars respectively in 2005–06" (Chandra et al. 2008, 500). Some 40 percent of pharmaceutical production was exported (Ishigami and Satō 2011, 238).

# 11 The Structure of Indian Society and Economic Growth

## From Village to City: The Rural and Urban Classes

The 1940s non-farming sector labour market was broadly composed of three tiers which were essentially anchored in the class structure of rural society (see Chapter 2). The first tier was typified by skilled workers in the engineering and metalworking industries. They were comparatively high-waged, allowing them to settle permanently in the city with their families, detached from rural society. These workers had advanced through several years of apprenticeship and then into their specified jobs. These were divided into grades, which they moved up through with annual pay rises. The second tier was represented by cotton mill workers, like cotton mill workers in Bombay (Mumbai), semi-permanent labourers who came from the agricultural castes in village society. They incorporated their generational reproduction of labour with agriculture and village society, returning there, for example, after retirement. Their wages occupied an intermediate position between those of skilled workers in the engineering and metalworking industries and labourers, low compared with the former, but higher than the latter. These low-paid labourers, many of whom worked in the jute industry and bidi manufacturing made up the third tier. They were from the lowest classes of village society, landless farm labourers or petty farmers owning miniscule pieces of land. Though they moved to the cities, their wages were set at agricultural levels, which were very poor, making it difficult for them to take dependent family members with them. It was common for their families to remain in their places of origin, where they formed an intrinsic part of the generational reproduction of labour in the rural community. If family members did go to live in the city, they usually made their living through holding down multiple jobs. Besides the jute and bidi industries, such labourers worked on plantations and in mining, in many industries in the unregistered sector, as coolies in registered factories in the engineering and metalworking industries, and in cotton mills. Most of these labourers hailed from the rural low-class workforce.

There was not much difference between the wage rates for the lowest strata in India's industrial employment structure and among urban and non-farm workers and those of farm labourers, since agricultural wages determined the basic wage level. Above them were workers who came from the middle and

DOI: 10.4324/9781003341550-15

upper sections of the rural village. Wages for skilled workers were two to three times higher. This multi-tiered labour market structure, which corresponded to stratified rural society, continued fundamentally unchanged after Independence.

### *Urban Employment and Rural Society: South India*

Let us examine the structure of urban employment based on a 1980 field survey in M village, the wet village within commuting distance of Tiruchirapalli in Tamil Nadu, referred to in Chapter 6. Before doing so, I would first like to explain briefly the education system in that state. Five years of primary education are followed by five years of middle school, after which the SSLC is taken. Its results fundamentally determine the course the student then takes. The minimum mark required to pass is 35 percent. Depending on the results achieved, students may continue to higher secondary school (two years) and then on to university (three years) and perhaps the master's programme at graduate school (two years). Alternatively, they may go to a polytechnic (three years) to receive a diploma or to an ITI to receive vocational qualifications as turners, mechanics and so on (one to three years).

Tiruchirapalli and its environs have developed as one of the most important industrial centres of South India. In 1980, BHEL employed some 14,000 permanent labourers and 1,200 casual labourers, the Southern Railway Workshop in Tiruchirapalli had 6,000 employees and the Dalmia Cement Plant and the Ordnance Factory had around 1,600 each. Seven other smaller factories engaged more than 100 staff each. Government offices, especially the Electricity Board, provided important employment opportunities for villagers, including the landowning Brahmin class.

Workers from around M hamlet employed in urban areas in an around Tiruchirapalli can be classified into two categories: Permanent employees in large factories and government offices, and workers in MSEs and shops. The categories differ both in the conditions of employment and in the socio-economic background of the workers. First, permanent workers in the large factories were generally paid better wages than those in the second category. In 1980, most earned more than Rs 500 per month, while the majority of those working in shops and small factories received less than Rs 300 per month. Second, workers in large firms were ranked into classes and could expect to be promoted not only to a higher grade within the same class but also to a higher class. At BHEL for example, skilled workers consisted of four grades. They were first posted to the lowest rank of the skilled worker class, Grade IV. They usually spent around three years in Grade IV, five years in Grade III, six years in Grade II and six years in Grade I. Third, employees in large firms were generally in continuous service, much longer than what was usual in the MSEs. Villagers seldom resigned from such work, except to retire.

These three features are to be found in large Japanese firms as well. The fourth though differs from the Japanese case in that workers in large firms in India were clearly sorted according to job type. In principle, new workers for each job type were directly recruited externally. It was thus very difficult to rise internally to a higher class in the company. Though there were some differences, workers were generally ranked in one of four classes: Executive (officer) class, supervisor class, skilled worker class and unskilled worker class. Minimum qualifications were required for each class, and companies usually recruited qualified workers from outside, as we have seen. At BHEL, for instance, new employees in the supervisor class had to have a diploma from a polytechnic and skilled workers needed to be graduates of ITIs. In many large factories, even unskilled workers were required to have the SSLC or to have reached the eighth grade. New employees worked on probation as trainees for one year and were then posted to the job in the lowest grade. Executive class employees might be appointed to a rank in this class from the beginning, usually in the lowest, such as an engineer.

A worker's career was to a large extent determined by his qualifications and the kind of employee class in which he was first engaged. It took workers many years to rise through the grades within their own job specification, but promotion to a higher class was possible only after about 20 years. Nevertheless, it was very difficult for a skilled worker to be moved up to the level of supervisor, and only about one tenth of candidates were said to advance in this way.

The wage structure was also differentiated. For example, in BHEL around 1980, the basic salary paid to a Grade IV skilled worker started at Rs 395 per month. This increased by Rs 10 annually. It took about fifteen years for him to receive a basic salary of Rs 580, which was the basic salary of a supervisor upon appointment. Executives received Rs 750 as their starting salary. For those wishing to work in large companies and government offices, their lives were mainly directed by their qualifications and the work they had secured based on them.

By comparison, the employment conditions of workers in MSEs and shops were greatly inferior. Such work included truck drivers, salesmen in shops, workers in small factories such as rice mills, a metal factory and an ice-cream factory, day labourers and watchmen in large firms, and cleaners in bus companies. Wages in 1980 were lower here than for permanent employees in large firms and government offices, at around Rs 300 per month. Respondents said that it was not possible to live in an urban area on a monthly income of less than Rs 350. Given that an agricultural labourer was paid on average Rs 10 per day, the income of an urban worker in this category was little different, making it hard for him to live an independent life easily there. There was no graded service system as in the large firms, and however long a worker was employed, his wage level would not rise above Rs 300. Due to low wages and poor labour conditions, as well as no system of promotions, the length of workers' service was short, not exceeding five years.

The labour market in Tiruchirapalli and its environs was two-tiered: Workers in large firms and government offices on the one hand and workers in MSEs and shops on the other. Roughly speaking, the former belonged to the formal sector and the latter to the informal. Formal sector employment was not monolithic, but divided according to education level with different career paths (executive, supervisor, skilled worker and unskilled worker). There were marked differences between the classes in salaries and labour conditions; as we have seen, the starting wage in each ascending class was twice that of the lower.

The stratified class structure of rural society corresponded with employment hierarchies in urban areas. Landholding Brahmin families in M village gave their sons a university education, and many of them gained employment in the formal sector in the white-collar classes of executive or supervisor. Many members of forward castes like the Pillais and the Chettiars took ITI qualifications or technical diplomas and found work as supervisors or skilled workers in large factories. In 1980, there were comparatively few urban workers from among the backward castes like the Muthurajas and the SCs; many of these, with a few exceptions, worked in non-farm employment in the informal sector in the vicinity of the village, such as the artificial diamond polishing industry and rice straw trading.

A similar parallel connection between a family's socio-economic status in rural society and the ranks of their urban jobs was again observed in my 2007 re-survey of the same village. Table 11.1 shows the occupation distribution according to household of Pillais and Chettiars, Muthurajas (backward castes, OBCs), and SCs. Of the Pillais and Chettiars, 45 percent were engaged in jobs earning more than Rs 5,000 per month, as government workers, skilled workers in large firms and professional work. The employment rate of Muthurajas and SCs in this group was lower, at 24 percent and 31 percent respectively. The Pillais and Chettiars also occupied a relatively large proportion of the under Rs 5,000 group, working as bus drivers and conductors in the formal sector. This means that around two thirds of urban employees from advanced castes in the village had jobs in the formal sector. By contrast, formal sector employment among the Muthurajas and others was a little over 35 percent and among SCs just over 55 percent.

The example of this South Indian village shows that higher castes such as Brahmins worked as supervisors or executives in white-collar jobs, that many from the advanced castes worked in the formal sector as government workers, in industry and in professional work, and that the majority of workers from the backward castes who attained urban employment worked in the informal sector. The SCs worked in lower class occupations in the formal sector or in the informal sector.

A survey of a Tamil Nadu village conducted by Keiko Sato (2011) also reveals that many workers from wealthier, landholding households in the village held white-collar jobs and a similarly large number of workers from the lower middle class had blue-collar jobs (37). "Roughly speaking, the monthly salary observed among the workforce from the study village was Rs. 10,000–50,000 for white-collar workers, around Rs. 5,000 for blue-collar workers, and Rs. 1,200–2,500 for daily laborers" (47). Blue-collar workers in urban work received a much bigger wage than daily labourers, and white-collar workers earned many times more than blue-collar workers.

*Table 11.1* Workers according to occupation in M hamlet, 2007 (%)

| | | *Pillais, Chettiars* | | *Muthurajas etc.* | | *SCs* | |
|---|---|---|---|---|---|---|---|
| | | *Men* | *Women* | *Men* | *Women* | *Men* | *Women* |
| A group | Farm operation | 4 | 0 | 18 | 4 | 4 | 2 |
| | Milk production | 1 | 6 | 1 | 0 | 0 | 0 |
| | Farm labourer | 10 | 13 | 26 | 53 | 40 | 72 |
| | Farm labourer + farm operation | 0 | 0 | 2 | 0 | 1 | 0 |
| | Trading in village or vicinity | 5 | 6 | 2 | 2 | 1 | 2 |
| | Business in village or vicinity | 10 | 0 | 2 | 2 | 6 | 0 |
| | Village handcrafts, services | 5 | 13 | 5 | 13 | 6 | 2 |
| | Artificial diamond polishing | 8 | 19 | 3 | 11 | 0 | 1 |
| | Total | 42 | 56 | 59 | 84 | 58 | 79 |
| B group | Construction labour | 0 | 0 | 4 | 2 | 1 | 1 |
| | Low-class urban work (e.g. watchmen, autorickshaw drivers) | 10 | 13 | 9 | 4 | 8 | 2 |
| | Total | 10 | 13 | 13 | 5 | 9 | 3 |
| C group | Urban trading | 0 | 0 | 0 | 0 | 4 | 5 |
| | Salesmen, calculator operators and so on | 10 | 13 | 6 | 5 | 3 | 5 |
| | Urban business (including owners of auto rickshaws) | 0 | 0 | 1 | 0 | 1 | 0 |
| | Total | 10 | 13 | 7 | 5 | 8 | 10 |
| D group | Nurses (less than Rs 5,000) | 0 | 0 | 0 | 2 | 0 | 2 |
| | Teachers (less than Rs 5,000) | 0 | 0 | 0 | 2 | 1 | 3 |
| | Electricians (less than Rs 5,000) | 1 | 0 | 5 | 0 | 2 | 0 |
| | Lorry drivers, for example (less than Rs 5,000) | 0 | 0 | 3 | 0 | 1 | 0 |
| | Bus drivers (less than Rs 5,000) | 6 | 0 | 2 | 0 | 5 | 0 |
| | Conductors (less than Rs 5,000) | 6 | 0 | 1 | 0 | 4 | 0 |
| | Total | 13 | 0 | 11 | 4 | 13 | 5 |

| | | | | | | | |
|---|---|---|---|---|---|---|---|
| E group | Drivers (more than Rs 5,000) | 1 | 0 | 1 | 0 | 3 | 0 |
| | Conductors (more than Rs 5,000) | 2 | 0 | 1 | 0 | 3 | 0 |
| | Electricians (more than Rs 5,000) | 1 | 0 | 0 | 0 | 0 | 0 |
| | Others (more than Rs 5,000) | 6 | 0 | 0 | 0 | 0 | 0 |
| | Shop managers, for example (more than Rs 5,000) | 2 | 0 | 1 | 0 | 1 | 0 |
| | Nurses (more than Rs 5,000) | 0 | 13 | 0 | 0 | 0 | 0 |
| | Teachers (more than Rs 5,000) | 0 | 6 | 0 | 0 | 0 | 1 |
| | Office workers, other white-collar workers (more than Rs 5,000) | 0 | 0 | 1 | 0 | 0 | 0 |
| | Total | 13 | 19 | 5 | 0 | 6 | 1 |
| F group | Skilled workers in large firms, government workers | 2 | 0 | 2 | 0 | 3 | 0 |
| | Supervisors in large firms | 2 | 0 | 0 | 2 | 0 | 0 |
| | The professions | 4 | 0 | 1 | 0 | 1 | 1 |
| | Retired with pension | 4 | 0 | 1 | 0 | 1 | 0 |
| | Employed abroad | 1 | 0 | 1 | 0 | 0 | 0 |
| | Total | 13 | 0 | 5 | 2 | 5 | 1 |
| | Sum total (aggregate average) | | 100 | 100 | 100 | 100 | 100 |

Source: Author's survey (2007).

### *Urban Occupational Rank Divisions: Pune*

We can observe a similar parallel connection between a family's socio-economic status in rural society and the occupational ranks of their urban jobs throughout India as a whole. Deshpande and Palshikar (2008) classify occupations as follows (Appendix 1, p. 69):

UPPER: Class I officers, higher professionals, large-scale business, small-scale, medium- and large-scale industrialists.

UPPER MIDDLE: Class II officers, small business, own small business based on modern skills (with three to four employees) small-scale business of transport, small-scale business in the construction sector.

MIDDLE: Class III employees, skilled workers in class III occupations, skilled workers in organised sector, own business based on traditional skills, pensioners, farmers with landholdings of five acres and above, call centre employees, goldsmiths, priests.

LOWER MIDDLE: Class IV employees, skilled workers in unorganised sector, semi-skilled workers, petty business, carpenters, blacksmiths, weavers, tailors, watch repairer, coppersmith, potter, barber, washermen, painters, masons, cooks, work with small financial institutions, farmers with 1 to 4.99 acres of land, part-time or full-time service + small business, lottery and other stall owners, rickshaw owners and drivers.

LOW: Watchmen, unskilled workers, women engaged in home-based petty business, workers in warehouses, waiters, drivers, (salesmen, carpenters, tailors, masons, cooks, painters, barbers, weavers – employed), glass bangle makers, cobblers, milkman, farmers with land below one acre, landowners + agricultural labourers.

VERY LOW: Beggars, prostitutes, landless agricultural labourers, workers engaged in jute sack stitching, bidi workers, construction labourers, sweepers, domestic workers, babysitters, casual labourers, ragpickers, basket makers, butchers, boys distributing newspapers.

We can say that the "upper" and "upper middle" in this classification approximately correspond to the middle class studied in Chapter 10 and the "lower middle" and below correspond to the informal class.

The connection between social caste/class and occupation shown in the South Indian examples is confirmed by a 2007 survey of the inhabitants of Pune, Maharashtra (Deshpande and Palshikar 2008). Of the respondents, 77 percent of the upper caste worked in jobs classified as upper, upper middle and middle, with 54 percent in the upper two, corresponding to "officers". Members of the Maratha-Kunbis, a large group of Maharashtrian agricultural castes, mainly worked in occupations classified as middle, which included skilled workers, and 60 percent of these households were in the upper middle, middle and lower middle groupings. Though 22 percent of OBC households held jobs described as middle, 54 percent had jobs categorised as lower middle and below, corresponding to labourers in the informal sector, which may therefore be considered the main occupation of OBCs (see

Chapter 9). The SCs as a whole worked in an even lower classification, with 72 percent of households engaged in occupations labelled as lower middle and below (Table 11.2). To summarise, occupations of the upper-caste households (e.g. Brahmins) centred on upper middle, those of the agricultural castes on the middle and those of the OBCs and SCs on the lower middle and below. The socio-economic stratification of rural society has been basically

*Table 11.2* Occupational profile of four generations

| | *Grandfather* | *Father* | *Respondent* | *Son/Daughter* |
|---|---|---|---|---|
| ***Upper Caste*** | | | | |
| Upper | 11% | 16% | 29% | 38% |
| Upper middle | 34% | 33% | 25% | 27% |
| Middle | 39% | 25% | 23% | 25% |
| Lower middle | 6% | 13% | 6% | 2% |
| Poor | 6% | 8% | 12% | 7% |
| Very poor | 5% | 6% | 5% | 2% |
| Sample number | 118 | 276 | 216 | 92 |
| ***Maratha-Kunbi*** | | | | |
| | *Grandfather* | *Father* | *Respondent* | *Son/Daughter* |
| Upper | 0% | 2% | 8% | 16% |
| Upper middle | 11% | 12% | 22% | 26% |
| Middle | 19% | 36% | 21% | 29% |
| Lower middle | 37% | 33% | 17% | 13% |
| Poor | 9% | 9% | 15% | 12% |
| Very poor | 24% | 8% | 7% | 4% |
| Sample number | 54 | 306 | 142 | 68 |
| ***OBCs*** | | | | |
| | *Grandfather* | *Father* | *Respondent* | *Son/Daughter* |
| Upper | 2% | 2% | 3% | 11% |
| Upper middle | 15% | 12% | 19% | 16% |
| Middle | 16% | 25% | 22% | 21% |
| Lower middle | 41% | 36% | 33% | 35% |
| Poor | 18% | 18% | 15% | 14% |
| Very poor | 8% | 7% | 8% | 3% |
| Sample number | 100 | 202 | 161 | 63 |
| ***SCs*** | | | | |
| | *Grandfather* | *Father* | *Respondent* | *Son/Daughter* |
| Upper | 0% | 0% | 3% | 3% |
| Upper middle | 3% | 4% | 8% | 4% |
| Middle | 9% | 23% | 17% | 16% |
| Lower middle | 13% | 24% | 24% | 27% |
| Poor | 16% | 17% | 16% | 27% |
| Very poor | 59% | 32% | 32% | 23% |
| Sample number | 93 | 203 | 169 | 75 |

Source: Deshpande and Palshikar 2008, Tables 11, 12. 13. 14.

reproduced in the urban setting: The lower tiers of rural society have shifted to the urban informal classes, whereas the rural elite people now form the upper and middle classes of the urban population.

## Education and Social Mobility

The compelling Pune survey facilitated the study of occupational mobility over four generations (Deshpande and Palshikar 2008). The first finding of consequence is that all castes appear to have experienced a rise in occupational ranking. The Maratha-Kunbis stand out in this regard, but among the SCs too, whereas 59 percent of the grandfather's generation worked in "very poor" jobs, by the fourth generation this number had decreased to 23 percent and 16 percent had "middle" occupations. This reflects the rising socio-economic status over the long term of these castes, presumed to be landless (see Chapters 5 and 6). The OBCs too evidently improved their occupational ranking over the generations. This socio-economic climbing of the lower classes was, as we have seen, a strong foundation for the purchasing power of the "rural and urban-informal economies" zone. The second point of interest is that although the OBCs and SCs, whose occupational ranking had been very low in their grandfather's time, crept up the social ladder, they have been greatly limited. It is still a formidable challenge for SC "sons and daughters" to move beyond work classified as lower middle, that is, work in the informal sector. Though some "sons and daughters" of the forward castes advanced their occupational ranking to middle and above, most remain in lower middle jobs. Third, at the time of the survey, 38 percent of the "sons and daughters" generation in upper-caste households were in occupations classified upper, and 27 percent in those labelled upper middle, giving weight to their identity as the urban middle class. More than 40 percent of Maratha-Kunbis can similarly be designated.

Overall, according to the Pune survey, while there was a certain mobility between classes in urban–rural class relationships, the rural class structure was still being reproduced within an urban setting even after four generations. Even when the lower classes of rural society move to cities, they remain within the informal classification. When the rural upper classes, on the other hand, relocate, they do so as an urban upper class. Though there are certainly instances where members of the rural lower classes have advanced to the urban upper class, such cases are by no means common. Upward social mobility has not been strong enough to eliminate the boundary between the upper and lower tiers of people in Indian society.[1]

### *Social Mobility and Education*

Much attention had been given to those factors directly inhibiting social mobility and most studies agree that education is key.[2] As previously described, specific educational qualifications are required for each kind of job in the formal sector (large firms, government offices), depending on the class of employment (executive, supervisor, skilled worker, unskilled worker). This is a system unlike that in Japan's factories during the period of high growth, where middle school and high school graduates found unskilled work first and then trained to do skilled and ultimately managerial work. In India, educational qualifications are crucial in determining a person's future.

The case of the auto components industry (Chapter 10) demonstrated that there has been a gradual rise in the educational standard and qualifications needed for employment since 1980. At the time of my village survey of 1980, a person could almost certainly find work in the formal sector with the SSLC. However, my resurvey in 2007 revealed that to do so then it was virtually necessary to have a long-term educational attainment, like a tertiary education.[3]

Education affects not just the urban labour market but also income levels. As Table 9.13 shows, 70 percent of graduates have middle or high incomes. There is a strong correlation between high educational qualifications and high pay, even in the informal sector.

Sato (2011), in a study of a village in Tamil Nadu, makes it very apparent just how essential a higher education was for acquiring secure, remunerative non-farm jobs. Top marks were required in the necessary examinations to enter a well-regarded college or university. Many parents in wealthy households would therefore send their children to private schools from pre-school level to be taught in English. The entrance fee and the annual tuition fee of the pre-school were Rs 2,000 and Rs 6,000 respectively, equivalent to a several months' wages for an agricultural labourer. The annual tuition fee at the college/university ranged from Rs 60,000 for a Bachelor of Science degree to Rs 260,000 for a Bachelor of Information Technology. With the monthly income of day labourers in the village around Rs 2,000 and of blue-collar workers approximately Rs 5,000, these costs greatly exceeded their annual income and were far beyond their ability to save for. Even white-collar workers with monthly incomes of above Rs 10,000 found education expenses a struggle. Access to credit sources was essential. Even after graduation, to get white-collar work especially in government service, a recommendation from a relative or a friend of the family was required, and it was the custom here to pay Rs 50,000 in thanks. In one example, the very large education costs for the first son were borrowed from relatives; when he graduated, he went to work in Saudi Arabia to support the education of his younger brother. Poorer families sold livestock to raise money for education. Being loaned such large sums of money was a necessary condition for the son to graduate and get a job. Even when members of the village upper classes who owned large amounts of farmland went to work in urban areas, they found well-paid, stable employment as white-collar workers. Thus the village class system was reproduced in urban employment.[4]

The relationship between rural classes and non-farm employment makes it problematic for the lower classes who make up much of the rural population to leave the villages wholesale and move to the cities. In the case of M village, with the rapid growth of non-farm employment, a fairly high proportion of members of forward caste households like Chettiars and Pillais obtained secure and remunerative employment in the formal sector as a result of higher education, including university. By contrast, only a fraction of children from the backward castes and the SCs went to university, so even if members of these communities acquired non-farm employment, it generally tended to be insecure and with wage rates comparable to agricultural pay. Earning a steady living only from non-farm wages would have been a considerable burden for them.

Of the backward caste Muthuraja households, 37 percent farmed full-time, either in running their own farms, working as agricultural labourers, or in a combination of the two. If we add to this the 15 percent chiefly involved in farm work but with some non-farm work on the side, slightly more than half of households were engaged principally in agriculture. The figure comes to 78 percent if we include those households where farm work was subsidiary to non-farm jobs. Similarly, 32 percent of SC households were engaged in farming full-time and 10 percent combined farm and non-farm employment, meaning 42 percent of these households predominantly worked in agriculture. Adding the 29 percent of households where farming was supplementary, we have 72 percent engaged in agriculture in some way (with the overwhelming majority being agricultural labourers). Therefore, in the case of the Muthurajas and the SCs, the growth of non-farm employment did not take workers away from farming; the bulk of households remained attached to agricultural occupations while undertaking non-farm work. The household unit functioned as a side business (Table 11.3).

*Table 11.3* Household distribution of main occupation in M hamlet, 2007

| | *Pillais, Chettiars* | *Muthurajas, etc.* | *SCs* |
|---|---|---|---|
| 1. Agricultural management (AG) | 2% | 7% | 2% |
| 2. Agricultural labourers (AL) | 3% | 9% | 25% |
| 3. AG + AL | 3% | 20% | 5% |
| Total (mainly agriculture) | 9% | 37% | 32% |
| 4. AG + non-farm work | 0% | 6% | 2% |
| 5. AL + non-farm work | 3% | 7% | 7% |
| 6. AL + AG + non-farm work | 0% | 2% | 2% |
| Total (farm work main,, non-farm work subsidiary) | 3% | 15% | 10% |
| 7. Non-farm work + AG | 14% | 10% | 9% |
| 8. Non-farm work + AL | 3% | 8% | 20% |
| 9. Non-farm work + AL + AG | 0% | 8% | 1% |
| Total (non-farm work main, farm work subsidiary) | 17% | 26% | 29% |
| 10. Business | 3% | 4% | 7% |
| 11. Professional | 3% | 1% | 2% |
| 12. Other non-farm work | 55% | 18% | 20% |
| 13. Artificial diamond polishing | 9% | 0% | 0% |
| Total (non-farm work alone) | 0% | 0% | 0% |
| TOTAL | 71% | 22% | 28% |

Source: Author's survey (2007).

This situation illustrates the obstacles faced by members of the rural lower classes who wished to leave the village completely and settle in urban areas reliant upon a purely non-farming based income. A survey of six villages in Tiruchirapalli District in 2005–2006 revealed that of the 238 households surveyed in 1979–1980, 31 had left the village and 5 were no longer known there. Assuming that those 5 are regarded as having left the village, still no more than 15 percent had left over 25 years (Djurfeldt et al. 2008). Even if non-farm employment soared and non-farm income became the core of village economy, for the majority of villagers a complete departure from farming was not an option. Leaving the village therefore reflected tough circumstances. John Harriss, citing H. Bernstein (2004), describes how the labouring classes maintain a living through small-scale and insecure informal sector employment and self-employment, spread across different sites in both urban areas and villages (Harriss et al. 2010, 61; Harriss et al. 2012, 54). This is perhaps the dominant reason behind the low number of households conclusively quitting farming and village.

## A Two-Tiered Society: Urban Middle-Class Society and the "Rural and Urban-Informal Economies" Zone

Indian society is effectively two-tiered in structure. On the village side, the two tiers consist of a very small dominant class which owns most of the land and a majority of landless agricultural workers and tenant farmers. In the case of urban society, the division separates a middle class that derives from the village upper classes and an informal lower class from bottom rungs of village society. Upward social mobility, though it does exist among the poor, has not been strong enough to eliminate the boundary between the upper and lower levels of Indian society.

Though further studies of various districts are needed, it is possible to suggest that within this two-tiered structure we may discern a trend towards permanent migration from villages as the upper classes in village society households move to cities and become the urban middle class.[5] From the end of the nineteenth century in South India, Brahmin households had been slowly shifting their major bases of life to urban areas and post-1980 economic growth has accelerated this movement. They have gradually disposed of their land, but the rate of landholding reduction has seen little change since 1980. More exploration is required on this point but it appears that these migrating village elites are reluctant to sell off all of their land when they take up residence in the cities.

The situation is very different for migrating members of the village lower classes. Failing to get a job in the urban formal sectors through lack of educational qualifications, they can get only insecure jobs with low incomes in informal industries. They earn a fraction of the income of the white-collar, urban middle class, and they have no health insurance or pension. Moreover, it is very difficult for them to reproduce themselves over the generations in the urban setting. They continuously depend on both non-farm earnings from informal employment and agricultural income mainly from labouring, making it almost impossible for them to completely leave rural life behind. This is the backdrop against which, as discussed in Chapter 9, the "rural and urban-informal economies" zone has been formed. It is an integral part of the explanation behind the low rate of population decline in rural India. It is therefore likely that the two major tiers of Indian society will eventually come to consist of two population groups: The urban middle and upper classes, and the non-elite groups of people living in the "rural and urban-informal economies" zone.

## Notes

1 Kiso (2012), in an important study tracing changes in employment in the next generation of workers who lost their jobs in the Ahmedabad cotton mills, points out that social mobility is by no means high and that class differences in occupation are maintained over the next generation. Kumar et al. (2002b) also point out that there is low inter-generational fluidity between occupational classes and that there has not been any great change in the relationship between caste and class of occupation, based on data collected in 1971 and 1996.

2 A worker in Coimbatore stated, "My classmate who went on to a polytechnic and got an LTM diploma is now my supervisor" (Ramaswamy 1983, 136). For the importance of education as a determining factor in establishing hierarchies in industry, see Breman 1999.

3 Lanjouw and Murgai 2009 speak of the very high educational standard required of people seeking non-farm employment.

4 Hnatkovska et al. 2012, who studied differentials in education, work, income and consumption between 1983 and 2005, found that though on the whole there was significant convergence between SC/ST levels and non-SC/ST levels in these areas, in terms of employment in white-collar work and higher education the differential had grown to some extent. This is in accord with my findings.

5 Sato (2011) gives several examples of wealthy households in the village acquiring white-collar work and moving permanently to urban areas.

# Conclusion

## Towards Further Development

### The Historical Formation of the Two-Tiered Structure

As the Indian economy grew after 1980, the two-tiered arrangement of rural society developed without fundamental change into a two-tiered social and economic structure that straddles village and city. The village social structure, described in Chapter 1, where a very few people owned most of the cultivable land and the majority of villagers were tenant farmers or employed as agricultural labourers, has remained basically unaltered, despite the land reforms referred to in Chapter 5. Staff – such as managers, technicians and highly skilled workers – in the large corporate sector of urban industries and services who needed to be educated inevitably came from the landholding classes. They could afford the expenditure. To secure these human resources, employers had to provide wages high enough to correspond to the income of the village landowners. Simultaneously, the inflow of labour for jobs that did not require a high educational level – unskilled workers in the formal sector and labourers in the informal sector – came from the rural lower classes, and their wage levels were determined by those of agricultural labourers (Chapters 2 and 9). The gulf between the wages and working conditions of these two groups of urban workers formed in response to village social stratification.

Pre-Independence economic change, including industrial development, was premised along the divided lines of rural society. Economic growth since Independence, postulated to have encouraged the partial weakening of this two-tiered structure, has in fact reproduced it. Rises in agrarian output and the increase of non-farm employment, together with growing aspirations by the lower classes for social advancement, made possible by improved real incomes as agricultural wages rose, led to the weakening control of village elites and the expansion of the rural market. This in turn fostered a rise in the growth rate of the Indian economy from the 1980. Since rural demand, centred on the non-farming sector, was oriented towards low-cost "quasi-branded goods" that had no guarantee of quality, there was a consequent expansion of informal sector industries and services (Chapters 7 and 8). As a result, the informal sector absorbed an enormous workforce from rural areas as cheap,

DOI: 10.4324/9781003341550-16

low-educated labour well adapted to producing the quasi-brands that the market demanded. Given such manpower requirements, there was probably little motivation for the rural lower classes, lacking the economic resources to fully educate their children, to remain in schooling for more than the few years of primary education desired for employment in the informal sector. Thus the lower classes continued as they had in village society, the basis of cheap labour, only now supplied to the urban informal sector.

The rural lower classes face manifold obstacles if they wish to escape from poverty. They are typically bound to make their living from a combination of income from agricultural labour and MSEs and the small amounts they earn from employment in the urban informal sector. This means, however, that demand for non-agricultural sector goods and services continues to be for low-cost quasi-branded goods, and so they remain the foundation for the ongoing development of the informal sector. In other words, there is a mutually complementary relationship between the two.

Since the 1980s and 1990s, the consumer durables and communications industries have, due to economic liberalisation, swollen through joining the markets associated with the "rural and urban-informal economies" zone and with the urban middle class, comprising entrepreneurs in the informal sector, government workers and the executives in large firms (Chapter 10). Those who fill management and higher-level employee positions in these industries are well-educated members of households belonging to the upper classes of society, including the rural. The formal sector, like the informal, acts as a foundation that is stratified both socially and economically in terms of both markets and supply of personnel. The question is, can Indian economic growth continue, given that this stratified structure is fundamentally being reproduced?

## Social and Economic Stratification and Economic Growth: Merging the Tiers

The above description does not mean that Indian economic growth was accelerated thanks to the stratification of Indian society. The opposite is the case. It is my contention that it was the weakening of hierarchical relationships through lower-class resistance towards the village elites that was the core factor in the expansion of the rural market. The economic base of the lower classes expanded as the wage for agricultural labour rose and the landless acquired miniscule pieces of land with the whittling away of the elites' monopoly on village landholding. It is difficult to imagine that the rural market could have expanded otherwise. It is impossible to comprehend the size and type of the lower-class demand for non-farm goods and services without taking into account their aspirations for social mobility and struggle against the hierarchical social order. The weakening of caste hierarchies also played an important part in the formation of an entrepreneurial class, as we have seen. As Varshney (2012) and others have emphasised, it was because caste hierarchies were largely undermined in South India that various castes, high and low, entered retail and business in large numbers, contributing to the region's economic growth. The waning of class relationships in rural society is vitally important for understanding India's present high growth.

Post-Independence development of the large urban corporate sector was linked in market terms mainly with demand from the government and the elite classes. Since the 1980s, its expansion has also been linked with "growth from below", with the evolution of the "rural and urban-informal economies" zone that emerged out of the breakdown of class relationships. In this sense, the development of two tiers created the basis for a new growth in the Indian economy, as they co-mingled as a result of the policy of economic liberalisation. A similar cross-merging can be seen in the formation of capital, if only partially. As we discussed in Chapter 10, within a system where old corporate capital derived from trading capital was dominant, farming castes and others with their base in agricultural development advanced into industry and trading in regions were capital domination by Marwaris and others was weak, and from them emerged a group of entrepreneurs who led the development of technology-intensive industries. These new capitalists who materialised through the "democratisation of capital" played an important role both in the economic reforms and in the later economic growth. Thus in the formation of capital too we can see the emergence of a new structure for development through the cross-merging of the two tiers.

## The Class Structure as a Constraint on Economic Growth

The growth of the Indian economy may have been spurred on by a certain weakening of class divisions, but these divisions were basically replicated in the process. Post-1980 economic growth advanced on the basis of a socio-economic structure that had a class character. Yet, this stratified social structure may well impose limitations on the future Indian economic growth.

First, and most importantly, the class structure places constraints on the further growth of the domestic market in the non-farm sector. This sector, which includes consumer durables from the formal sector, depends, as we have pointed out, on the "rural and urban-informal economies" zone, and the problem here is that the core of this market is the rural and urban poor. As this study has shown, with virtually no change in the pattern of landholding in rural areas, it is unlikely that the majority of classes can become independent as small-scale landed farmers. In the cities too, as long as people continue to work as labourers in the informal sector, they have no option but to go on labouring for low wages in employment that offers no future security. The living standard of people in the "rural and urban-informal economies" zone has certainly improved in the past few decades, but as the Pune survey showed, most of the very poor could rise no further than "lower middle" over the generations. There remains a considerable distance to cover before the rural and urban working poor reach the "middle class", where the reproduction of secure and autonomous households is possible. It is therefore extremely improbable that the rural and urban-informal economies" zone will be able to move forward from the present expanding market for cheap consumer durables to one for expensive durables, like passenger cars. There are fundamental differences here from East Asia, where land reforms virtually did away with absentee landlordism and agriculture came to be centred on independent farmers.

Second, the mass demand for goods and services, based on preferences from the rural and urban-informal economies" zone, has been towards quasi-branded commodities, cheap goods without quality guarantee, produced mainly in the informal sector. As long as most of the people in this zone remain the working poor, such preferences are not likely to change. Though it is not impossible that a market here could arise for a quality product meeting national standards, which would make producers in informal industries raise technical and quality standards and improve their industrial structure, change even then would be incremental. The present structure of a segmented informal sector, manufacturing low-cost goods without quality guarantee, will continue for a long time to come.

Third, there are limited possibilities for labour-intensive industries, adapted to meet the domestic demand for quasi-branded goods, to develop an export market. As discussed in Chapter 7, the export apparel industry lacks in-house training systems but depends on migrating, less trained workers. Therefore its products penetrate only international low-end markets. This is in sharp contrast with their Chinese counterparts, which, with well-developed in-house training systems, have expanded their products to higher-end markets.

Fourth, Indian firms are highly socially stratified and managers and workers generally have completely different social backgrounds. This has a great bearing on worker commitment. Kiyokawa (2003), a monumental study of factories in China and India, pointed to the weaker commitment of Indian workers compared with their Chinese counterparts. This may be attributed to the employers' disinterest in improving the quality of the workforce, as well as to problems of communication on the floor due to the different social classes of workers and management. This affected both attitudes to functional work practices and the growth of competitiveness. The contrast between China and India in comparative wage levels and educational qualifications between middle management and worker was stark; whereas there was little difference in China, in India there was a great disparity. In a homogenised society like Japan, which is both egalitarian and competitive, workers are highly committed. China too, being likewise egalitarian and competitive, and valuing education and training, may be expected to display higher levels of commitment than India. Kiyokawa, considering the growing gap in recent years between the industrialisation levels of China and India, understands the characteristic distinctions between the two countries to have come into play as the consequence of economic liberalisation. This indicates that India's class-based social structure, reproduced in the corporate internal composition, hamstrings industrial development.

## Outlook

This work has studied the process by which the Indian economy, stagnant in the first half of the twentieth century under colonial rule, grew after Independence and entered a period of rapid growth after 1980. It has identified, against a backdrop of the activities of a broad range of people, three critical factors which contributed to the formation of the foundation for this growth. First was the socio-economic rise of the rural lower classes, in which resistance to the social order and a desire for a more equal society were important constituents. Second was the post-Independence rise in agrarian output, underpinned by the experience of the agricultural classes from the end of the nineteenth century of efforts to raise productivity. Third was the post-Independence process of state-led import-substitution, in the context of the colonial period independence movement which sought to form a self-sustaining national economy. It is therefore entirely feasible to say that Indian economic growth was the result, in ways both expected and unexpected, of long-term activities by a broad section of Indian people, including the lower classes, to realise self-sustaining economic development and an equal society.

Though the social and economic class structure of Indian society was not dismantled in this process, certain important indications of change are emerging. The social and economic domination of village elites has deteriorated considerably. There are some villages in South India where social reform has occurred to such an extent that no one social group can dominate. Important changes have been seen regarding landholding in some villages; whereas Brahmins were once dominant as the main landholders, now SCs have grown to be the largest landholding group in them (Harriss et al. 2010, 2012). A number of village surveys have revealed a trend towards small-scale farming based on family labour, as a result of a labour shortage and soaring wages that have made farming operations based on employed workers difficult (Djurfeldt et al. 2008). Today, aspirations for socio-economic mobility among the lower classes are very strong, and even among the lower classes in rural society there has been an upsurge in recent times for good quality education, despite the harsh economic environment. As the study of occupational mobility over four generations in Pune shows, there are very few cases of people rising from the lower classes to the middle class. New inclinations towards in-house training and education that were noted in Chapter 10 are still chiefly restricted to technology-intensive industries. However, such programmes represent positive potential as systems to raise the commitment of workers.

For the Indian economy to overcome the limitations presented by the social structure and to continue to develop, a central question concerns the way in which the "rural and urban-informal economies" zone, made up as it is of vast numbers of the working poor, can change and what socio-economic level those living in it can achieve in order to live self-sustaining lives. Significant here is the degree to which farmland has moved between the classes and how dominant smallholders, traditionally the core of the lower classes, have become. Also important is whether or not workers in the urban informal sector will become independent of the villages and reproduce themselves in the cities, as a result of increased wages, employment security and old age pensions. Is there a possibility that the way will open for those living in the "rural and urban-informal economies" zone to establish themselves in a secure and self-sustaining lifestyle, so that they, the largest market for manufactured goods and services, will demand not only quantity but quality? This would bring about not only the quantitative expansion of the manufacturing and service sectors, including the informal, but also improvements in technical, educational and living standards.

The constraints upon Indian economic growth are considerable, but it is vital to seek out potential ways in which the Indian people can carve out a path to new and continued growth, breaking boundaries using the cumulative effect of long-term experience.

# References

## Primary Sources


*Census of India, 2011, Houses, Household Amenities and Assets, Figures at a Glance*, Government of India, 2012. http://censusindia.gov.in/2011census/hlo/Data_sheet/India/Figures_Glance.pdf Accessed August 11, 2016.

E & O 6144/1936. From T. Ainscough to A. Edgcumbe, 24 August, 1936.

E & O 7532/1936. From the Secretary of State for India to the Secretary of State, Government of Burma, 24 September 1936.

*Economic Survey, 2010-11*(http://indiabudget.nic.in)p. 246. Online http://indiabudget.nic.in/budget2011-2012/es2010-11/echap-10.pdf (accessed August 7, 2016).

Government of India, No. 2211, Development, 13 December 1929.

*Preliminary Report on the Survey of Cottage Industries in the North Arcot District*, Madras, 1929.

*Preliminary Report on the Survey of Cottage Industries in the Salem District*, Madras, 1929.

Government of India, Ministry of Commerce and Industry, Development Commissioner (Small Scale Industries), *Small Scale Industry Analysis and Planning Report, No. 18, Hosiery Industry (All India)*. New Delhi, 1958.

Government of India, Ministry of Telecommunications and IT, Department of Telecommunications. *Annual Report 2010-11*. New Delhi, n.d.-a http://www.dot.gov.in/sites/default/files/English%20AR%202010-11_1.pdf Accessed August 11, 2016.

Government of India, Ministry of Telecommunications and IT, Department of Telecommunications. *Annual Report 2012-13*. New Delhi, n.d.-b http://www.dot.gov.in/sites/default/files/Telecom%20Annual%20Report-2012-13%20(English)%20_For%20web%20(1).pdf Accessed August 11, 2016.

Government of India, Ministry of Labour. *Agricultural Labour Enquiry: Report on Intensive Survey of Agricultural Labour*, 1955.

Government of India, Labour Bureau, Ministry of Labour, Employment and Rehabilitation, *Report on Family Living Survey among Industrial Workers 1958-59, Coimbatore*, Delhi, 1967.

Government of India, Ministry of Rural Development, *Annual Report, 2006-7*. Downloaded. n.d. http://rural.nic.in/sites/downloads/annualreport/anualreport0607_eng.pdf

Government of India, Ministry of Textiles, Market Research Wing. *Highlights of Consumer Purchases of Textiles*, Vol. 1, 1985.

Government of India, Ministry of Textiles, Market Research Wing. *Export and Management Capabilities of the Indian Garments Industry*. Indian Institute of Foreign Trade, Mumbai, c. 1999.

Government of India, Ministry of Tourism and Culture, Department of Tourism, Market Research Division. *Indian Tourism Statistics 2004*, ca 2006. http://www.tourism.nic.in/CMSPagePicture/file/marketresearch/ITS2004.pdf (accessed 9 August 2016).

Government of India, National Sample Survey Organisation. *Informal Sector in India, 1999-2000, Salient Features*. NSS 55th round (July 1999-June 2000). n.d. http://mospi.nic.in/rept%20_%20pubn/459_final.pdf (accessed August 20, 2016)

Government of India, Planning Commission. *Report of High Level Group on Services Sector*. New Delhi, March 2008.Online http://planningcommission.nic.in/reports/genrep/rep_ser.pdf (accessed August 7, 2016).

Government of India, Planning Commission, *Report of the Expert Group to Review the Methodology for Estimation of Poverty*, 2009. http://planningcommission.nic.in/reports/genrep/rep_pov.pdf (Accessed August 22, 2016).

Government of India, Ministry of Statistics and Programme Implementation, Central Statistical Office. *Statistical Yearbook India, 2011*, 2011. http://mospi.nic.in/mospi_new/upload/statistical_year_book_2011.htm (Accessed September 1, 2016)

Government of Madras. Proceedings of Board of Revenue, No. 28, 12 Feb. 1921.

Government of Madras, Government Order No. 1714, Miscellaneous, Development Department, 10 Sept. 1930, "Report of the Madras Youth League."

Hemingway, F.R. *Madras District Gazetteers, Tanjore*. Madras, The Superintendent, Government Press, 1906.

Hemingway, F.R. *Madras District Gazetteers: Trichinopoly*. Madras, The Superintendent, Government Press, 1907.

*Housing Condition in India: Housing Stock and Constructions: NSS 58th Round (July 2002-December 2002)*, Report No. 488. n.d. www.ilo.org/surveydata/index.php/catalog/195/download/2051

India, Department of Commercial Intelligence and Statistics, *Large Industrial Establishments in India*, 1924, 1937.

Indian Tariff Board, 1934, Vol.1. "Representation on behalf of the Hosiery Manufacturing Association of Bengal for Protection to the Hosiery Industry" Delhi, 1934.

Labour Investigation Committee, Government of India. *Report on an Enquiry into Conditions of Labour in the Engineering and Minerals and Metals Industries in India*. Manager of Publication, Delhi, 1946a.

Labour Investigation Committee, Government of India. *Report on An Enquiry into Conditions of Labour in the Cotton* **Mill Industry** *in India*. S.R. Deshpande, Delhi 1945-46.

Labour Investigation Committee, Government of India. *Report on an Enquiry into Conditions of Labour in the Jute Mill Industry in India*. S.R. Deshpande. Delhi, 1945-46.

Labour Investigation Committee, Government of India. *Report on an Enquiry into Conditions of Labour in the Bidi, Cigar and Cigarette Industries*, The Manager of Publications, New Delhi, 1946b.

Madras Revenue Proceedings, Government Order, No. 102, Revenue, 10th January 1910.

NCAER. "Domestic Tourism Survey". Sponsored by the Ministry of Tourism and Culture, the Government of India, 2002-03. *statistics.unwto.org/sites/all/files/pdf/domestic.pdf*

NCAER. "National Survey of Household Income and Expenditure", 2005.

National Commission for Enterprises in the Unorganised Sector, *The Challenge of Employment in India: An Informal Economy Perspective*, Vol. 1, The Main Report, New Delhi: Government of India, 2009. http://nceuis.nic.in/The_Challenge_of_Employment_in_India.pdf (accessed September 20, 2016).

Ramiah, K. *Rice in Madras: A Popular Handbook*, Superintendent, Government Press, Madras, 1937.

Rao, D. Narayana. *Report on the Survey of Cottage Industries in the Madras Presidency*. Madras, 1929.

Rao, D. Narayana. *Preliminary Report on the Survey of Cottage Industries in the East Godavari District*, Madras, printed by the Superintendent, Government Press, 1929.

Reserve Bank of India, *Reports on Currency and Finance: Special Edition, Vol. III, 2005-06*, date 31 May 2007, "IV. Credit Market".

Row, T. Venkasami. *Manual of District of Tanjore in the Madras Presidency*. Madras, 1883.

Slater, G. ed. *Some South Indian Villages*. Oxford: Oxford University Press, 1918.

*Statistical Appendix for South Arcot District*, Madras, Superintendent, Government Press, 1932.

*Statistical Appendix and Supplement to the Revised District Manual (1889) for Coimbatore District*, Madras, 1933.

Thomas, P.J. and K.C. Ramakrishnan, eds. *Some South Indian Villages: A Resurvey* with Analysis and Observations. University of Madras, Madras, 1940.

*Travel and Use of Mass Media and Financial Services by Indian Households, NSS 54th Round (Jan-June* 1998*)*, Report No. 450.

*Wages in Kind, Exchange of Gifts and Expenditure on Ceremonies & Insurance in India, 1993-94, 5th quinquennial survey of consumer expenditure, NSS 50th Round, July 1993-June 1994*, Report No. 428. n.d.

**Secondary Sources**

Ahluwalia, Isher J. *Industrial Growth in India: Stagnation since the Mid-Sixties*. Delhi: Oxford University Press. 1985.

Athreya, V.B. *Vadamalaipuram: A Resurvey*. Working Paper No. 50, Madras Institute of Development Studies, Madras, 1984.

Athreya, V.B. "Gangaikondan," Working Paper No. 56, Madras Institute of Development Studies, Madras, 1985.

Athreya, Suma S. "The Indian Software Industry and Its Evolving Service Capability". *Industrial and Corprate Change* 14, 3 (2005): 393–418.

Athreya, V.B., G. Djurfeldt and L. Staffan. *Barriers Broken: Production Relations and Agrarian Change in Tamil Nadu*. New Delhi: Sage, 1990.

Attwood, Donald W. *Raising Cane: The Political Economy of Sugar*. Boulder, CO, San Francisco and Oxford: Westview Press, 1992.

Bagchi, Amiya Kumar. *Private Investment in India, 1900-1939*. Cambridge: Cambridge University Press, 1972.

Baker, Christopher John. *An Indian Rural Economy, 1880-1955: The Tamilnad Countryside*. Delhi: Oxford University Press, 1984.

Balakrishnan, Pulapre. "Benign Neglect or Strategic Intent? Contested Lineage of Indian Software Industry". *Economic and Political Weekly* 41, 36 (2006): 3865–72.

Balakrishnan, Pulapre. *Economic Growth in India: History and Prospect*. New Delhi: Oxford University Press, 2010.

Balakishnan, Pulapre and M. Parameswaran, 2007. "Understanding Economic Growth in India: A Prerequisite". *Economic and Political Weekly* 27–28, July 14, 2007.

Banerjee, Abhijit V., Paul J. Gertler and Maitreesh Ghatak. "Enpowerment and Efficiency: Tenancy Reform in West Bengal". *Journal of Political Economy* 110, 31 (2002): 239–280.

Bardhan, Pranab. "Introduction". In *Conversations between Economists and Anthropologists*, ed. Bardhan, Pranab. Delhi, OUP, 1990, pp. 1–12.

Bardhan, Pranab K. *Awakening Giants, Feet of Clay: Assessing the Economic Rise of China and India*. Princeton, NJ: Princeton University Press, 2010.

Baru, Sanjaya. "Continuity and Change in Indian Industrial Policy". In *Industry and Agriculture in India Since Independence*, ed. T.V. Sathyamurthy. Delhi: Oxford University Press, pp. 115–134. 1995.

Baru, Sanjaya. "Economic Policy and the Development of Capitalism in India: The Role of Regional Capitalists and Political Parties". In *Transforming India: Social and Political Dynamics of Democracy*, ed. F.R. Frankel, Z. Hasan, R. Bhargava and B. Arora. New Delhi: Oxford University Press, 2000.

Basile, Elisabetta. *Capitalist Development in India's Informal Economy*. Oxford and New York: Routledge, 2013.

Basu, Kaushik. "China and India: Idiosyncratic Paths to High Growth," *Economic and Political Weekly* 44, 38 (2009): 43–56.

Besley, Timothy and Robin Burgess. "Land Reform, Poverty Reduction, and Growth Evidence from India". *The Quarterly Journal of Economics* (May 2000): 389–430.

Bhagavan, M.R. "Capital Goods Sector in India", *Economic and Political Weekly* 9 March 1985.

Bhalla, Sheila, Anup K. Karan and T. Shobha. "Rural Casual Labourers, Wages and Poverty". In *Chronic Poverty and Development in India*, ed. Asha Kapur Mehta and Andrew Shepherd. New Delhi: Sage Publications, 2006.

Bhargava, Sanjay. "Indian Business Houses in the 1990s". *The Economic Times*, 17 June 1993.

Bhashin, Reena. "Dynamics of Migration and Poverty in Ludhiana City". In *Distressed Migrant Labour in India: Key Human Rights Issues*, ed. Gopal Iyer . New Delhi: Kanishka Publishers and Distributors, 2004.

Bhattacharya, Prabir C. "The Informal Sector and Rural-to-Urban Migration: Some Indian Evidence". *Economic and Political Weekly* 23 May 1998.

Bhowmik, Sharit K. "A Raw Deal". *Seminar* 491, July 2000.

Bhowmik, S.K. *Street Vendors in the Global Urban Economy*. New Delhi and London: Routledge, 2010.

Binswanger-Mkhize, Hans P. "The Stunted Structural Transformation of the Indian Economy: Agriculture, Manufacturing and the Rural Non-farm Sector". *Economic and Political Weekly*, 48, 26 & 27 (29 June 2013).

Biradar, R.R. *Rural Non-agricultural Employment in India*. New Delhi: Concept Publishing Company, 2009.

Blaikie, P., J. Harriss and A. Pain. "The Management and Use of Common-Property Resources in Tamil Nadu, India". In *Making the Commons Work*, ed. D.W. Bromley. San Francisco: Institute for Contemporary Studies, 1992, pp. 247–264.

Blyn, George. *Agricultural Trends in India, 1891-1947: Output, Availability, and Productivity*. Philadelphia: University of Pennsylvania Press, 1966.

Bokil, M.S. "Privatisation of Commons for the Poor: Emergence of New Agrarian Issues". *Economic and Political Weekly* 31, 33 (1996): 2254–2261.

Borbora, Saundarjya. "Tourism: Its Growth and Impact on Employment Generation". In *Tourism in India and India's Economic Development*, eds Kartik C. Roy and Clement A. Tisdell. New York: Nova Science Publishers, 1998.

Bosworth, B., Susan M. Collins, and Arvind Virmani. "Sources of Growth in the Indian Economy" NBER Working Paper No. 12901. Printed in *India Policy Forum 2006/07*, vol. 3. New Delhi: Sage, 2007, 1–50.

Brar, Karanjot Kaur. *Green Revolution, Ecological Implications*. Delhi: Dominant Publishers & Distributors, 1999.

Brara, Rita. *Shifting Landscapes, the Making and Remaking of Village Commons in India*. New Delhi; New York: Oxford University Press, 2006.

Breman, Jan. *Patronage and Exploitation: Changing Agrarian Relations in South Gujarat, India*. Berkeley: University of California Press, 1974.

Breman, Jan. "The Study of Industrial Labour in Post-colonial India – The Formal Sector: An Introductory Review". *Contributions to Indian Sociology* 33, 1–2 (February 1999): 41.

Cain, P.J. and A.G. Hopkins. *British Imperialism: Innovation and Expansion, 1688–1914*. London and New York: Longman, 1993.

Cawthorne, Pamela M. "Of Networks and Markets: the Rise and Rise of a South Indian Town, the Example of Tiruppur's Cotton Knitwear Industry". *World Development* 23, 1 (1995): 43–56.

Chambers, R., N.C. Saxena and T. Shah. *To the Hands of the Poor: Water and Trees*. London: Intermediate Technology Publications, 1989.

Chandavarkar, Rajnarayan. *The Origins of Industrial Capital in India*. Cambridge: Cambridge University Press, 1994.

Chandra, B., M. Mukherjee and A. Mukherjee. *India Since Independence*. New Delhi: Penguin Books, 2008.

Chandrashekhar, C.P. "Aspects of Growth and Structural Change in Indian Industry". In *Industrial Growth and Stagnation: The Debate in India*, ed. Deepak Nayyar. Delhi: Oxford University Press, 1994.

Chandrasekhar, C.P. Explaining Post-reform Industrial Growth. *Economic and Political Weekly* 31, 35/37 (1994): 2537–2545.

Chandrasekhar, C.P. "Six Decades of Industrial Development: Growth of the Manufacturing Sector in India from the 1940s". In *Shaping India: Economic Change in Historical Perspective*, eds D. Narayana and Raman Mahadevan. New Delhi: Routledge, 2011.

Chari, Sharad. "The Agrarian Origins of the Knitwear Industrial Cluster in Tiruppur, India". *World Development* 28, 3 (2000): 579–599.

Chari, Sharad. *Fraternal Capital: Peasant-Workers, Self-made Men, and Globalization in Provincial India*. Stanford: Stanford University Press, 2004.

Chari, Sharad. "Social Labour and the Geography of Work in Tiruppur, Tamil Nadu". In *Colonial and Post-colonial Geographies of India*, eds M. Saraswati Raju, Satish Kumar and Stuart Corbridge. New Delhi: Sage Publications, 2006, pp. 141–161.

Charlesworth, N. *Peasants and Imperial Rule: Agriculture and Agrarian Society in the Bombay Presidency, 1850-1935*. Cambridge: Cambridge University Press, 1985.

Chatterji, Basudev. *Trade, Tariffs and Empire: Lancashire and British Policy in India, 1919-1939*. Oxford: Oxford University Press, 1992.

Chattopadhyay, K.P. *A Socio-economic Survey of Jute Labour*. Calcutta: University of Calcutta, 1952.

Chattopadhyay, Raghahendra. "An Early British Government Initiative in the Genesis of Indian Planning". *Economic and Political Weekly* 22, 5 (31 January 1987): PE19–PE29.

Chaturvedi, C. and J. Chataway. "The Indian Pharmaceutical Industry: Firm Strategy and Policy Interactions". In *The New Asian Innovation Dynamics, China and India in Perspective*, eds G. Parayil and A. D'Costa. Basingstoke: Palgrave, 2009.

Chaudhuri, B. "Eastern India". In *The Cambridge Economic History of India Volume 2: c. 1757-1970*, eds Kumar, Dharma and M. Desai. Cambridge: Cambridge University Press, 1983, 86–177.

Chaudhuri, K.N. "Foreign Trade and Balance of Payments (1757-1947)". In *The Cambridge Economic History of India Volume 2: c. 1757-1970*, eds Dharma Kumar and M. Desai. Cambridge: Cambridge University Press, 1983, 804–877.

Chaudhuri, Sudip. "The Pharmaceutical Industry". In *The Structure of Indian Industry*, eds A. Sen, S. Gokam and R. Vaidya. New Delhi/New York: Oxford University Press, 2004.

Chopra, Kanchan. *Agricultural Devlopment in Punjab, Issues in Resource Use and Sustainability*. New Delhi: Vikas Pubishing House, 1990.

Chopra, Kanchan and S.C. Gulati. "Environmental Degradation, Property Rights and Population Movements: Hypothesis and Evidence from Rajasthan". *Environment and Development Economics* 3 (1998): 35–57.

Chowdhury, Nuimuddin. "Information and Communications Technologies". In *Appropriate Technology for Sustainable Food Security, 2010 Vision Focus 7*, Brief 6 of 9, ed. Per Pinstrupp-Andersen. Washington DC: IFPRI, 2001.

De Corta, L. and D. Venkateswarlu. "Unfree Relations and the Feminisation of Agricultural Labour in Andhra Pradesh, 1970-1995". *The Journal of Peasant Studies* 26, 2–3 (1999).

Centre for Science and Environment. *The State of India's Environment 1982, a Citizen's Report*, eds A. Agarwal, R. Chopra and K. Sharma. New Delhi: CES, 1982.

Centre for Science and Environment. *The State of India's Environment 1985, the Second Citizen's Report*, eds A. Agarwal and Sunita Narain. New Delhi: CES, 1985.

Centre for Science and Environment. *The State of India's Environment 1999, the Citizen's Fifth Report*, eds Agarwal, Sunita Narain and Srabani Sen. Centre for Science and Environment, New Delhi, 1999.

Damodaran, Harish. *India's New Capitalists: Caste, Business, and Industry in a Modern Nation*. Basingstoke: Palgrave Macmillan, 2008.

Das, K (2003): "Income and Employment in Informal Manufacturing: A Case Study". In *Informal Economy Centrestage: New Structures of Employment*, eds R. Jhabvala, R.M. Sudarshan and J. Unni. (New Delhi: Sage Publication).

Dasgupta, Sukti. "Structural and Behavioural Characteristics of Informal Service Employment: Evidence from a Survey in New Delhi". *The Journal of Developmental Studies* 39, 3 (2003): 51–80.

Datt, G. and M. Ravallion. "Shining for the Poor Too". *Economic and Political Weekly* 45, 7 (2010): 55–60.

D'Costa, A.P. "Restructuring of the Indian Automobile Industry: The State and Japanese Capital". *World Development* 23, 3 (1995): 485–502.

Deshpande, Rajeshwari and Suhas Palshikar. "Occupational Mobility: How Much Does Caste Matter?" *Economic and Political Weekly* 43, 34 (23-29 August 2008): 61–70.

Dewey, Clive. "The End of the Imperialism of Free Trade: The Eclipse of the Lancashire Lobby and the Concession of Fiscal Autonomy". In *The Imperial Impact: Studies in the Economic History of India and Africa*, eds Clive Dewey and A. G. Hopkins. London: The Athlone Press for the Institute of Commonwealth Studies, 1978.

Dewey, Clive. "The Government of India's 'New Industrial Policy', 1900-1925: Formation and Failure". In *Economy and Society: Essays in Indian Economic and Social History*, eds K.N. Chaudhuri and Clive Dewey. Delhi: Oxford University Press, 1979, pp. 215–257.

Dhawan, B.D. *Ground Water Depletion, Land Degradation and Irrigated Agriculture in India*. New Delhi: Commonwealth Publishers, 1995a.

Dhawan, B.D. "Magnitude of Ground Water Exploitation". *Economic and Political Weekly* 8 April 1995b.

Dholakia, R.H. (2007), "Understanding Indian Economic Growth: Some Observations", *Economic and Political Weekly* 42, 34 (25-31 August 2007): 3509–3511.

Djurfeldt, Göran, Venkatesh B. Athreya, N. Jayakumar and R. Vidyasagar. "Agrarian Change and Social Mobiity in Tamil Nadu". *Economic and Political Weekly* 43, 45 (Novermber 2008).

Dorin, B. and F. Landy. *Agriculture and Food in India: A Half-century Review, from Independence to Globalization*. New Delhi: CSH, 2009.

Drèze, J.P. and A.K. Sen. (eds.) *India: Development and Participation*. Oxford University Press, 2002.

Duraisamy, P. and S. Narasimhan. "Migration, Remittances and Family Ties in Urban Informal Sector". *The Indian Journal of Labour Economics* 3, 1 (2000): 111–119.

Eapen, Mridul. "Rural Non-Farm Employment: Agricultural versus Urban Linkages – Some Evidence from Kerala State, India". *The Journal of Peasant Studies* 28, 2 (2001): 67–88.

Ecological Economics Unit. Institute for Social and Economic Change, Bangalore, 1999.

Fan, S., P. Hazel and T. Sukhadeo. *Linkages between Government Spending, Growth, and Poverty in Rural India*. Research Report No. 110. International Food Policy Research Institute, Washington, DC, 1999.

Foster, A.D. and M.R. Rosenzweig. "Technical Change and Human Capital Returns and Investments: Evidence from the Green Revolution." *American Economic Review*, 86, 4 (1996): 931–953.

Foster, A. D. and M.R. Rosenzweig. "Does Economic Growth Increase the Demand for *Schools*? Evidence from Rural India, 1960-2000". In *Indian Economic Prospects: Advancing Policy Reform*, ed. A.O. Krueger. University of Chicago Press, 2002.

Foster, Andrew D. and Mark R. Rosenzweig. "Agricultural Productivity Growth, Rural Economic Diversity, and Economic Reforms: India, 1970–2000". *Economic Development and Cultural Change* 52, 3 (April 2004): 509–542.

Freebairn, Donald K. "Did the Green Revolution Concentrate Incomes? A Quantitative Study of Research Reports". *World Development* 23, 2 (1995): 265–279.

Fujita, Kōichi. "Nōson no binkon to kaihatsu no kadai" (Rural Village Poverty and Topics for Development). In *Binkon to kaihatsu* (Poverty and Development), eds Esho Hideki, Hosaka Mitsuhiko, Nogami Hiroki. Tokyo: Nihon hyōronsha, 2004.

Fukazawa, H. "Western India". In *The Cambridge Economic History of India Volume 2: c. 1757-1970*, eds Dharma Kumar and M. Desai. Cambridge: Cambridge University Press, 1983, 177–206.

Fuller, C.J. *The Camphor Flame: Popular Hinduism and Society in India*. Princeton: Princeton University Press, 1992.

Ganguly, Sumit and Rahul Mukherji. *India since 1980*. Cambridge: Cambridge University Press, 2011.

Ghose, Kamal Kumar (1969). *Agricultural Labourers in India: A Study of Their Growth and Economic Conditions*. Calcutta: Indian Publications.

Gidwani, Vinay and K. Sivaramakrishnan. "Circular Migration and the Spaces of Cultural Assertion". *Annals of the Association of American Geographers* 93, 1 (2003): 186–213.

Gill, Kavery. *Of Poverty and Plastic: Scavenging and Scrap Trading Entrepreneurs I India's Urban Informal Economy*. New Delhi: Oxford University Press, 2010.

Gokarn, Subir and Rajendra R. Vaidya. "The Automobile Components Industry". In *The Structure of Indian Industry*, eds Subir Gokam, Anindya Sen, and Rajendra R. Vaidya. New Delhi/New York: Oxford University Press, 2004.

Gokhale R.G. *The Bombay Cotton Mill Worker*. Bombay: The Millowners' Association, 1957.

Gordon, James and Poonam Gupta. "Understanding India's Service Revolution". IMF Working Paper, WP/04/171, 2004.

Gorter, Pieter. *Small Industrialists, Big Ambitions: Economic and Political Networks on a Large Industrial Estate in West India*. Delhi: Oxford University Press, 1997.

Gorter, Pieter. "*The Social and Political Aspirations of a New Stratum of Industrialists: Local Politics on a Large* Industrial Estate in West India". In *Small Business Entrepreneurs in Asia and Europe: Towards a Comparative Perspective*, eds Mario Rutten and Carol Upadhya. New Delhi: Sage Publications, 1997, pp. 81–114.

Gough, Kathleen. *Rural Society in Southeast India*. Cambridge: CUP, 1981.

Guhan, S. and Joan P. Mencher. "Iruvelpattu Revisited". *Economic and Political Weekly* (4 and 11 June 1983).

Guhan, S. and K. Bharathan. *Dusi, A Resurvey*. Working Paper No. 52. Madras: Madras Institute of Development Studies, 1984.

Guhathakurta, S. "Economic Independence through Protection? Emerging Contradictions in India's Small-Scale Sector Policies". *World Development* 21, 12 (1993): 2039–54.

Hamaguchi, Tsuneo and Nishiguchi Akio eds. *Shinpan Indo keizai* (Indian Economics, New Edition). Kyoto: Sekai shisōsha, 1990.

Hansda S.K. and P. Ray. "Employment and Poverty in India during the 1990s: Is there a Diverging Trend?". *Economic and Political Weekly* 50, 27 (2006): 3014–3023.

Haque, T. and A. S. Sirohi. *Agricultural Reforms and Institutional Changes in India*. New Delhi: Concept Publishing Company, 1985.

Harnetty, Peter. "'Deindustrialization' Revisited: The Handloom Weavers of the Central Provinces of India, c. 1800-1947." *Modern Asian Studies* 25, 3 (July 1991): 455–510.

Harriss, J. *Power Matters*. Oxford: Oxford University Press, 2006.

Harriss-White, B and J. Harriss. "Green Revolution and After, the 'North Arcot Papers' and Long-term Studies of the Political Economy of Rural Development in South India". Queen Elizabeth House Working Paper No. 146. Oxford: Oxford University, Department of International Development, 2007. http://www3.qeh.ox.ac.uk/pdf/qehwp/qehwps146.pdf Accessed 13 August 2016.

Harriss-White, B. and S. Janakarajan. *Rural India Facing the 21st Century*. London: Anthem Press, 2004.

Harriss, John, J. Jeyaranjan, K. Nagaraj. "Land, Labour and Caste Politics in Rural Tamil Nadu in the 20th Century: Iruvelpattu (1916-2008)". *Economic and Political Weekly* 45, 31 (2010): 47–61.

Harriss, John, J. Jeyaranjan and K. Nagaraj. "Rural Urbanism in Tamil Nadu, Notes on a 'Slater Village': Gangaikondan, 1916–2012". *Review of Agrarian Studies* 2, 2 (July–December 2012): 29–59.

Hayami, Yūjirō. "Indo Derii-shi ni okeru haihin kaishūgyōsha: Toshi binkonsō no bunseki" (Waste pickers and collectors in Delhi: A study of the urban poor). *Keizai kenkyū* 56, 1 (2005): 1–14.

Hayami, Y., A.K. Dikshit, and S.N. Mishra. "Waste Pickers and Collectors in Delhi: Poverty and Environment in an Urban Informal Sector". *Journal of Development Studies* 42, 1 (2006): 41–69.

Haynes, Douglas. "The Logic of the Artisan Firm in a Capitalist Economy: Handloom Weavers and Technological Change in Western India, 1889-1947". In *Institutions and Economic Change in South Asia*, eds Burton Stein and Sanjay Subrahmanyam. Delhi: Oxford University Press, 1996.

Haynes, Douglas. *Small Town Capitalism in Western India: Artisans, Merchants and the Making of the Informal Economy, 1870–1960*. Cambridge and New York: Cambridge University Press, 2012.

Hazell, P. and S. Haggblade, "Rural-Urban Growth Linkages in India". *Indian Journal of Agricultural Economics* 4, 4 (1991): 515–29.

Hazell, Peter and C. Ramasamy. *The Green Revolution Reconsidered: The Impact of High-yielding Rice Varieties in South India*. Baltimore: Johns Hopkins University Press, 1991.

Heston, A. "National Income". In *The Cambridge Economic History of India Volume 2: c. 1757-1970*, eds Dharma Kumar and M. Desai. Cambridge: Cambridge University Press, 1983.

Hnatkovska, Viktoria, Amartya Lahiri and Sourabh B. Paul. "Castes and Labor Mobility". *American Economic Journal: Applied Economics* 4, 2 (2012): 274–307.

Hutton, J.H. *Caste in India, Its Nature, Function and Origin*. Bombay: Oxford University Press, 1977.

Inoue, Kyōko. *Industrial Development Policy of India*. Tokyo: Institute of Developing Economies, 1992.

Inoue, Takashi. "Tojōkoku ni okeru josei no nenreibetsu idōritsu no suii to sono tokuchō" (Changes in Women's Age-Specific Migration Rate in Developing Countries and their Characteristics). In *Tojōkoku no jinkō idō to jendā* (Gender and Population Migration in Developing Countries), ed. Hayase Yasuko. Kyoto: Akashi shoten, 2002.

Ishigami Etsurō. "Indo Tekkōgyō no hatten to henyō: senpatsu ikkan mēkā, shinkō ōte mēkā oyobi shōkibobumon teiritsu no kōzu" (Development and Restructuring of the Indian Steel Industry: The Triple Structure of Main Producers, Secondary Producers and Small Scale Producers). In *Ajia-shokoku no tekkōgyō: hatten to henyō* (The Steel Industry in Asian Development and Restructuring), ed. Hajime Satō. Chiba: Institute of Developing Economies, 2008, pp. 159–202.

Ishigami, Etsurō. "Sangyō seisaku to sangyō hatten" (Industrial planning and industrial development), in *Gendai Indo, Minami Ajia keizairon* (Economic theory in modern India and South Asia), eds Ishigami Etsurō and Satō Takahiro. Tokyo: Minerva, 2011, pp. 149–82.

Ishigami Etsurō and Satō Takahiro eds. *Gendai Indo, Minami Ajia keizairon* (Economic Theory in Modern India and South Asia). Tokyo: Minerva, 2011.

Itō, Shōji. "Dokuritsugo no dokusen shihon no hatten to keizaiteki jūzoku" (Post-Independence Development of Monopoly Capital and Economic Dependence). In *Indo gendaishi no tenbō* (Outlook on Modern Indian History), ed. Nakamura Heiji. Tokyo: Aoki shoten, 1972.

Iwatani, Ayako. "Roten ha mooru wo yume miruka – gulobaru ka suru indo ni okeru rotenshou bijinesu no genzai" (Do Hawkers dream of Mall? Hawker Business in Globalized India). In *Gulobarizeishonzu – Jinruigaku, Rekishigaku, Chikikenkyuu no genba kara* (Globalization from Anthropology, History, and Area Study), eds Mio Yuko and Tokoro Ikuya. Tokyo: Kobundo, 2002.

Jeffrey, Craig and Jens Lerche. "Stating the Difference. State, Discourse and Class Reproduction in Uttar Pradesh, India". *Development and Change* 31 (September 2000): 857–878.

Jhabvala, Renana, "Roles and Perceptions". *Seminar* 491, July 2000.

Jodha, N.S. "Social Science Research on Rural Change". In *Conversations between Economists and Anthropologists*, ed. P. Bardhan. Delhi, OUP, 1989.

Joseph, K.J. "The Electronics Industry". In *The Structure of Indian Industry*, eds A. Sen, S. Gokam and R. Vaidya. New Delhi/New York: Oxford University Press, 2004.

Joseph, Mathew and Nirupama Soundararajan eds. *Retail in India: A Critical Assessment*. New Delhi: Academic Foundation, 2009.

Kagotani, Naoto. "Nichū sensō mae no Nihon no keizai gaikō: dainiji nichiin kaishō (1936-37) o jirei ni" (Japanese economic policy before the Second Sino-Japanese War: A Case Study of the Second Japan-India Trade Negotiations [1936-37]). *Jinbun gakuhō* (Kyoto University), 77 (1996).

Kalirajan, K.P. and S. Bhide. "The Post-reform Performance of the manufacturing sector in India". *Asian Economic Papers* 3 (2005): 126–157.

Kanitkar, A. "Entrepreneurs and Micro-enterprises in Rural India". *Economic and Political Weekly* 29, 9 (1994): 25–30.

Kapur, Devesh, Prasad Chandra Bhan, Pritchett Lant and Babu D. Shyam. Rethinking Inequality: Dalits in Uttar Pradesh in the Market Reform Era. *Economic & Political Weekly* 45, 35 (2010): 39–49.

Kashyap, S.P. "Growth of small-size enterprises in India: Its nature and content". *World Development* 16, 6 (1988): 667–681.

Kashyap, S.P., R.S. Tiwari and D.R. Veena. *Facets of an Urban Economy – Economic Base Study of Ahmedabad*. Ahmedabad: Sardar Patel Institute, 1980.

Kathuria, Sanjay. "Competitiveness of Indian Industry". In *Indian Industry: Policies and Performance*, ed. Dilip Mookherjee. Delhi/New York: Oxford University Press, 1995.

Kathuria, Sanjay. *Competing through Technology and Manufacturing Strategy: A Study of the Indian Commercial Vehicles Industry*. New Delhi: Oxford University Press, 1996.

Kaushik, A. 2005. "Nature of land market interventions in India." Institute for Sustainable Development, Noida.

Kessinger, Tom J. *Vilyatpur: 1848-1968. Social and Economic Change in a North Indian Village*. Delhi: Young Asia Publishers. 1979 (originally published by University of California Press, 1974).

Kingdon, G.G. "Does the Labour Market Explain Lower Female Schooling in India?" *Journal of Development Studies* 35, 1 (1998): 39–65.

Kiso, Junko. "Factory Workers and Their Mobility in Ahmedabad City". In *The Other Gujarat: Social Transformations among Weaker Sections*, ed. T. Shinoda. Mumbai: Popular Prakashan, 2002.

Kiso, Junko. "Job Loss and Job Opportunities of Factory Workers in Ahmedabad: Flexible Labour Rethink". In *Globalisation, Employment and Mobility: The South Asian Experience*, eds H. Sato and M. Murayama. Basingstoke: Palgrave Macmillan, 2008, pp. 31–61.

Kiso, Junko. *Indo no keizai hatten to hito, rōdō* (People and Labour in India's Economic Growth). Tokyo: Nihon hyōronsha, 2012.

Kiyokawa Yukihiko. *Kiroku: tojōkoku ni okeru kōjō chōsa to hihonhyōgosa no kanri, Indo no jirei kara* [Factory surveys in developing countries and non-sampling errors]. Discussion paper Series A No. 432. The Institute of Economic Research, Hitotsubashi University, Kunitachi, Tokyo, 2002.

Kiyokawa, Yukihiko. "Ajia ni okeru kindaiteki kōgyō rōdōryoku no keisei: keizai hatten to bunka narabi ni shokumu ishiki" [The Form of the Modern Factory Labour Force in Asia: Economic Development, Culture and Work Commitment]. Tokyo: Iwanami shoten, 2003.

Knorringa, Peter. *Economics of Collaboration: Indian Shoemakers between Market and Hierarchy*. New Delhi; London: Sage, 1996.

Kochanek, Stanley A. "Liberalisation and Business Lobbying in India". The Journal of Commonwealth and Comparative Politics 34, 3 (1996a): 155–173.

Kochanek, Stanley A. "The Transformation of Interest Politics in India". *Pacific Affairs* 68, 4 (Winter 1996b): 529–550.

Kochhar, K., U. Kumar, R. Rajan, A. Subramanian and I. Tokatlidis. *India's Pattern of Development: What Happened, What Follows* International Monetary Fund Working Paper WP/06/22, 2006.

Kohli, Atul. "Politics of Economic Growth in India, 1980-2005: Parts I & II". *Economic and Political Weekly*, 1 and 8 April 2006.

Kohli, Atul. *Poverty Amid Plenty in the New India*. Cambridge: Cambridge University Press, 2012.

Kollannavar, Giriyappa, D. Chandramouli and B. Krishnama Naidu. "Artisan Footwear Industry – Impact of Technology Transfer and Globalization". In *Rural Development in India: Scope for Industrial Development*, eds Y. Gangi Reddy and Shankar Chatterjee, New Delhi: Serial Publications, 2010.

Kulshereshtha, A.C. and Gulab Singh. "Contribution of Unorganised Sector in the Indian Economy". *Manpower Journal*, 34, 3 (October-December 1998): 45–67.

Kumar, Dharma. "Agrarian Relations, South India". In *The Cambridge Economic History of India Volume 2: c. 1757-1970*, eds Dharma Kumar and M. Desai. Cambridge: Cambridge University Press, 1983.

Kumar, Dharma ed. with the editoral assistance of Meghnad Desai. *The Cambridge Economic History of India Volume 2: c. 1757-1970*. Cambridge: Cambridge University Press, 1983.

Kumar, N. Ganesh. "Some Comments on the Debate on India's Economic Growth in the 1980's", Working Paper No.1015, Indian Institute of Management, Ahmedabad, March 1992. *Indian Economic Journal* 39, 4 (April-June 1992): 102–111.

Kumar, Parmod. "Marketed Surplus of Different Crops Across Farm Size: A Study in Haryana". *Indian Journal of Agricultural Economics* 54, 4 (October-December 1999).

Kumar, Parmod. *Farm Size and Marketing Efficiency, Pre- and Post-Liberalization*. New Delhi : Concept Publishing Co., 2007.

Kumar, S., A. Heath, and O. Heath. "Determinants of Social Mobility in India". *Economic and Political Weekly* 37, 29 (July 2002a): 83–87.

Kumar, S., A. Heath, and O. Heath. "Changing Patterns of Social Mobility". *Economic and Political Weekly* 37, 40 (October 2002b): 91–96.

Kumar, Praduman, Mruthyunjaya, and Madan M. Dey. "Long-term Changes in Indian Food Basket and Nutrition". *Economic and Political Weekly*, XLII, 35, September 1, 2007.

Kurosaki, Takashi. "Indo Pakisutan Banguradeshu chōki nōgyō seichō" (Long term agricultural growth in India, Pakistan and Bangladesh). Global COE Hi-Stat

Discussion Paper Seies 125. Research Unit for Statistical and Empirical Analysis in Social Sciences (Hi-Stat). Hitotsubashi University. March 2010. On line. https://hermes-ir.lib.hit-u.ac.jp/rs/bitstream/10086/18361/1/gd09-125.pdf

Kurosaki, T. "Economic Inequality in South Asia". In *Routledge Handbook of South Asian Economics*, ed. Raghbendra Jha. Oxford, UK: Routledge, 2011, pp. 61–75.

Kurosaki, Tadashi. "Long-term Agricultural Growth in India, Pakistan, and Bangladesh from 1901/02 to 2001/02". Research Unit for Statistical and Empirical Analysis in Social Sciences (Hi-Stat). Hitotsubashi University. On line 2014: http://www.ata.boun.edu.tr/ahec/conferencepapers2014/Kurosaki.pdf

Lal, D. "Agricultural Growth, Real Wages, and the Rural Poor in India". *Economic and Political Weekly*, Review of Agriculture 11 (June 1976).

Lall, Sanjaya. "Trade in Technology by a Slowly Industrializing Country: India". In *International Technology Transfer: Concepts, Measures and Comparisons*, eds N. Rosenberg and C. Frischtak. New York: Praeger, 1985, pp. 45–76.

Lambert, Richard D. *Workers, Factories, and Social Change in India*. New Jersey: Princeton University Press, 1963.

Lanjouw, Peter and Abusaleh Shariff. "Rural Non-farm Employment in India: Access, Incomes and Poverty Impact". *Economic and Political Weekly*, XXXIX, 40 (2 October 2004).

Lanjouw, P. and R. Murgai. "Poverty Decline, Agricultural Wages, and Non-Farm Emloyment in India, 1983-2004". Policy Research Working Paper, No. 4858. World Bank, Washington, DC, 2009. *Agricultural Economics* 40, 2 (March 2009): 243–263.

Leadbeater, S.R.B. *The Politics of Textiles: The Indian Cotton-Mill Industry and the Legacy of Swadeshi, 1900-1985*. New Delhi: Sage Publications, 1993.

Lynch, Owen M. *The Politics of Untouchability*. New York: Columbia University Press, 1969.

Madheswaran, S. and A. Dharmadhikary. "Income and Employment Growth in Service Sector in India". *The Indian Journal of Labour Economics* 43, 4 (2000): 835–864.

Mahalanobis, P.C. *Papers on Planning*, eds P.K. Bose and M. Mukherjee. Calcutta: Statistical Publishing Society, 1985.

Majumder, Bhaskar. "Import Substituting Industrialization in the Indian Economy: A Critical Evaluation". *Indian Journal of Economics* 71, 38 (October 1990).

Mani, Sunil. "Growth of India's Telecom Services (1991-2007): Can It Lead to Emergence of a Manufacturing Hub?" *Economic and Political Weekly* (19 January 2008).

Marjit, Sugata and Saibal Kar. "Firm Heterogeneity, Informal Wage and Good Governance". *Review of Development Economics*, Wiley Blackwell, 16, 4 (2012).

Mascarenhas, R.C. *Technology Transfer and Development, India's Hindustan Machine Tool Company*. Boulder, CO: Westview, 1982.

Mayer, P.B. "Is There Urban Bias in the Green Revolution? Report on a Field Trip to North Thanjavur". *Peasant Studies* 11, 4 (Summer 1984) 213–235.

Mazumdar, Krishna. "Disproportional Growth of Service Sector in India: 1960-1990". *The Indian Economic Journal* 43, 2 (October-December 1995).

Mazumdar, Mainak. *Performance of Pharmaceutical Companies in India, A Critical Analysis of Industrial Structure, Firm Specific Resources, and Emerging Strategies*. Springer, 2013.

Mazumdar, Dipak and Sandip Sarkar, "Growth of Employment and Earnings in Tertiary Sector, 1983-2000". *Economic and Political Weekly* XLII, 11 (17 March 2007).

Mazumdar, Dipak and Sandip Sarkar. *Globalization, Labor Markets and Inequality in India*. London: Routledge, 2008.

McCartney, Matthew. *India - The Political Economy of Growth, Stagnation and the State, 1951-2007*. Routledge 2009.

Mehta, Niti and S.P. Kashyap. "An Approach Towards Identifying Sunrise Industries: A Regional Perspective". Paper presented at workshop on *Employment in the Rural Non-farm Sector*. New Delhi: Institute of Applied Manpower Research, 2002.

Mencher, Joan P. *Agriculture and Social Structure in Tamil Nadu: Past Origins, Present Transformations and Failure*. Durham, N.C.: Carolina Academic Press, 1978.

Mitra, Arup. *Urbanisation, Slums, Informal Sector Employment and Poverty: An Exploratory Study*. Delhi: B.R. Pub. Corp., 1994.

Mitra, Arup. *Occupational Choices, Networks and Transfers: An Exegesis Based on Micro Data from Delhi Slums*. Delhi: Manohar, 2003.

Mizushima, T. "Changes, Chances and Choices, The Perspective of Indian Villagers". *Socio-Cultural Change in Villages in Tiruchirapalli District, Tamil Nadu, India, Part 2, Modern Period -1*, ILCAA, Tokyo University of Foreign Studies, Tokyo, 1983.

Moench, M.H. "Chasing the Watertable: Equity and Sustainability in Groundwater Management". *Economic and Political Weekly* (1992a): 171–177.

Moench, M. "Drawing Down the Buffer". *Economic and Political Weekly* 27, 13 (1992b): A7–A14

Mohan, R. "Industrial Policy and Controls". In *The Indian Economy, Problems and Prospects*, ed. Jalan, Bimal. Viking, 1992.

Morris, David. *The Emergence of an Industrial Labor Force in India: A Study of the Bombay Cotton Mills, 1854-1947*. Berkeley and Los Angeles: University of California Press, 1965.

Morris, D. "The Growth of Large-Scale Industry to 1947". In *The Cambridge Economic History of India Volume 2: c. 1757-1970*, eds Kumar, Dharma and M. Desai. Cambridge: Cambridge University Press, 1983, pp. 533–676.

Mosse, David. *The Rule of Water, Statecraft, Ecology and Collective Action in South India*. New Delhi: Oxford University Press, 2003.

Moulik, T.K. and Ranjan Moulik. "Structural Changes in Rural Economy – Gujarat". In *Encyclopaedia of India and Her States* (6), eds Verinder Grover and Ranjana Arora. New Delhi: Deep and Deep Publications, 1996.

Mukherjee, Dipa. "Informal Manufacturing Sector in India: Pre and Post Reform Growth Dynamics". MPRA Paper No. 4866. (2004).

Mukherjee, Mridula. *Colonializing Agriculture: The Myth of Punjabi Exceptionalism*. Delhi: Sage, 2005.

Mukherjee, S. and S. Mukherjee. "Overview of India' Export Performance: Trends and Drivers". Indian Institute of Management Bangalore, Working Paper 363 (April 2012): 1–63.

Munshi, Shoma. "Yeh Dil Maange More… Television and Consumer Choices in a Global City". In *Patterns of Middle Class Consumption in India and China*, eds Christophe Jaffrelot and Peter van der Veer. New Delhi: Sage (2012).

Munshi, Kaivan and Mark Rosenzweig. "Traditional Institutions Meet the Modern World: Caste, Gender, and Schooling Choice in a Globalizing Economy". *The American Economic Review* 96, 4 (September 2006).

Nadkarni, M.V. *Farmers' Movements in India*. Ahmedabad: Allied Publishers, 1987.

Nadkarni, M.V. "Crisis of Increasing Costs in Indian Agriculture, – Is there a Way Out?" *Economic and Political Weekly, Review of Agriculture* (24 September 1988): A114–A119.

Nadkarni, M.V. *The Political Economy of Forest Use and Management*. New Delhi: Sage, 1989.

Nagaraj, R. "Industrial Policy and Performance since 1980, Which Way Now?" *Economic and Political Weekly* (30 August 2003): 3713.

Nagaraj, R. "India's Recent Economic Growth, A Closer Look". *Economic and Political Weekly* 43, 15 (12 April 2008): 55–61.

Naidu, K. Maju Shri. *Growth of Footwear Industry in India, Problems and Prospects*. New Delhi: Serials Publications, 2009.

Nair K.N. and Aridarm Banerjee. "Structural Changes in Land Distribution and Implications for Improving Access to land", in *Shaping India, Economic Change in Historical Perspective*, eds D. Narayana and Raman Mahadeven. New Delhi: Routledge, 2011, pp. 46–66.

Nakamura, Hisashi, 1982. "Disintegration and Re-integration of a Rural Society in the Process of Economic Development: The Second Survey of a Tank-based Village in Tamil Nadu". *Studies in Socio-Cultural Change in Rural Villages in Tiruchirapalli District, Tamilnadu, India, No. 5*, Institute for the Study of Languages and Cultures of Asia and Africa.

Nakamizo, Kazuya. *Indo bōryoku to minshushugi: Ittōyūi shihai no hōkai to aidentitei no seiji* (Violence and Democracy in India: The Collapse of One-party Dominant Rule and Identity Politics). Tokyo: The University of Tokyo Press, 2012.

Nakatani, Sumie. "Atarashii komyunitei no shutsugen – Raajastaan nōson ni okeru Raamdevu shinkō to junrei" (Appearance of a New Community – Ramdev Faith and Pilgrimage). *Minami Ajia kenkyū* 21 (2009).

Nakazato, Nariaki. *Agrarian Sustem in Eastern Bengal, c. 1870-1910*. Calcutta: K. P. Bagchi and Co., 1994.

Nakazato, Nariaki. "The Transfer of Economic Power in India: Indian Big Business, the British Raj and Development Planning, 1930-1948". In *The Unfinished Agenda: Nation-building in South Asia*, eds Mushirul Hasan and Nariaki Nakazato. New Delhi: Manohar, 2001, pp. 247–307.

Nara, Tsuyoshi and Tsukasa Mizushima. "Neikuramu mura chōsa hōkoku I" (Social Change I a Dry Village in South India, An Interim Report). *Studies in Socio-Cultural Change in Rural Villages in Tiruchirapalli District, Tamilnadu, India*. Tokyo: Institute for the Study of Languages and Cultures of Asia and Africa, 1981.

Natarajan, L. 1998. *India Market Demographics Report, 1998*. New Delhi: National Council of Applied Economic Research.

Nayak, Paramananda and H. Kopresachari. "Changing Patterns of Textile Consumption in India: A Case of Andra Pradesh". *Exprfess Textile*, (October–December 2002).

Nayyar, Deepak. "Economic Growth in Independent India: Lumbering Elephant or Running Tiger?" *Economic and Political Weekly*, 41, 15 (15 April 2006).

Nayyar, Gaurav. *The Service Sector in India's Development*. Cambridge: Cambridge University Press, 2012.

Ōji, Toshiaki. "Indo, Panjabu ni okeru nōson no tenkai to midori no kakumei – Amurittsūa-ken Gagarubāna-mura o jirei toshite (Village development and the Green Revolution in the Punjab, India: Gaggar Bhana, Amritsar District)". *Shirin* 57, 5 (1974): 25–78.

Okada, Aya. "Skills Development and Interfirm Learning Linkages under Globalization: Lessons from the Indian Automobile Industry", *World Development* 32, 7 (2004): 1265–1288.

Okada, A. "Skills Formation for Economic Development in India: Fostering Institutional Linkages between Vocational Education and Industry". *Manpower Journal* (Special Issue on Vocational and Professional Education, edited by Jandhyala B G Tilak), 41, 1 (2006): 71–95.

Okada, Aya. "Small firms in *Indian* software clusters: Building global competitiveness". In *High-tech Industries, Employment and Global Competitiveness*, eds S.R. Hashim and N.S. Siddharthan. London and Delhi: Routledge, 2008.

Osella, Filippo and Caroline Osella. "From Transience to Immanence: Consumption, Life-cycle and Social Mobility in Kerala, South India", *Modern Asian Studies* 33, 4 (1999).

Pandit, D. 1969. "Myths around Subdivision and Fragmentation of Holdings: A Few Case Histories". *Indian Economic and Social History Review* 6.2 (1969): 151–163.

Parikh, Kirit S. and R. Radhakrishna eds. *India Development Report*. New Delhi: Oxford University Press, 2005.

Park, YoungWon and Paul Hong. *Building Network Capabilities in Competitive Environments. Practices of Global Firms from Korea and Japan*. Baton Rouge, London, New York: 2016.

Patel, Kunj M. *Rural Labour in Industrial Bombay*. Bombay: Popular Prakashan, 1963.

Pathak, Akhileshwar. *Contested Domains, The State, Peasants and Forests in Contemporary India*. New Delhi: Sage, 1994.

Pedersen, Jorgen Dige. "Explaining Economic Liberalization in India: State and Society Perspectives. *World Development* 28, 2 (2000): 265–282.

Pothana, V. "Rural-Urban Migration and Development: Myth and Reality". In *Growth of Urban Informal Sector and Economic Development*, ed. M Koteswara Rao. Vol. 2. Delhi: Kanishka Publishers Distributors, 1994.

Raj, K.N. "Some Observations on Economic Growth in *India* over the Period 1952-3 to 1982-3". *Economic and Political Weekly* (13 October 1984).

Raj, K.N. et al. *Essays on the Commercialisation of Indian Agriculture*. Delhi: Oxford University Press, 1985.

Rajakumar, J. Dennis. "Corporate Financing and Investment Behaviour in India". *Economic and Political Weekly* (17 September 2005): 4159–4165.

Raju, R. Satya. "Socio-Economic Aspects of Construction Labour in India". In *Growth of Urban Informal Sector and Economic Development*, Vol. 2, ed. M. Koteswara Rao. Delhi: Kanishka Publishers Distributors, 1994.

Ramanujam, M.S., M.C. Goel, Surendra Prasad, I.C. Awasthi, U.S. Bhandari and S.K. Yadav. *Employment in the Informal Sector (A Study of Selected Towns)*. Institute of Applied Manpower Research. New Delhi: Agricole Publishing Academy, 1994.

Ramaswamy, K.V. "Small-Scale Manufacturing Industries in India: Some Aspects of Size, Growth and Structure". Paper 105, Indira Gandhi Institute of Development Research, 1994.

Ramaswamy, K.V. "The Search for Flexibility in Indian Manufacturing". *Economic and Political Weekly* 34, 6 (1999): 363–368.

Ramaswamy, K.V. "Economic Reforms, Industrial Structure and Performance: The Case of *Consumer Durable* Goods Industry in India". In *Economic Reforms and Industrial Structure in India*, ed. Shuji Uchikawa. New Delhi: Manohar, 2002.

Ramaswamy, Uma. *Work, union, and community: Industrial Man in South India*. Delhi: Oxford University Press, 1983.

Rani, G. Swaroopa and S. Galeb. "Organisation and Economic Performance of Manufacturing Activities in Urban Slums of Hyderabad City: A Case Study of Sandal Making Activity". *The Indian Journal of Labour Economics* 41, 3 (1998): 539–553.

Rani, G. Swaroopa and S. Galeb "Manufacturing Activities in Urban Slums: A Case Study of Sandal Making in Hyderabad". In *Informal Sector in India, Perspectives and Policies*, eds Amitabh Kundu and Alakh N. Sharma. New Delhi: Institute for Human Development, 2001, pp. 196–214.

Rani, Uma and Jeemol Unni, *Urban Informal Sector: Size and Income Generation Processes in Gujarat*, Part II, Report No. 3, National Council of Applied Economic Research, 2000.

Rao, C. H. Hanumantha. *Agricultural Growth, Rural Poverty and Environmental Degradation in India*. Studies in Economic Development and Planning Institute of Economic Growth (India), No. 59, Delhi: Oxford University Press, 1994.

Rao, M. Koteswara ed. *Growth of Urban Informal Sector and Economic Development*, Vol. 2. Delhi: Kanishka Publishers Distributors, 1994.

Rao, M. Koteswara and K. Gangadhara Rao. "Socio-Economic Characteristics of Labour in Urban Informal Sector: A Case Study". In *Growth of Urban Informal Sector and Economic Development*, Vol. 2, ed. M. Koteswara Rao. Delhi: Kanishka Publishers Distributors, 1994a.

Rao, M. Koteswara and K. Gangadhara Rao. "Socio-Economic Status of Migrant workers in Informal Sector: A Case Study". In *Growth of Urban Informal Sector and Economic Development*, Vol. 2, ed. M. Koteswara Rao. Delhi: Kanishka Publishers Distributors, 1994b.

Rao, M. Koteswara and M. Prasada Rao (1994). "Migrant Labour in Informal Sector: A Case Study," in Rao ed. 1994.

Rao, S.L., ed. *Consumer Market Demographics in India*. Revised edition. New Delhi: National Council of Applied Economic Research, 1994b.

Ravallion, M. and G. Datt. "How Important to India's Poor Is the Sectoral Composition of Economic Growth?" *World Bank Economic Review* 10, 10 (1996): 1–25.

Ravindranath, N.H. and D.O. Hall. *Biomass, Energy and Environment: A Developing Country Perspective from India*. Oxfore: Oxford University Press, 1995.

Ray, R. *Change in Bengal Agrarian Society, 1760-1850*. New Delhi: Manohar, 1979.

Ray, Rajit K. and Ratnalekha Ray. "The Dynamics of Continuity in Rural Bengal under the British Imperium". *The Indian Economic and Social History Review* 10, 2 (1973): 103–128.

Rodges, G. and J. Rodgers. "Inclusive Development? Migration, Governance and Social Change in RURAL BIHAR". *Economic and Political Weekly* 46, 23 (2011): 43–50.

Rodrik, Dani and Arvind Subramanian. *From "Hindu Growth" to Productivity Surge: The Mystery of the Indian Growth Transition*, IMF Working Paper, WP/04/77. 2004

Roy, Satyaki. *Small and Medium Enterprises in India, Infirmities and Asymmetries in Industrial Clusters*. London and New York: Routledge, 2013.

Roy, Tirthankar. *Artisans and Industrialization: Indian Weaving in the Twentieth Century*, Delhi: Oxford University Press, 1993.

Roy, Tirthankar. "Development or Distortion? "Powerlooms" in India, 1950-1997". *Economic and Political Weekly*, XXXIII, 16 (18 April 1998) 897–911.

Roy, Tirthankar. *Traditional Industry in the Economy of Colonial India*. Cambridge studies in Indian history and society (5). Cambridge: Cambridge University Press, 1999.

Roy, Tirthankar. "Acceptance of Innovations in Early Twentieth-Century Indian Weaving". *Economic History Review*, 55, 3 (2002a): 507–532.

Roy, Tirthankar. "Consumer Non-Durable Goods Industries: Growing Market and Increasing Competition". In *Economic Reforms and Industrial Structure in India*, ed. Shuji Uchikawa. New Delhi: Manohar, 2002b.

Roy, Tirthankar. "The Textile Industry". In *The Structure of Indian Industry*, eds Subir Gokam, Anindya Sen, and Rajendra R. Vaidya. New Delhi/New York: Oxford University Press, 2004.

Roy, Thirthankar. "Roots of agrarian crisis in interwar India". *Economic and Political Weekly* 41, 52 (2006): 5389–5400.

Roy, Tirthankar. *Economic History of India, 1857-1947*. 3rd edition. New Delhi: Oxford University Press, 2011.

Roy, Tirthankar ed. *Cloth and Commerce, Textiles in Colonial India*. New Delhi/ Thousand Oaks/London: Sage Publications, 1996.

Rutten, Mario. *Farms and Factories: Social Profile of Large Farmers and Rural Industrialists in West India*. Oxford: Oxford University Press, 1995.

Sarkar, Siuli. *Kolkata Hawkers: A Chronicle of Deprivation, Discontent and Struggle*. Kolkata: Worldview, 2009.

Sastry, D.V.S., Balwant Singh, Kaushik Bhattacharya, and N.K. Unnikrishnan. "Sectoral Linkages and Growth Prospects: Reflections on the Indian Economy". *Economic and Political Weekly*, 38, 24, (14 June 2003): 2392–2397.

Satyanarayana, A. *Andhra Peasants under British Rule: Agrarian Relations and the Rural Economy, 1900-1940*. New Delhi: Manohar Publications, 1990.

Satō, Keiko. "Employment Structure and Rural-Urban Migration in a Tamil Nadu Village: Fosucingon Differences by Economic Class". *Southeast Asian Studies* 49, 1 (June 2011): 22–51.

Satō, Takahiro. "Indo no fudōsan ichiba to shisan kakaku baburu" (Real Estate Markets and Asset Price Bubbles in India). INDAS Working Paper No. 4, March 2011.

Seminar. Special issue on street vendors. No. 491. 2000. www.india-seminar.com/2000/491.htm

Sengupta, A., K.P. Kannan, and G. Raveendran. "India's Common People: Who Are They, How Many Are They and How Do They Live?". *Economic and Political Weekly* 43, 11 (2008): 49–63.

Shah, Amita. *Employment Linkages of Industrialisation in backward Rural Economy, a Case Study of Ankleshvar Industrial Estate in Gujarat*. Ahmedabad: Gujarat Institute of Development Research, 2001.

Shah, Tushaar. *Taming the Anarchy: Groundwater Governance in South Asia*. Washington, DC: RFF Press, 2009a.

Shah, Tushaar. "Climate Change and Groundwater: India's Opportunites for Mitigation and Adaptation". *Environmental Research Letters* 4, 3 (2009b) 1–13.

Shah, Parth J. and Naveen Mandava. *Law, Liberty and Livelihood: Making a Living on the Street*. New Delhi: Academic Foundation, 2005.

Sharma H.R. *Agrarian Relations in India: Patterns and Implications*. New Delhi: Har Anand Publications, 1995.

Sharma, R.N. "The Politics of Urban Space". *Seminar*, No. 491 (July 2000).

Sharma, A.N. "Agrarian Relations and Socio-economic Change in Bihar". *Economic and Political Weekly* 40, 10 (2005): 960–972.

Sharma, R. N., and K. Sita. "Hawkers and Vendors in Mumbai, India". *Indian Journal of Social Work* 69, 3 (2008): 339–368.

Shimane, Yoshie. "Jiba kigyō no kiban ga chūmoku sareru Indo jidōsha sangyō no hatten" (The Development of the Indian Automobile Industry focusing on the Base of Local Enterprises). In *Hendō suru Indo keizai* (The Changing Indian Economy), ed. Uchikawa Shūji. Chiba: IDE-JETRO, 2006, pp. 268–293.

Shiva, Vandana. *The Violence of the Green Revolution, Third World Agriculture, Ecology and Politics*. London and New Jersey: Zed Books Ltd,/Penang, Malaysia: Third World Network, 1991.

Shrinivasan M. *A Decade of Agricultural Development in India*. Bombay: Asian Studies Press for Indian Institute of Asian Studies, 1965.

Shukla, V. "Rural Nonfarm Activity – A Regional Model and Its Empirical Application to Maharashtra". *Economic and Political Weekly* 26, 45 (1991): 2587–2595.

Siddiqi, Asiya. *Agrarian Change in a North Indian State: Uttar Pradesh 1819-1833*. Oxford: Oxford University Press, 1973.

Singh S. Pal. "Bicycle Industry since Independence: Growth, Structure and Demand". *Economic and Political Weekly*, 25, 34 (1990): 98–109.

Singh, Amarjit. "India." A Country Report Presented at the Study Meeting on Agricultural Diversification and International Competitiveness, Asian Productivity Organisation, 16–23 May 2001, Tokyo, Japan.

Singh, Bishwa Nath. "Employment Generation in India's Service Sector". *The Indian Journal of Labour Economics* 43, 4 (2000): 877–882.

Singh, Surjit. "Employment in Restaurant and Hotel Sector in India". *The Indian Journal of Labour Economics* 43, 4 (2000).

Singh, Surjit. "Informal Tourism Sector: Insights from Two Cities". In *Informal Sector in India: Perspectives and Policies*, eds Amitabh Kundu and Alakh N. Sharma. Institute for Human Development & Institute of Applied Manpower Research, New Delhi, 2001.

Singh, N. and M.K. Sapra. "Liberalization in Trade and Finance, India's Garment Sector". In *Trade Liberalisation and India's Informal Economy*, eds B. Harriss-White and A. Sinha. New Delhi: Oxford University Press, 2007.

Sinha, Rajeev Ranjan Kumar. *Dynamics of Land-Caste Relations in India*. New Delhi: Manak Publications, 2009.

Sivakumar S.S. and Chitra Sivakumar. "Class and Jati at Asthapuram and Kanthepuram: Some Comments Towards a Structure of Interests". *Economic and Political Weekly*. Annual Number, (February, 1979).

Sivasubramonian, S. *The National Income of India during the Twentieth Century*, Delhi: Oxford University Press, 2000

Sivasubramonian, S. *The Sources of Economic Growth in India 1950-1 to 1999-2000*. New Delhi: Oxford University Press, 2004.

Sivertsen, Dagfin. *When Caste Barriers Fall. A Study of Social and Economic Change in a South Indian Village*. New York: Humanities Press, 1963.

Specker, Konrad. "Madras Handlooms in the Nineteenth Century." *Indian Economic and Social History Review* 26: 2 (1989). Reprinted in Roy 1996.

Sreeramamurty, Kudamala. *Urban Labour in Informal Sector*. Delhi: B. R. Publishing, 1986.

Sridharan, E. "The Political Economy of the Middle Classes in Liberalising India", ISAS Working Paper No 49, 2008 (https://www.files.ethz.ch/isn/92166/48.pdf accessed 24 August 2016).

Stokes, Eric. "Agrarian Relations, Northern and Central India". In *The Cambridge Economic History of India Volume 2: c. 1757-1970*, ed. Dharma Kumar with the editoral assistance of Meghnad Desai. Cambridge: Cambridge University Press, 1983.

Streefkerk, Hein. *Tools and Ideas: The Beginnings of Local Industrialization in South Gujarat, 1970-2000*. New Delhi: Manohar Publishers, 2006.

Subrahmanya, M.H. Bala. "Small Industry, and Globalisation: Implications, Performances and Prospects". *Economic and Political Weekly* 2004: 1826–1834.

Sugimoto, Yoshio. "Shōhi sareru kiseki – Minami Indo, Veeraanganni seidō no medeia senryaku" (Miracle as consumption – the media strategy of the Basilica of Our Lady of Good Health in Velankanni in South India). In *Shōhi pataan no chōki hendō to shakai kōzō, shakai ishiki – Minami Indo no jirei o chūshin ni* (Long Term Fluctuations and Social Change and Social Consciousness – Centring on South India), ed. Yanagisawa Haruka. Chiba University, 2010.

Sundaram, K. *Weakening Welfare: The Public Distribution of Food in India*. New Delhi: LeftWord Books, 1998.

Suryanarayan, M.H. "How Real Is Secular Decline in Rural Poverty?" *Economic and Political Weekly* 35, 25 (2000).

Suryanarayan, M.H. *Nutritional Norms for Poverty: Issues and Implications*, Concept paper prepared for the Expert Group to Review the Methodology for Estimation of Poverty, Planning Committee, Government of India, New Delhi, 2009.

Suryanarayan, M.H. "Economic Development and Inequalities". In *Growth, Inequality and Social Development in India: Is Inclusive Growth Possible?* ed. R. Nagaraj. New York: Palgrave Macmillan, 2012.

Suryanarayanan, S.S. "Service Sector and Employment". *The Indian Journal of Labour Economics* 43, 4 (2000).

Suzuki, Nobutake and Junjiro Shintaku. "Indo no keizai hatten to Indo kigyō, Nihon kigyō no monozukuri" (Analysing Manufacturing in Indian Firms and Japanese Firms in India within Indian Economic Development). MMRC Discussion Paper No. 294. Manufacturing Management Research Center, March 2010.

Swaroopa, G. Rani and S. Galab. "Organisation and Economic Performance of Manufacturing Activities in Urban Slums of Hyderabad City: Case Study of Sandal Making Activity". *Indian Journal of Labour Economics* 41, 3 (1998): 539–553.

Taniguchi, Shinkichi. "The *Zamindar*'s Estate-control on the Eve of the Permanent Settlement in Bengal (1773) – A Case Study of a Middle-size *Zamindari* in Northern Bengal". *The Calcutta Historical Journal* 18, 2 (1996): 1–41.

Tewari, Meenu. "Intersectoral Linkages and the Role of the State in Shaping the Conditions of Industrial Accumulation: A Study of *Ludhiana's* Manufacturing Industry". *World Development* 26, 8 (1998): 1387–1411.

Tewari, Meenu. "Successful Adjustment in Indian Industry: The Case of Ludhiana's Woolen Knitwear Cluster". *World Development* 27, 9 (1999): 1651–1671.

Tiwari, R.S. *Informal Sector Workers, Problems and Prospects*. New Delhi: Anmol Publications, 2005.

Tomlinson, B.R. *The Political Economy of the Raj, 1914-1947: The Economics of Decolonization in India*. London: Macmillan, 1979.

Trehan, Prerana. "The Big Fat: Indian Wedding". *The Sunday Tribune*, Spectrum section, 29 August 2004. (http://www.tribuneindia.com/2004/20040829/spectrum/main1.htm. Accessed 11 August 2016.)

Tsujita, Yuko and Hisaya Oda. "Caste. Land. And Migration: A Preliminary Analysis of a Village in an Undeveloped State in India". IDE Discussion Paper No. 334. Tokyo: Institute of Developing Economies, 2012.

Twomey, Michael J. "Employment in Nineteenth Century Indian Textiles." *Explorations in Economic History* 20 (1983): 37–57.

Tyabji, Nasir. *The Small Industries Policy in India*. Calcutta and Oxford: Oxford University Press, 1989.

Tyabji, Nasir. *Industrialisation and Innovation, the Indian Experience*. New Delhi: Sage, 2000.

Uberoi, Patricia. "Aspiration Weddings: The Bridal Magazine and the Canons of 'Decent Marriage'". In *Patterns of Middle Class Consumption in India and China*, eds Christophe Jaffrelot and Peter van der Veer. New Delhi: Sage, 2008.

Unni, Jeemol. "Agricultural Labourers in Rural Labour Households, 1956-57 to 1977-78 – Changes in Employment, Wages and Incomes". *Economic and Political Weekly* 23, 26 (1988): A59–A68.

Unni, Jeemol. "Diversification of Economic Activities and Non-Agricultural Employment in Rural Gujarat". *Economic and Political Weekly* 31, 33 (1996): 2243–2245 + 2247–2251.

Unni, Jeemol. "Non-Agricultural Employment and Poverty in Rural India: A Review of Evidence". *Economic and Political Weekly* (28 March 1998).

Unni, Jeemol. "Urban Informal Sector: Size and Income Generation Processes in Gujarat", Part I, SEWA-GIDR-ISST-NCAER, Report No. 2, National Council of Applied Economic Research, New Delhi, April 2000.

Unni, Jeemol. "Economic Reforms and Labour Markets in India: Organized and Unorganized Sectors". In *Labour Market and Institution in India: 1990s and Beyond*, ed. Shuji Uchikawa. New Delhi: Manohar, 2003.

Unni, Jeemol and Uma Rani, "Employment and Income in the Informal Economy: A Micro-perspective". In *Informal Economy Centrestage: New Structures of Employment*, eds Renana Jhabvala, Ratna M. Sudarshan and Jeemol Unni. New Delhi: Sage, 2003.

Upadhya, Carol. "The Farmer-Capitalists of Coastal Andhra Pradesh". *Economic and Political Weekly* 23, 27 and 28 (1988): 1376–1382; 1433–1442.

Upadhya, Carol "Capital Flows, Business Networks and Entrepreneurs in the Indian Software Industry". *Economic and Political Weekly* 39. 48 (27 November 2004): 5141–5151.

Vidyanathan, A. "Some Aspects of Inequalities in Living Standards in Rural India". In *Poverty and Income Distribution in India*, eds T.N. Srinivasan and P.K. Bardhan. Calcutta: Statistical Publishing Society, 1974, pp. 215–241.

Vaidyanathan, A. "Labor Use in Rural India – A Study of Spatial and Temporal Variations". *Economic and Political Weekly* 21, 52 (1986): A130–A146.

Vaidyanathan, A. "Second India Studies Revisited: Food, Agriculture and Water". Madras Institute of Development Studies, Madras, January 1994a.

Vaidyanathan, A. "Employment Situation: Some Emerging Perspective", *Economic and Political Weekly*, 29, 50 (10 December 1994b): 3147–3156.

Vaidyanathan, A. *India's Water Resources: Contemporary Issues in Irrigation*. New Delhi: Oxford University Press, 2006.

Varshney, Ashutosh. "Two Banks of the Same River? Social Order and Entrepreneurialism in India". In *Anxieties of Democracy: Tocquevillean Reflections on India and the United States*, eds. Partha Chatterjee and Ira Katznelson. Delhi: Oxford University Press, 2012.

Veeramani, C. "Sources of India's Export Growth in Pre- and Post-reform Periods". *Economic and Political Weekly* 42, 25 (2007).

Venkatachalaphy, A.R. "'In Those days There Was No Coffee': Coffee-Drinking and Middle-Class Culture in Colonial Tamilnadu". *Indian Economic and Social History Review* 39, 2 & 3 (2002).

Verma, Rubina. "Structural Transformation and Jobless Growth in the Indian Economy". In *The Oxford Handbook of the Indian Economy*, ed. Chetan Ghate. New York: Oxford University Press, 2012, pp. 276–310.

Vijayabaskar, M. "ICTs and Transformation of Traditional Workplaces: The Case of the Indian Automobile Industry". In *ICTs and Indian Economic Development: Economy, Work, Regulation*, eds Aahwani Saith and M. Vijayabaskar. London, New Delhi: Sage 2005, pp. 386–413.

Vijayabaskar, M. "Conceptualising Contemporary Formal-Informal Dichotomy: An Explanatory Essay Based on Emerging Evidence from Tamil Nadu, Southern India". Presented at International Conference on "Actualities of Indian Economic Growth at Rural-Urban Crossroads" held at the University of Tokyo, 15 and 16 December 2012.

Vijayabaskar, M and J. Jeyaranjan. "The Institutional Milieu of Skill Formation: A Comparative Study of Two Textile Regions in India and China". In *Industrial Dynamics in China and India: Firms, Clusters, and Different Growth Paths*, eds Moriki Ohara, M. Vijayabaskar and Hong Lin. Hampshire: Palgrave Macmillan, 2011.

Wadley, Susan S. *Struggling with Destiny in Karimpur, 1925-1984*. Berkeley, CA: University of California Press, 1984.

Wadley, Susan S. "The Village in 1984". In *Behind Mud Walls: Seventy-five Years in a North Indian Village*, eds William H. Wiser, Charlotte Viall Wiser with chapters by Susan S. Wadley and a Foreword by David G. Mandelbaum. Berkeley, Los Angeles, London: University of California Press, 2000.

Wadley, S.S. and B. W. Derr. "Karimpur 1925-1984: Understanding Rural India through Restudies", in *Conversations between Economists and Anthropologists*, ed. P. Bardhan. Delhi, OUP, 1990.

Wagle, D.M. "Imperial Preference and the Indian Steel Industry, 1924-39." *Economic History Review* 34 (1981): 120–131.

Wallack, Jessica Seddon. Structural Breaks in Indian Macroeconomic Date," *Economic and Political Weekly* 38, 41, (11 October 2003).

Whitcombe, Elizabeth. "Irrigation". In *The Cambridge Economic History of India Volume 2: c. 1757-1970*, eds Dharma Kumar and M. Desai. Cambridge: Cambridge University Press, 1983, pp. 677–737.

Wiser W. and C. Wiser. *Behind Mud Walls, Sevety-five Years in a North Indian Village*. Berkeley and Los Angeles, University of California Press, 2000 (updated and expanded edition).

Wishwakarma, R.K. "Informal-Formal Sector Linkages: Its Implication for Employment Policy", *Manpower Journal* 29, 3 (October–December 1993).

World Bank. 2007. *India - Land Policies for Growth and Poverty Reduction*. Washington, DC: World Bank. http://documents.worldbank.org/curated/en/2007/07/8208651/india-land-policies-growth-poverty-reduction

Yanagisawa, Haruka. "Juhasseikimatsu Minami Indo ni okeru tochi hoyu kankei "Igirisu kain Indo mondai tokubetsu iinkai daigo hōkoku"" (Land Possession in South India in the 19th Century seen through the Fifth Report From the Select Committee on the Affairs of the East India Company, House of Commons). *Toyo bunka* 50–51 (March 1971a): 139–165.

Yanagisawa, Haruka. "Indo zairai orimonogyō no saihensei to sono shokeitai (1) Menkōgyō ni okeru kōjō seido no kakuritsu to no kanren" (The Reorganization of the Handloom Industry in India [1] Development of a Factory System in the Cotton Textile Industry). *Ajia keizai* 12, 12 (1971b): 51–69.

Yanagisawa, Haruka. "Indo zairai orimonogyō no saihensei to sono shokeitai (2) Menkōgyō ni okeru kōjō seido no kakuritsu to no kanren" (The Reorganization of the Handloom Industry in India [2] Development of a Factory System in the Cotton Textile Industry). *Ajia keizai* 13, 2 (1972): 32–54.

Yanagisawa, Haruka. "Indo ni okeru chin rōdō no sonzai keitai – 'Rōdō chōsa iinkai hōkoku' ni miru" (Modes of Wage Labour in India through the Report of the Labour Investigation Committee). In *Indo no keizai seikaku to shokaisō*, ed. Yamaguchi Hiroichi. Tokyo: Ajia keizai kenkyūjo, 1975.

Yanagisawa, Haruka. "Tōai ichiji Nichiin kaishō o meguru Ei-in kankei" (Anglo-Indian Relations in the Course of the First Indo-Japanese Trade Negotiations). *Keizai to bōeki* 129 (1980): 30–47.

Yanagisawa, Haruka, 1983. *Socio-economic Changes in a Village in the Paddy Cultivating Area in South India* (Socio-Cultural Change in Villages in Tiruchirapalli District, Tamilnadu, India, Part 2, Modern Period, No. 2), Institute for the Study of Languages and Cultures of Asia and Africa.

Yanagisawa, Haruka. "Mixed Trends in Landholding in Lalgudi Taluk: 1895-1925." *Indian Economic and Social History Review* 26: 4 (1989).

Yanagisawa, Haruka. *Minami-Indo shakai-keizai-shi kenkyū* [Studies in the Socio-Economic History of South India]. Tokyo: University of Tokyo Press, 1991.

Yanagisawa, Haruka. "The Handloom Industry and Its Market Structure: The Case of the Madras Presidency in the First Half of the Twentieth Century." *Indian Economic and Social History Review* 30: 1 (1993). Reprinted in Roy 1996.

Yanagisawa, Haruka. *A Century of Change, Caste and Irrigated Lands in Tamilnadu 1860s-1970s*. New Delhi: Manohar, 1996a.

Yangisawa, Haruka. "Elements of Upward Mobility for Agricultural Labourers in Tamil Districts, 1865-1925". In *Local Agrarian Societies in Colonial India: Japanese Perspectives*, eds Peter Robb, Kaoru Sugihara, Haruka Yanagisawa. Richmond, Surrey: Curzon Press, 1996b (Reprint Routledge 2013).

Yanagisawa, Haruka. "Ei-in keizai kankei to Indo kōgyōka no ichisokumen – Dainiji Nichiin kaichō (1936-37 nen)" (An Aspect of Anglo-Indian Economic Relations and Indian Industrialisation: The Second Indo-Japanese Trade Negotiations). In *1939 nendai no Ajia kokusai chitsujō*, eds Akita Shigeru and Kagotani Naoto. Hiroshima: Keisuisha, 2001.

Yanagisawa, Haruka. "Growth of Small-Scale Industries and Changes in Consumption Patterns in South India, 1920-1950". *Economic Journal of Chiba University* 19, 3 (2004): 127–163.

Yanagisawa, Haruka. "Some Key Aspects in Understanding Historical Changes in South Indian Society: Lanholding and Non-farm Job Opportunities". *Studying Village Economies in India* (2008a).

Yanagisawa, Haruka. "The Decline of Village Common Lands and Changes in Village Society: South India, c. 1850–2000." *Conservation and Society* 6, 4 (2008b): 293–307.

Yangisawa, Haruka. "Growth of Small-Scale Industries and Changes in Consumption Patterns in South India, 1910s-50s". In *Towards a History of Consumption in South Asia*, eds Douglas E. Haynes and Abigail McGowan. Oxford: Oxford University Press, 2010, pp. 51–75.

Yanagisawa, Haruka. "Indo no kyōdō riyōchi no rekishiteki henyō to shinrin" (Forests and Historical Changes in the Common-Use Land in India). In *Shinrin hakai no rekishi* (History of the Destruction of Forests), ed. Inoue Takako. Tokyo: Akashi shoten, 2011a.

Yanagisawa, Haruka. "Village Common Land, Manure, Fodder, and Intensive Agricultural Practices in Tamil Nadu from the Mid-Nineteenth Century". *Review of Agrarian Studies* 1 (2011b): 23–42.

Yanagisawa, Haruka. "South Indian Village Common Land in Transition: Including a Comparison with the Japanese Case". *Community, Commons and Natural Resource Management in Asia*, ed. Haruka Yanagisawa. Singapore: Singapore University Press, 2015.

# Index

Note: *Italic* and **bold** page numbers refer to figures and tables; page numbers followed by "n" denote endnotes.

For Product Safety Concerns and Information please contact our EU representative GPSR@taylorandfrancis.com
Taylor & Francis Verlag GmbH, Kaufingerstraße 24, 80331 München, Germany

www.ingramcontent.com/pod-product-compliance
Lightning Source LLC
LaVergne TN
LVHW010550300926
849162LV00002B/296
*9781032377216*